TORN:

THE MELISSA WILLIAMS STORY

Will Melissa choose the
path of least resistance
or will she continue on a
path that keeps her torn
and caught in
the middle?

By: Ella Campbell

"The Battle Is Not Yours. It Belongs to the Lord."

www.trafford.com
North America & international
toll-free: 844-688-6899 (USA & Canada)
fax: 812 355 4082

I Dedicate This Book ......

To the most important people in my life – Chenaya, Jonathan, Devion, Stefani, Brianna, and Justice.

To my sisters and brothers for all the memories growing up in Monroeville, AL.

To Yolanda Adams, Shirley Caesar, Creflo Dollar, Greg Powe, Marvin Sapp, Kirk Franklin, Donnie McClurkin, Oprah Winfrey and Tyler Perry. Your music, ministry, and life has inspired me in so many ways to complete this book. Keep doing what you do because your light forever shines for others to see the way to achieve greatness.

To My Special Friends – you know who you are.

The Introduction

"Torn: The Melissa Williams Story"

Remember those years when we thought our lives would always be happy and fun. During those times of our lives, we were lead to believe that we were invincible and that things would never change. How wrong were we about that?

Throughout the following pages, many of you will be able to relate to the good, the bad, and the ugly and will be reminded of those times when you, yourself, sneaked out of the house in the wee hours of the morning, or told a little "white lie" to your parents about where you were going or who you were going with, or even those times when you allowed yourself to lose your virginity in the backseat of a car. Regardless to the act that you committed, you will be able to relate to the young lady, Melissa, and see how her journey in life led her to be ultimately "caught in the middle".

In this day and time, there is always a war going on in one way or the other. Raging fire is how I have heard it put in a song by the Florida Mass Choir. But I am reminded from a scripture in the Bible that taught me that the sufferings of this present time are not worthy to be compared to the glory that we will receive.

After reading this book, you will undoubtedly gain more strength to be able to go through the wars in your very own life. You will understand that you are never alone. When times get tough, that is the time to really exercise your faith and hold on! Walk with Melissa through her journey of life. Just like she will find out, you will also remember that 'the battle is not really yours, it belongs to the Lord'.

"Melissa's High School Years"

As a varsity cheerleader, Kiwanis Club sweetheart, SHARE club member, and a class officer, it seems as if life just can't get any better for Melissa. She is dating one of the hottest guys in school. He proudly lets Melissa wear his letterman jacket, and has no problem letting everyone know that she is his girlfriend. Over lunch and in the hallways, the main topics of discussion are Janet Jackson's latest video and whether she is a better singer and/or performer than Whitney Houston.

Going to the clubs during the week has become a regular thing for Melissa and her friends. Their main excuse to get out of the house is that they are "out studying". Because there isn't a dance club in Middleton, they have to travel to Asbury to go dancing. Neither is there a movie theatre, beaches, or anything of the sort. To get by, they substitute the beach for a lake, and the movie theatre for sleepovers. No matter what, they always find a way to make life in Middleton exciting.

Melissa's life changes forever when on a nice spring evening, close to summer break, she and her girlfriends decide to go to the club on a school night, when, in fact, they are supposed to be studying for finals at a friends' house. Once they make it to the nightclub, they hook up with their male friends and decide to share the night dancing, drinking and having fun. Melissa and her friends are the coolest because they always find male friends to hang out with no matter where they travel.

On this particular night, Melissa specifically remembers being in the club studying for her Government Finals, and dancing in between songs. Melissa knows that this isn't cool! As much as she wants to be out with her friends having fun, she is not crazy enough to flunk out of school doing it. It's getting late and the night is quickly coming to an end. Melissa and her friends know that they have to get home before their parents start to worry. But, they are having too much fun to leave. On their way home, Melissa and her friends let their creative juices flow and come up with a brilliant plan that convinces their parents and they return to the club. There are four girls in the car, but this decision changes Melissa's life forever.

CONTENTS

GOD DOESN'T MAKE MISTAKES

Chapter 1	"First Signs of Trouble"	1
Chapter 2	"It All Goes Wrong and Thank God"	14
Chapter 3	"Off to College"	21
Chapter 4	"It's Not His Fault!"	27
Chapter 5	"What's Wrong?"	31
Chapter 6	"Jesus Love You, This I Know"	35
Chapter 7	"Back To School"	41
Chapter 8	"Wouldn't You Do It For Me?"	44
Chapter 9	"Angels From Above"	46

IS IT REAL LOVE?

Chapter 10	"I Really Like This One"	53
Chapter 11	"Tell It Like It Is"	60
Chapter 12	"Back to Church"	64
Chapter 13	"Dana Has What?"	66
Chapter 14	"This Man is the Truth!"	79
Chapter 15	"Mark Who?"	82
Chapter 16	"Kalin Meets My Family"	95

FAMILY COMES FIRST

Chapter 17	"And Now It's My Turn"	97
Chapter 18	"We Don't Cuddle Tonight"	104
Chapter 19	"Amber's A Winner!"	108
Chapter 20	"I Just Can't Leave Them!"	111
Chapter 21	"Not Again!"	117
Chapter 22	"Laura is What?"	129
Chapter 23	"Not My Children!"	135

WHAT DOESN'T KILL YOU MAKES YOU STRONGER

Chapter 24	"Back to Middleton"	152
Chapter 25	"He Died. Why Should You?"	158
Chapter 26	"Rita to the Rescue"	164
Chapter 27	"Don't Believe Him!"	169
Chapter 28	"Keep Your Nose Clean"	181
Chapter 29	"What A Pitiful Sight!"	188
Chapter 30	"Hurt My Baby and It's Over!"	193
Chapter 31	"Liberty and 'Justice' For All"	204
Chapter 32	"He's Gone!"	210
Chapter 33	"As Long As He's With You"	219
Chapter 34	"Back in Court for the Finale!"	227

TROUBLE DOESN'T LAST ALWAYS

Chapter 35	"Why Did I Do That?"	230
Chapter 36	"Ms. Rita Brings Trouble"	234
Chapter 37	"I Don't Understand Teenagers"	236
Chapter 38	"Go Buccaneers!"	238
Chapter 39	"Why Are You Saying These Things?"	241
Chapter 40	"Why Did He Run?"	246
Chapter 41	"Stuart's New Friend"	251
Chapter 42	"Is There A Problem?"	261
Chapter 43	"Fire Her or I Will!"	269
Chapter 44	"Dejavu or What?"	272
Chapter 45	"Is There Probable Cause?"	280
Chapter 46	"Tell It To The Judge!"	288
Chapter 47	"Nothing Else Matters"	294
Chapter 48	"Nothing To Live For Anymore"	308
Chapter 49	"Please Don't Take Them!"	318
Chapter 50	"Cry If You Need To!"	335

THIS BATTLE BELONGS TO THE LORD

Chapter 51	"Fifteen Minutes Left"	341
Chapter 52	"Move on Counselor!"	351
Chapter 53	"How Do You Know Her?"	356
Chapter 54	"And, How is the Main Witness?"	375

Chapter 55   "Nothing Else We Can Do" 382
Chapter 56   "I Can't Do That!" 390
Chapter 57   "Ordered to Attend" 395
Chapter 58   "Letter For You" 401
Chapter 59   "Is He Flirting With You?" 409
Chapter 60   "Cindy, Don't Go There!" 419
Chapter 61   "Dear Ms. Melissa" 422

CHAPTER 1

"First Signs of Trouble"

"**M**elissa, why do you keep throwing up?" says Brittney, my next door neighbor. Brittney is speaking to me from the other room, because I am wrapped around the porcelain toilet.

"I don't know. I guess I have a virus or something", I respond. "I have never experienced anything like this and can't understand why I am throwing up every time I eat something."

"Yeah, a 9-month virus", she softly says. I don't know quite what to think about her comment nor do I care because my head is still in the toilet. "Melissa, why don't you let me take you to the doctor just for precaution because I think that you might be pregnant?" she asks. *Pregnant? Where in the world would she get such an outrageous idea? Of course I am sexually active but why in the world didn't I remember to have Wil wear a condom? Could this be true? Could I be "pg"? No way! Getting pregnant is just not part of the plan.*

Without hesitation, I agree to go to see the doctor. I guess it is better to know than not to know. Because Brittney is older than I am and is a senior next year, I figure she will certainly know her way out of this mess. I always go to her when there is something bothering me. She and Laura are the only friends that I trust to hold on to this type of information. Brittney, too, has found herself in some tight situations. We always have each other's back through the thick and the thin. So, this is no exception. She picks up the phone and before I know it, she has made an appointment for me to see her doctor. I can hardly wait to finally put an end to the madness of possibly being pregnant.

With so many thoughts running rampantly through my mind, I start to remember all of the gossip I have heard just walking through the hallways about girls who end up pregnant. Many of them end up getting abortions or dropping out of school. I have to admit it, but my choice, if I am found to be pregnant, will definitely be to get an abortion. But, this can't be why I am throwing up. Oh God no!!

With the appointment coming up and all, I can't sleep, eat, or anything. The anticipation of my doctor visit is really starting to be somewhat overwhelming. I can't tell my little secret to anyone because I don't know what will happen nor do I know what to expect.

Brittney decides to attend the doctor visit with me. Brittney has so graciously prepared me for the doctor visit. *Hmmm, how does she know so much about these visits anyway?*

"Melissa, when you go in there, they are just going to have you pee in a cup, check out your vital signs, and the doctor will examine you", she explains.

"I have to pee in a cup, for what?" I ask, sounding like a young child to her mother.

"They have to do all of that to see if you are pregnant", she explains.

"And, what else?"

"The doctor will have you lay back on the table and he will examine you, sweetheart. It won't hurt. Just sit back and relax", she continues.

"How do you know so much about this stuff?" I ask, looking for an answer. Before she has a chance to answer me, the nurse calls my name.

"Melissa Williams", the nurse says. I follow her to the back and wave goodbye to my friend. Right before the door closes, I can see that Brittney has already picked up one of the magazines sitting on the table in the waiting area. Even though she decides to stay in the lobby, it is so comforting just knowing that she is here with me.

The visit is going just as Brittney told me it would. *Is this something that is taught in Health class that I missed? How does she know so much? It is almost as if she has been here herself?*

The visit takes approximately 45 minutes and I am back in the lobby with Brittney.

"So, how did it go?" she asks, as I join her on the sofa.

"It was everything you said it would be. I was so scared."

Deep into our conversation, I look up and see the nurse heading our way.

"The doctor will see you now". We follow the nurse down to the doctor's office where he is waiting for me. He looks up as if he is ready to deliver the news. *Will it be good news or bad news? If it turns out that I am pregnant, will this be a good thing or a bad thing? Will I be able to handle whatever news he is coming to deliver?*

"Can my friend come in?"

"Sure, if you don't mind. It is up to you."

"Brittney, please come in with me."

The doctor begins to speak. "I don't know if this is good or bad for you young lady but the test results show that you are definitely pregnant", he says, as if he is delivering the news to an excited couple or something. *I can't be pregnant!*

"What!" I say, with a look on my face that immediately lets the doctor know that I am not excited about being pregnant. I look over at Brittney and she has her hand over her mouth. She is just as speechless as I am. But the funny thing is that just days before, she was quite certain that this was the reason for me throwing up my guts.

What in the world am I going to do? How in the world will I ever be able to tell my mother? She is going to be so disappointed in me. She, too, was a teenage mother and I just repeated history again. The people at the church will be so disappointed in me. I am disappointed in me. What in the world was I thinking? Why didn't I have Wil wear a condom that night? Or was it even Wil's baby? I was with Michael the week before that. How do I know exactly who the father is?

The doctor can see that I definitely have a lot going on in my head right now. He is probably wondering why I am not here with my mother, but I am sure that we are not the first teenagers who have come into his office without a parent. We are both very stunned about this news. He begins to give me the alternatives for pregnancy.

"Melissa, if you have doubts about wanting to have this baby and raise it yourself, there are other options such as abortion or adoption. You should go home and speak with your parents about this and between you and them, you can decide what is best for you and the baby", he explains.

Does this man not understand that my mother is going to kill me? She is not going to ask any questions. She is just going to start yelling and cursing and yelling some more. Or better yet? Maybe she will call all the women in her missionary group and, perhaps, they will pray the baby out of me, I thought.

This news has me feeling very frustrated, afraid, and desperate. At this point, I will do anything to wake up and find out that this is just a bad dream and that none of this is really happening. Brittney tries to comfort me by telling me that everything is going to be okay. I can't fathom the idea of having a child. I won't have a child. I will make all of this go away and nobody will ever have to know my little secret.

We finally leave the doctor's office and on the way home, there is complete silence in the car. I don't know what I would do without Brittney. She had to borrow her father's car to take me to the appointment. I am so hungry, but I don't want to chance it by eating anything right now because I will only throw it up anyway. I can't seem to get the events of my last sexual encounter with Wil out of my head. The thought of it continues to flash before me. I am not sure why Brittney is so quiet, but I am definitely thinking of what my next move will be. *Who will I go to now to make this all go away?*

After making it back home, I walk in the door and speak to everyone as if I had not just moments earlier been told that I am an expectant mother. What in the world will they think when they find out my secret? I have to call my other closest friend, Laura. Laura and I have been friends since kindergarten and if I had to leave everything I own in this world to anyone, I would leave it to Laura. She is a no-nonsense kind of girl. Nobody messes with her. She is somewhat of a bully, especially to anyone who thinks they want to start trouble with her friends. Laura is also older than me. She is mixed with black and Italian and has long curly hair. She is beautiful and always has some guy trying to get her number. Although she could be stuck up, she chooses not to be that way, but, instead is very likable and friendly.

"Hello!" she says, with the radio blaring in the background.

"Laura, hey girl, how are you? What are you up to?"

"Nothing. Just chilling. I just got off the phone with this boy who wants to take me out Friday night. Now, how is he going to do that and he knows he has a girlfriend? Boys are something else!", she says with a hint of sarcasm.

"Girl, who are you fooling? You know I know you! You only like the boys who have girlfriends anyway!" We both laugh behind this comment.

"So what's up with you Meme? Sounds like something's up", she says.

"Laura, I have bad news", I begin to say.

"Ok, what is it? What's wrong?" she asks.

"Remember when I told you that "B" was going to hook me up with her doctor to see why I was throwing up and stuff?"

"Yeah, and what happened with that?"

"I am pregnant, Laura! My mother is going to kill me as dead as I can be!"

"Oh no! Are you serious? Are you kidding me, Meme? Don't worry. We will figure it all out. Don't cry. But, what are you going to do?" she asks.

"I don't know. I know that I don't want to have a baby right now in my life. I am too young. How in the world will I take care of a baby? My mother can't afford it right now, either."

"OK, so if you don't have it, that means that you will have to have an abortion", she says.

"That is right! I will just have to get an abortion and move on with my life as if this never happened", I respond.

"Go on with your life like it never happened?" she asks. "Once you get that abortion, your life will never be the same. Don't kid yourself. It will never be the same!"

"So, do you think the abortion is the best idea or what do you think?"

"I am not sure what to think right now. I can't believe that you weren't more careful."

"Do you personally know someone who has had an abortion?"

"Of course I do."

"And?"

"Honestly, most of the girls who get the abortion are all doing just fine today. As a matter of fact, some of them have had more than one", she responds.

"And did they all turn out okay?"

"Yes. I don't know of anyone having complications with the abortion, if that is what you are asking. It is a dangerous procedure and you should carefully think about this before making that decision. Oh, I almost forgot! You remember Ms. Maureen who lives around the corner? She actually got an abortion and died from the complications. Everyone thought she died from something else, but it was actually an abortion that killed her."

"Oh, that is great! Why don't you just scare me to death? I am sure of one thing and it is that I do not want to have a baby at this time. In my mind, this "thing" growing inside of me is just as much a virus to me as anything."

"So, is it Wil's baby?" she asks.

"Yeah, I think so."

"You think so?" she asks. "So how many times did you get with him?"

"Just that one time."

"Well, it doesn't take but one time", she comments. "Does he know that you are pregnant?"

"No, I haven't told anyone. I just found out myself."

"What do you think he is going to say?" she asks.

"I wish that I knew."

"So, how did you two hook up? He lives all the way in Asbury for crying out loud."

"It was three weeks ago when me, Janet, Brittney, and Janay went to the nightclub."

"Yeah, I think I remember that. You all went during the week and on a school night, right?" she questions.

"That's right! We had gone to the club already and had our little fun, but no, we just had to go back! And when we did, Wil and his friends were still there and we all hooked up. Wil had been bugging me all night for sex. And honestly, I just got tired of him asking, so I decided to give it to him right in the backseat of the car. I didn't even bother to take off all of my clothes. It was too much of a hassle. And the sad part about it is that there was nothing special about it at all! There were no fireworks. All I was thinking about was getting back inside to dance."

"So you had sex with him one time and got pregnant?" she asks.

"Yep! And honestly, it really was a waste of my time! That night is not worth this hell that I am going through right now. It wasn't even good to me."

"Girl, how in the world can you joke at a time like this?"

"I have to laugh to keep from crying."

Laura and I talk for hours about my little situation. But, in the end, she decides to support me no matter what I decide.

A couple of weeks have passed since I found out that I was pregnant and I have not made much progress one way or the other. Through the grapevine, I heard about this woman who manages a local restaurant who is looking to adopt a baby because she can't have any children. I think it's worth a shot. What do I have to lose anyway?

The following week, I decide to pay the lady a visit just to get a feel for her and to see what she thinks of the idea of taking my baby to raise as her own.

Again, Brittney has to get her father's car to take me to the restaurant. Once we arrive, she decides that I should go in and speak to the lady by myself. She and I agree that she should stay in the car and wait for me to return.

Once inside the restaurant, I see that the employees are extremely busy taking orders from the customers, while children are running around and playing with their bunny ears. The place smells like Easter candy.

Luckily, one of the employees finally takes notice that I need some help and approaches me.

"May I help you?"

"Yes, I am here to see Cheryl, the manager."

"Sure, she will be right with you". I don't know what to expect. *Will she deny it? Will she accept my offer? What kinds of questions will she ask me? I don't have an idea of what types of questions to ask her. Maybe I will first find out if it is true about whether she can have kids. Does she plan to marry? Will my baby have a father in the picture? Will she let me see the child?*

This is getting crazier by the minute! All of this is because I had sex with a boy ONE TIME and there is a possibility that I may end up being this child's mother! Cheryl finally comes out and I am pleasantly surprised. She looks to be a middle-aged woman, very attractive, very friendly, and very kind. She looks almost too young to raise a child. She almost looks like a kid herself.

"Hi, my name is Cheryl and I understand you want to speak with me", she says, extending her hand out to me.

"Yes, Cheryl, I am here to speak with you about a private matter. Can we talk in private somewhere? She looks somewhat puzzled and starts to look me over trying to decide if speaking with me is worth her while.

"Of course, follow me to my office". She leads me down a hallway into her office. I can see the pictures on the wall of previous employees who have earned awards, the Minimum Wage Poster, and the restaurant's mission statement. She seems curious to know why I am there. "Please have a seat."

"I apologize for barging in on you at work, but I have something very important to talk with you about. I heard through the grapevine that you can't have children." Before I can say another word, she throws up her hands as if she is ready to call a truce or something.

"Wait a minute!" she shouts. "I can't believe that you would come here to my place of business to discuss this with me. That is my personal business!"

"Cheryl, I don't mean to be rude or to upset you. I am here because I have a proposition for you. Three weeks ago, I went to the doctor and found out that I was pregnant and I am only 16 years old. My mother doesn't even know that I am pregnant yet and I don't want to have a baby. I don't necessarily want to abort the baby but I can't afford a baby right now. I still have to finish high school and I have dreams of going on to college", I explain.

Throughout the conversation, Cheryl starts looking away. She looks in the ceiling, at the pictures on the wall. It seems as though she is doing everything that she can to avoid eye contact with me. I can't really tell what is on her mind. She might want to throw me out of her office.

"I can't have children", she admits. "I have wanted nothing more than to give birth to my own child, but when I was younger, my father raped me and my mother made me abort the baby. My mother took me to a woman who did abortions with a wire hanger and her "homemade surgery" ruined any chances that I have for giving birth to my own child. I would love to adopt your baby and give it a good life", she says.

Cheryl and I are both crying. I don't know if I am crying because of what she has experienced in her past or if I am just happy that I may have found a home for my baby.

"If you don't mind, I have some questions for you, Cheryl."

"Sure, ask away!"

"First question; are you married?"

"No. I am not married. I live with a woman. She is my lover. I am bi-sexual. I sleep with men and I sleep with women. I have not decided which I will end up marrying. I am attracted to both of these sexes", she admits.

I am not crazy at all about Cheryl's answer. *Bisexual!* My child may or may not have a father in the picture, but possibly another woman. *Two mothers? Will this cause my daughter to think that something is wrong with her?*

"Next question, do you believe in God?"

"I believe that God exists. I don't go to church because the people in the church only care about what you are wearing when you walk through the doors. They never get a chance to know you. They just judge you period. I don't want to be around any of that. I listen to my gospel songs and I watch "church" on television. I don't have time to sit up in anybody's church. My mama used to have us in church every Sunday – me, her, my brother Kevin, and my father – but it didn't stop my father from raping me. Where was God?" she says, as a tear drops from her eye.

I can tell that Cheryl is still very hurt by what happened to her as a young lady. *Does she still have a relationship with her mother and father? Where is the man that did so much harm to her?* I want to ask her all of these questions but why would she be honest with me about her personal business? She just met me. I am not sure if I really want to know about it anyway.

"If you don't mind my asking, where are your parents now?"

"My mother is dead and my father is in a nursing home", she answers.

"Do you ever go see him?"

"Hell no! I hate him and will never see him again", she yells. "I hate that bastard for what he did to me. I don't care if he falls dead right in his tracks."

"Well, that is all the questions that I have for now. I can see that you are upset and I don't want to make it any worse. I am just trying to find a better solution for my baby than to abort it."

"I am truly sorry for getting upset but I would love the opportunity to take your baby. I have always wanted to have children but never could. I would take care of the baby. I can certainly provide for the baby. Here's my number if you have more questions for me", she says. She hands me her number on a post it note and stands up from her desk to give me a hug. Cheryl politely walks me to the door.

"Thanks again, Cheryl" I say, as I walk away.

When I make it back to the car, Brittney is sitting in the car listening to WBLX, the Beat of the Bay. They are playing one of my favorite songs from Salt and Pepa, "Push It". She is startled when I pull on the door and get in. She can tell that I am not that happy either.

"How did it go?" she asks.

"Not well at all. That woman has issues. She may have a job and can provide for a baby, but she has tons of baggage. And not only that but she is bisexual!"

"Bisexual?" Brittney asks, with a puzzled look on her face.

"Yes, bisexual! She said that she likes men and women and is just not sure which she will end up married to. She lives with a woman now who is her lover. God knows that I am not trying to judge her, but I don't think this is the best environment for my baby."

"Wow – now that is messed up!" Brittney comments.

"Yeah I know. She was raped by her father when she was younger and her mother made her get an abortion and the lady who did it used a wire hanger and it messed her up from being able to have children. Understandably so, but she is filled with hatred for her father and I have been taught that no matter what, you have to love everybody and I want my baby to know that and live that and if she is around people who hate others, she will too."

"Wow! Now that is messed up!"

"Oh well, back to the drawing board. I already know that I am not going to give this woman a call. So, I don't need this!" I tossed her number out the window. *Geez, I wish I could toss myself out the window and just fly away into the wind.*

We finally make it home. "Hey Melissa, would you like to come in?" she asks. I really want to go in but I know that Brittney has other things in mind and I am not in the mood for it.

"No, I have lots on my mind. I need to go home." She walks away and goes inside her house waving goodbye.

When I get in the house, my youngest nephew, Sean, is on the phone. When he finally gets off the phone, I dial Laura's number and she finally picks up after three rings or so. "Hello", she says.

"Hey girl, I have lots to tell you."

"What is wrong? Are you okay?"

"Yes, I am fine. I went to talk to the lady at the restaurant about adopting my baby and she has issues! Check this out. She is bisexual, lives with a woman, and can't have children because her father raped her and her mother made her get an abortion and the lady who did it used a wire hanger", I explain, not even taking a breath in between.

"What!" she exclaims. "Girl, you need to just let that idea of adoption go the hell away. That is not going to happen and you know it!" she says.

"Of course, I have already come to that conclusion. She gave me her phone number, but I have already tossed it out the window."

"Good, because with all of that mess going on, you might as well have your baby and raise it yourself", she comments.

"What did you just say?"

It seems as though Laura hasn't been listening when I explain to her that I just can't have a baby. There is just no way! As much as I don't want to admit it, but she is right about the fact that this woman's life is just messed up, but I am not sure about the "raising the baby myself" idea. I do know that this is really starting to take its toll on me. This is draining my energy and almost feels like a waste of time. *Am I going through all of this to end up having the baby anyway?*

Having a baby will mean that I will have to completely give up life as I currently know it to be - the cheerleading, the clubs, the sleepovers, and the girlfriends. *Who will want to be around me with my belly sticking out? What guy will be interested in me now?* I have to make a decision and I have to make a quick one. At this point, my decision is one of two; either have the abortion *after* cheerleader camp or *before*. I don't know what prompts me to want to speak to Mrs. Knowles about the abortion and the pregnancy but I somehow find the courage to want to do so. I'll speak to her tomorrow after practice. I will just have to pull her to the side and hopefully none of the girls will pay attention to us as we discuss this matter. After such a long day, it is time to close my eyes and try to go to sleep.

Right before practice, I pull Mrs. Knowles off to the side and speak with her about my situation. Our cheerleader sponsor is very down to earth. We talk to her about everything from sex to dating and back to sex. She gives us good advice about boys. I can say that I don't always like her advice because she is usually telling me to stop doing something that I am doing. I remember one time when she pulled me into her office to tell me to stop dating this one guy just because he was of a different race. I don't usually like to be told who to date and the truth of the matter is that she might as well had told me to do it!

"Mrs. Knowles, I have to tell you something."

"Is everything okay at home?" she asks.

"In a way. Please promise me that you won't tell my mother. Promise me that this is just between the two of us", I plead with her.

"Meme, you know how I am about keeping secrets from parents."

"I know, but this one is a matter of life and death. Will you help me or not?"

"Ok, go on."

"Well, you see, I got myself pregnant and I have not told my mother yet. I am working on getting money for an abortion and I really need your help!"

I can clearly see and feel the disappointment. I already know why she is disappointed. I am disappointed in me too. She is always encouraging each of us to make better choices. I don't really want to hear that at this point.

"Oh, Meme, I am so disappointed. Who is this baby's father? Is it someone from here?" *I already know how she feels about me dating boys of the opposite race. I am sure that she is thinking I got myself pregnant by one of the white boys.*

"You don't know the baby's father and no, he isn't from here." I don't want to admit to her that I'm not quite sure who the father is. The less she knows, the better. "Mrs. K, I just want to just have the abortion and carry on as if this never happened. To get the abortion, I need $75."

"You know that I don't believe in abortions, right?" she mentions.

"I know that, but I am asking this huge favor. I am too young to be a mother. You know how much I love cheerleading and I am not ready to give all of it up just to be pregnant. Will you please help me with this? No one will have to know that you gave me this money."

"I like you a lot Melissa and that is why I will help you out this time, but you better not tell anyone that I had anything to do with this", she demands. "Do we understand each other?"

"Yes ma'am. Nobody will know about this."

"There is one other thing. Don't do it this week. Wait until after cheerleader camp to get this operation. I don't want you to start hemorrhaging while we are at camp. This will be our little secret."

I am relieved that this whole ordeal is almost over. Pretty soon, I will have this "thing" out of me and my life can go back to nomal. It is finally starting to feel like there *is* a light at the end of the tunnel. How can I be so happy about ending this child's life? I am not exactly proud of myself right now. What I do know is that I will still be a cheerleader. And besides, Wil will never have to find out that I *am* or *was* even pregnant.

Cheerleader camp is off to a start, and as usual, it is lots of hard work out in this 98 degree weather in the middle of the summer. The camp scouts are on the prowl again looking for the cheerleaders who they will use as models at the end of camp for the Cheerleader Uniform Fashion Show. I am picked again for the 4th time! For a brief moment, I am able to forget about the idea that I am carrying a child.

I want so badly to share my news with Lisa, my roommate, but I just can't do it. Lisa and I always room together during Cheerleader Camp. I don't know if she can tell that I am a little pre-occupied, but if I do like we normally do and "pig out" on some Oreo's and milk, then hopefully, she won't notice anything differently. *I just hope that I am able to do it without throwing up. That will probably blow my cover!*

None of the cheerleaders have a clue as to what is *really* going on with me. Camp finally comes to an end and it is time to face the real world again. My reality is that I am 16 years old and will get an abortion next week. Because my mother doesn't know about this, I will have to go through one of the hardest things in my life *without* my mother by my side comforting me. I am terrified and feel so alone.

A few days later.

Oh my goodness! In the morning, I will travel to Marin to kill this child that is growing inside of me. I have had to grow somewhat heartless just to go through with this. How embarrassing it would be to walk around the school campus in maternity clothes! I just can't do that! What would everyone think? What would my family and friends say about me if I ended up making this terrible mistake of having a baby in high school? It is just too much stress to even think about.

This is it! I am scheduled to be in Marin by 2pm. Laura can tell that I am nervous because I am not as talkative as usual. I was told that I am not allowed to eat anything before the procedure. Because I can't eat, Laura decides that she won't eat anything either. Before leaving Middleton, Brittney tries everything to keep me from going through with the abortion. Her final attempt is that she takes this time to share a secret of her own with us.

"Melissa, is there a chance that you will change your mind about this?" she asks.

"No, I have to do this."

"Why do you feel as though this is the only option?"

"I don't feel like this is the only option, but I know for sure that it is *my* only option. Come on! We have been talking about this for 2 or 3 weeks already and you know how I feel about this whole thing. Why is it now that you are so concerned?"

"I have something to confess to you. The truth is that I got pregnant last year and that is why I understand how you are feeling. My parents didn't ask me how I felt about the pregnancy or whether I even wanted the baby or not. They made the decision for me to get an abortion. We went to Marin and I got the abortion like they wanted and I have never been the same. That is why I don't want you to go through with this", she says, as tears begin to fall down her face. "I am not trying to scare you or anything but I don't want you go down there and get this abortion."

"I am going through with this. There is no turning back now. All I need from you is to let my mother know where I am just in case I don't make it back", I say, giving her a hug and fighting back the tears.

"Melissa, please take it easy and I will see you when you get back", she says, as I walk away.

Laura and I get into the car with Tony, who has to travel to Marin for business. He lets us go along for the ride and has agreed to drop us off at the Clinic. He doesn't ask us any questions about our plans and we don't tell him anything either.

"Melissa, you know that I love you and will go anywhere you need me to go, but honestly, I agree with Brittney. I don't think that you should do this either."

Is she serious or what? All of this time they were both in agreement with me and the day that I am scheduled to get this over with, they start talking with me about not getting it done. I thought I could depend on these two. I thought they had my back. I thought they actually agreed with this decision of mine. Why do I feel so angry right now? Doesn't matter anyway – it's too late!

"Laura Walters, are you serious?"

CHAPTER 2

"It Goes Wrong and Thank God!"

*L*aura and I finally make it inside the lobby, after passing through all of the protesters outside. One of them, ever so clever, manages to slip a brochure in my hand that reads, **"God Can Turn Your Wrong Into a Right".** I don't want to read it. I know what it is going to say. I decide to lay the brochure to the side and just forget that it is there. Walking into this abortion clinic feels like walking straight into hell, if there is such a thing!

We walk in and see that there are two chairs that are empty right next to each other. We take these seats and immediately pick up a "People" magazine, with the beautiful Janet Jackson gracing the front cover. This issue features her new album that is about to drop. Janet is absolutely beautiful! With a little time on our hands, I look around and notice that there are kids in this office that look young enough to be my little sisters. They look so afraid. I notice this one girl who looks like she is about to cry. Next to her is an older woman reading a magazine, looking like she is completely bothered by having to be in such a place.

I wonder how *she* ended up pregnant. Did *she* have to go through what Ms. Cheryl went through? Was it a boyfriend or what? Is she scared? Does she know what is about to happen to her body? I am not sure if I understand what is about to happen or if it is going to hurt. How will I feel when it is all over? I keep thinking about what Brittney said before we left. Does she *really* know what she is talking about?

"Laura, how am I going to do this without my mother finding out I was here? She will kill me dead in my tracks if she finds out that I arranged this abortion and came here without her permission. I know that I am putting my life in danger but there is just no way that I am going to have a baby. It doesn't fit into my life right now."

"I don't know how we will keep it from her. Change your name or something. Nobody knows that we are here but me, you, Brittney, and Ms. Knowles. You know that she isn't going to tell anyone."

"I will have to give a different name because I don't want anyone to recognize Melissa at all. What do you think about Pamela Knight?"

"OK, that is geeky, but it will have to do", she responds.

Pamela Knight it is! I sign in under this fake name and wait patiently to be called. I can't think of a fake social security number so I guess I will just have to use my own.

"Pamela Knight!" the receptionist yells. After a few times, I finally realize that she is actually calling my name. This is it! *Oh God, please watch over me. I know that this is wrong, but please watch over me as I go through this procedure. I can't move. This is the hardest thing I have ever done in my life. Amen.*

This is, no doubt, the scariest thing I have ever done in my entire life. Do I really want to do this? Am I going to end up regretting this for the rest of my life like Brittney said that I would? Is it going to hurt? I will never ever put myself in this type of position again because this is just too hard for any one person to have to deal with.

Okay Melissa, if you are going to change your mind, this is the time to do it! The nurses have come into the room, ready to administer the anesthesia for the procedure. The nurse instructs me to take off my clothes and to put on their gown. She takes my temperature and listens to my heart with the stethoscope. It is so cold against my skin. I can feel my bare back being exposed in this gown.

While the nurse is preparing the anesthesia, the doctor comes in and begins to examine me. He starts making small talk with me about my age, the grade I am in, the activities that I am involved in, etc.

"How old are you young lady?" he asks.

"16."

"Do you realize that you are the oldest child in here today? The youngest kid out there is 11 years old. You young girls are getting pregnant just to have something to call your own."

"Wow!"

"Ms. Knight, when was your last menstrual cycle?" he questions.

"I am not sure. Why?"

"I am sorry to tell you this, but after examining you, I believe that you are too far along than what we allow for a simple abortion, so we are going to have to do a sonogram just to determine how many weeks you are before we can proceed", he says.

"What?" I say in disbelief.

I know exactly what is going on here. It was the cheerleader camp week that threw everything off. If I had not listened to the cheerleader sponsor, I would have been here and it would all be over now. What in the world am I going to do now? This is not going as planned. I should be almost on my way home getting ready to hang out with my friends, but, instead, I am still here in this office.

"Yes ma'am, once you have entered into another stage of the pregnancy, it then becomes more risky, which increases the costs of the procedure, as well as more paperwork that you will have to sign", he explains. "If you still want to have this abortion procedure, you will have to bring in $200 more dollars to complete the procedure."

Where in the world am I going to get $200 more dollars? The only person I know who lives in Marin who could give me more money is my cousin, who I am so sure will call my mother and let her know that I am here. I have to do something. I don't want to blow it so I will have to get back to Middleton and rethink my plan.

"OK, thanks. I will just have to return later to complete the procedure. I need to go and pick up the balance of the money."

"Ok, Ms. Knight, get dressed and inform the ladies at the desk of your intentions", he says, while removing his gloves.

When I make it back into the waiting room, Laura is right there with open arms to console me and when I tell her that I didn't get the abortion, she almost seems relieved. When I explain to her why I didn't get the abortion, she tries to comfort me by saying that "it just isn't meant to be".

Wrong answer buddy! That is not what I want to hear, I thought. I want her to help me come up with our next plan so that I can return to complete the procedure. This is one time when I really wish that I was surrounded by a heartless friend. I wonder what Wil would think if he knew I was here to abort his baby.

"I have a plan", I say to Laura, as we are walking through the parking lot. I am going to call Wil and let him know that I am pregnant and that if he doesn't want to pay child support for the rest of his life, he had better come up with the rest of the money that I need to get the abortion."

"Melissa, seriously, do you think that Wil will just give you money if he doesn't know if it is his baby or not?" she asks.

"I don't know but I have to try something. I can not have this baby. I just can't!"

"We can figure it out when we get back to Middleton. For now, let's just get something to eat because I am starving", she begs.

"OK, let's get something to eat but promise me that when we make it back to Middleton, you will help me figure this thing out so that we can get back here and get this over with."

"OK, I promise!"

It is almost as if Laura is starting to believe as if this abortion thing is just not going to happen. I don't want to start feeling like it's not going to happen, but I have to admit that I am starting to lose hope. In the end, I just may have to have this baby. But that means that I will be another teenage statistic and finish high school as a mother. This is certainly not what I intended for my life. Who would have thought? I never wanted to have children. It was just not part of the plan for me.

We finally make it to Burger King. We both order the Whopper Value Meal, except that mine ends up in the toilet. The morning sickness is still kicking in. Laura enjoys her meal, though. On the way back to Middleton, Laura and I agree to just relax and not speak of what happened. We have already agreed that our plan is to get back home, get the rest of the money and return to complete the procedure.

We are back in Middleton and go straight to Laura's house to try and figure out how we will get $200 to complete the abortion. With Laura by my side, I muster up the courage to call Wil and request his assistance, but he did just what Laura said that he would do. He went religious on me and decided that he didn't believe in abortions and would not agree to the procedure. He admits that even if he did have the money, he wouldn't give it to me because he can't be sure that the baby is his. *What a jerk! How stupid could I have been to sleep with this idiot! Oh, he doesn't believe in abortion but he believes in sex before marriage!!* It looks like I am on my own with this one or so it seems!

Laura and I flop down on her bed and carefully discuss what has happened so far and what we will do next. I have to relax! I decide to give Brittney a call with an update. I am sure that she is patiently waiting by the phone. "B, we're back!"

"Melissa, I have something to tell you before you go home. Your mother called and was looking for you. She kept questioning me about where you were and I had to tell her the truth. My mother forced me to tell her the truth and said that she would whip my behind if I didn't tell your mother what was going on with her child. So, I told her that you went to Marin for an abortion. She was very upset, but I had to tell her", she confesses.

"You are kidding, right?" I ask. By this time, Laura sits up on the bed as if she wants to know what was just said.

"Sweetheart, I am so sorry. I didn't mean to betray you this way, but she and my mother cornered me and I just couldn't look at your mother and lie. She was in tears, Meme."

There is really nothing more to be said. I don't know if I am pissed or relieved. Am I upset that she told my mother what I was up to or am I more upset that I didn't get the abortion completed? Now, I am starting to feel as though I should just give this whole thing up, realize that I have made a mistake, have this baby, love this baby, and move on with my life. I can still make something of my life. There are so many people who have made this mistake. But, I will wear shame for being pregnant. People will point the finger at me and I won't be able to handle that type of criticism. Regardless of what will happen, it is starting to feel as though I don't really have a choice at this point.

The phone rings and because I am so deep in thought, I almost miss the call. Laura comes down the hall to let me know that my mother is on the phone.

"My mother is going to kill me! Oh no – I don't want to speak to my mother. I can't face her right now. I know that she is going to blast me out for having made such a decision and not only that, but trying to go through with it. This will certainly be the end of the road for me."

Laura puts her hand over the mouthpiece and demands that I get the phone and talk to my mother. "It is time now, Melissa. Honey, it will be okay."

"Hello."

"Honey, how are you?" my mother asks. She sounds as if she doesn't have a clue where I was all day.

"Fine", I respond.

"Are you ready for me to pick you up?" she asks, sounding like it's just another fine day or something.

"No, I want to stay here tonight."

"Not a good idea. You are coming home with me tonight", she says. *How can I face my mother with what I have done today? What will she think of me now? Will she ever be able to trust me again?*

We live only 5 minutes away and I know that my mother will be here shortly. Laura just looks at me and says, "Meme, don't worry, it will all work out like it should."

My mother is pulling into Laura's driveway and my heart suddenly skips a beat. She has finally made it into the living room where I am waiting on her. Laura and her mother give us a little privacy to talk. She doesn't say anything about the abortion, which I think is quite strange. The silence is driving me crazy.

"Ma, you know where I was today, right?"

She responds softly, "Yes, I do and the moment that I found out where you were, I started praying and I knew that you would not have that abortion", she admits. *How can she possibly know that it wouldn't go through? I thought. Does she know something that I don't know?*

How can she be so calm at a time like this? Does she not understand what I am saying? I just said to her that I want to kill the baby that is growing inside of me. That should have triggered some type of emotion in her, but, instead, she remains calm.

"Meme, let's go home, honey. Please thank Mrs. Walters for having you over."

After saying goodbye to Laura and her mother, we head for home. On the way home, my mother asks if I want to speak to our pastor about this situation.

I think to myself, why in the world would I want to speak to him? What can he possibly say to me that he shouldn't have already said to his own daughter? No one knows this but she was with me the night I got pregnant. Janay stood at the back of the car while Wil and I got it on in the backseat of the car. I am pretty sure that I don't want to hear anything he has to say.

"No, I just want to go home. Thanks, though. I am not having a baby. I can't. I just want you to know that. I am going back to Marin and I am going to have this abortion and I don't care what you say."

My mother responds, "You are not going back to Marin to have an abortion. You are going to have that baby because it is not the baby's fault that you got pregnant. Just have the baby and I will help you take care of it. I give you my word on that."

Because my mother does not trust whether I will return to Marin or not, she and other family members decide to take turns watching me so to speak. At the time I got pregnant, I was living with my sister at her apartment, but my mother makes me come back home until I am too far long to have an abortion and then she allows me to go back to continue to live with my sister.

The summer is over and it is time to return to school, but this time, I will enter my senior year of high school as a "nobody". I won't be on the Cheerleader squad. I won't be on the Student Council. I won't be the most popular girl in school anymore. But, what I will do is shop for maternity clothes and baby furniture. My life will be totally different. The only thing I have to look forward to is giving birth to my first child.

Throughout the pregnancy, I experience tremendous moments of sadness. My friends are hanging out and no longer include me in on anything. Guys who would have killed to get my number are no longer interested. It is as if I have gone from the most popular girl in school to "Melissa who". The only people who will spend their Friday nights with me are Laura and Brittney on their way to the football game or the nightclub. They always find time to spend with me just to show that not everyone is against me.

Nine months later, my beautiful baby girl is born and I name her Christy Leigh Williams, who weighs in at 7 pounds, 10 ounces. Laura, Brittney, and the entire cheerleading squad show up at the hospital with their gifts for my baby.

I wonder how Cheryl would have felt if I had been able to give her a baby. It hurts to know what she has experienced, but my daughter means everything to me. I am so happy that she made it into the world.

CHAPTER 3

"Off to College"

My life may not be the most admired one, but during the spring of that same year, I graduate from high school, right along with my classmates. Graduation night is a little different for me, though. While all of my friends are out having dinner with their parents, or having small celebrations at their homes, I am home with my daughter spending as much time with her as possible knowing that I will be attending school in the Fall. Besides, hanging out with my friends is just not that important to me on graduation night. In my own little way, I celebrate my graduation night with the most important person in my life. When she looks at me, she doesn't see anything wrong with me. She doesn't judge me. She just loves me, faults and all.

Marin College's Fall session is beginning soon and my enrollment is completed. My major will be Communications, with a concentration in Broadcast Journalism. Someone has to take Oprah's place one day! I have to leave my baby behind but she is in the best of hands. She is with my mother. I know that every chance that I get to go home, I will do just that.

My classes have begun and I start meeting new friends. They are not as cool as Laura and Brittney, but they will have to do for now. Because Brittney is across the way at University of Marin, we still see each other on the weekends.

Leaving my Communications 101 class, I run into this guy named Kevin and we hit it off right away. Kevin is an upper classman and is absolutely gorgeous. I want to get to know him better. The feeling is mutual. We start eating together in the cafeteria. He starts walking me to class. We even take long walks around campus. I am not surprised when he finally invites me into his room, which is clearly against the rules.

"Melissa, sweetheart, I have a surprise for you", he says, after leaving the cafeteria one day.

"Surprise for me! Really? What is it?"

"I want to spend some quiet time with you in my dorm room", he answers. "What do you think?"

"Isn't that against the dorm rules?"

"Of course it is, and ---" he says, throwing his shoulders up. "Don't you want to see the surprise I have for you?"

"Why can't you show it to me outside your dorm room?"

"You will want to be inside for this surprise", he says with his sly grin.

Kevin finally convinces me to break the rules and join him in his dorm room for the evening. After the security guard has made his final rounds, I have now made it into Kevin's room. He gives me a tour of his room and within minutes, we end up on his bed having great sex. After tonight, we start spending quite a bit of time together. Kevin starts showing up at my classes and my work-study job to walk me home. I have to admit it. I am getting a big kick out of the attention that he is showing me. We even skip classes to be together. As much fun as we are having, Kevin and I are very careful to use protection. I just don't want anymore children right now. But, just when I think that things are really tight between us, I find out that Kevin is human.

One Sunday, after arriving back on campus, Kevin's new friend, Roslyn, makes sure that I am made aware that she spent the weekend with Kevin. This news has struck a nerve! I have to break it off with him because he won't embarrass me this way!

Kevin continues to pursue me, even though I don't want him anymore. He can't get it through his head, though. One day, he catches up with me as I am leaving my Broadcasting class. "Melissa, what is your problem? What did I do wrong?" he asks.

"Why don't you ask your little girlfriend? Maybe Roslyn will be able to explain it to you. Listen, I don't have time for this. Please leave me alone. I don't want you anymore!"

"So, is she why you are upset? Ok, yeah I fucked that girl, but she means nothing to me. You are the one I am out here with. You are the one that I spend time with getting to know. You don't see me sitting around trying to get to know her. It is you that I want!"

"Really? I can't tell! Listen. I need to focus on my studies. I didn't come to college to fall in love and spend all my time with just one guy. Let's just see other people and move on, Kevin."

"Fine! Well, fuck you then!"

Kevin doesn't move on, but instead, he starts acting like a mad man and threatens anyone who gets close to me. None of the guys want to be seen with me because they are afraid that he will taunt them. He is doing everything he can to make my life here at college a living nightmare.

Aside from all of this unnecessary drama, I am excelling in all of my classes. My professor is giving me extra help because he really believes that I have a good chance at being the next 'Oprah Winfrey'. He meets me after class to give me some special tips and insight into the Internships so that I can start building my career the right way. He says that I will eventually have my own show with the College's Communications Department by the time I am a senior. Luckily for me, he is the head of that program. To stay on point with everything, I do my best to avoid Kevin. Through his basketball buddies, he usually finds out what my shifts are at the library and shows up at the end of my shifts to walk me to my room. It is starting to feel as if he is doing this just to keep tabs on who may be waiting there for me. This scares most people, but I know that he is harmless.

Three Weeks Before Summer Break Begins.

Tonight is a celebration and not even Kevin is going to mess it up. It's the debut of my program, "Fun In High School", that is set to air on PBS. This is from one of my communications classes where we are assigned to a local high school to go out and get footage and bring it back to the Communications Lab, edit it, and load it onto the Master Tape. It comes on at 6:30 p.m., right after dinner. To celebrate, my friends have decided to come over to my lobby and we plan to watch it together. I am so excited! It is still hard for me to watch myself on television. By the cheers and applause, I can see that my friends think that I did a great job! The show is a huge success! There are 2 more episodes to go! Now that the show is over, it is time for bed. I head upstairs to my room, but just before shutting off my light, I can hear someone yelling my name and it's coming from below my window. I look outside and it is Kevin! He acts like he is drunk or something. He is asking for me to come down because he needs to talk to me.

"Melissa, I need you! Please come down now! I need to talk to you. It won't be long. I just need to holla at you for a minute! Come on girl! I need to talk to you right now! Please, Melissa!" he continues to yell.

"I might as well go down. He is not going to stop", I say to my roommate, Jennifer.

"Melissa, don't do it! Don't go anywhere with that fool! Let him yell! He is making a fool out of himself!" she says.

"What harm can it do? I will just be a minute. I won't go off with him or anything. We will just talk. I just don't want to hear the yelling anymore."

"Alright, Melissa, whatever!" she says, rolling back over in her bed.

At one time, I was really excited about this guy and it will be nice to just see what he has to say to me. It may be interesting. Against my roommate's wishes, I decide to go downstairs to speak with Kevin. Besides, it's the end of the semester and we will all be going our separate ways soon. I won't see him again until next Fall, so I figure it is okay to visit with him for a few minutes. What harm can it do?

"Kevin, what do you want?" I say, finally making it outside.

"I just want to talk to you", he says, slurring his words.

"You're drunk, Kevin! I don't want to be out here with you like this."

"Come on. Let's just go for a walk. I just want to spend some time with you. Don't you love me anymore?"

"Ok! If it will shut you up! Fine. Let's walk."

Kevin and I decide to go to the Activities Center to play pool with some of his friends. There's a group of students hanging outside the center. It is such a beautiful evening. It seems as if there are a million stars painted across the sky. Without thinking, I decide to go past the Activities Center. We walk beyond the point where there is any visibility. I have no idea what Kevin is planning for us. *Is he trying to display his romantic side or what, I wonder.*

Kevin has a different set of plans. Out of nowhere, he grabs me by the hands and pulls me into the wooded area and pushes me to the ground and starts to rape me. He takes my hands and pins them over my head. He uses one had to pin me down and the other hand to pull up my mini-skirt. He rips off my panties and enters into me very hard. The pain makes me gasp for air. Throughout the process, he is asking me who I had been 'fucking'. He even makes a reference that I must have been 'fucking Jesus or somebody'. He finally has an orgasm and is finally finished. I attempt to scream but nobody hears me. His long body just overpowers me.

"Now there, that wasn't so bad, was it?" he asks, as he is zipping his pants.

Did this thing just happen with Kevin? Is he standing there with that smirk on his face as if he just won the lottery or something? What in the world is this guy thinking? Does he not understand that I did not want to have sex with him? Does he understand that "no" in this case definitely meant "no"?

He gets up and leaves me right there and orders me to get up and go. It is hard to stand up. It is almost as if putting one foot in front of the other one is such a hard task. I finally regain enough composure to get up and leave. I slowly walk back to my room with grass in my hair and this is when I discover that I am also missing an earring. *Why didn't I listen to Jennifer?*

When I return, Jennifer can tell that something is wrong. There's grass in my hair and my earring is missing and I am crying. "What did he do to you? I told you not to go with him!" she exclaims.

"What do I do now?" I ask, as tears quickly fill my eyes.

We both decide that I should take a shower and get some rest. I can't fall asleep, so my roommate and I sit up talking for awhile. Summer break is approaching and this will be behind us and we will never have to speak about this ever again. I just want to go to sleep and forget about this. She promises to never disclose what happened tonight to anyone.

"Melissa, I know that you don't want to, but I really think that you should speak with a counselor when you get home, just to get through this", she suggests.

"I will be just fine. But, thanks for being concerned. Just go to sleep."

I close my eyes knowing that I will have to totally erase what just happened out of my head altogether. It doesn't matter anyway. In two weeks, we will all meet at breakfast and say our goodbyes to one another for the summer. I will not have to face Kevin anymore and that is just fine with me. Maybe he won't return next Fall or maybe I won't return. I never want to see this guy again.

Two weeks have almost passed and I haven't heard from Kevin at all. I don't think I have even seen him around the campus. The final event for this Session is a Bar-B-Que in the Dining Hall. My friends and I are all hanging out, and Kevin just walked in and is heading our way.

"Hey, Melissa! You looking good today baby doll. Make sure you have a good summer and I will see you in the Fall", he says. *I can't believe this idiot said anything to me after what happened between us. What nerve!*

****

For the first time in 8 months, I am back in my old room in Middleton with "B" talking about the "old times". We just finished eating some pizza and for some reason, it doesn't settle well in my stomach, which sends me rushing to the bathroom. Brittney follows me into the restroom. "Melissa, why are you throwing up?" she asks.

It's like dejavu or something! I don't even have to go to the doctor this time. I just know that I am pregnant and instantly become nervous, scared, and angry. I am not in this situation because I made a decision to sleep with a guy but the guy made this decision for me. What in the world am I going to do? How am I going to tell my mother that I am pregnant? I am certainly NOT going to tell her how this came about to be. I just can't tell her. My roommate, Jennifer, is the only one who is armed with the truth about that night and she promises never to tell anyone.

CHAPTER 4

"It's Not His Fault!"

*I*am constantly throwing up and either my mother doesn't notice it or she already knows it and just doesn't want to confront me about what is going on with me. She never asks, so I never tell her anything. Day in and day out, I am dealing with what happened just three weeks before we dismissed for the summer. I can't seem to get it out of my head. I can't disclose this truth to anyone. They won't understand. There will be too many questions and I don't want to have to deal with this.

Because I am so angry with Kevin, I start having thoughts that, perhaps, I should share this information with him. I think that he should know what his actions caused. If I am going to go through this nightmare, he should have to go through it also. With the support of my friends, they are able to get Kevin's contact information out in California. Apparently, he is in California spending his summer with his fiancée, Marshawna, who lives in California. I had no idea that he had a fiancée! He certainly didn't act like it at school.

While I am here everyday throwing up my guts, he is living the good life out in California with his sweetheart. My friends are just as shocked as I am to discover that Kevin is engaged to be married. After careful thought, I decide to give him a call. I don't care if she answers, nor do I care if he hates me for this, but he needs to know what he did to me.

"Hello", the woman on the other end says.

"Hello, with whom am I speaking?"

"This is Marshawna", she responds. "Who is this?"

"Oh, I am sorry, Marshawna, but this is Melissa. Is Kevin available?"

"And who are you?" she asks.

"I am a friend from college. I have some very important information to share with him. So, if you don't mind, I would really like to speak with him right now. It's rather urgent."

"Sure, hold on", she says. My stomach is starting to ache. I haven't practiced this conversation enough because I really don't know how to tell him that he has a baby on the way.

I can clearly hear muffled voices in the background as if Marshawna is questioning him about getting a call from a female from college. He finally comes on the phone after a couple of minutes.

"Hello."

By the way he says "hello", I can tell that he has no idea that it is me on the other end of the phone.

"Kevin, this is Melissa and I have news for you."

"Ok, what is it?" he asks. "…and make it quick!"

"Here it is. I am pregnant and it is your child", I blurt out, without a care in the world.

"Man, get the fuck outta here", he says, very angrily. "You must be out of your mind if you think that I believe that you are pregnant with my child. You were going back and forth to Middleton every weekend. How do I know who you were fucking up there?"

"It is your baby, ok. Remember two weeks before we left for the summer and how you insisted that we have sex? Because of that, I am now pregnant with your child. You don't have to believe me, you asshole, but this is your child, you son of a bitch. You did this to me and you know it!"

At this point, I am extremely angry with him and begin to cry.

Marshawna must have overheard the conversation because she grabs the phone out of Kevin's hand hoping to get more information.

"Excuse me, but what the hell are you saying? Are you saying that you are pregnant with Kevin's baby? How could that be? He is engaged to be married to me."

"Sweetheart, Kevin and I had a relationship for a short time at school. He and I were sleeping together almost everyday. I hate to tell you this, but I was in his dorm room on several occasions. We spent quite a bit of time together and he never mentioned anything about you. I am sorry that you have to hear about it this way. It is what it is."

There is complete silence on the phone.

"Keep talking", she says. "I want to hear everything! Don't stop now!"

I can hear Kevin in the background ordering her to get off the phone with me". *Should I tell her about how her fiancée forced me to have sex with him?*

"I was really falling for him, Marshawna. We had a good time together. I *just* found out that you are his fiancée. I never knew that he was seeing anyone else because he never mentioned anything about you. And, I know that you don't want to hear this, but he certainly didn't act like there was a fiancee in the picture. He didn't just sleep with me at Marin College, but others as well. At one time, Kevin and I had made a pact that we would be together as long as we were both on campus. But, when I found out that he was with this other girl, I left him alone! But he couldn't take it. He started stalking me at school and threatening other guys who were interested in me. And the worst thing of all is that just three weeks before we were dismissed for summer break, Kevin raped me."

I can hear a big gasp on the other end of the phone.

"I told him that I did not want to have sex, but he insisted. He may give you a totally different version of what happened, but this is the true version. I don't want to be in a relationship with him, but just want him to know that he got me pregnant."

"So what do you want from him?" she asks, with a bitter tone in her voice. "What do you hope this call will do for you? I hate you bitch whores who lay down with another woman's man like he is yours. I am so fucking tired of this."

"I don't want anything from him. I just wanted him to know. Sweetheart, I know that you are angry and shocked right now, but *I* am not your problem."

By this time, I can tell that she is totally fed up with the whole situation and demands that Kevin leave her house. I didn't realize that this news would cause this much commotion. She is crying and screaming and asking him how he could do this to her after all she had done for him. He finally grabs the phone out of her hand.

"You bitch! How dare you call this house? Don't ever call here again!" he screams.

It is always a surprise how men tend to react when they are caught in their lies. All of a sudden, they become such 'woosies'. Not only is she made aware that he cheated on her while he was away at school, but she knows that he has a tendency to take sex from women who say "no".

The truth of the matter is that whether he steps up to the plate or not, I am still pregnant and it is *finally* time for me to come to grips with my current situation. I need to come clean and tell my mother the truth. She will be disappointed. The truth is that I am so afraid and wish that I never had to deal with anyone in the real world ever again. Being in this predicament, an abortion should have been the answer but for some reason, I don't even consider this as being an option this time.

Each morning, I wake up to face the challenge of being able to keep my food down. Morning sickness is kicking my butt! I just can't seem to find the energy to put my feet on the floor. After all of this time, I still haven't made an appointment at the gynecologist to get my prenatal vitamins. I am just too devastated!

"Mom, I have to talk to you."

"What about, Melissa?" she asks.

"Have you noticed that I have been sluggish lately and throwing up?"

"Yes, I have noticed it and I already know that you are pregnant again. You don't have to tell me. Don't you think I know my child?"

"When did you notice?"

"Couple of weeks after you came home for the summer. A mother knows."

"Are you mad at me?"

"I am not mad at you, but I wish that you would just make better choices about sex. I wish that you would stay focused and do what it is that you have to do and stop wasting all of your time worrying about boys", she chastises.

I want to tell her that I was trying to make a good choice. I want to tell her that I stopped accepting Kevin's offers for sex, but that he forced sex on me and even when I tried to do right, this trouble still followed me. To do that, I will open a can of worms and a big deal would be made about what Kevin did and I truly want to forget about that night. I don't want to bring it up ever again!

"Yes, mother, you are right. For whatever reason, I continue making these bad decisions and end up paying a big price for it. I am so sorry that I have disappointed you once again."

Although I am happy that my mother and I are finally able to talk about the situation at hand, I am still not ready to go visit a doctor. More and more time passes and I am still somewhat depressed. I am moping around the house feeling sorry for myself. Enrollment for the fall classes will begin soon and I won't be there. It isn't fair! I bet that Kevin will be there!

CHAPTER 5

"What's Wrong?"

*A*pproximately 8 months into the pregnancy, I finally decide to make an appointment with the gynecologist. Dr. Rogers gives me the news that I am suffering from low iron and that I need to take medication to build my iron before having this baby. A month later, I give birth to a 10 pound baby boy. I look into his beautiful eyes and the first name that comes to mind is "Kameron". He is such a perfect baby. He has beautiful hair, round cheeks, fat fingers, and beautiful lips. And he looks just like Kevin!

When the phone rings, the nurse answers and hands it over to me. I had an idea that as soon as the news that my baby is born makes it through the campus, Kevin would be calling.

"Hey Melissa, how are you doing sweetie?" says Erin, my college friend who helped me to locate Kevin's whereabouts.

"I am doing fine. I am just a little sore."

"I bet you are! The baby is *only* ten pounds. I think I would be sore also."

"So, have you seen him?"

"Of course I have seen him. As a matter of fact, he is right here and wants to talk to you", she says.

I don't have a chance to object to speaking with him because he is already on the phone. "Hello Melissa."

"Hello Kevin. How are you doing? I guess you heard that you have a son and his name is Kameron."

"Great choice; I love it. When do you think I will be able to see him?" he asks.

"I am not sure. We will talk about that later. So, now you want to acknowledge that this is your baby?"

"Let's just say that my mother helped me to see the light. I admitted being intimate with you and that it is certainly possible that the baby can be mine and she told me to 'do the right thing' by you and my baby. So, that is what I am trying - -."

Before he is able to finish his sentence, I interrupt him. "Hey, I am sorry Kevin. The doctor just came in and looks like he wants to talk to me so I will have to talk with you later. You can call me here at the hospital if you would like to speak to me. I will talk to you later."

I quickly drop the phone onto the receiver because I am eager to hear what the doctor has to say about me and the baby going home.

"Melissa, I have some disturbing news for you and I want your mother to be here so that she will help you understand what is going on with your son", he announces.

Almost frantically, I blurt out, "What is wrong with my baby? Is he going to die or something?"

"Where is your mother?" he asks, not acknowledging what I just said.

"She should be back any moment."

Just as I say this, my mother walks into the room. She must have gone to the cafeteria because she has the coffee in a cup holder with several napkins wrapped around it.

"Oh great, Mom, you are here. The doctor is just about to deliver news about my son. Apparently, there is something wrong with him."

"Listen, we did some tests because we couldn't understand why your son was spitting up bile. It appears that he has a hole in the upper and bottom chambers of his heart. This is something that usually happens in infants, but these holes normally close on their own after a short period of time. Your son's holes are just too big and there may have to be an operation to save his life."

"Oh my God! This must be because I didn't get prenatal care, right? I did this to him. This is my fault, isn't it?"

My mother immediately comes to my rescue and wraps her motherly arms around me to comfort me. She starts humming words to a hymnal and rocking me in her arms as if I am a 4 year old toddler who just scraped up her knee. Although I appreciate it, I am unable to get those words out of my head that the doctor just spoke.

"No, this is not your fault", the doctor consoles. "This is just a birth defect that sometimes happens. There will need to be more extensive tests run on him, but unfortunately, we are unable to run those tests here at this hospital. He will have to be transferred to Marin and they will take much better care of him over there." *Did he just say Marin? That is where Kevin is. I mean, he did just say that he wants to see his son. I hate that it has to be under these conditions, but at least, he will get to see him.*

"Ok, so when do we leave?"

"Unfortunately, your son is being released but you will have to stay here to recuperate. You still haven't had a bile movement and you aren't healing as quickly as I'd like you to. Once you do that, you will be released. Until that time, you will remain here in the hospital. We have already made arrangements for your son to be transported out of here this afternoon. I will have the nurse bring your son to you for you to say goodbye to him."

The doctor and nurses leave the room to give us a moment to digest the news just delivered. I don't know what to feel right now. In some way, I feel betrayed by God. I feel like he is punishing me for having sex with a guy after I had made a commitment to serve Him. *Why in the world is this happening to me?* "Momma, is he going to die?" I ask, starting to cry.

"You heard what the doctor said. They should be able to correct this with surgery. He will be fine."

I hate to admit it but I am afraid for my son. I begin to wonder if my actions will cause him to die. I do; however, feel a little better after me and my Mother pray. I am already starting to miss him and he hasn't left yet. By the time our prayer ends, the nurse is walking into the room carrying my son. She hands him over to me. He looks so peaceful wrapped in the blanket.

"Hey there little guy", I say to him. "It's mommy. Aren't you just a perfect picture of a baby? Well son, you have to leave me now, but it is just temporary. The doctors want you to be seen by other doctors who have more experience just to make sure that you are doing okay. I am always with you, baby. You will be fine. I will be there as soon as possible. But guess what? You will be over in Marin where your father is. Who knows? Maybe he will be able to come over and see you after he gets out of school."

I am holding his hand and speaking with him as if he really understands what I am saying to him. It doesn't matter. He needs to feel his mother's comforting and soothing voice in the same way that my mother comforts me when I am hurting. Within a short period of time, the nurse returns for Kameron. She takes him from my arms and prepares him for his trip to Marin, which is only two hours away. I can already feel the tears coming.

"You know that he is going to be just fine, Melissa", my mother says. "They will take good care of him. Don't worry about it. You need to get better so that you can join him and be there for him." As much as I know that my mother is right, I don't want to move at all. I'd rather continue to blame myself for my son's condition. If I had not eaten 'baby powder' and non-food items, maybe my son would still be here with me.

The phone rings and it is Kevin. "Well hello, Melissa. It is Kevin. How are you doing?"

"I am doing okay, but I have news for you."

"What is it?" he asks.

"Your son is on his way to Marin", I explain. "The doctors want him to get more tests done because he has been spitting up bile. They say that he has a hole in the top and bottom chambers of his heart."

"Oh my goodness!" he responds. "That is terrible! How could you let this happen? Why didn't you take better care of yourself? Are you that stupid or what? And because of you, my son may die."

Kevin's mean words hurt so deeply. He isn't doing anything that I wasn't already doing to myself. He is right to blame me for what has happened to Kameron. It is my fault. After he calms down, he eventually asks for the name of the hospital where Kameron is headed.

"Marin University Hospital. He will be in the Neo-Natal section of the hospital. He will be there by 3 pm. Please take care of my son."

"You mean, our son, right?" he asks.

Kevin agrees to go over to the hospital to be with *our son*.

"Will you please call me and let me know how he is doing? I can't sit around and wait for the doctors to tell me anything. Look at it this way. At least you will get to meet your son. He really is a perfect baby."

"I can't wait to meet him", he says, just before hanging up the phone. *'Why didn't you do something?", "How could you let this happen?" These words echo in my ear and continue to pierce my heart even after he has hung up the phone.*

CHAPTER 6

"Jesus Loves You, This I Know!"

"*E*xcuse me ma'am, my name is Kevin and I am looking for the Neo-natal section. My son was brought here from Middleton", he explains.

"This way, sir", she directs. Kevin follows this nurse into the Neo-Natal section. And you are?" she asks.

"I am the baby's father", he answers.

"I thought so. I can see the resemblance. He is such a cute baby and big, too!"

"Well this will be my first time meeting him because I wasn't in Middleton when he was born. But, I am glad to *finally* get a chance to meet him." As Kevin gets closer to his son's incubator, he becomes more and more anxious. Kevin walks past a few babies that are small enough to fit in his hands and becomes nervous. When he finally makes it to his son's bed, he begins to weep. Kevin is having a hard time seeing his son hooked up to the machines.

While my son lay in Marin fighting for his life in the Neonatal Intensive Care Unit, I am still in Middleton. The doctor won't release me until I show some signs of improvement. After a week, I am finally released and although I am more than ready to go to Marin to be with Kameron, my mother convinces me to go home and get some rest and promises me that we will go tomorrow.

The following day, we travel to the hospital to see Kameron. When I walk into the hospital and see my son hooked up to the machines, I suddenly become afraid. This is a very troubling experience because he looks so healthy but is so ill. The doctors carefully explain to me that my son is experiencing a birth defect called **ASD/VSD**. It is a form of a congenital heart disease. This simply means that there is a hole in the top and bottom chambers of his heart. They explain to me that the holes are too big to close on their own and that they will monitor him and will decide when or if he will qualify for open heart surgery. He is born as a 10 pound baby, but is beginning to drastically lose weight. They explain that he needs to gain weight, not lose it. They go on to say that if he continues to lose weight, they will have to operate on him right away.

It seems like the more I pray, the worse he gets. After just two months, the doctors all agree that my son's condition is worsening and that they will have to send him to Bauerville for a possible open heart surgery. They want the pediatric cardiologists there to look at him and determine if he needs the open heart surgery or the bypass surgery.

Is he strong enough to hold up to a major surgery? He is only 2 months old. Within two weeks, we are on our way to Bauerville. The trip only lasts for 4 hours but it is starting to seem like 8 hours. Kameron looks so content in his car seat. My mother seems so nervous. She must be because she starts saying things that I just do not want to hear. "Melissa, I want to talk with you about something", she begins to say.

"Ok", I respond.

"I want you to understand that God giveth and He taketh away", she says.

I know where this conversation is headed. She is trying to prepare me in the event my son doesn't return home. I am not accepting that. "Mom, I understand what you are trying to do. My son *is* coming home and will be just fine. I know it! I won't hear that nonsense that you are saying. My son is going to live through this, ok!"

"OK baby, I hear you. I was just trying to help."

"Then, if you want to help, pray for my son", I respond. "Agree with me in prayer for his health to be renewed if you want to do anything for me."

After the long drive, we finally make it to the hospital and he is taken directly to the pediatric intensive care unit, where they are already expecting Kameron. He meets with the team of cardiology specialists and they unanimously agree that he should go ahead and have the open heart surgery.

"But, he has lost so much weight since his birth. Is he strong enough to go through this open heart surgery?"

The head doctor is from Arabia and speaks with a very strong accent. "I wouldn't agree to this if I didn't believe that he would be fine, Ms. Williams", he says, with such confidence. Although this is my first time meeting this doctor, I feel so safe with him. He truly makes me feel that I can trust him with my son.

Surgery will take place in two days! Kameron is first on the list. I decide to give my mother a call and give her the news. She says that she will put it before the church so that they will remember him in prayer.

"I am very proud of you, Melissa, for how you are handling all of this and on your own, I might add", she says.

"Mom, I learn from the best and one thing I know is that I am never alone. You have always taught me to trust God. You said that prayer changes things."

I can tell that my mother is somewhat moved by my comments. Because she is not the kind of person who likes to display her emotions, she makes an excuse to get off the phone with me. "Well, let me get off the phone to cook. These grandkids are all hungry."

"OK, Mother. I will talk to you later."

For some strange reason, I get this idea that Kevin may be interested in knowing about his son so I decide to call him to share the news with him about Kameron. I call his mother's house only to learn that he is back in California with Marshawna.

"Hello", Marshawna says.

"Hello Marshawna, this is Melissa. May I please speak with Kevin?"

"Hold on. Kevin, telephone!" she says.

Kevin comes to the phone shortly. "Kevin, I just wanted to give you a call with an update about your son's condition. The doctors have decided to do the open heart surgery in a couple of days. They feel that he is strong enough to handle the operation."

"Ok, great, what do you want me to do?" he says so abruptly.

"I was just telling you! I thought you would want to hear about your son's condition! Excuse me!"

"I don't know what the hell you want me to do about it. I am here so you just need to handle it", he says. Before he finishes his sentence, I bang the phone in his ear. There is no way that I will waste anymore of my time dealing with this man. I don't need him anyway. All I need right now is my peace with God.

****

The next day, I arrive at the hospital to find my son crying and whining. Because he is not allowed to eat anything before surgery, he is just a little frustrated from being hungry. I pick him up and hold him closely. Nothing else in the world matters right now. All that matters at this moment is my son. The Arabian doctor who is performing the surgery has just walked in and whispers something in the nurse's ear. He turns to me and tells me that it is time for my son to go.

"Before you take my son away, will you please do me a small favor?"

"Sure, Ms. Williams", he answers.

"I would like for you, me and the nurse to hold hands and pray." He looks at the nurse and she looks back at him and they both agree without hesitation.

"Dear Lord. Thank you for waking us up this morning in our right minds. Thank you for these doctors and nurses who will now care for my son. Lord, I pray that you give them wisdom to know what to do. Lord, please make my son strong for this surgery. Send the angels to encamp around his bedside. Let the angels play with him and make him comfortable. These and other blessings I ask in thy son Jesus' name. Amen."

I kiss my baby on his forehead and tell him that I love him and that I will see him when he gets out of surgery. The doctors and nurses disappear down the hall with my baby and all I know is that I believe that it is God's plan for him to return.

The surgery is a success! After a week, my son is being released from the hospital. The doctor prescribes several medications that I will have to make sure that he gets on a daily basis. I will have to stay awake all night just to make sure that I give him his medication at the time that he is supposed to get it. This goes on and on and so do the checkups until he is given 'thumbs up' from all of the doctors.

When Kameron and I make it back home, Brittney and Laura pay us a visit. They both come with gifts for Kameron. Laura walks in with a huge teddy bear that has a big red heart in the middle of its chest. Punching the middle of the heart will send the bear into a singing frenzy. He sings special songs like, "Jesus Loves You", "He's Got the Whole World in his Hands", and it says a very special prayer. The bear is so special and I know that Kameron will feel so comforted with this bear alongside him in bed. Brittney walks in with a frame that has a picture of me holding Kameron after he was born. Underneath the picture, she had it engraved, "A Mother's Love". It is so beautiful. I thank them both for their gifts.

"Melissa, I have to go because I am meeting some of my friends at the move theatre. I never get to see them because we are, of course, at different schools. We agreed to come home for the weekend and meet up to see the new movie. And you know we have to drive 45 minutes away just to see a movie", Laura explains.

"Sure, no problem, have fun and be safe." Before leaving, Laura reaches over and kisses Kameron on the forehead.

"So, do you like the gifts?" Brittney asks.

"Of course I do. They are both so special. Thank you so much."

"Hey, I was wondering if you would like to sneak away for a moment while Kameron is asleep. I have to show you something", she says. "Your mother said that she would watch him for a few moments. I really want you to see something."

Brittney and I decide to take a break and walk over to her house. Her parents aren't home. They have gone out for their regular Saturday night dinner and the house is completely empty. Brittney leads me to her bedroom and goes underneath the bed and pulls out a videotape. From the doorway, I can clearly see that it is titled, "Me". "Have a seat!" she instructs. I take a seat in the chair next to her bed. She flops down on her freshly made bed and switches the remote to "play".

The video starts and you can tell right away that this is made by amateurs. The music sounds like "porno" music. The first person that I notice is Brittney and she is surrounded by a couple of guys who look like they are just about to undress her.

"Girl, is that you?"

"Yes, it is me. Isn't this cool?"

"You made a sex video, Brittney? Are you crazy? Who else has a copy of this?"

"Nobody!" she shouts. "Calm down and watch it."

"I don't want to watch this, sweetheart. Why did you make a video like this?"

"It was fun. And besides, I was paid to do it."

"Paid? You were paid for this?"

"Yes, I was paid to do this. I know the guys in the video, so it was cool. And, no, I won't disclose them. That is why they have masks over their face. Just relax, please."

"Do you not remember what happened to Kendra Merengo who made that video? She ended up ruining her reputation and giving up her crown after she was found out. I don't want to see that same thing happen to you."

"Melissa, relax."

Before I know it, I am looking up at this video and one of the guys is parting her legs prepared to give her oral sex. She seems to really enjoy it. I hate to admit it but I start to imagine myself in the video receiving this same pleasure that Brittney is receiving. It has been a long time since I have been intimate with anyone. It has taken awhile for me to get past my experience with Kevin. The video ends. Just watching Brittney, I can tell that she is very proud of herself for making this video. "It wasn't that bad, right?" she asks.

"Goodnight, Brittney. I have to get back home. I will see you tomorrow. I will let myself out."

CHAPTER 7

"Back To School"

Kameron is doing much better, so now I have the opportunity to return to Marin to pick up where I left off. I re-enroll and begin the following fall session. At some point, I know that I will eventually see Kevin again on campus. I do not let him know that I am returning. He doesn't seem to have any interest in his son so I don't bother to communicate with him either.

Kevin and I try to avoid each other as much as possible. I see him in the cafeteria, in the library, and in the gym. It is a small college campus so there is just no getting around it. The inevitable finally happens. He catches me when I am by myself and makes a comment when we see each other in the cafeteria.

"You look great", he says.

"Thanks."

"So, how's my son?"

"Let's not go there. But, I have a question for you. How's your fiancée? That seems to be the only person you really care about anyway. Since you asked, we are both doing just fine without you."

"So, it's like that, huh?"

"Yes, it's just like that!" Kevin walks away because I am sure that he doesn't want to get into it with me right now.

On a different note, my professor has signed me up to be a spokesperson for "Say No to Drugs." Being this spokesperson means that I will get the opportunity to go to all the local high schools encouraging the students to stay off drugs. My grade is based on how effective my speech is and the feedback that I get from it. My professor tells me that I am a "natural up there". Doing this causes my schedule to be pretty hectic and I certainly don't have much time for a social life. Spring Break is approaching and I am going home for a quick break. I really miss my children.

It's Homecoming Weekend in Middleton and I decide to go solo to the game. I am not solo for long because I was just introduced to a friend of a friend. His name is Abernathy Richards and they call him, "Rock". He is such a sweet guy, not to mention, a few years younger than me. But, he really knows how to put a smile on my face. We decide to hit some of the "after parties". And of course, we end up spending the night together.

After this weekend, I spend several more weekends together with "Rock". He doesn't seem to have a problem with the fact that I already have two children. His mother does, though. As a matter of fact, she forbids him to see me, but he does anyway. We continue to see each other in spite of the fact that neither of our parents wants us to be together. We are attracted to each other and it is very obvious.

Every chance that we get, we are intimate. It is as if we just can't keep our hands off of each other. When I am not in Middleton, I miss him and I can't wait to come home to be with him. He seems to have a little bit of experience in the lovemaking department. With the age difference, I am sure that he wastes no time in bragging to his friends about our intimate connections.

As crazy as it is, "Rock" and I continue to have sex without protection, over and over again. I should be more responsible than this, considering the fact that I already have two children. After several months, I discover that I am pregnant, AGAIN! This will be my third child.

"Rock, I have news for you", I say to him one night while eating dinner.

"Oh yeah, what is it? Let me guess. You want to tell me how sexy I am in bed, right?"

"Well, you are all that, but no, that is not what I want to tell you", I respond. "We are pregnant. I know that this is not the news that you want to hear being that you are still in high school."

"I am shocked!" he responds.

"I don't know why. It's not like we use protection to prevent this. I should know better because I already have two children. I am so sorry. That "pulling out" thing doesn't always work. We were very careless, Rock."

"You didn't do this by yourself. I could have made sure that we were being more careful. This is not entirely your fault, Melissa. Listen, I love you and I think –", he says, before I interrupt him.

"I want to move to Florida with my sisters and just have the baby there. I can't do it here again. I am too embarrassed. And besides, I won't be able to go back to school right now. I have to leave and I need for you to understand."

"Melissa, why would you want to move away now that you are carrying my child? I will be here for you. I won't abandon you like the others did. As soon as I graduate, I will get a job and take care of you and all of your children. I love you. Please don't leave me", he pleads. "Don't you love me?"

"Yes, I do love you, but you are so much younger than me. It just won't work!"

"It won't work? It worked just fine when we were making love!"

"I can't, Rock! I just can't!"

"Melissa, if you leave Middleton and move to Florida, this relationship is over. I won't be able to stay true to you. I won't have you away in Miami with our child living your life without me. Don't you love me the way that I love you?"

"Rock, I love you more than you will ever know. You have been the only guy who has been there for me. You went against all odds just to be with me, but this isn't about you. I am too ashamed to stay here and have a third child. I appreciate the fact that you would go through this with me, but I have to do what is best for me", I explain.

"The bottom line is simple, Melissa. If you leave, our relationship is over", he says, while turning away from me.

"Baby, I love you. I will never forget you. Just know that you were not just a fling with me. I really wanted to be with you for the rest of my life like we discussed. Goodbye, Rock."

No matter how much I love this guy, I have to get out of here. I have to do what I think is best for me, my unborn child, and the two children that I already have.

When I make it home, I pick up the phone and call my sister. "So, Rachel, make room for me and my two children because I am coming to Miami."

CHAPTER 8

"Wouldn't You Do It For Me?"

*M*y third child will soon be born. In the meantime, I babysit for my sisters, Rachel and Diana, who have also just recently moved to Miami. But, shortly after arriving in Miami, I find out that my sister Diana is under investigation by an organization called Children Come First. I am not sure who they are or what they do, but whatever it is, she is very upset about it.

Apparently, someone called the abuse hotline and reported that my sister was leaving her children home by themselves and that they are outside most of the time getting into all sorts of trouble. "Diana, is there anyone around who could have watched the children for you?" I ask. She seems to be pretty upset after her visit from the social worker.

"No, everyone has to work. These women around here do what they have to do. Most of them have to leave their children at home, but just haven't gotten caught yet. What do they expect? I am a single mother. I don't make enough money to pay someone to watch them so I have to leave them home!" she explains. "I do the best that I can!"

"Honey, don't cry. It is going to be okay. I got it! I have a solution! I will say that I was in the house watching the kids and the people who called just didn't know about it."

"You would do that?"

"Of course, I will. I can't sit by and watch my sister lose her children. This isn't entirely your fault. And by the way, who is *Children Come First?*"

"We call them CCF for short. They are the folks who come around and will take your kids if you aren't doing what they think you should be doing", she explains. "People will call on you and they will come out to see what is going on in the home and if they don't like what they see or even if they don't like *you*, they will remove your children and there is nothing you can do about it."

"That sounds crazy to me! So, how do I reach them?"

My sister hands me the contact information for the social worker and I decide to give her a call to carry through with my plan to help my sister.

"Hello, this is Mrs. Avila, how may I help you?" she says.

"This is Melissa Williams and I am calling on behalf of Diana Williams. I understand that you have an open case regarding her children being left at home alone. I am calling to let you know that I was watching her children. They were not home alone."

"And you are?" she asks.

"I'm sorry. I am her sister, Diana Williams. As I was saying, I was there with them. They would, oftentimes, go outside when they weren't supposed to and I would punish them when I found out. But, they were always here with me", I explain.

"Really?" she asks.

"Yes ma'am, I am there everyday with those kids. I watch my other sister's kids also. So, whoever called you was mistaken", I explain.

"Are you sure?" asks Mrs. Avila. "Would you testify under oath regarding this matter?

"Of course, I would."

The following evening, Diana receives a call from Mrs. Avila informing her that they are dropping her case due to the fact that she did have someone watching the children. Her release form reads, "no indicators of abuse found".

My sister is relieved! Because of my testimony, she will not have to live under the careful watchful eye of CCF. She is so happy that she decides to take me out for dinner at Red Lobster's.

"Thanks so much for looking out for me. They were all over me about leaving the children home alone. I don't know what I would have done if they had taken my children from me. You saved the day for me. I was so scared. But God knows that I had to leave them home because I have to work to provide for them, being that their sorry ass father won't send me any money to care for them."

"Well, you would have done it for me, right?" I ask, not looking up from dipping my fries in the ketchup.

"Sure."

CHAPTER 9

"Angels From Above"

*A*lthough Rock is back in Alabama and getting along just fine, he and I are also getting along fine as friends. He is just as much a part of this pregnancy as I am. He wants to know everything that is going on with his baby. Rock is thrilled that he will be a father soon. He says that his mother is starting to come around about the baby, but she still wants to be sure that this baby is, in fact, Rock's child before she will welcome it into her life. But Rock claims that she has already been telling the other family members that she is going to soon be a grandmother.

The closer the baby arrival date, the more Rock and I talk. Today is January 23rd, which is also Kameron's birthday. How awesome it will be for my baby to be born on its brother's birthday! Rock and I are on the phone and right in the middle of our conversation, a sharp pain hits me all of a sudden.

"Oooohhh, that was a good one", I say, with my eyes looking up to heaven as if Rock can see what I am doing.

"What's wrong?" he asks.

"Your baby is pretty active in there. I think it wants out right away. That would be so cool if he were born tonight because this is also Kameron's birthday. I have to go now, but I will be in touch with you if we end up having a baby tonight."

Instead of just staying in bed waiting on the labor to progress, I decide to watch some television. TV Land is running a marathon of "Good Times". One of my favorite episodes is on. It's the episode where Keith and Thelma get married and right now, Michael is singing. My bags are already packed and until my contractions are at least 30 minutes apart, I am going to just sit here and keep watching television. A couple of hours have passed and it is finally time to go!

"Rachel, it is time to go now", I say, very calmly. "Please call Rock for me and let him know that we are headed to the hospital. His number is on my nightstand."

"Will do", she responds. She gives him a call to give him the news that we are heading out on our way to the hospital and that we may end up with our baby tonight. He is thrilled. I can hear him screaming through the phone.

"OK, I am coming", she responds. She grabs her glasses, her book, and helps me to the car. After getting settled in, we are finally on our way to Miami General Hospital. At this point, the contractions are at least 45 minutes or so apart. We finally get to the hospital after what seems like hours. Now that the labor is starting to get more and more intense, I feel like we are closer to having a baby. As soon as I get into my hospital bed, the nurse hooks me up to the monitor. The baby's heart rate is normal. I am starting to dilate and I am up to about 5 cm at this point. The nurse comes in and takes my vital signs but doesn't say a word. Her silence leads me to believe that all is fine. Moments later, the doctor walks in with the nurse next to his side.

"Melissa, we checked your vital signs and it looks like you have a fever. I am not sure where this is coming from but just to be on the safe side, we will not give you any type of medications because we need to make sure that the baby is safe. Your urine is a brownish color as well. We don't know what is going on, but we will be getting the baby out as soon as possible", he explains. *Surely, he can't be talking about not getting any anesthesia!*

"Doctor, does that include anesthesia?"

"That is correct! Giving you *any* type of medication can possibly harm the baby and we won't take that chance. So, just relax, breathe, calm yourself and let's get ready to have this baby", she advises.

"Rachel, did you hear what the doctor just said?"

"No, what happened?"

"The doctor just explained that I have a fever and that my urine is brownish in color. She is not quite sure what this is all about and decided that I shouldn't have any type of medications just to make sure the baby is safe. So that means that I will have to deliver this baby without anesthesia."

"You will be alright, Melissa. Just breathe."

Many contractions later, I am finally dilated to 10cm and it is time to deliver this baby. The doctor returns to the room with a team of nurses.

"Doc, I am sorry but I can't have this baby without first getting some anesthesia."

"Oh yes ma'am you will; you will breathe and you will push and before you know it, we will have a baby here tonight", she responds, while putting the mask over her face. "Now, I just need you to slide all the way down, put your feet in the stirrups and push only when I tell you to push", she says with authority.

"Ok, Ms. Williams, it is now time to push", she instructs. I take a deep breath and push with everything that I have. The pain is intense! This hurts like hell!

After twenty minutes or so of pushing and pulling, my baby boy is born into the world. He is registered in as 7 pounds 6 ounces! Once the nurse put my baby in my arms, I feel so much better! My first thought is that he looks just like "Rock". He is so cute! His eyes finally meet mine and life just can't get any better than it is right now. Rachel is relieved that it is over and so am I. She cheers me on throughout the entire process. I don't think that I could have gotten through it without her being there. She immediately starts making phone calls. Apparently, she took Rock's number from the nightstand because he is the first call that she makes. I can hear parts of her conversation to him. Rock must be so thrilled because Rachel is smiling and laughing throughout the conversation. Although I am excited about the arrival of my new baby, I decline to speak to Rock because my chest is in excruciating pain. I don't really want to say anything because I feel that it will soon go away. These pains are very familiar. Throughout the pregnancy, I oftentimes dealt with these chest pains and it was always diagnosed as "gas". I have spent several evenings in the emergency room behind these "gas" episodes.

Rachel walks out of the room, but she is still on the phone. Once the baby is taken away to the nursery, the nurse finally notices that I am tugging at my chest. Within the hour, the doctors order the sonogram and I am on my way into the X-Ray room. With the bright lights towering above me, I need to think about pleasant things just to make it through this process. I start thinking about my new baby and all the fun I had getting him here. I start thinking about Rock and what he really means to me and how I wish he were here with me. At least he is involved in his child's life. So far, he is the only concerned father. How ironic! He is also the youngest father.

The nurse starts taking pictures of my front, side, and back until she is all done. She probably doesn't realize it but I see her gasping for air as she begins to read some of the X-rays. I can't deny it, but her reaction to what she is seeing does make me a little nervous.

"What is it? What is wrong? What do you see?"

"You will have to speak with the doctor", she responds. "I am not allowed to discuss this X-ray with you. The doctor will explain everything."

Before long, the doctor comes into my room and lets me know that I am full of gallstones. She carefully explains that a few of them are in my bile duct and need to be removed immediately. Rachel just walked in and hears what the doctor is saying that needs to be done and also agree that the doctor should do whatever is necessary to make me better. Things happen pretty quickly and before I know it, I am already starting to count…"100, 99, 98, 97, 96 . . ." I recite, as if fading into a cloud.

Because I am starting to wake up now, it can only mean that the surgery is over! Moments later, the doctors come in to speak with me. They explain to me that this was an emergency that they had to perform in order to remove the gallstones from my bile duct and that they will have to go in later to remove the gall bladder because it is basically destroyed and with it being that way, it can potentially poison my system. They explain that my eyes are starting to turn yellow as a result of these conditions. I need something for pain but the nurse explains that I will have to wait until I get to my room upstairs.

My mind starts wondering about my new baby son. I haven't figured out what his name will be. I finally decide on Darren. After surviving the recovery room, it is now time to go upstairs into a more stable room. I can't wait to finally be in a real room so that I can get something to eat, watch television and see my son. When I finally make it into my room, my sister is already there waiting for me, along with the doctor.

"Ms. Williams, I have some news for you", he begins. *Dejavu is kicking in right now. This reminds me of the day the doctor came in to deliver news about Kameron. All of a sudden, I quickly remember how that felt.*

"Oh no, what is wrong with my baby?"

"Let me finish. We examined your son and it appears that he has an irregular heart beat; a heart murmur is what we call it. We will continue monitoring him to see if the condition worsens or if it stays the same", the doctor explains. The doctors walk out of the room and Rachel and I are left there to talk about what he just said. The only problem is that I am speechless. I have nothing to say. I don't know whether to scream or whether to cry. I sit in the bed as if my world has suddenly come to an end. The only thing that comes to mind is the news that I received about Kameron's heart condition and what we went through with that.

"Melissa, you know that it will all be okay."

"Sure", I say, without taking my eyes off the clock on the wall. "I just want to see my baby." Rachel leaves to go see what is going on with my son at the nursery and to see about them bringing him to me for me to visit with him. While deep in thought, in walks a nurse.

"What is wrong?" asks the nurse. She is wearing the usual white uniform that most nurses wear, but she has on a blue jean jacket, which is a little different and strange to me. I don't really care right now. When she comes into the room, I notice how friendly she is. I am not in a good mood, so why is she? I don't have anything to smile about right now. So, her happiness is really upsetting me.

"You look upset", she says. "What is wrong?"

"I just got news that my son has been diagnosed with a heart murmur and I just can't go through this again. See, my first son ended up having open heart surgery when he was just 2 months old and I just can't do this again. Not to be rude, but why do you care anyway? I really don't want to talk about this."

"Sure, I understand. Would you like to pray?" she asks sweetly. My comment to her makes me feel bad because she is just trying to be nice.

I reluctantly answer, "Sure, why not?" She begins to pray for me. When she finishes, she leaves the room and I am left with my mouth wide open. I can't believe that a nurse has taken time out of her day just to pray with me. Before she leaves the room, she encourages me to call the doctor to see how my son is doing.

Even though I have agreed to call, I know that I won't call until after Oprah goes off. Chris Tucker is on the show today promoting Rush Hour 2. He is so fine! The show is over and the credits are rolling, so I decide to pick up the phone to contact the doctor to check on my son as the nurse has instructed. "Sir, I am just calling to see how my son is doing."

"What perfect timing! Your sister was just here to get your son and we were right in the middle of doing his tests. When we finished, we couldn't believe our eyes! Your son's heart murmur is gone! It is as if it never existed. Your son is on his way to your room. Congratulations Ms. Williams. We have never seen this before", he explains.

All of a sudden, memories of my time at Beaulah Baptist come to mind. I remember when, right the before the preacher gets ready to preach, we would sing a song from the Hymnal Book. I can still see the older missionaries sitting on the front pews. My friends and I would want the pews to fill up quickly so that we could have a chance at sitting in the balcony. And the funniest times of all was when Ms. Lucy would try to sit in the pulpit with the ministers. Thoughts of choir rehearsals, play rehearsals, and Red Baron meetings all come back to memory. *Is this what it was all about? Is this what prayer was all about?* The Bible teaches us to believe what we pray and we'll have it.

Think about the miracle I just experienced. The nurse walked into my room, prayed for my son, and now he is healed. I have to call her to give her the good news. I know that it is her prayer that changed my son's condition. I am so grateful to her for taking the time to pray for him. I push the button, labeled "nurse", thinking that this will get me to the lady who just prayed for my son. The voice at the other end does not sound like the lady who was just in my room praying for me so I feel like I have to ask for my nurse. "Hi, this is Melissa, in room 240 and I would like to speak with my nurse, please."

"Yes, Melissa, what can I do for you?" she responds.

"No, I mean *my* nurse."

"Sweetheart, I am *your* nurse."

"Well, are you the lady who was just in my room praying with me?"

"No, I wasn't just in your room praying with you. What do you need?"

"I don't mean to sound crazy right now, but there was a lady who was just in my room praying with me after I told her all about my son's condition. She had on a nurse's uniform with a blue jean jacket. She had blonde hair. I didn't catch her name, though."

"Melissa, I am your nurse and I have been your nurse all day and I was not just in your room praying for you", she says, hesitantly. "And besides, there is nobody here dressed like that. I am sorry, but I don't know who she was. Is there anything that I can do for you?"

"No, no thank you. Sorry to bother you."

"It's no problem", she responds.

Who was the lady that was just in my room? Was she an angel sent by God to remind me that He is still real? Am I seeing things? Did I just make this up or what? And if it was an angel, why in the world would she waste her time on me? Why would God send an angel just to pray for my son and to see him healed? Where did the mystery woman go? And who was she? And why didn't she stick around?

While deep in thought, Rachel walks into the room with my son. I am so happy to see him that I just start crying. My sister seems puzzled but realizes that the doctor must have given me the news about my son's condition. "See Melissa, I told you that everything would end up okay", she comforts. "The doctors told me that the baby's heart murmur was gone after they tested him."

"Yes, but something else happened here today."

"What now?"

"An angel came to my room and prayed for my son to be healed. She has now disappeared. Nobody knows who this woman is. She claimed to be my nurse, but my nurse says that she is my nurse and they are not the same people", I explain.

My sister is just as shocked as I am. She, too, is speechless and begins to cry tears of joy. Darren seems to be quite amazed with all of this emotion because he starts smiling and looks in the corner of the room as if he has seen a clown or something. I have reached my own conclusion and that is that the lady who came into my hospital room today to pray for my son was an angel. It all makes sense to me now that she is gone. She was very beautiful and smiled quite a bit. Her voice was wavy like the ocean and she was so soft and peaceful. What I remember more than anything from the encounter was the peace that filled the room when she entered and the comfort that I felt when she left. Needless to say, my son leaves the hospital on January 24th healed from an irregular heartbeat.

CHAPTER 10

"I Really Like This One!"

Without the financial support of either of the fathers, without having a place to call my own, and without a job, I am now faced with having to care for three children on my own. The last thing I heard about my children's absentee fathers is that Wil is now a Corporal in the Marines, Kevin is a psychiatrist, and Rock is in his first year of college. I can't depend on these men, so I have to get a job and I need one right away! Acting and modeling sounds like a good choice for me right now. So, why not! Although I don't have any skills at this, I figure that it won't be long before I do.

Much to my surprise, this new career is taking off quite well for me. I am participating in fashion shows all over Miami and becoming quite popular I might add. I continue to work out at the gym because I am preparing myself for the upcoming New York trip. This is the time when models across the country all come together to hopefully get picked up by some of the top agents in the country. To help fund my trip, I decide to sponsor a dance in Middleton, where my biggest supporters are. Believe it or not, but people actually purchased giant sized portraits of me. The article in the local newspaper about the dance didn't hurt either. I made enough money at the dance to completely fund my trip. That's why I love the family back home.

Although I am busy with classes, raising my children, and watching my nieces and nephews while my sisters work, I still find time to have a social life. I have started going out on dates and is most often, the guys from my class. In this industry, I get the chance to meet some really hot guys. And from time to time, I hook up with the girls from class and we go out for drinks. It all takes me back to sweet, sweet Middleton.

During one of the fashion shows, I meet Stevie, who is a well known model/comedian. Stevie is absolutely gorgeous! It won't surprise me if he isn't already in a very committed relationship. Stevie is that guy that you take home to Momma. He is every mother's dream for their daughter; he's smart, funny, and fine and I do mean fine as hell! Stevie and I start spending quite a bit of time together. He *is* aware that I have children and doesn't seem to mind. I really like this one. He is exactly the type of guy that I can actually see myself falling in love with and marrying one day. The way he is with me reminds me of Rock.

Stevie and I both love visiting museums and learning about other cultures. We have so much in common. It is like a dream come true with him. We are spontaneous together. It is nothing for us to just get up and ride off to Orlando or to Tampa. And sometimes, when we are too tired to drive back to Miami, we will stop in at our favorite hotel and get a room together. He has never said that he is exclusive with me, but I am certainly hoping.

One of our favorite restaurants in Celebration is Di'Antonio's. The ambience is so romantic. Stevie and I love to visit when they have "Live Jazz" night. Believe it or not, but the employees actually ask for our autographs when we show up there because someone keeps this rumor going that we are celebrities. On this particular weekend, Stevie and I decide to leave Di'Antonio's and get a room at The Gaylord Palms. The hotel is simply amazing! This is where celebrities visit when they are in town. The last time I stayed here was when Tom Joyner had his Labor Day Cruise Vacation. Stevie invited me to join him because he was asked do perform a comedy act. We had a great time that weekend! I have to admit that it was pretty awesome meeting Tom Joyner and his staff. They were so much fun!

It's late and both of us have been drinking, so we decide that it isn't such a smart idea to drive back to Miami tonight, but get a room instead. Whenever we stay here, Stevie and I always get the same room that overlooks the courtyard. I have had a few drinks and Stevie has had even more than me. I must not be too drunk because when Stevie bends down to get him something to drink out of the refrigerator, I notice that his penis is erect. I hope we don't let this moment go to waste. The mood is right and I want him right now!

"Melissa, would you like something to drink?" he asks.

"Sure, hand me a Smirnoff, please." He brings over my drink and ends up on the sofa right next to me. After a few sips of our drinks, Stevie places my feet in his lap and starts rubbing them. I don't know if it's the Smirnoff or what, but I am already starting to relax. Stevie has moved in closer and places his hands underneath my skirt and pulls off my pantyhose. He starts playing with my toes, one at a time, before putting them in his mouth. So that we can get more comfortable, Stevie picks me up to place me on the king size bed. Stevie is making me feel so good that I grab my breast nipple and play with them until they become hard. He takes over and kisses them gently. His already erect penis is growing. I reach for it and massage it. Our desire for each other is so overwhelming that we tear each other's clothes off. I straddle him and realize that I have him right where I want him. He likes it when I take charge and make love to him. Stevie's chest turns me on. I bury my head in his chest and use my tongue to kiss his beautiful body. I am down at his midsection, and before I know it, his manhood is deep in my mouth. I want to taste all of him. We continue pleasing each other throughout the rest of the evening until we finally decide to get some rest so that we will have enough energy to drive back to Miami on tomorrow.

When we make it back to Miami, Stevie starts to get more and more acting and modeling assignments, which takes him away from me more and more. Unfortunately, this is just the nature of the business. Sadly enough, our times together are few and far between. Busy or not, we still find ways to connect, even if it's nothing more than a quickie during his lunch break.

After a couple of months of hooking up and having sex without protection, I am not surprised when I don't see my period. I can't tell him that we are pregnant. He is just too busy with his career to have to deal with this. But, just to confirm, I will go ahead and take the pregnancy test and when the results read, "positive", I am not surprised. There is no need to ponder about this. I might as well prepare myself for baby number 4. *How in the world can anyone make this many mistakes? What am I thinking? Why don't I choose to be more careful when it comes to sex?* This feels just like a very familiar episode from high school when Brittney and I went to the doctor and learned that I was pregnant. It was clear then that I wanted to end that pregnancy and it is even clearer to me that I want to end this pregnancy as well. I need to find the nearest abortion clinic and end this pregnancy as soon as possible. Within minutes, I am on the phone with the Eastside Abortion Clinic making an appointment, with the consideration that I have to film a commercial next week.

****

Today is my appointment and I feel very nauseous. I don't know if it is because I am going alone this time or if I am just scared, or if I feel guilty about ending this pregnancy without even telling Stevie. Nonetheless, this needs to be done. I am finally moving in the direction I have always wanted and I can't bring it to a halt because of an unwanted pregnancy. Let's face it! I already have 3 children, Christy, Kameron, and Darren. They are ages 6, 4, and 2. It doesn't take a blind man to see that I don't need another baby right now.

I wonder what Laura would tell me if she were here with me. *Would she agree with my decision or would she tell me that I should at least tell Stevie about the pregnancy?* I won't ever know the answer to this question because she is not here and I am pulling into the parking lot. I will admit this. There is something about this appointment that just doesn't set right with me, but I am not sure what it is. Although I am feeling somewhat disturbed about the appointment, I still want to go through with it. I safely make it past the protesters outside. I am now inside being greeted by the receptionist at the front desk. After just 15 minutes, I am already in the room getting undressed and slipping into the gown handed to me by the nurse. "How are you feeling today, Melissa?" the nurse asks.

"As well as can be expected", I respond.

"The doctor will be in shortly. So, just relax." While waiting, there is music playing over the intercom. This seems to be a strategic way of getting patients to relax because once you get to this point, it seems to get a little harder. The song playing over the intercom is "Endless Love". This song takes me back to my 10th grade year when I was so in love with Brian, or so I thought. He would sing this song to me all the time. I specifically remember a special moment that we shared. It was after a Friday night football game and everyone had left the stadium. Brian and I slipped back into the stadium. As usual, we kissed and kissed, but this time, we decided to go a little further. I decided to let him slip a finger inside of me. We had not, yet, decided to go all the way, but he seemed to enjoy this just as much. Brian was my first love and he was my first lover. And you never forget that! I often wonder what he is doing these days. The last thing I heard about him was that he was playing with the New York Yankees, married, with 2 children and living happily in Texas. Deep down inside, I am happy for him. While deep in thought, the nurse and doctor enter the room. "Good morning Ms. Williams, how are you?" the doctor asks.

"Fine, sir, thanks."

"OK, so you want to end your pregnancy, right?" he asks.

"Yes sir, I do. I already have 3 children and I am not married and just don't want to have another one", I explain. "I am moving along in my career as a model and this is certainly not the time to have another child."

"Does the baby's father know?" he asks. I am somewhat surprised that he asks this question.

"No", I say, without any further explanation. During the time that the doctor is making small talk with me, he examines me. The nurse is in the distant corner preparing the IV for the procedure. "Ms. Williams, we have a problem", he explains.

"Problem? What do you mean?"

"After examining you, I can see that you have - - - ", he begins, before I interrupt him.

"Let me finish. Exceeded the number of weeks to have a standard abortion", I say.

"So, you've heard this before?" he asks.

"Yes, I have."

"I will have the nurse order a sonogram for you just to be sure", he offers.

"Don't worry about it. Thanks, Doctor." *Is this dejavu or what?* This is the same thing that happened when I am had my first abortion experience. I wonder how far along I am than what I need to be. "Doctor, just out of curiosity, how much too far am I?"

"One week too far", he explains. "Had you been here a week or so ago we could have completed the procedure." *No way! One week too far! That is also the same thing that happened the first time. My commercial had saved my baby's life. Because I wanted to shoot my commercial and because I wanted to go to cheerleader camp, I was prevented from getting two abortions. Was it just not meant to be?*

I leave the abortion clinic not really knowing how to feel about what has just happened. On one hand, I am glad that I am prevented from having an abortion, but on the other hand, I am disappointed because there is no way I will now be able to continue in this career at this time. I will have to pass this dream up for now. It looks like I am going to have another baby. *But do I tell Stevie or do I just allow enough time to pass and hope he just find out on his own? I am so confused right now! I might as well tell him and hope for the best.*

When I finally gain the courage to tell Stevie, he doesn't believe that the baby belongs to him. To say the least, he does not support my decision to move along with the pregnancy. All of a sudden, he is too busy to spend time with me now. While I am attending my regularly scheduled appointments for pre-natal care, he is still doing his fashion shows, comedy acts, and short films. My intentions are not to ruin his career with this interference. I want him to live out his dreams and I will just continue to do what I have to do. I have seen women do this over and over. So, I already know that I won't be the first woman who is forced to raise her children alone, and I am for certain that I won't be the last to do it either. It doesn't make me feel any better when I walk into a local convenience store and see Stevie featured on the cover of an Ebony magazine, with a beautiful blonde woman right by his side!

****

On December 20th, I recognize these sharp pains that are piercing my body right now are labor pains. Within 12 hours, I have given birth to a beautiful baby girl, who I name Sharell. She is perfect! I am in love when she smiles back at me, with her deep dimples that just melt your heart and make you forget that there is anything wrong in the world. I should call Stevie. He has not been here for the pregnancy, but just maybe he will want to know that he has a beautiful daughter. I have already called him several times and left messages for him, but he has not returned any of my calls. After several weeks, I finally receive a call from Stevie and he wants to meet with me and talk. Even though I wanted him to come at first, I am not so sure anymore, but in the end, I agree to meet with him. We have agreed to meet out at Sands Lake, where we have countless hours together. He admits that he is curious about Sharell and wants to see her. Within 30 minutes or so, he is walking up the stairs to my apartment and the first thing I notice is that he is wearing the cologne that he knows drives me crazy. It has been quite a while since I have seen him and it doesn't surprise me that he looks good enough to eat.

"She is very beautiful. You were right! She looks just like me."

"Look at those dimples. She just makes you melt, right?"

"Yes she does. She is a beautiful baby, but so is her mother."

"Well, thanks." My babysitter is here so we head out to Sands Lake to talk. I can't help but think about all that good times that we have shared out here. I remember when he challenged me to jump in the lake completely naked and I did it! We were always doing crazy things. He has an appointment to get to in a couple of hours so we decide to go in separate cars.

"So, did you think about all the good times we have shared out here as you were driving?"

"How did you know that? I certainly did", I respond.

"Melissa, I wanted you to come out here to tell you that I am moving to California permanently. I just signed on to a big movie deal that will have me out there for at least a year, so I figure that I might as well make it my new home. You don't have to say anything. I know that you love me. I love you too, but I have to make this move for my career. I know that you might not believe this but I will miss you", he explains.

"I am happy for you Stevie. I really am! I will miss you, but I understand that this is something that you have to do for yourself. That reminds me. I saw you on the cover of Ebony with your new girl."

"Oh, that was nothing! That was for publicity. I am focusing on my career right now. A serious relationship is the last thing that concerns me right now", he replies.

"What about you? Are you going to be alright here in Miami? Are you going to continue modeling? You are really good and should consider making a career out of it also", he says.

"Well, I have quite a few little ones who need me right now."

"Speaking of little ones, what are your plans for Sharell? Are you going to sue me for child support or what? I would just like to prepare myself if this is your intention."

"Stevie, I love you and I don't want to do anything that will keep you from living your life as you should. I will take care of my daughter. You just go on and live your life." We sit on the pier and continue talking until it gets late and we both realize that it is time to say goodnight. We also decide that it is easier to just say goodnight instead of making it complicated with a passionate night of lovemaking. Even though we are extremely attracted to one another, sex would only complicate matters even more right now. So, instead, we just kiss and say goodbye, not knowing if or when we will see each other again.

"I wish you the very best, Stevie."

"Thank you, Melissa. I will be in touch with you after I make it to California", he says. Stevie has already turned to walk to his car. He doesn't notice, but crocodile tears are already falling down my face. *Deep down in my heart, I know that he will get out there in California and forget all about us. It was still a great ride with him and hopefully our paths will cross again. I just hope that he will one day find it in his heart to search for his daughter.*

CHAPTER 11

"Tell It Like It Is!"

Now that Stevie is gone, I am a little depressed. I really miss him. He hasn't called yet and he probably won't call either. I might as well stop sitting by the phone. I am sure that he sees beautiful women by the dozens and Miami is the last thing on his mind. My reality is that I have four children, no job, no skills, no career, no husband, no boyfriend – nothing! I don't have a good feeling about men right now. I don't keep in touch with my girlfriends back home. For whatever reason, it feels like all the people that I love eventually leave.

My family members and friends constantly tell me that it is going to be very difficult for me to hold down any type of relationship with a man because of my children. I know that I have to work to provide for my children and can't afford to sit around and wait for these men to do anything for my children. I finally land a job with Town Center Steel. It doesn't pay a lot, but it is good for me. The family who has afforded me this opportunity treats me like part of their family. We have the same last names, so we pass off perfectly as kin. After proving myself over and over to Mr. Williams, I finally earn a new position as Bids Director. Not only do I gain more responsibility, but my paycheck is a little better.

After a few months, I get my first promotion! With this new promotion, I am now able to move my family to a much better community. It is definitely time to move on. I remember a time when I was followed home by a complete stranger, but I was smart enough to not go to my home so that he would know where I live. He eventually stopped following me. I also remember when an intruder broke into my apartment and stole my television and my children's bikes. And the worst thing that has happened to me at this community was when I had to hire a girl in the neighborhood to watch my children, who neglected my children and chose to smoke pot all day, instead.

It's moving day! I am thrilled and so are the children. This new community is so convenient. It's closer to my job and most importantly, the mall! However, there is one thing missing. I wish that I was sharing my life with someone. I have to admit it, but I am a little lonely. To satisfy that loneliness, I have decided to put an ad in the local newspaper looking for a mate. At first, it is exciting, but when the calls start coming in from freaks, it is not longer fun. There isn't one guy who I feel that I want to see or even talk to again. We just don't have anything in common. It seems that one thing that they all want is to have sex with me, but nothing more than that. I want more than that from a partner. I guess I will just have to keep waiting.

My birthday is approaching and I don't have any definite plans, but Lena has made it clear that I will not be alone because she has already made all the plans for my big day. She says that all I have to do is just look pretty because the night is on her! Lena has ordered pizza for the children and has also paid for my babysitter for the evening.

****

We have finally made our grand entrance into the Nightclub. It is jumping and is packed with young, middle-aged, and older women all looking for the same thing. The DJ is playing all of the latest hits. The bar is filling up quickly because tonight is a 2 for 1 night. My friends and I are regulars at the night club, but to be on the safe side, Lena called in advance to reserve our favorite table. She didn't miss anything! She remembers my chocolate covered strawberries, dipped into a lime tasting margarita. Ms. Jennie has prepared at least 5 dozen of them. They are delicious!

Lena doesn't stop there. She has also made arrangements for a stripper to dance for me. I should have figured it out when the club announcer tells the DJ to turn down the lights. "Alright, let's get this party started right! We have a special surprise for a special someone here tonight. She is celebrating her 24th birthday and the word on the street is that she likes chocolate! Baby girl, Melissa, how about some Chocolate Thunder!" he yells.

The music starts and the song, "Do Me Baby", the Prince version, comes on and standing before me within 30 seconds is the finest chocolate man I have ever seen. If I had it my way, I would take him right here and right now!

"Lena, you got me girl! You got me!" I yell to Lena, while Chocolate Thunder is performing right in front of me. My friends are enjoying this pleasant surprise just as much as I am. When he stands in front of me doing his thing, I don't have a problem putting my hands right in his chest. To my surprise, he flips me around and is grinding up against me from behind. I am enjoying this attention.

"You look beautiful tonight, sweetheart", he whispers in my ear.

"Thank you."

"Happy Birthday, My Beautiful Queen!"

Chocolate Thunder kisses me on the cheek and dances off into the crowd.

"Wheeeeeewww! Lena, what a pleasant surprise! That brotha is fine as hell!"

"Well, guess what? I have also made arrangements for you to spend some time with him after the show to do with him what you want", she says.

"Are you serious? Is he a gigolo or something?"

"Well, yes he is! Dancing isn't his only gig. He's yours if you want him."

"I don't think so."

"Are you sure about that?" she asks.

"I am sure. It is tempting, though, but I think I will have to pass on the all night sex with this sexy chocolate man."

Although the night is going just perfectly, all of a sudden, a strong chill is taking over and I feel sleepy. All I want to do is lay my head on the table and fall asleep. I haven't had that much to drink, so I don't think I'm drunk. *And, why am I starting to see things? Do my friends notice me at all? I really don't want Lena to think that I am bored, but this feeling is overtaking me.* I must have dozed off to sleep, because when I finally wake up, there is a man standing over me. He looks a little different. By saying differently, I mean that he is walking with a limp. I look around to see if my friends notice him but they appear as if they don't notice him at all. This feels too much like an out of body experience. He looks at me and says, "What are you doing here?"

I look puzzled and ask, "Are you talking to me?"

He says, "Yes I am talking to you; what are you doing here?"

"Oh, it is my birthday and I am out with my girlfriends and I am having fun!" I say, trying to convince him.

He so boldly responds by saying, "You don't belong here."

"Excuse me", I reply. "I don't belong here?"

I have to admit that I am somewhat offended when he makes that comment. "You don't know me! Who are you?"

He never gives me a name but just keeps saying to me that I don't belong there. He neither looks nor sounds like anyone that I know. *But, where has he come from? And why aren't my friends stepping in to give this guy a piece of their minds?* He realizes that he isn't getting anywhere with me and he eventually walks away. Before he leaves, he gives me $20 and says 'happy birthday'. When I finish talking to him, I ask my friends if they saw the man that I was just talking to and they say, "no". How could they not see him? He was just standing right here.

There are so many questions that I still have to ask this mystery man. I need to find him to ask him why he feels that I don't belong in the club and to find out how he knows that without knowing me. *Does he know something that I don't know? Who sent him to give me that message?* I step down from the barstool to look for him, but there is no sight of him anywhere! He has disappeared into the night. I begin to ask other people in the Club to see if they saw him. It almost seems as if I am the only person who did! I decide to walk back into the bar area and my friends are still there drinking and having fun.

"Melissa, what is wrong with you?" asks Lena. "You look like you have seen a ghost". I am sure that they are able to see the puzzled look on my face. It is hard not to hide my emotions. There is no way that I will be able to explain what just happened. They will certainly think that I am crazy or just drunk or something. I will have to keep this one to myself to share with them at a much later time. From this night on, I will always remember the look on the crippled man's face as he said, "you don't belong here". There was something comforting in his eyes. I walked into this Nightclub one way, but I am leaving with a totally new perspective on my life.

CHAPTER 12

"Back To Church"

Now that I have given up the club life that I have been a part of for the last 10 years or so, I decide to start going back to church so that I can get closer to God. For some reason, the idea of feeling like I have to have someone in my life is no longer that important to me anymore. I have a newfound passion for gospel music, Joyce Meyer books, and watching Creflo Dollar on television.

"Melissa, I notice that you have been reading your Creflo Dollar books on lunch break. Would you be interested in going to church with me sometimes?"

"Sure, I would love to", I respond. "Are you going this Sunday?"

"I go every Sunday. Give me your address and I will pick you up and please be on time!" Phillip jokes. Phillip is second in charge behind Fred. He came here from Orlando to work from Fred. Apparently Fred and Phillip know each other from Disney. Rumor has it that Phillip is loaded with money!

"Great! I will see you then."

Phillip picks me up every Sunday. But, before he drops me off at home, he almost always stops and picks up food for me and the children. He says that he does this because it is just the right thing to do. I hope that he isn't expecting anything in return because I am not interested in him at all, or any other man for that matter.

****

The sermon today is titled, *"Who's Your Daddy?"* It makes me think about my father and how I am missing out on being a part of his life. I know that this is not the Daddy that the minister is speaking about, but I still miss my father all the same. As usual, Phillip stops at Publix to pick up dinner for me and the kids. Before he gets out of the car, he grabs my hand and looks into my eyes and says, "Melissa, I have something to tell you."

"What is it, Phillip?"

"I have fallen in love with you. I truly believe that God sent me to be your husband", he says. "He knows that you need someone to take care of you and your babies, so He needed to send a real man to do just that. I have more than enough money to care for you and these kids. So, what do you say?"

Without being concerned about what I look like, my mouth drops open. I don't know what to say to this at all. Nobody has ever said this to me this way.

"My husband? Phillip, I am flattered by this. I truly am. I have to be honest with you, though. I am not looking for a husband right now. Maybe one day, I will, but certainly not now. I appreciate all that you do for me and my children, but we are not on the same page with this. I would love for us to continue to be friends", I respond.

"Just friends? All you want to be is friends? I have been here for you and probably better than anyone has, so I have a problem with just being friends. It will be hard for me to be around you knowing that I want you and can't have you. I think that it's best if we not hang around each other", he says.

"I can't believe this. So, just because I don't want anything intimate with you, we suddenly have nothing in common. Is that what you are saying, Phillip?"

"I guess so."

"If that is how you want it, then that is how it will be." Because I am not ready to accept Phillip's hand in marriage, he is no longer interested in being my friend anymore. After the Sunday incident, we only speak at work but nothing more than that. He walks by me in the hallway as if he never spent time with me at all.

CHAPTER 13

"Dana Has What?"

D o you believe in "love at first sight"? I don't either. With all that I have experienced, I have grown accustomed to men coming in and out of my life. That is more and more likely to happen now that I am a single woman with 4 kids. I am not considered a great catch. My ideas about men are just that they only want one thing from me. At this point, I'm not sure if there will ever be a man who will come into my life and truly love me the way that I need a man to love me.

Because of my slight depression, Lena decides to put a BBQ together at her house. She, of course, invites all of her family. Lena is known for having six of the finest brothers in Miami. I have only met a few of them, but there is one in particular that she is always talking about and hopefully, he will show up today. Lena and I are putting out the plastic chairs for the guests, when this gorgeous guy walks up to us. "What's up sis? How are you and who is this beautiful woman standing here looking all delicious in this beautiful lime green outfit?"

"Melissa, meet Mark and Mark, meet Melissa", she announces. "This is my brother that I am always telling you about. This boy is so crazy."

"Well hello Melissa. You are so beautiful!" he compliments. "I wonder what I would have to do to get to know you a little better."

I am shocked with how flirtatious he is already. But I like him! "Hello Mark and thanks for the compliment."

I hate to admit it, but Mark is out of this world. He is gorgeous and has the body of a god. He is funny and really knows how to give a girl a compliment. I really like being around him. Lena makes an excuse to leave so that I can talk to him. "You're welcome, sweetheart."

"Are you always this crazy?" I ask Mark, as he pulls up a chair next to me.

"It's just that you make me so nervous. I know that I am fine and all, but you are looking at me like you want to just take me right here!" he says. We laugh so loudly that Lena looks over to make sure that I am okay.

"Right! Where is your girlfriend, Mark? I am sure that you have one. Did you leave her home or what?"

"Something like that", he answers.

"What about your boyfriend? I am sure that you have one."

"Actually, I am single, Mark. I am not feeling too good these days about men, so I have learned to keep my distance."

"Are you more interested in women?"

"Hell no! I am just by myself right now. That's all."

"Well, it was nice to meet you and I look forward to seeing you again", he says. Mark looks into my eyes as if he is trying to figure out what I am thinking. He picks up my hand and kisses the top of it. I am glad that he doesn't notice that my palms are sweaty and how fast my heart is racing. I have to maintain my cool because this *is* my friend's brother. Mark is distracted when his brother, Darren, calls out to him to get in on the next game of Spades. He lets them know that he is coming, but before he leaves, he winks at me as he walks away.

I decide to get up and mingle with the other guests. Lena invited our friends from work and we are standing around talking, but I can't seem to keep from focusing in on Mark. He is very interesting and I already know that I want to get to know him better. I find Lena in the kitchen mixing her perfect Sweet Tea. "Girl, your brother is fine as hell!"

"Child, please", she responds. "He is very charming to the ladies, if you know what I mean."

I don't really know what she means, and I don't care either.

"Is he always this crazy?"

"Yes, he is", she answers. "Wait a minute! You like him, don't you? Don't get ahead of yourself. He lives with a woman and has 3 children with her", she warns.

"Is he thinking of marrying her?"

"I can't say what he is thinking, but you might as well say that they are married. They have been together for several years. She is the mother of his children and I know that he loves his children."

"Oh, I am sure that he does. It is always good to see a man who takes care of himself and his family. That is all."

"Ok, okay, then. That better be it. I can't have you messing with my brother. I don't want to see you get hurt."

It can't be all that bad, can it? I decide against listening to Lena's advice and let my desire for Mark get the best of me. She isn't aware of it but after this first introduction to Mark, he and I start seeing each other. Lena is not going to be happy if she finds out because she has already told me how she feels about it. Before he leaves the barbeque, I make sure that we exchange phone numbers. He stops by, often, to see me when he is in the neighborhood. I make him promise not to disclose our relationship to his sister. He agrees. I even introduce him to my children and my mother, which is a big step for me. The last guy my mother met was Rock and she wasn't crazy about him at all. She always wanted me to marry Brian from high school. He still visits her in Middleton when he goes home.

Mark and I have been dating for quite some time and have taken our relationship to another level. We are sleeping together and he stays over some nights. I have grown to really care for him and have even fallen in love with him. The fact that he lives with another woman is enough to make our relationship strained. But I am willing to accept it because I really like him.

Why in the world would I want to be with a man who is obviously with someone else? Why have I allowed myself to accept this type of behavior from any man? It may seem strange but I really love him. Deep down I want to believe that this man is not really in love with this woman and that he is really just with this woman because of their children, just like he says all the time. To make what we have work, he comes up with any excuse to be with me. We shop together, go to the local amusement parks together, go for walks on the beach together and share activities with my children. There is no reason for me to believe that he doesn't want to spend his life with me. We have become somewhat inseparable. Mark has finally come up with something to test my love. Tonight, right after I finish putting the children down to bed, Mark calls me with a very tempting proposition.

"Melissa, Dana will be out at the hospital tonight. Why don't you come over to visit me at the house?" he asks during an early evening conversation.

"Are you crazy? Why in the world would I come over to this woman's home to visit you? That is insane!"

"Because I really want to see you", he responds. "And besides, I told you that our relationship is not really like that. I am only here for the children. She is the mother of my children and that is all. We are not intimate. I sleep on the couch and think of you every night."

I know that I should not even consider this, but I really want to see him and if he is crazy enough to invite me to their home, then just maybe there isn't anything going on between the two of them. "OK. I will come. Call me a cab and I will see you in less than an hour."

"Done", he says cheerfully. After hanging up the phone with him, I realize that it is too late to turn back now so I get dressed. I make sure to put on the sweet smelling perfume that he likes. I pack lightly and wait for my cab. My neighbor from downstairs agrees to come watch the children while I go out for a few hours.

Within an hour, I am standing at his doorstep, where he answers the door and greets me with the most sensual kiss anyone can imagine. This guy really makes me feel good. He makes me feel like the most beautiful woman alive. This is certainly how every woman should feel. This just feels right.

After making it inside, he carefully gives me a tour of the house. I am not surprised when the tour ends in the bedroom and before I know it, he is already starting to undress me, making sure to kiss every single inch of my body, whispering the words, "I love you". I am falling deeper and deeper. He has started to kiss me in all the right places and it doesn't matter to me if I am in their house or not. He is here with me right now. *Am I really in another woman's bed? Am I actually having sex with Mark in the same bed that he is probably sleeping in with another woman? How do I know that he isn't sleeping with Dana? Is he telling me the truth about why he is still living in this house with her?*

Mark and I make love over and over again. He can't get enough of me. We make love in the bedroom, in the shower, in the family room, and in the garage on top of his car. I don't want the evening to end, but it is time for me to get back home before Dana returns and gets the surprise of her life. After a shower together, Mark calls me a cab. I jump in and head home. I am exhausted. He really put it on me tonight. On the way home, I replay all the events of tonight over and over in my head. I suddenly realize that Dana never called home to give Mark an update on their daughter. But at the same time, Mark didn't call to check on his daughter either. I feel horrible because I didn't even ask him about his daughter. As much fun as I had tonight with Mark, there is a part of me that feels bad about being intimate with him in another woman's home.

The cab has finally pulled in front of my apartment. And as soon as I walk in the front door, the phone rings. "Hello."

"How is my sexy chocolate?" Mark says on the other end. I just wanted to make sure that you made it in okay and to tell you that I miss you already and can't wait to see you again", he continues.

"I am doing just fine, now that you have given me what I needed so badly."

"Did you get enough?" he asks. "I mean, I have more to give you, sweetheart."

"I am sure you do, but for now, let's say goodnight. I am tired. I am going straight to bed."

"Well, okay, then. Hey, I love you, Melissa, and thanks for making me a happy man", he says.

"I love you too, Mark." After such a connection with Mark, I am sure that things between us will get better and who knows, maybe even marriage. He sees now that I will do anything for him. *Mrs. Melissa Roberts! I like the sound of that. And will Lena come around then?* He has to marry me now. Recently, when my mother visited, Mark told her that he wants to marry me one day. I just need to keep supporting him and being patient and before long, he will be mine and only mine. For the next few days, it is life as usual but I am starting to realize that Mark has not called me. He has never done this. This is a little weird to me.

I have called his phone several times and can't reach him. Desperation is starting to kick in, so much so that I ask Lena about his whereabouts. She doesn't seem to understand my desperation but admits that she has spoken with him a few times and that he was at their mother's house today.

"Why are you asking about Mark?" Lena asks. "Are you seeing him, Melissa?"

"It's not what you think! He and I just crossed paths one day and struck up a conversation and I would see him in the neighborhood sometimes."

Deep down inside, I don't think that Lena is buying my story. I must not have been too convincing because she sighs and says, "Just be careful, Melissa."

The fact that she doesn't say anymore gives me the okay to continue talking about Mark. I am desperate so I decide to give her a little more information. Lena is my friend and right now, I need her to get me through this so I can figure out what is going on with Mark.

"Lena, here's the truth. I have been seeing your brother quite a bit. I am sorry that we have been leading you to believe that nothing was going on. You are my friend and I don't want anything to put a damper on our friendship. I love him. But he hasn't called me in a while and now I am concerned", I confess.

At first, she doesn't say a word, but she finally breaks her silence. "I hope that you know what you are doing."

"Ok, so now that I have gotten that off my chest, can you please call him and tell him to call me?"

"I will. Don't worry about Mark. He is a very busy person", she says. "I am sure that he will call you at some point. If I see him, I will tell him that you are asking for him. I will warn you of this, though. It is hard as hell to get to him when she is not around. She is always hanging onto him wherever they go. I don't see how he was able to get out of the house to be with you. There are times when she follows him when he leaves the house. That's why you have to be careful!"

"Is she a stalker or something? What would she do to him if she found out that he was having an affair on her and with me?"

"Honestly, there is no telling what she would do if she found out he was having an affair. I do know this. When she started going to church, she completely stopped having sex with Mark and told him that if he wanted sex from her, he would have to put a ring on her finger. *I thought, how would he do that if his plans are to marry me? That is what he told my mother.*

Deep down in my gut, I am starting to feel that something is wrong. This is not like him to just not call me. *Where is he and what is going on?*

Days later, my phone rings and the caller ID reads, Mark Roberts. As much as I want to make him wait, I rush to the phone.

"Hello."

"Hello, Melissa. How are you?"

"I am fine, but I am missing you! Where the hell have you been, Mark? What is going on?"

"Sweetheart, we need to talk. Can I come over now?"

"Of course. You never have to ask me if you can come over."

"Great. I will be there in about 15 minutes."

I don't like the tone of his voice. I wonder if he found out that I was going out with Lionel on the weekends when he wasn't here. He has to know that I do not like being alone on the weekends when he is playing the family man. Guys are so trifling! *Would Lionel have told him? How will I explain this to Mark if I am confronted with this? Do I even feel like I should explain anything to him at all?* He isn't married to me. He isn't even committed to me only.

Within the hour, Mark is at my doorstep with a very serious look on his face. He walks through the door without kissing me and worse than that, without acknowledging the children, which is something that he never does. Mark walks straight to my bedroom and sits in the chair next to my bed. When he does this, it is my cue that something is seriously wrong.

Since he and I have been sleeping together, he has never sat in that chair, unless it was for sexual purposes. Mark always greets me with a kiss at the door, he always plays with the children first, and he never sits in the chair next to the bed. He is definitely not acting the same.

"Melissa, I have something that I have to say to you and it is not easy for me to say", he begins. "I really love you and I think that you are truly an amazing woman, but sweetheart, you deserve so much better than me. You deserve a man who will give you what you need. You deserve someone who can be here for you and your children and I just can't do that right now", he continues. *Is he breaking it off with me because of Dana?*

"Are you serious with me right now, Mark? We just spent a wonderful evening together. You said to me that you loved me. You even told my mother that you wanted to marry me. What happened? What did I do wrong?" I ask, while fighting back the tears.

"Baby, please don't cry", he says, while trying to console me. "I know that this hurts but it is truly for the best. I know that you don't understand right now but one day you will understand. You will find someone who is good for you because you are a wonderful woman. I am so sorry, Melissa", he says, while walking away. "I just can't do this anymore. I can't live a lie like this anymore. My family needs me. I have to tend to their needs now."

"I need you! I don't want anyone else! I want you! I love you! I need you in my life! Why are you doing this to me? How can you come into my life like this and play games with my heart?"

"Melissa, it was not a game for me. I need you to understand - -", he says before I interrupt him.

"Understand! How can I? We just shared an amazing evening together! You told me that you loved me and wanted to be my husband one day! You said that shit! And now you walk in here and tell me it's over! Fuck you Mark! I hate you!" The tears are flowing down my face. He is fighting to get away from me and has started to cry right along with me. I barricade the door, but he pushes right past me. He just wants out, but I am preventing him from leaving. I need him to say that he is just kidding and that this is all a joke, but it doesn't happen. *Why can't I just let him leave? Why can't I hold on to some small amount of dignity and let this man leave?*

Within half an hour, Mark is already in his car leaving me behind, sobbing and embarrassing myself in front of my neighbors. When his engine finally starts, I know that there is no turning back. He doesn't even look back to see if I have gotten off the ground or to see if I make it inside the house. He drives away, leaving more than just a broken heart behind. I am sitting on the ground, sobbing, until his car is completely out of sight.

My neighbor, Lisa, walks outside when she hears all of the commotion. "Meme, please get up and go back inside", she says, while assisting me off the ground. "Come on honey. Let him go. God has someone for you. You do not have to be out here like this. Think about your children who are standing in the doorway looking at you. Let the man go, honey!"

I manage to find the strength to take Lisa's advice and go back to my apartment. My children are asking me what's wrong and why "Sweet Daddy Mark" made me cry. Although I am very angry that he hurt my feelings, I am even angrier that he is gone from my children's lives. I vow never to introduce another man to my children.

Later that evening, Lena calls to see if Mark finally contacted me. I admit to her that he called, but I don't tell her about the events that took place moments ago. I don't want her to know how bad I really have it for her brother and to hear her say, "I told you so". She has warned me over and over. She did tell me when she introduced me to her brother that he already had someone. I knew what she told me but I wanted to believe what he told me instead.

"Melissa, are you okay? You don't sound happy like you normally do."

"No, I am fine", I respond, while fighting back the tears.

"Ok, since you don't feel like talking, I will call you later."

After getting off the phone with Lena, I really want to be alone so that I can properly sort this out. *What just happened here? What did I do wrong? We were getting along just fine or so I thought.*

Now that the children are finally in bed, I give Lionel a call because I need to forget about what has just happened.

"Lionel, what's up with you tonight?" I ask, trying to hold back the tears.

"Nothing. I don't have to go to work at the club tonight. They let us off because the boys from Ft. Lauderdale are doing a show tonight. It's definitely going to be packed", he answers. "Why, what's up?"

"I need you to come over and spend the night with me. I don't want to be alone tonight."

"Do you want to talk about it?"

"Not really. I don't really want to do much talking. I just really need you to take care of this pain that I am feeling between my legs."

"Is it like that baby girl? What has you in so much pain?" he asks.

"Like I said, I don't want to talk about it. Can you come over or not?"

"Slow down baby! I will be over soon. Give me about 45 minutes. I have to run a quick errand first."

"Let yourself in through the back. My children are home and I won't have you waking them up."

"Ok, see you later, sweetheart."

Lionel shows up looking good and smelling good as usual. He is wearing a shirt that shows off his tight abs and chiseled arms. He knows that I love his body. He knows that once I catch a glimpse of it, I am only 10 seconds away from tearing his clothes off of him. Besides, I have to get my mind off Mark. He has left me for good and it hurts like hell.

"Hey baby girl", he says, as he walks right into my bedroom. I am already waiting on him. He walks over to me and grabs me from behind and pulls me close to him. He smells so good. Looking into his eyes briefly takes my mind off of Mark. He can tell that I am in great pain. It shows in my eyes, I am sure. He can clearly see that something has truly upset me. He has never seen me like this. He doesn't dare ask because I have already told him that I don't want to discuss it. Besides, he doesn't want to ruin the moment.

"I am here now, sweetheart. Lionel will make it all better. He leads me to my bed and spreads my legs apart. He kisses me all over, from my toes to the top of my head. We spend the rest of the evening together. By the time my children wake up, he is already gone. He knows that this is part of the deal. He knows that I am very careful when it comes to my children seeing different men coming in and out of my bedroom. For some reason, the thought of losing Mark is putting me in more pain right now after having had sex with another man. Lionel is gone for now and Mark won't return and according to him, it is because I deserve someone better.

How can he do this to me? How can he build me up so much and make me feel so beautiful and then hurt me like this? What did I do to deserve this? Oh God, why? What did I do to deserve this?

A few days later, Lena calls and for the first time, her happy voice annoys the heck out of me. "Melissa, you are not going to believe what happened", she begins.

"Good or bad?"

"It depends on how you look at it", she answers. "It's about Mark!"

"What happened?"

"Mark and Dana got married on yesterday. They didn't tell anyone; they just went down to the courthouse and got married. We are all shocked and had no idea that they were even thinking about getting married. Did he say anything to you about this when he called?"

"What? Are you serious they got married? I am shocked! I don't know what to say. I had no idea. He didn't say anything at all about this!"

"Well, I knew it would happen one day", she continues. "I told you not to fall for him because he was already with someone else. Honey, men are something else, aren't they? You just can't put your all into them."

"I know what you mean, but I am doing just fine. We are just friends and nothing more. I am happy for him. I just wonder why all of a sudden he decided to marry her."

"Girl, didn't I tell you? Men are something else!"

Days go by and the pain just intensifies. I can't talk to Lena about how I am feeling because she is the person who warned me about falling for her brother in the first place. The fact is that he has moved on and I am left to deal with this sharp dagger that remains in my heart. I can't sleep. I don't want to eat. I just want Mark. I belong only to him. My body belongs only to him and it needs him. Because he is such a good lover, I am sure that Dana is wrapping her entire body all over him and enjoying the benefit that once belonged to me.

****

It is Sunday morning and my children are at church with the neighbor. I should have gone to church with them, but I guess I would much rather stay home and feel sorry for myself. The television is on but I am not really listening to it. The phone rings. *Who can this be? I thought.* The caller ID reads, *Mark Roberts.* I catch myself in mid-thought as I am looking at the phone. After a few rings, I finally pick it up and find the strength to say, "Hello".

"Hello beautiful", the person on the other end says.

"Who is this?"

"Come on now. Don't tell me you don't know my voice", he responds, as if he didn't just stick a dagger in my heart. "Baby, I love you."

"Mark, is that you? Why the hell are you calling me?"

"Melissa, please don't hang up", he pleads. "Can I come over to talk to you? There is something very important that I need to tell you", he says.

"I don't know what the hell else you could say to me. You have already broken my heart and left me to deal with this pain. What else can be said? You made a decision about which it is that you want."

"Melissa, please", he pleads.

"Fine! You have 15 minutes and not a minute more. I don't have time for this crap."

Within half an hour, Mark is standing at my door trying to get a smile on my face with his jokes and humor, but it isn't working this time.

"Mark, what do you want with me? You have hurt me so much and I really don't want to see you right now, let alone talk to you. What do you have to say to me?"

"I love you, sweetheart", he says. "May I please come in?"

"Love me? You have only 15 minutes and then, I want you out of my house."

"Melissa, I have always loved you", he begins. "I miss you and I am so sorry that I hurt you this way. When my sister introduced me to you, I was so angry with myself that I was already in a relationship. There aren't too many women out here like you. You make me feel so important. I told her to never tell you this but I told her that I loved you and she tried to forbid me from pursuing a relationship with you. I guess I did just what she said I would do. You don't deserve this because you were so good to me. But, I still believe that you deserve better than me." By the time Mark finishes, I am already sobbing and in tears with my head held down. He grabs my face and places it in his palms so that I can see that he is also crying.

"How in the world could you have married her when you claim you weren't even having a relationship with her? You lied to me, my mother, and my children. Boy did you have us all fooled? You made a fool out of me! How could you do that?" He wipes the tears away from my eyes.

"I had to marry her. Oh my God, I had to marry her! Melissa, she is dying with cancer and there is one thing that she always wanted and it was to be my wife. Sweetheart, because of the cancer, the doctors have given her only one year to live. And, I just can't leave her now and let her die alone. I want life to be as normal as possible for her. I don't want to put my kids through anything else right now." The entire time that Mark is explaining everything to me, my head is lowered. I can't bear to look at him and see the sadness in his face. I can already hear it in his voice.

"I don't know what to say."

"Please tell me that you forgive me and that you will wait for me", he pleads.

"You mean wait until she dies?" I ask, looking up briefly.

"If that is how you want to put it", he responds.

"Why should I put my life on hold for a man who may or may not marry me in the end?"

"We love each other, right?" he asks.

"I thought we did! To be honest with you, I really want more with my life at this point. I thought that we had something special but I see that we don't. We can be friends."

"Fuck that! I don't want to be friends with you. I won't be able to control myself if I see you with someone else. I want all of you, Melissa. You are the woman that I think about when I am with her. It is your face that I see when I look at her. It was your lips that I kissed during the wedding ceremony. How horrible is that? I can't help myself. I love you so much!" His voice is heightened as he says each word. In his passion of words, he grabs my arm and doesn't realize that he is hurting me.

"Mark, let me go and please leave my apartment! Now! There is nothing else to talk about at this point. Congratulations on your marriage, but please, just go!"

"I am sorry", he says. "I am so sorry that I hurt you. Please forgive me."

"Mark, I think that you should leave now. I just don't think that it is a good idea for you to be here right now. And besides, *where is your wife?*"

"Please don't do this", he continues to plead. "I had to marry her. Please give us a chance. Because she is the mother of my children, I felt pressured to do the right thing by her", he explains. "Because of my love for my children, I feel that this is the only thing to do. I am so sorry that you got hurt in the process. I feel horrible about that. You have to believe me. Please understand that I love my children more than anything in this world."

"Then, you don't really need me, right?"

After going back and forth, he finally agrees to leave but under one condition. "I need to make love to you, Melissa. I need to taste you one last time. I need to feel your warm body on top of mine. I hurt you and I am sorry. Please, baby, let me make love to you", he pleads.

"Are you serious, Mark? You are crazy as hell! You come in here and break my heart, marry **another** woman, but you want to "make love" to me. You must think I'm a fool!"

"Melissa, you know that you want me just as badly as I want you. You know that we make good music together. Baby, please", he begs. He is right about that. I do want him. My body aches for his touch. This is something that I have wanted for weeks now. I have to do this, but I feel sorry for Dana. Here I am, now wanting to make love to her husband because of my selfish desires. She doesn't deserve what I am about to do.

It is not completely my fault that I fell in love with him. He had a hand in it also. I will sleep with him now and this will be the last time. Mark and I don't waste any time getting each other out of our clothes. We make love and I know that this is the last time I will see him. Although it is not the moral thing to do because he is a married man, he and I need closure and we find it in each other's arms on this Sunday morning.

CHAPTER 14

"This Man Is The Truth!"

Six Months Later.

Several months have passed and Mark is beginning to be a distant memory in the back of my mind. Believe it or not, I find a way to laugh again. I am going out with other guys and getting back in the swing of things. I finally decide to give Lionel the boot because I was getting bored with him. Although sex with him is out of this world, I realize that I want something more for myself. I want someone who can love my children. I want a man who will one day find himself at the local pharmacy picking out sanitary napkins for me if he has to do so.

From time to time, I ask Lena about Mark and she constantly reminds me that he is taking one day at a time. One time I ask her about both Mark and Dana and she tells me that Dana is starting to get worse. She admits that he really needs a friend right now more than ever. She encourages me to call him, but I just can't do it. I was in love with him at one time and if I speak with him, all the old feelings that we shared will once again become fresh in my mind.

"Melissa, his wife is getting worse. The cancer is progressing quickly. Mark has lost so much weight. He doesn't eat, doesn't sleep and is always at the hospital", she explains.

"I am so sorry to hear about this. She is just too young. It just doesn't seem fair."

"I know. Tell me about it. Mark really needs you to call him. He doesn't want to talk to anyone but you. He won't open up and talk to anyone in the family. We have all tried! He just keeps asking for you. Please call him", she begs.

"Maybe I will call him later. Someone is at the door. I will call you back", I say, before hanging up. It is Lionel at my door. I almost forgot about my tickets that he promised me for the upcoming event at Celebrities Night Club, "Stripper's Desire". This is when all the hottest male strippers come together for the biggest strip event ever. Lionel is still good for something. Right as he is leaving, the phone rings.

"Hello."

"Hey baby", the person on the other end says.

"Is this Mark?"

"Yes and I need you right now", he says. "Didn't Lena tell you to call me?"

"Mark, what is wrong and why are you calling me?"

"I am going to be honest with you. I need to make love to you. I haven't had sex in 3 months or so. She can't do it anymore. The radiation is starting to make her feel sick all the time and she is not up to it", he admits.

"Mark, I can't do this", I respond. "You really need to be there for your wife right now. I don't feel-."

Mark interrupts, "Melissa, she is ok with it. She is aware that she can't satisfy me and knows that I need to be satisfied. Sweetheart, she admitted to me that she has known all along about us. One night, she had me followed and that is how she found out. So, I ended up telling her the truth. I admitted to her that I love you and that what we share, it just happened. She understands that you make me feel things that I didn't know existed. Because of her illness, she has made it known that she understands that I need sex and having sex with you is fine with her as long as I don't leave her", he explains.

There is total silence on the phone. What he has just said has me so shocked that I end up dropping the phone on the floor. *What am I doing? I can't resist him any longer. My body is addicted to him. I want to reach out to him and hold him in my arms and kiss all of his pain away.* When I find the strength to pick up the phone, Mark is calling out to me. "Melissa, are you still there?"

"I am here. I am without words. I don't know what to say to you."

"Say, come over", he suggests.

"I need you, too, Mark. I need you badly", I respond. "Please come over."

Within 30 minutes or so, Mark is knocking on my door. When he sees that it is already open, he walks right in to find me in the bedroom already naked and waiting on him. There is absolutely no hesitation on my part to give him what he needs. We make love and it feels right! To make the evening even more perfect, my sister has taken the children to her house.

So, you can guess that without any distractions, we get up the following morning and have great conversation over breakfast and we never discuss Dana or anything about her cancer. This day remains special to both of us. Although I am enjoying it, I know that after awhile, this loving moment will end and he will be back at his wife's side giving her what *she* needs. "Sweetheart, you know that I have to leave now", he says, as he stands to leave.

"I love you, Mark. I am here for you whenever you need me. I do understand that you have to leave. Go, do what you must do."

"I love you, too, Melissa. You are one hell of a woman and I will always love you. I want you to be my wife. I want you to just be patient", he says.

"Mark, I can't ---", I begin to say before he interrupts me.

"Shh. Goodbye, sweetheart." He walks out the door and drives away. A feeling of sadness comes over me as I watch him leave. His car has turned the corner and I go to my bedroom and lie across my bed and look up at the ceiling. *I wonder what my life could have been like if Dana never became ill. He would still be here and perhaps, we would be getting ready to make love again.*

CHAPTER 15

"Mark Who?"

*A*t Town Center Steel, Fred is starting to let me bid jobs for him. He has also decided to put me in charge of the Annual Minority Business Leadership Meeting. This has become a big event over the years. Each year, one of top producing minority businesses takes on the task of hosting it. This year, it is Town Center Steel's turn and Fred is turning it all over to me, with a budget of $15,000. Fred's plan is to eventually hand over details such as this to me. Although his daughter works here too, he doesn't feel that she is responsible enough to handle it. He is; however, holding her responsible to assist me with this Event.

He hands me a list of his special guests who should attend. Although he offers suggestions on some locations, he ultimately agrees that it is up to me to decide where this event will take place. I have decided that the event will be held at the Marriott Hotel on Martin Luther King Blvd in Downtown Miami. One by one, the invitations are sent out to each guest. Special guests from Tallahassee, Montgomery, and Baton Rouge will arrive in the company's rented limousines. The event will be formal. I have arranged for the limos to pick up the guests from the surrounding hotels. Many of the guests decide to stay at the Marriott Hotel, but others have opted to stay at neighboring hotels. The event will be catered by *Houston's*.

****

The day of the event has finally arrived. My formal gown is simply beautiful. It is emerald green and is rented from Oxford's, a very well known boutique for parties such as these. Because I am the event planner, I am given all of the accessories for free. Rushing as usual, I head over to my friend's beauty salon to get my hair done. She tops it off with a French manicure and pedicure. My friend, Felicia gives my makeup a look of perfection. I am ready for a good time now!

Right on schedule, the company limo picks me up and carries me over to the Marriott. Tara, the boss's daughter, meets me at the front entrance because she is assigned to be my assistant for the evening. She is certainly not doing it for free. She gets a hefty bonus from her father for tonight. She is hoping to purchase a big ticket item and her father told her that she would have to work for it. She is actually making $500 just to show up and do what I need her to do. Tara and I are standing at the front entrance to the ballroom inviting in all the guests, when there is one guest who shows up that is not on the list.

"Hello ladies. My name is Kalin Thomas and I was invited here this evening by Fred", he says in a matter-of-fact kind of way.

"Tara, I don't see Kalin's name on the list, do you?" I say, without looking up to see him.

"It may not be on your list because I am his special guest. I am his interior designer and he personally invited me", Kalin explains.

Before he can say another word, I look up to see that his eyes match my dress. He is absolutely gorgeous and has a smile that will make any woman melt. I can't take my eyes off the mystery man.

"Oh yeah, that is right! My dad told me to remind you that there would be a Kalin Thomas coming who won't be on the list", she remembers. "We are so sorry sir. Please come in and you can have a seat at Table G. Have a wonderful evening."

He walks away to find his seat. "Tara, who the hell is *that*?"

"Oh, Melissa, you are so crazy. Don't lose your cool now. Don't go getting ghetto on me. You look too good", she says, with a slight laugh keeping her eyes on the guests who are still coming in.

"Now, that man is beautiful! He has the most gorgeous eyes. They look like they are the color of my dress. Who wouldn't want to wake up next to him in the morning?"

By now, all of the guests have arrived and are all seated in the ballroom. Tara and I have placed our seats at the back of the room just so we can keep our eyes on everything that is going on. Mr. Fred is very particular about his events. They have to be very professional. He is trying to see if I can handle myself.

The leadership meeting is officially underway. Christopher Wiggins, one of Miami's gayest guys is serving as the Emcee for the evening. He always does a good job. I had to spend a little more than I wanted for him, but he is worth it. During the meeting, I can not concentrate on anything but Mr. Kalin Thomas. I catch myself focusing in on him the entire evening. *I have to find a way to strike up a conversation with him. I am not going to leave this place without finding out more about this mystery man. My mind is wandering and wondering if he is married, gay, or seeing someone. I won't leave here tonight until I find out.*

"Good evening everyone!" he begins. "What a beautiful crowd we have here this evening! Whew, ya'll look good! Give it up for Ms. Melissa Williams and her assistant Tara Williams for putting on such an awesome event here. Ladies, you did your thing with this one! Give them a round of applause!" he says, as the crowd cheers.

Christopher introduces the board and takes the meeting agenda play by play. The guests are served and seem to enjoy the food. I can't eat because I need to make sure to be available for any mishaps. I notice that Kalin is enjoying himself as well. *I wonder what he would think if he knew that I was watching him and fantasizing about meeting him. I hate to admit it but my mind is wandering way too much! In my mind, I am thinking, "Mark Who?"*

The meeting is finally over and it is a success! Guests will talk about this year's Minority Meeting until next year this same time. I was very careful not to miss anything. When all the guests get back to their rooms, they will have a "thank you" card and chocolates waiting in their rooms. I had Tara get the room numbers for all the guests and arrange for Godiva Chocolate Baskets be delivered to all of our guests, with Town Center Steel's business cards in them.

I can see that Kalin is getting up to leave so I have to make a move over to him. "Leaving already? It's still early", I say to Kalin as he is heading towards the exit doors.

"It's just that I have an early morning appointment", he explains.

"I see! How do I contact you if I ever want to use your services?" *I know this is lame but it is the best I can come up with in such a short notice.*

"Of course. Please take my card", he says, as he hands me a card. I notice that the first name on the card is Kayla Thomas. *I hope that Kayla is either his mother or his sister.*

"So, Kayla Thomas, is this your sister or mother?" I ask, almost dreading the answer to the question.

"No. Kayla Thomas is my wife", he says, as if he is proud of it.

"Wonderful! How sweet!" At this point, I don't really care about anything else that he has to say.

"It's a family business that we have had for several years. My wife is friends with Mr. Williams' wife and that is how I learned that he was looking for an interior designer."

"Oh yeah, that is right! That is great", I say, as if I can't wait to get away from him. "It was nice meeting you and please, have a great evening, Mr. Thomas."

"Thank you. You enjoy the rest of the evening as well", he says, as we go in separate directions. There is no doubt in my mind that this will be my conversation with the mystery man because he is "married" and that is off limits. *Who am I kidding? I wouldn't mind to have him in my bed, even if it is just for one night!*

I am exhausted! On the way home in the limo, I start thinking about what it could be like to be married to a man like Kalin. He is gorgeous, successful, confident, and did I say gorgeous? I wonder if he is in love with his wife. I wonder what he thinks of me. He didn't seem interested in me at all.

Back at work on Monday, I am still talking about Kalin. I know that Tara is tired of hearing me go on and on about him. Every chance that she gets, she makes sure to remind me that he is a married man and then reality kicks in. That is the only thing that will keep me from speaking about him. I just remembered that he gave me his business card. I want to call him but I know that I can't because he is married. I just want to know him and be in his space one more time. But I need an excuse to call him. What will I say to him anyway?

"Tara, I have a meeting with the boss, so if anyone calls for me, please take a message or send them to my voice mail."

"Sure, Melissa", Tara responds.

Fred and I are working on a bid for a project that is coming up for the rebuilding of the Miami Dolphins Stadium. If Fred gets all the steel work for this project, this will certainly put us in the money! They need some minority companies to bid on the job to get some of the work. Through my contact at the Bidding Office, I can see what the competitors are bidding so that I can give a better bid. When I get back to my work area, Tara is already packing up and getting ready to leave for the day.

"Did anyone call?" I say to her.

She responds, "Well that guy that you went so crazy over called", she says, with a smile on her face. "He didn't ask for you, though. He only called to speak to my Dad."

"Really?" Tara can clearly see the disappointment in my face as she is telling me about Kalin's call. She does; however, suggest that I give him a call to confirm his appointment with Mr. Fred for some interior designer work at his house.

The phone rings and I am nervous. After a few seconds, what I presume to be his wife, answers the phone. "Hello, thank you for calling "No Place Like Home", it's Kayla speaking, how may I help you?"

"Hello and good morning. This is Melissa Williams from Town Center Steel and I am calling to confirm an appointment that Mr. Thomas has with Mr. Williams. Is he available?"

"Sure, hold on", she responds. A few moments pass and he picks up the phone.

"Hello", he says.

"Yes, Mr. Thomas, this is Melissa Williams and I am calling you to confirm your appointment with Mr. Fred Williams for Thursday at 2pm. Does this time work for you?"

"Yes that is fine", he answers. *Does he remember that I am the lady from the event the other night? I wonder.*

"Okay, I will let Mr. Williams know that this time is okay. If you have any questions, just give him a call."

"Ok", he says. *He really doesn't remember. Now I am crushed!* Right before hanging up the phone, he says, "Hey, can I call you sometime?"

I answer, "No, I don't think that it's a good idea."

He begs, "Please, I would really love to speak to you."

Again I say, "No, I really don't think that it's a good idea." *I thought, one more time and I am giving in for sure.*

"May I please call you sometime; I would really like to talk to you, just as friends", he asks again.

"Ok, just as friends?"

"Yes, just as friends", he answers.

I gladly give him my home number. The rest of the day becomes a blur in my memory. All I can think about is the conversation that I will have with Kalin tonight. *I can't imagine what he wants to talk to me about. Does he want a booty call or something? Where was his wife just now when he was speaking with me?*

Before going home, I decide that it's going to be a KFC dinner tonight. Once the children are fed and off to bed, I can then prepare myself to get my call from Kalin. The rest of the evening will belong to us. As soon as I walk in the door, I recognize that the voice message light is blinking on the phone. *Did I already miss his call? I hope I didn't.* It is Kalin! His voice message ends up being a short version of him singing, "Sparkle in your Eyes". I can't believe what I am hearing. Did he sing a song for me? I wonder if he's done this type of thing for other women as well. Although I am happy, I am also very skeptical about his intentions. *I mean, he is married!*

Later on that evening while finishing up the dishes, the phone rings and it is Kalin! Although I am excited, I have to be careful to not seem desperate and needy. I don't want him to think that I am sitting here waiting on him to call, even though I have thought of nothing other than this all day.

"Hello", I say, as if I am not expecting a call.

"Hello, beautiful", he says. "Did you get my message?"

"Yes, I did. Can you hold for a moment?" I ask, sounding like I am right in the middle of something.

"Sure, I will hold", he responds.

I finally return to the call with him, where he is patiently waiting. Kalin and I sit on the phone and talk for hours about our lives and how we both ended up in Florida. For the first time in awhile, I don't think about Mark nor do I think about his wife's illness. I don't think about my sister's issues or anything else for that matter. All I care about is getting to know more about Kalin. Unbelievably so, his wife's name doesn't come up at all. When we finally get off the phone, it is time for bed but I can't sleep for thinking about him. I wonder how he will allow himself to have such a deep conversation with me if he is happily married. I am sure that I will find out soon enough.

The following day at work, he calls me and the day after that and the day after that. When he calls, I find myself making the kids stay quiet because I don't want him to know all about me, just yet. In time, he will find it all out and hopefully by then, he will have already fallen in love with me. I haven't told him that I have children. I am having so much fun getting to know him and I don't want anything to spoil that. Eventually, I will have to tell him and eventually, he will have to give me the story about his wife.

One evening while we are on the phone, my youngest child, Sharell, finds a way to get away from the others and ends up in the room with me where I am on the telephone talking to Kalin. After she gets out of the room, the others follow. And now, all 4 of the children are right at my feet causing a commotion.

"What is that noise, Melissa?" Kalin asks.

In all of my conversations with Kalin, I have never mentioned to him that I have four children. There is no time like the present. It is now time for me to tell him my truth and see how he responds to it. With a very defensive tone, I say, "my children".

"I didn't know that you had children", he responds.

"Ok, so there you have it. There is my truth. I have four children. Their names are Christy, Kameron, Darren, and Sharrell, and if you w---", I continue, before being interrupted.

"Well, actually, Melissa, I love children", he says, with a soft touch. "I guess there is no time like the present for me to tell you about the situation with my wife."

"I am listening."

"She and I are getting a divorce. The marriage is over and has been for quite some time. I still live at home with her but I sleep on the couch. We are no longer intimate", he explains. *This sounds just like Mark when he explained to me about his situation of living with Dana. Should I believe Kalin? How do I know if he is telling me the truth or not? He didn't actually come out and tell me this, now did he?*

I can't believe that he is unable to work things out with his wife. He seems like such a genuine person and I can't believe that his wife wouldn't want to make it work with him. Even though I am happy that he wants to be committed to me, I still feel sad for his current wife because I loved him from the moment that I laid eyes upon him. Kalin and I continue to talk for weeks on the phone before I invite him over to meet my children.

"So, what does your schedule look like on Thursday evening?"

"I will be where you want me to be, my love", he answers.

"Well, I would love for you to meet my family."

"What time?" he asks.

"I'll say 8:00 or so." I really want to see if he is all about me or if this will simply end in a "booty call". It is better that I find out the truth about Kalin once and for all. I am curious to see how he reacts to my children and more importantly, how they respond to him.

"Great, I will be there around 7:30 or so", he says. The next few days, I mentally prepare myself for Kalin to meet my family. The last time I introduced my children to a man friend was with Mark and the last thing they remember about him is that he made me cry.

The doorbell rings at approximately 7:45p.m. I am somewhat nervous about answering the door because this visit could change everything that we share already. It is very important that he is comfortable with my life. And as much as I want him, I have to consider the needs of my children. "Well hello my love", he says after I open the door. "You still look as beautiful as I remembered."

Kalin shows up with flowers. I have never met a man who has bought flowers for me! It is so hard to resist this mystery man. He says all of the right things and just looking into his eyes makes me believe that he means every word.

Sharell is just a toddler and she is just learning to walk. She connects with Kalin right away. He seems to be comfortable around the children and is simply a natural! He moves around and spends time with each one of them, but Sharell ends up in his arms. The two of them standing there together is the most beautiful thing I have seen in a long time. Kameron and Darren seem to appreciate him as well. It is a picture perfect moment. Here is this man who I just met and in love with already and he is standing here being accepted by the most important people in my life. He only counts three children! He realizes that one is missing. I explain to him that Christy is in Middleton with my mother. He is eager to meet her as well. After putting the children to bed, Kalin and I retire to my bedroom for conversation.

"So, how did I do?" he asks.

"I think they like you. You are a natural with children. Do you have any children?"

"No, just my stepson, Phillip, that I am raising with my wife, rather Kayla", he responds.

"It's quite okay to call her your wife. You *are* still married to her."

I know that I am treading on dangerous ground because I have not been intimate with a man in quite awhile, but I feel like I can handle it with no problem. Kalin sits in the chair next to the bed. I am finding it very difficult to make eye contact with him for fear of giving in to my own desires, which are to make love to this mysterious man even if he never comes back. I desire him like I have never desired another man in my life. Although I am sweating bullets, Kalin is being a complete gentleman. He doesn't seem to have any problems with being in the bedroom alone with me. He hasn't tried to kiss me or anything.

Our conversation lasts all night long. When we awake the next morning, I am still in my clothes and so is he. Last night, we fell asleep in each other's arms on top of the bed. I can't believe it! I actually made it through the night! He didn't try to take advantage of me but he maintained the respect for me and my children. The more and more that I grow to know him, the more I *want* to know about him.

The next day, Kalin calls me just to say hello and to tell me that he enjoyed our evening together. *But we didn't have sex. What was there to enjoy, I wonder.* "Since we had such a lovely evening, I would love for you to stop by after work."

"I would love that too, Melissa", he responds. He decides to come by after his shift ends that night. I am battling with whether I should be completely honest with him about what I am feeling. I think I have no other choice but to be honest with him.

"Kalin, you know that I have thoroughly enjoyed our time together. I think you're wonderful and ---", I begin, before being interrupted.

"You're giving me the axe already!" he exclaims.

"No, I just feel that it is more appropriate for you to date me after you have settled this thing with your wife. I am falling in love with you and if you're not serious about me, then I think –." Kalin reaches over and grabs me and kisses me very gently on the lips.

"I love you, Melissa Williams. I already know that I want to be with you for the rest of my life. I need you. You complete me. I will move out of the house and get my own apartment if that makes it better. How about that?" he asks. I can't believe that he gave in just like that. I am not used to this. I am starting to believe that just maybe, he really does love me.

"That would be fantastic! Are you sure that it is over between you and your wife?"

"I am very sure." After we talk long and hard about the "extra" bills, we agree that it's better for Kalin to just move in with me and the children.

On moving day, I hate to admit it but I am very nervous because even though I have been in numerous relationships, I have never been in one where the man and I end up living together with my children. *Am I ready to share my space like this? What if I can't live up to the expectations that he has? What if he doesn't like my cooking? What if he doesn't like the way I clean?* I have never been under the same roof with a man on a permanent basis and now I will be sharing my bed with him every day. This is quite odd but exciting. I have to talk to him about what I am feeling.

Kalin and I are very open in our conversations. We talk about everything! That is why I feel comfortable in sharing with him my doubts and concerns. As usual, he makes me feel comfortable and assures me that all will be okay. He constantly reminds me that he is not here to disrespect me nor my children and that he simply wants to share his life with us. Days and nights pass and Kalin and I have not been intimate. *Is there something wrong with me? Is he in our bed thinking of his ex-wife?* I don't want to guess any longer so I ask him to tell me what is wrong. "Kalin, do you find me sexy?"

Kalin rolls over and looks into my eyes and says, "Melissa, I find you very sexy and tempting, but I made a promise to you and that was to respect you and to not push you into anything", he answers, as he holds my hand and looks into my eyes.

It is at this moment that I realize that I can no longer resist him. I want to hold him, and I want to go far beyond that. Honestly, I want to make love to him and I never want to stop. We end up sharing the most wonderful evening together holding each other and fulfilling each other's desires, **without** having sexual intercourse. But then, the phone rings. Kalin and I are so into each other that I don't acknowledge it at all. If it is important, they will certainly leave a message.

The next morning, I get up and realize that he is still there when I hear the water running in the bathroom. "Good morning, Mrs. Thomas", he jokingly says. *I thought, wow, I really like the sound of that. Mrs. Thomas. No man had ever given me his last name except when I was in 8th grade. I wonder if he can see himself as my husband and me as his wife.*

"Good morning, Mr. Thomas." You can certainly tell that something really wonderful is starting to happen between the two of us. I decide not to make a comment about him calling me Mrs. Thomas. I decide to act as if I don't hear him.

"Melissa, the phone is beeping. Don't forget to check the message", he reminds me. "That must be the call that came through last night when we were so caught up with each other." We both laugh. When Kalin goes into the bathroom to finish brushing his teeth, I decide to listen to the message.

"Hello Ms. Williams. It is Mark and I need you girl. I really miss you so much. Dana's health is really getting horrible. I think that her time must be coming near to the end. I feel so sorry for her. I really need you sweetheart. Please give me a call on my cell phone. I am going out with the fellas tonight and we will be in your neighborhood so please hit me up so that I can come see you. I love you".

What am I supposed to feel after hearing this message? Do I still love Mark or has my love for him been replaced with the feelings that I am developing for Kalin? With all of our conversations, I totally forgot to discuss my little arrangement with Mark. Things are going too good with Kalin and I am not about to ruin it with this foolishness. Besides, Mark is married and there is no commitment with us, just occasional sex, more like therapy for him during this rough time. So, as far as I am concerned, there is really no need to say a word. Kalin calls from the other room, "Honey, is everything okay?" he asks, after noticing the concerned look on my face.

"No, everything is just fine. That was just Tara calling me to tell me about the change of plans for our appointment on tomorrow", I explain. *Did I just lie to Kalin for the first time?* I am done with that part of my life and all I want to do is be in Kalin's life. Mark will get the message when I don't return his calls.

The kids are getting used to the idea of having Kalin around. He makes sure to spend quality time with them and I appreciate this more than anything. One night while he and the kids are downstairs watching "The Lion King", I decide to head upstairs to take a nice long bubble bath to collect my thoughts. *How in the world can Mark come around like this now? There was a time when I would have jumped at the idea to be with him and to be his wife, but not anymore. I gave him love and he didn't appreciate it. I need to move on from Mark to find my true happiness.*

Kalin finally puts the children to bed and makes his way into the bedroom, where he finds me already in bed. "You know, honey, I really like that movie. It's a very good family movie that teaches real core values about love. Darren and Sharell fell asleep, but Kameron hung in there with me until the end."

I feel a little awkward because the evening prior had been really wonderful and I am afraid that we will start to find fault with one another and it will be all over before it gets started. It is hard to accept that any man can love me and want to be my partner for life. To my surprise, Kalin gets up from his side of the bed and gets down on his knees next to my side of the bed. He takes my hands in his, looks into my eyes and says, "Melissa, I want to spend the rest of my life with you and these children", he proclaims. "Can I? I know that I am still legally married but I am done with her and I want you to be my wife."

I don't know what to say. I have never had a man want to do that with me and certainly not with me **and** my children. *Should I tell him about my previous arrangement that I had with Mark? Will he understand that I was just doing this to help my friend? Or will he think that I was just being a whore?*

"Yes!" I answer. "I would love to be your partner for life." So, technically, Kalin and I are engaged, but legally, he is still married to Kayla. Not knowing when the divorce will be final is *still* not enough to damper the evening. We make love over and over again until we are exhausted and neither of us can breathe. This becomes a regular routine for us. We can't keep our hands off of one another. I can't get enough of him and he acts as if I am the only woman on the planet. Every chance that we get, we are playing with the children, making love whether it is in the bedroom, in the bathroom shower, on the floor, in the closet, or wherever the urge comes across. I don't reject him at all.

I am spending so much time with Kalin that Mark is beginning to be a distant memory. I forget that Mark will eventually want to know why I have just stopped speaking with him. Kalin and I are together so much that the only time we are apart is when we both go to work. We love being in each other's company. My family is somewhat concerned as well as my friends. My explanation is that I am simply in love.

"Melissa, you don't know this guy that well and you are already madly in love with him?" asks Diana. "I mean you got him all in your apartment and leaving him there when you are gone. You even have him watching your children", she comments.

"I know that and I do know him", I answer. "I spend lots of time with him and the children all adore him. If you don't believe me, just ask them. He's a really good guy."

Before Diana can say another word, the phone rings and the caller id reads, FT. LAUDERDALE WATER COMPANY! It's Mark! I might as well take the call so that I can tell him the truth. "Hey, I have another important call that I have to take. We will talk later, ok", I say.

"Alright Meme", she says, before hanging up. I switch over to pick up the call from Mark.

"Hello."

"Well, well, well, it is about time", he says, surprised that he actually has me on the phone.

"Mark, there is something that I have to tell you."

"Melissa, she died last night", he blurts out, before I can think of how to break the news to him. I can tell that he has been crying.

"What?!"

"I am so sorry Mark. Were you there with her?"

"No, but she was with the children. She died very peacefully. I had left the house to try to call you and when I returned, the children were crying and I knew then that it was over. She had already made arrangements with Wilkins Funeral Home. I am at peace but I really need to see you. I need you right now."

"Mark."

"Melissa, I need you. Please don't blow me off tonight. If there is a time that I need you, I need you right now", he says. "We don't have to be intimate. I just need you to hold me. Please don't leave me now!"

"Mark, I am with someone now and I am in love with him. I won't be able to meet with you in that way anymore. I am so sorry, but he is a really good man and I don't want to mess up what we have", I explain. There is complete silence on the other end of the phone. "Are you there?"

"I don't believe this. I thought that you loved me. I thought that we had an understanding. You have been giving my love to another man and now that we can be together, you are not able to be there for me. Does he know about our *arrangement*?"

"Please don't do this, Mark. Please don't be mad at me because I wanted someone to love *me*. Kalin is wonderful to me and I really want to be with him. I am so sorry about Dana, but I can't run off to give you sex right now. I will be the best friend for you right now, but I can't be *that kind of friend* right now. Come on! Let's just talk about what you are feeling."

"Forget you, Melissa Williams. Go on with your happy little life and just forget all about Mark! I don't need you anymore!" he yells.

Before I can say another word, he has slammed the phone down. I don't want to call him back but I feel badly for him and his family. But Kalin is my family now and I can't hurt him either.

CHAPTER 16

"Kalin Meets My Family"

"When do we meet him?" Diana asks.

"For Thanksgiving", I answer. "We will have Thanksgiving at our house and everyone can finally get to meet Kalin."

"Our house? So, he lives with you now?" Diana asks.

"Yes he does. Please don't start with me, ok? He is here now. This is my life, remember? Please let me live it. I care about this man and I want to spend the rest of my life with him."

"And you are sure about that?" she asks.

"Yes I am. Just support me, sis. That is what I need right now. But, I do have to go because I have an appointment at the hair salon."

"Ok, sis. I will see you on Thanksgiving."

Kalin will meet my family soon. He is just as excited to meet them as I am for them to meet him. I know that they will find him adorable just as I have. I hope that my mother is happy for me that I have finally met someone who loves me *and* my children. She will be happy, for sure, to see that not all men just want to have sex. Here is a man who is not the biological father to my children and is acting as if he is. *What mother would not want a son-in-law like that, I thought.*

My family has finally arrived in Ft. Lauderdale and announce that they will be over around 5:00 or so. When Kalin picks me up from work, he is so nervous about meeting my mother that I almost feel so badly for him. Nothing else matters to him except for being accepted by my mother. It is all he has talked about since I told him the family was coming.

We have made it to the apartment and my family is already inside waiting on us to arrive. As soon as we walk in, all eyes are on Kalin. I can't blame them because he is such a gorgeous man, except this is not why they are eyeballing him.

"Kalin, is it?" my mother asks, almost rudely.

"Yes, ma'am", Kalin responds, looking puzzled.

"Your wife called and said for you to call her back", my mother says, without making eye contact with him. I don't know what hurts worse. *Is it that Kalin is still legally married to this woman or is it that my family found it out this way or is it that my mother embarrassed him so terribly in front of the entire family?* As horrible as it is, Kalin handles it like a trooper.

"Thanks for the message", he says, while walking upstairs to our bedroom.

"Kalin, don't take it personally", I say, trying to console him.

"She hates me, Melissa", he says. "She hates me for sure now. She will never think that I will be good enough for you. This is the thing that she will remember about me. How can I convince her now that I love you?"

"Honey, one thing you need to remember and that is that I love you and that is all that matters between me and you, you got that?"

"I got it."

"Do you still want to be with Kayla?"

"Of course I don't. I am with the woman that I love and cherish and that is you, Ms. Williams", he responds.

"Okay, then. That is good enough for me and it has to be good enough for them. Now let's go downstairs so that you can meet my family."

"Okay", he agrees.

Kalin and I go back downstairs and I introduce him to my nieces, nephews, cousins, sisters, and brothers. They engage him in friendly conversation, but you can tell that the "wife" thing is still on their minds. I can sense that my mother's first impression of the man who will become my husband is not a very pleasant one. Unfortunately, there isn't anything I can do to change it.

Over the next few weeks, I find myself having several conversations with my family about my personal relationship with Kalin. They don't think he is the right guy for me because he is married and hasn't divorced his wife yet. I know why they feel this way. They are just trying to protect me and look out for my best interest. But the truth is that I love him and I want to be with him. They will just have to learn to love him and support my decision.

CHAPTER 17

"And Now It's My Turn"

O ver the next few weeks, Kalin and I make some changes. Because Kalin and I live together now, it just makes sense to me that he watches the kids during the day and I watch them at night. With him around, I no longer need my current babysitter, so I decide to discontinue my service with her. As can be expected, she is not happy with this decision because it decreases her income. I have decided to leave my job with Fred at Town Center Steel. He tries everything to get me to stay, but I have tendered my letter of resignation, but have agreed to stay with him to train my replacement. It has nothing to do with this job because I love it and I love them, but I have always wanted to put a hand into Real Estate and property management and was recently offered a comfortable position with Landstone Realty.

"Melissa, telephone's for you", says Tara.

"Who is it?"

"It sounds like Kalin."

"Hello."

"Hello, honey. I just want you to know that I just punished Darren and Kameron because they were supposed to be right outside playing on the porch and they sneaked off down to the pond and almost jumped in. I found out because the manager saw them and brought them back to the apartment", he says, very nervously.

I don't know quite what to think. Although I am concerned for my children more than anything, Kalin assures me that they are okay. Is he comfortable with watching the children? Will this push him away or what?

"Are the kids okay now?"

"Yes, they are fine. They are sleeping now," he answers.

"Are you okay?"

"Yes, I am fine. I just wanted you to know what happened."

"Thanks. I will see you when I get home."

"Okay, I love you", he says.

"I love you too."

I can tell that Kalin is somewhat nervous about this situation with the children. He always seems concerned about the children and I have no reason to believe that he would intentionally cause harm to them whatsoever.

After this incident, a week or so has passed and there is a knock at the door. On the other side of the door is a petite woman who introduces herself as a social worker for the Children Come First Organization. That name rings a bell! These are the same people who were investigating my sister when I first arrived here in Miami. I specifically remember how I lied to them so that Diana wouldn't have to lose her children due to poor supervision, even though she was doing what she had to do. *I guess it's my turn now.* Being that she is standing here, that means that someone must have called them, but why?

"Good morning Ma'am. My name is Patrice Nettles and I am here from Children Come First. May I come in, please?" she asks.

"Sure, please come in."

"Ms. Williams?" she asks, looking around the apartment.

"Yes, how may I help you?"

"Our office has received a call that your children are being abused by a Kalin Thomas, who is your live in boyfriend. The report says that you just stand by and do nothing and continue to allow him to abuse them" she explains.

"Are you serious?" I exclaim. "Who would call and say this about us? I love my children! My children are well taken care of."

"So who lives here?" she asks.

"Me, my 3 children and Kalin", I respond, as Kalin stands by and listens.

"So Kalin, are you the children's father?" she asks.

"No, I am not their biological father, but I love them very much as if they were my own children", he answers.

"Our alleged report reads, and I quote, "Kalin disciplines the children while the mother is away and leaves bruises on them", she reads from her file.

"Ma'am, Kalin called me the other day because the children slipped away from the front porch and ended up at the pool area and had to be returned home by the apartment manager. He called me at work to tell me what happened", I explain.

"Okay, but did he discipline them?" she asks, almost interrupting me.

"Yes, I did. What is the problem?" Kalin asks, directing his attention to Ms. Nettles.

"We need to talk in the other room, ma'am", she says, pointing to the room closest to the dining room.

"What is the problem?" I ask, without offering her a seat.

"Ma'am, your children are your children. Kalin is not their father and does not have the authority to discipline them. He needs to reserve that for you to do", she explains. "I need to look at the children and make sure that they are okay. We will do our investigation and will let you know of our findings."

"Kids, please come down. There is someone who needs to see you", I yell to the children upstairs. They are upstairs watching television in our bedroom.

One by one, they make their way downstairs and go into the room with Ms. Nettles. She is in the room with them for a brief moment and returns with her folder closed and a nod that agrees that the children are okay.

"Ma'am, we will be in touch with you", she says, as she is packing up her briefcase. "Nice to meet you, Kalin."

Although she is gone from the apartment, there is still a huge hole that is left in my heart. *Who could have possibly called these people to complain that I did or allowed any harm to my children? I love my children with everything that I have. There is no way I would allow anyone to harm them? Is this right? Can people just call and make this type of accusation against you? Who would do this to me?*

The night doesn't quite end once Patrice leaves. The police show up! Officer Heathrow speaks with me and Kalin regarding the allegation and determines that there is no evidence of abuse, just as Ms. Nettles discovered. Apparently, CCF doesn't take too kindly to discipline being administered by a non-biological parent.

For the next several days, there is speculation as to who could have placed that call. I don't have any type of conclusions to draw from because everyone that I know certainly knows that I love my children. Will I be able to get a report from CCF regarding this allegation or is that confidential? I decide to give them a call to find out.

"Hello, Patrice Nettles, please."

"This is she. How may I help you?"

"Hi, this is Melissa Williams and I was wondering if it is possible to get a copy of the report that was just recently closed regarding the allegation?"

"Sure, you will have to come down to the office to get a copy of the full report", she explains.

"Ok, is there a fee?"

"Yes. $1 per page."

"So, how many pages are in the entire file?"

"10 pages or so", she responds.

"Fine, I will be in to pick up my copy."

I can hardly wait to get my hands on this report to see who could have called CCF on me and Kalin. The trip to their office seems like a long one. When we finally arrive, I walk down the hall to the area named "RECORDS". Across the desk is a plump lady who has on way too much lipstick.

"Yes, how may I help you" she asks.

"I am here to get a copy of a report that was filed against me", I explain.

"Well you know that it is going to cost you $1 per page, right?" she asks, as if I won't be able to afford to pay for it.

"Yes, I am aware of that."

"Wait a minute", she says very rudely. "I need you to sign something else first."

Before I can receive the packet of information, I have to sign a document that reads, CONDITIONS FOR RECEIVING ABUSE REPORT. After reading the document, I have learned that I will be charged with a misdemeanor if I use any of the information in the report *against* the organization. Without much thought, I sign the document. The lady behind the desk returns with the report. I need a name or some kind of clue as to who called! Speed reading through it, I finally run across the name, DIANA WILLIAMS.

"DIANA WILLIAMS, my sister!" I gasp. "There must be a mistake!"

There it is right before me that the culprit to my nightmare is my sister. How could she have done this? Why did she do this? I am so devastated finding this out. Now, I really don't know what to think.

Back at home, the children are back to normal. They don't miss a beat! They still love Kalin and so do I. Our family will not fall apart because of this incident. We continue to act as normally as possible. We continue to show each other love. But, in the back of my mind, I can't help but think that the reason for this has nothing to do with my children. Diana and the rest of my family just don't like Kalin and totally despise the idea that he wants to play the father role in my children's lives.

Over the next couple of weeks, I find myself having to constantly reassure Kalin that I am not angry with him. He feels a little self conscious about the incident. I explain to him over and over again that he did what a normal parent would have done. He is so hurt that he is being accused of abusing my children when he and I both know in our hearts that abuse is certainly not the case.

Because it is the right thing to do, we move on past this experience and choose to put it out of our minds. Besides, the children still love him and respect him. My family is not coming around as much, which is fine by me until one day the phone rings and it is my sister, Diana. *How does she have the nerve to call me after knowing what she has done? She probably doesn't know that I know that she called CCF, when I was the very one who kept her from going through the same nightmare. I know that I have to forgive her. Our mother always taught us that family comes first. We have always been that way. She has also taught us forgiveness and that is what I have to do right now. Nothing happened as a result of her calling, so we might as well move on from this.*

"Melissa, how are you?" she asks. I really want to say something to her about calling CCF on me, but I decide against it. She must have her reasons for doing it. There was not much harm done.

"I am doing fine. How are you?"

"Doing well. Is Kalin still there?" she asks

"Yes, he is still here. Should he be somewhere else?"

"Do you really want me to answer that question or do you want me to tell you what you want to hear? Why are you in denial about this man, Melissa? I don't trust him. I think that he has other motives for wanting to be with you. Why did you have to go and let him move into your place? You will never be able to get rid of him now. And you are now letting him spank your kids? Are you crazy?" she asks, sounding as if she is getting frustrated with me.

"This is my life. Let me live it the way I want to live it. I love Kalin and I really believe that he loves me. Why can't you be a big sister and just be happy for me? Is that too much to ask?"

"I would be happy for you if I felt like you were with someone who cares about you *and* your kids. I just think that he has something else on his mind. That's all!"

"But Diana, the man is here with me! He could have any woman he wants, but he has chosen to be with me. He cooks and cleans and takes very good care of the children. The kids love him!" I say, defending Kalin's honor.

"It's more like they are afraid of him. That is what I think. And for some reason, their mother can't see it."

"Please change the subject. I don't want to talk about this anymore. Is that why you called?"

"No. I called to see if you would let me take my nieces and nephews to the Zoo", she says.

"You know what? The kids could use an outing today. I think it will be fun for them."

"Great. I will be there in about 30 minutes or so. Please have them ready."

My sister has arrived and the kids are very excited to go to the Zoo. It has been at least a couple of years since I have taken them to the Zoo. They wave goodbye as my sister buckles them into the seatbelts. Sharell is still in a car seat.

"So, I can't believe you allowed the children to leave with their Aunt", Kalin says as the car turns the corner.

"Why wouldn't I let them go?"

"Let's see. This is the same woman who called CCF on us. This is the same woman who thinks you shouldn't be with me", he responds.

"But this woman is my sister and that won't ever change. And, besides, my children love the Zoo. Why would I deny them the opportunity to go out and enjoy themselves? Everything will be just fine. But, I do have an idea of what we can do now that we have the house to ourselves", I say, as I sit in his lap and face him. Kissing him certainly takes my mind off the kids and anything else going on around us.

Kalin and I make love right here on the floor next to the floor model television. It was a nice break for us being able to spend some quality time with each other. It has to end now because my sister just called to let me know that she is just minutes away from the house.

Right as we are putting the kids down to bed, Kalin looks me in the eyes and says, "Melissa, do you know that I would never do anything to hurt these kids?"

"Kalin, I know that, honey."

"I really mean it and it hurts that your family or anyone would think that I would do that", he says.

"Don't worry honey, I love you and trust you and that is all that matters. When *I* start to doubt you and lose trust in you, then that is when you need to worry."

We both agree to never discuss what happened with Children Come First ever again.

CHAPTER 18

"We Don't Cuddle Tonight"

*A*s a fresh start, we decide to move into a new townhouse that just recently became available. But first, Kalin and I have to go out to get some painting items from Home Depot. Instead of letting the kids tag along, we decide to call my nephew to watch them.

"Honey, I don't know how I feel about leaving the children home with Scott. Do you believe that he is responsible enough to watch the children?" he asks.

"They will be fine. Don't worry daddy."

After arriving to Home Depot, we discover that they are having a huge Paint Sale today. So, now I am able to get even more paint.

After picking up all that we need for our painting project, we head back home, only to discover that Scott is nowhere to be found. For whatever reason, he has left our children home alone.

"Christy, where's Scott?"

"He left, Momma. His friends came over and he left. He told us to lock the door and not to open it for anyone", she answers.

"See what I mean Melissa!" Kalin interjects.

"Well, we are here now. Everything will be just fine."

Because it's already late, Kalin and I decide to just fix dinner and put the painting project on hold until tomorrow. As much as I have tried to change the subject, Kalin continues to bring up what Scott has done. He feels justified in saying this because he didn't think it was a good idea to have Scott watch the children in the first place. I can see it in his face that he feels as though he may have made a mistake by deciding to become a part of my ready-made family. Because we don't cuddle tonight like we normally do, I am starting to prepare myself for Kalin finally deciding to leave us.

****

The following morning, we all decide to have cereal for breakfast, so that we can get an early start on our painting project. Right in the middle of putting on our painting gear, there is a knock at the door.

"Is Ms. Williams in?" asks the woman standing on the other side of the door.

"I am Ms. Williams. How may I help you?" I answer, with hesitation.

"Good morning ma'am. My name is Erica Stevens and I am here from Children Come First and we received a call from the abuse hotline. May I come in?" she asks.

"Sure. Come in, please." I am feeling as if my world has come to a complete halt. I can't believe that someone hates me this much. *This can't be Diana again! It just can't be! Her son was here with my children. Did he leave on purpose just to make me look bad again? Why!?!*

By this time, Kalin has joined us at the dinner table to discuss this matter. The investigator starts to explain why she is here. She begins by saying that someone called their Department alleging that Kalin and I left the house on Saturday and left the children alone. They also allege that the children are afraid of Kalin and that he is so controlling in that he gives them a bath and everything.

At this moment, I know in my heart that this is clearly my sister's work. She is my sister and I have to love her no matter what, but how much can one person take? It is painfully obvious that she is not crazy about Kalin, but why hurt me too?

As the investigator continues to speak, I am no longer listening. Does Diana remember what it felt like when CCF came to remove her children from her home? Doesn't she remember how I lied to save her from experiencing this pain? If she has a problem with something that I am doing, why can't she just come to me instead of calling these people on me?

"Ma'am, Kalin and did leave home on Saturday to go to the store. We took the youngest child with us and left my nephew here with the others. As a matter of fact, my sister's child is the one we left here with the children", I explain. "I don't know why he left. We gave him specific instructions on what to do while we were out. I hate to say it but I am starting to feel like they are trying to make me look bad. My sister knows that her son was supposed to be here watching the kids for me. I would never leave my children home alone like this", I continue to explain.

"I understand what you are saying, Ms. Williams, but the fact still remains that they were here alone and that is a problem for the Department. I will speak with the children now to see if there is any weight to these other accusations and I will inform you of my findings", she responds.

Away from us, Ms. Stevens speaks to the children to see if they give her the same story. And not only do they tell her that my nephew was home with them and left, but they also make it known that they are not afraid of Kalin. And for the record, Ms. Stevens makes a note in her report that there are no marks on the children, whatsoever.

The case is closed with only indicators of poor supervision.

"Melissa, why is your family doing this to us?" Kalin asks. "Is it that they just want me out of your life or what? Why do they hate me so much? Can't they see that I love you and I love these children? I know that I am not their fathers but I love them as if they are my own", he says.

Kalin is very hurt by all of this and it is obvious because he has never gone through anything like this with anyone in his entire life. I can't blame him for feeling offended as his name is being dragged through the mud. Why can't my family see the good in this man? Why is my sister trying to destroy my life? I just don't understand. I would never do this sort of thing to her.

"I know and I am sorry. I am truly sorry."

Days go by and we hear nothing from my family. Kalin's father, JT, is extremely confused about what is going on with Kalin. He is not happy with what his son is being accused of because he, for one, knows that Kalin truly loves us. I love him and don't want him to leave but I can see that my family is trying to make a point about him being here. I can't blame Kalin if he decides to leave after this.

"Melissa, I don't want your family in our home ever again", he says.

"And what will that solve? We have to continue to show love. I love my family and I can't just make them stay away."

"How am I supposed to feel knowing that your family can come around and call CCF whenever they get ready to call them?"

"I know how crazy this is getting. Remember that this thing happened to both of us and not just you. I can't just do away with them, Kalin. I will talk to my sister."

"Does this relationship mean anything to you at all? What if it were to end because of all this? Does that matter to you? Do you consider my feelings at all?"

"Of course it matters to me if you leave! I love you, Kalin. Can we just work this out?"

"Fine. Just know that there may come a day when you may have to choose, Melissa. If they continue to intervene in our life like this, you will *always* be caught in the middle."

CHAPTER 19

"Amber's A Winner!"

*A*fter putting the children down to bed, Kalin and I retire to bed ourselves. Because I need to convince him of my love for him, I make tonight very special for us. We take our time pleasing one another and I believe that this is the night that I get pregnant with our first child. A few weeks later, we officially find out that I am 6 weeks pregnant. Kalin is so happy that he gets on the phone and shares the news with everyone that he can remember. He gets on the internet and reads every article that he can find about expectant mothers and finds out that walking is the best thing for me to do during pregnancy, so every day after dinner, we take a walk through the neighborhood. Kalin doesn't stop there. He goes so far as to juggle his schedule around so that he is able to make it to all of my doctor visits.

After months of being pampered by my expectant boyfriend, I become familiar with the sharp, labor pains that I begin to experience on December 20th. Today is also Sharell's birthday. *I thought, no way!* First time was when Darren was born on Kameron's birthday and now this baby will be born on Sharell's birthday.

In the labor and delivery room, Kalin is the perfect boyfriend. He is so attentive to my needs and makes sure that the doctors and nurses handle me with care. When his daughter is being born, he stands there with tears in his eyes. This is a first time experience for me. My child's father is here going through this with me. I guess this is how God intended it to be. As soon as Kalin cuts the baby's chord, the doctors place his baby daughter in his hands. He holds her in his arms and kisses her forehead and whispers, "I am glad that you are here."

Kalin and I are the proud parents of a 7lb. 5oz. baby girl, who we name Amber. In my mind, the first night home will be sweet and full of great memories. But, it is far from that! She is not cooperating with my breast. She refuses to take it for her feeding time. Finally, after several attempts, she finally gets it. What a relief! This is something that Kalin really wants is for me to breastfeed our baby, so I am happy that she has finally cooperated.

The word has spread throughout the family that there is a new baby in the Williams' clan. My mother is a softie for her grandchildren and rarely misses any of their births. Word has it that she is planning a surprise visit to see our newest addition.

Without warning, my mother shows up bearing gifts for our little Amber.

"You didn't think I would miss my grandchild's new beginning, did you?" she asks, as she is walking into our townhouse with several packages.

"Mother, I am surprised to see you. When did you make it into town?"

"I had those grandkids of mine to bring me to Florida as soon as I found out that you were in labor. We may have had our issues in the past but I love my grandkids. Now, where is that baby?"

"Right this way", I say, as she follows me upstairs to her room.

Within minutes, my doorbell is ringing. I have no idea who it can be. When I open up the door, I am shocked that it is my sister and her sons. They, too, have come to take a peek at the new addition.

"Hello, sis. You look good to have just had a baby", she comments.

"Well thanks. Come in", I say. Kalin may not have been as thrilled to see them, but they are family and I will never turn them away.

By now, everyone is standing around Amber's crib and making comments of how beautiful she is and how she looks just like Kalin. "So I bet that Kalin is gushing right now?" Diana comments.

"Yeah, he is very excited and she is definitely daddy's baby. He gets up at night when she cries. He bathes her. After I pump the milk out of my breast, he feeds it to her by the bottle. He wakes me up to breastfeed the baby when she is hungry. He is very supportive, Diana."

Once the baby is finally asleep, we all sit in the family room and chat about fun family times. I bring out the family photo albums and suddenly, our home is, once again, filled with laughter. This feels just like old times, back in Alabama when there was a storm and all the televisions would have to be turned off, forcing us to communicate. Amber's birth has brought our family together, at least for today.

My six weeks for waiting to have sex are almost up when Kalin and I get a serious urge to give in to each other's desires. It seems like a year since he has made love to me. We can't wait another day. Surprisingly so,

Amber cooperates with us and is asleep for the entire evening. She must sense that mommy and daddy needs some time alone.

It is amazing to me how Kalin still makes me feel beautiful when I know that I am not beautiful at all. I now have stretch marks and breasts filled with milk but he loves on me as if I am the most beautiful woman in the world.

CHAPTER 20

"I Just Can't Leave Them"

"Hey honey, I met a very nice lady at work today."

"You did? Who is she?" he asks.

"Her name is Amy Stephens. She just recently moved in. She is not married and doesn't have any children. She came into the office today and rented one of our townhome suites and paid for the entire lease up front. Maybe I should invite her over one day."

"That is cool, honey", he agrees.

As the days pass, I am getting to know more and more about Amy. She reminds me so much of Brittney and Laura back in Middleton. Amy loves to write. She just recently wrote a book, titled, "Justice For A Reason". It is a book about this friend of hers that was wrongfully convicted and was literally days away from dying in the electric chair, when the show "60 Minutes" uncovered the truth about what really happened one Saturday evening in Alabama. A black man was accused of raping a white woman, while working at the Dry Cleaners'. He was charged and convicted for the rape, but the problem was that he didn't do it! The man got out of jail, sued the state of Alabama and won. He is a millionaire today because of it. She hands me a copy and I can't wait to read it. This is definitely my encouragement to write a novel one day.

"Hey honey. I am out of here. I am going to work now. I will be home for lunch to feed the baby."

"Great. I will see you then. I am going to *try* to get some sleep. I have an appointment to lay some tile this evening. Have a great day, sweetheart."

"You, too."

After giving Kalin and Amber a kiss, I head for the office. I am meeting my new assistant today, Cynthia Delgado. I hope she's nice.

A few days later, Amy invites me over for dinner because there is something that she claims is important for her to discuss with me. Of course, I agree. Amy is a great cook. Because I am eating at Amy's tonight, Kalin and the kids are on their own for the evening. Kalin's tile job is completed so he is able to watch the children.

For our dinner, Amy prepares steak and salad. It is delicious! Dinner is so good that I end up going in for seconds. She thinks of everything because, after dinner, we end up in her family room sipping on Merlot. I forgot how much I enjoyed doing this with Laura and Brittney. Although dinner is fabulous and our conversations are fun, Amy seems a little bothered about something.

"Amy, are you okay?"

"Melissa, there is something that I must tell you", she says.

"Sure, what is it?"

"Promise me you won't hate me after I tell you my secret. Promise me that you won't run out of here and never want to speak to me again!"

"Honey, I promise! There is nothing you can do to make me not be here for you. I promise you that! Now tell me."

"Ok. Here it is! At one time, I worked at the Baker Law Firm, off of 22nd. I worked there as a Legal Aid and was with them for 10 years. Believe it or not, but after all this time with them, they still didn't want to pay me what I was worth so I thought that I had to make it happen for myself. One of the more prominent attorneys at the firm, Larry Baker, had some very dark secrets, of which I had knowledge of. With times as hard as they are, I told him to pay me or I would tell. It backfired on me! He turned me in, confessed his sins, and now I am charged with extortion", she confesses.

"Yeah, I think I heard about this. So, that was you, huh?"

"Yes, that was me, but please don't believe everything you read in the paper. That bastard *was* cheating on his wife. I even walked in on him with his playmate. The twist in the story is that the 'mistress' was really a 'mister'. He was cheating on his wife with another man", she continues.

"Whoa!!!! It makes sense why he wanted to keep that under wraps!"

"Yeah, and because he turned me in, I have nothing now. I lost my job. They didn't give me any type of a severance or anything! And now, I am looking at doing some federal time, even if I cooperate with the prosecutors."

"Well honey, I am so sorry for that, but don't worry, everything will work out just fine", I say, while consoling her.

"What do you mean it will be alright? Not only am I going to prison but I also just found out that I am pregnant", she confesses, with tears finally flowing down her face and ruining her perfectly made face.

"Pregnant?" I ask, sounding surprised. "Sweetheart, children are a blessing and it doesn't matter when they get here. But, God can work it out for you."

"He is married!" she blurts out.

"Oh no! And what does he have to say about it?"

"He says that he doesn't care and that he will gladly give up his rights to the baby. He says that he no longer wants to have anything to do with me or my bastard child. Can you believe that? How could any man say that about his own flesh and blood?" she says, sobbing out of control.

"A real man would never say that! Screw him! We don't need him. That is alright! Did you tell your parents about this?"

"Yes, I told them, and guess what? They don't want to have anything to do with the child either."

"And, why not? It's their grandchild!"

"The man who got me pregnant is not only married, but is also well known and if people know about me, it will ruin his image. He is a well known minister. To keep me quiet, he takes care of everything that I need so that I won't say anything. This nice place, he pays for it; the car I drive, he bought it. The only thing he won't do is acknowledge his child. What an idiot, I know! So, because of my sins, they won't accept my child, their grandchild."

"Amy, I promise you that this will somehow work out. You will get through this. We will get through this. I just know it. You are a beautiful and smart lady and things will work out!"

Amy is getting more and more upset, so I reach over and dry the tears away from her eyes.

"And you still want to be my friend?" she asks.

"Of course. That doesn't change anything. Are you kidding? Why would that change how I feel about you? We all make mistakes. If there is anyone who understands that, it is definitely me."

Two weeks after our dinner together, Amy walks into the Broward County Courthouse and is sentenced to 3 years of federal time. She will do her time in Virginia and is required to leave immediately. Although I am saddened to hear of the verdict, I am at peace because she has prepared herself for this and is ready for this process to begin.

The Following Day.

The maintenance supervisor and I are making our rounds on the property and Kalin is calling. There must be an emergency because he knows not to call me at work.

"Hello."

"Melissa, there is an emergency phone call for you. It is Amy's attorney. He is saying that it is most urgent that you contact him right away. His name is Joel Santana and his number is 555-7114."

I hang up the phone with Kalin and immediately dial the number.

"Hello", he says.

"Hello. May I speak with Mr. Santana?"

"This is he."

"It's Melissa Williams. I understand that you needed me to ---", I begin, before being interrupted.

"Your friend, Amy Stephens, named you as next of kin if there is any type of emergency with her. She said that ---", he says before I interrupt him.

"Is she okay? Is Amy okay?"

"I don't know how to tell you this, but --", he begins.

"Please! Just tell me! Is she okay?"

"She attempted to kill herself today after sentencing."

"What?!! I can't believe that. She was fine when we last talked."

"People hide it very well. She was just not willing to do the time. She feels like such a disappointment", he explains. "She gave me specific instructions to speak with you as opposed to her elderly parents. She just doesn't want to disappoint you."

"I need to see her. Can you please get me in to see her? Oh my God! I can't believe this! Is she going to be alright?"

"The doctor says that she is going to be just fine."

"That's good. What about the baby? Did the baby make it?"

"What baby?"

Dear God, please watch over my friend, Amy. Forgive her father for what she has done. Please give her a peace that passes all understanding. Oh dear God, there is so much pain in this world. Lord, please make my friend better. Please send your angels into her hospital room right now and protect her from the enemy. In Jesus' name. Amen.

****

Ex-NFL Superstar, Michael Lawrence, is coming to Miami and needs a manager to run his condominiums on the east side. It sounds like a very sound opportunity. After meeting with me and believing in my leadership capabilities, he names me the Property Manager to oversee some of his properties, including apartments as part of the portfolio.

Believing that this is an opportunity of a lifetime, I am dumbfounded when Mr. Lawrence confirms the reports that are surfacing in the Media about his companies. They are all bankrupt! He has no money to pay his employees. Apparently, the bank has frozen all of his accounts. My heart suddenly skips several beats.

I can't believe that I uprooted my family for this. What a joke! What am I going to do now? The truth is that I have seen tougher times than this. There is a little voice in my head that encourages me to stick it out, which can *only* be the voice of God. I refuse to panic! As long as I can keep the apartment, I am going to stay. These residents have been treated so poorly and need someone who cares about their needs. I know that I have to be obedient to God's voice, so I agree to work for free until they can start paying again.

It's Monday morning and I am the only employee who has shown up for work. They have all decided for themselves that they can't afford to work for free. Although I understand and respect why they aren't here, I have to suck it up and call on the one person who I know will have my back.

"Kalin, I need your help."

"What is it honey?" he asks.

"Well, I am suddenly faced with a situation. None of the employees showed up this morning except me. Can you believe that?"

"Yes. I can believe it", he says, laughing carefully.

"I need your help."

"Honey, I don't know anything about maintenance work orders. I don't have this type of experience."

"I know that, but can you just try anyway?"

"Anything for you, Ms. Williams", he responds. "How is it that you always manage to get things out of me that I clearly don't want to do?"

For quite some time, Kalin serves as maintenance until the company hires a maintenance employee.

"Hello, my name is Ronnie and I am your new maintenance employee", he announces in a calm manner.

"Welcome aboard, Ronnie. I think that you and I will get along just fine."

For the next couple of months, Ron works with me at Trinity Gardens as the maintenance technician and we are successfully running this operation all by ourselves. He is also a strong mentor and often speaks to me about godly things. During this same time, Kalin and I befriend a couple, Lonnie and Cindy Collins. Then one day, we invite them all over for dinner one night. After dinner, Lonnie makes a strange request. He wants to pray for me and Kalin.

"Melissa and Kalin, I just want to say this but I don't want you to be offended. I believe that God is giving me a Word for the two of you", he begins.

"OK."

"There is a storm coming but do not be afraid for God is with you. Trust in His Word and do not be afraid. God wants you to know that He will be there in the midst of the storm with you."

Kalin and I are puzzled. We have no idea where all of this is coming from. Everything seems to be just fine. We have our new daughter, we are in love and life can't be any better right now."

CHAPTER 21

"Not Again!"

"**K**alin, are you thinking what I am thinking?"
"I don't know what to think after that", Kalin answers.

"Do you think that they are phony or do you think that they know what they are talking about?"

"I'm not sure", he answers.

Can you imagine what it is like to know that something is going to happen, but you just don't know what it is? How do you prepare yourself for something like this? I will be honest with you. I just don't know if I will be able to handle anything else.

I wake up today thinking of it as any other day. Work is a bit hectic because it is the first of the month and the rental payments are rolling in and 3-day notices have to go out! I am busy preparing for my day, getting the kids off to school and all the responsibilities of the morning. At the end of my work day, I walk into my house and Kalin is cutting his uncle's hair. The television is blaring from the other room where the children are obviously watching television. My nephews, Scott and Charles, are with them and speak to me as well. The first thing that everybody wants to know is what I am planning for dinner. Kalin shouts from the other room, "Me too!"

"Kalin, are you almost done so that we can just go and get some chicken? There is nothing here to cook that is already thawed out. I have a tenant meeting tonight and just need to get something on the dinner table pretty quickly."

"Okay, honey. We will go when I am done with Uncle Frank's haircut", he responds, not even looking up from what he is doing.

While Kalin is finishing with his uncle's haircut, the phone rings and it is for me. Cindy Collins is on the other end of the phone and she is inquiring about an apartment for her and her family. While on the phone with her, I can hear one of the children crying not knowing which one it is at the time. To muffle the noise, I go into the laundry room at the rear of the apartment. When I get off the phone, I realize that it is Sharell who is crying.

"What is wrong with Sharell?"

"She just got her butt whipped for writing all over the tile floor after I told her not to", Kalin answers from the other end of the hall.

"Okay, guys, we are going out to get the chicken and we will be right back."

As usual, Kalin has to use the restroom before leaving and Scott, my sister's son, pulls me off to the side and comments about Sharell's discipline. "Now Melissa, he did not have to whoop her like that", he says quietly. I don't want to get into this right now, so I tell Scott that we will discuss it later.

By this time, Kalin is out of the restroom and we are off to get the chicken.

On the way to the restaurant, Kalin and I briefly speak about Sharell's discipline. I mention to him what Scott said to me as we were leaving.

"I barely touched her", he says. "I only spanked her on her bottom and that was it. By the time we left, she had already stopped crying."

Kalin and I have to go to the ATM machine to get more money and when we approach the ATM machine, something in my heart changes. I feel a sudden urge to return home. I share these feelings with Kalin and he doesn't want to hear it. He does not want to be inconvenienced by having to return later to get the food but just wants to get it on this trip.

"Kalin, we have to go home right now."

"Melissa, what are you saying? Honey, we are right here and that would be insane to leave without the chicken", he responds.

"Something is wrong at home and I can feel it. Please, let's go now."

Because Kalin is driving, he decides to ignore my suggestion and go to KFC anyway because there are several hungry people back at the house. When we finally return, everything seems normal on the outside. So, we walk inside and for some reason, my children seem nervous and afraid. I look around and notice that Scott, Charles, and Sharell are all gone.

"Where is Sharell?"

"Come on guys! Speak up! Where is Sharell?" Kalin asks with a much deeper voice.

Almost in unison, they all say, "over to Auntie's house."

Right away, I grab the phone and dial my sister's number and my niece, Mary, answers the phone.

"Mary, where is Sharell?"

"She is here and we are not bringing her back to the house", she says angrily. It is no surprise to me that Mary is acting this way. She hates all men right now because her boyfriend cheated on her, leaving her with the two children to care for on her own.

"Where is Diana?"

"She is right here and she definitely isn't going to bring this child back over there. Kalin whipped this child too hard and you know it", she says.

"Will you guys please bring my child back home?"

"No we will not", she says.

By now, I am growing tired of pleading with them to return by child, so I decide to contact the police to see if they are able to persuade my sister to return my daughter to me. The police show up at our place looking for some answers. They seem eager in getting to the bottom of this fiasco. Kalin and I explain everything that happened within the last hour or so. We explain everything from when Sharell got disciplined up until the time that she was taken away from the house. Kalin walks into the bedroom to show the police officer the belt that he used to discipline Sharell. After taking down the notes from what Kalin and I have to say about what happened, the police officer leaves and heads over to my sister's house to look at Sharell to make a determination as to whether he believes the discipline was within reason.

While the police officer is gone, Kalin and I sit at the dinner table discussing what has just taken place. Deep down in my gut, I am starting to feel as though this may not turn out like we want. Although Kalin and I are honest with the police officer, it is still up to the officers' discretion. Honestly, I am nervous about what may happen when the officer returns.

What am I so nervous about? Am I afraid that Kalin is going to be arrested or what? I start having flashbacks about my other encounters with Children Come First. Isn't it okay to discipline your children without any involvement from the State? What if CCF was around when we were children? We always got spankings and there was no one around to protect us from it. And back then, it didn't have to be a parent that gave you a whipping. Even the neighbors were allowed to discipline you if it became necessary.

Being deep in thought causes me to almost not hear the officer knock at the door. I can't move. What if this officer comes in here and causes problems for us? Is he going to have my daughter with him or what?

After answering the door, the police officer walks in and looks directly at Kalin.

"Mr. Thomas, I am going to have to put you under arrest because I feel that the spanking was a little excessive", he says, while retrieving his handcuffs.

Kalin doesn't say a word. He immediately starts taking everything out of his pocket. The only thing he says is for me to "call his daddy". When the children realize what is happening, they are afraid and begin to cry.

What I am going to do now? I have never been in a situation like this in my life. How do I react? Should I cry or should I remain calm? My children need me and I have to remain strong. He didn't hurt Sharell and I know it. Of course she has a mark on her but I really don't think it is excessive. Why is this happening to him? Kalin has never gone to jail so I know that he must be afraid. I have to call his father and let him know what is going on right now.

"Ms. Williams, I want you to know that I feel that you should take your daughter to the hospital just to make sure that she is okay. Your sister is going to be bringing your daughter back to you and when she does, take her in to the hospital", advises the police officer.

The children are all starting to ask me questions about what is going on, where dad went, and why he was taken away. I can't think straight. I am in shock. I don't really know what to do about this situation. I am so used to Kalin being in the house and now he is gone.

Moments after the officer leaves with Kalin in the back seat of his car, my sister finally arrives with my daughter. When she comes into the apartment, she doesn't waste any time in making sure that we know how pleased she is that Kalin is on his way to jail.

"Melissa, the police officer says that Sharell should be taken to the hospital and we want to trail you to the hospital", she expresses to me.

"Sure, we are going to take her to Miami Community Hospital. You can just meet me there."

I know that I am not going to go to Miami Community because I don't want my sister involved in this any more than she has to be. I will go to Miami Southern Hospital instead. Why is she here in the first place? Where is she when her children need her? Why is she spending so much time worrying about me and my children when her very own sons need guidance and support? For crying out loud, they are smoking and selling marijuana and she is actually worried that my children are in danger.

Just as I go to pick up the phone to dial JT, the phone rings and he is calling me.

"Melissa, I got a call that my son was seen being arrested. Is that true? What's going on over there?" he asks.

"I was just about to call you. Kalin was just arrested and taken away for spanking Sharelle. The police believe it to be excessive and they took him away. I am so sorry —", I begin to say before he interrupts me.

"For spanking Sharelle? Are you serious?" he asks.

"Yes, sir. I am serious! The police just left and believe that I need to take her to the hospital to make sure that she is doing okay."

Before I can get the next sentence out of my mouth, he says, "I'm coming over. I will be there in fifteen minutes."

By the time that JT pulls into the driveway, Sharell and I are ready to go. The ride to the hospital is somewhat quiet, but once the idea sets into my mind that Kalin is gone to Jail, I begin to cry.

"It's okay, Melissa. Everything will be just fine. Hang in there and be strong", he counsels. "My son is strong. But, you have to hold it together out here."

"I know, but he doesn't deserve this. Since he has been with me, he is starting to get in trouble with the law. Has he ever gone to jail or ever been in trouble with the law before?"

"Not even for a traffic ticket", he answers.

Hearing this makes all of the blood rush to my head. I am looking out the window trying to figure out how I ended up here. In one instant, my life has changed. One minute, I am happy and blissful and enjoying my children and Kalin and the next moment, my life is turned upside down and for what!

After several hours of waiting in the hospital, Sharell is finally seen by the emergency doctor and is sent home. There are no broken bones or anything of the sort. My daughter is so content while playing in the waiting area. She has asked for "daddy" at least 3 times already. I can't understand what the fuss is about. We were never carried to the hospital after getting a spanking. We would have been in there all the time. The doctor simply says that Tylenol is appropriate if she complains of pain. From there, my father in law and I head home to come up with a plan to get Kalin released from jail.

Now, I understand why Lonnie had to pray for us. Somehow, he saw this coming! I wish I could have seen it coming. I would have done something to prevent it. After all of these incidents with Children's First, he is in jail! I watch the street lights go by and start to remember our much happier times. I start thinking about when our daughter was born and the look on Kalin's face as he cut the cord, or the time when we took the kids to the park and Darren ended up at the bottom of the sliding board with sand all over his face, or the time when Sharell had her very first birthday and she ended up sitting on top of her cake. Those times are much happier than this moment that I am having right now. *Will we ever have happy times again? Will this jail time force a separation with Kalin? How is he feeling right now? Is he scared?* He has never gone to jail for anything in his life. While deep in thought, Kalin's father interrupts.

"So, what are you thinking about?" he asks.

"Oh nothing! I am just thinking about how we will get Kalin out of that place."

"There is nothing that we can do tonight, but on tomorrow, we will figure this whole thing out. It will all work out just fine."

"Let me ask you a question."

"Sure, go ahead."

"What is wrong with disciplining your children? As a parent, don't I have that right to discipline them as long as I don't cause harm to them? Why in the world are we here right now? Why did we have to go to the hospital? Who has ever heard of that? We got whippings when I was growing up and there was nobody around to tell about it. Our parents didn't care what they hit us with or where it landed. Kalin didn't do anything wrong. He didn't hurt her. She got spanked on her bottom and she is just fine."

"There is nothing wrong with disciplining your child. These people are crazy! That is the thing that ruins children when they think that they can just do whatever they want to do. Parents are allowing this system to raise their children and when we were growing up, our parents did whatever *they* felt was necessary to raise us and dared anyone to say anything about it", he says.

"Goodnight Melissa. Try to get some rest and I will see you tomorrow", he instructs as I am getting out of the car.

"I will do my best."

****

The following day, JT and I find out that there is a bond set for $5,000. After speaking to a bail bondsman, we are able to get Kalin out of jail with $500. JT and I head over to pick him up, not really knowing what the conditions are for his release.

"Is that him coming this way?"

"Yeah, that's my son. I can tell that walk anywhere."

JT and I move closer toward Kalin. He looks so tired. He survived the night, though.

"Hey sweetheart, how are you? Are you okay? Did they hurt you in there?" I ask as I put my arms around him. He seems a little agitated. I thought he would be happier to see us.

"Good morning, Melissa. I am fine. Please don't make a fuss. How are the children?"

"They are fine. I am more concerned about you."

"Melissa, the Judge ordered a no-contact order on me. I can't be around you or our daughter, Sharell", he explains.

"What!"

"That's right. I can't violate the Order by the Judge, so when we get home, I will have to move out. I can't go back to jail. I am sorry that it has to be this way."

I am speechless. I am hurt. I am angry. I am sad. I begin to feel lonely all over again. Kalin seems as though he doesn't want to be with me. I guess I can't blame him.

I need to go downtown first thing tomorrow and find out why this went down this way.

****

After making it to the Courthouse and stopping at the seventh floor, I learn that the prosecuting attorney on this case is Larry Shatner. He is available, but I will have to wait because he is already in with someone else and quite a few people are waiting to meet with him. I will sit here all day if I have to do so just to get to the bottom of this fiasco.

"Melissa Williams", the receptionist finally announces after an hour or so.

I walk into his office to find a bald, short, scraggly looking guy sitting behind a desk, who doesn't even look up to acknowledge my presence.

"Good morning. How may I help you?" he asks, with absolutely no concern in his voice.

"Yes, sir. My name is Melissa Williams and I am here regarding the State of Florida versus Kalin Thomas. He was arrested two days ago and released last night."

"Sure. Give me a moment to locate that file."

As he stands up from his desk, I can see that he is even shorter than I imagined he'd be. He walks over to the file cabinet and pulls out the drawer. Thumbing through the files, he comes up with a file labeled, Kalin Thomas. He briefs himself and reads through the summary of the case. "And let me guess. You must be Melissa Williams?" he asks.

"As a matter of fact, I am."

"And you want to say how there has been a mistake and you should not have called the police?" he asks sarcastically.

"Can you tell me why the Judge ordered a no-contact order for me and my daughter?"

"You called the police because your husband spanked your daughter and now you want us to just let it go. Do you know how many women I see just like you in here – ", he begins to say before I interrupt him.

"Whooooaa, wait a minute! I didn't call the police because he was disciplining my daughter. I called the police because when he disciplined my daughter, my sister came to my home and took her away. I called the police to get assistance in bringing her back home to me", I respond.

"That is not what the report says", he says, looking at me as if I am not telling the truth.

"I don't care what your report says. I know why I called the police."

"So what do you want me to do about it?" he asks.

"I want the report to be changed to read exactly as it happened."

"That is not going to happen. You women play games with the State. You call in on these men and then they sweet talk you and get you to change your minds", he says.

"Sir, this is not the case here. You have to understand what I am saying. I didn't call the police on him! Because of this police report that was inaccurate, you made a no-contact order. Sir, this is his home, too. Where is he going to stay? He has nowhere to go!"

"Not my problem, ma'am. So, if you will excuse me, I have other things to do right now. Maybe you should tell your boyfriend to stop spanking your child."

I am not getting anywhere with this. He is not trying to hear it. He is not concerned at all about what I am trying to say. I finally leave Mr. Shatner's office feeling worse than when I arrived. I have to find a way to explain all of this to Kalin. How will he respond to this news? Will he want to just leave us altogether? I can't really blame him if he does.

I walk into my office the following morning to give him the news. He doesn't seem to be too bothered that he had to sleep in my office last night.

"Good morning, sweetheart. How are you?"

"I am okay. That sofa bed is not that comfortable", he answers. "Melissa, I have an idea."

"OK, out with it."

"Carl and Wendy are friends that I shared with Kayla and they don't live that far away and I know that they would not mind if I have to come and stay with them if I need to", he explains.

"Oh yeah, why are you so sure?"

"Listen, I am looking at this as an opportunity to get some work done, make some money for us, and keep busy and being there and working with Carl will help me to do just that", he explains.

"I don't want you to leave me. Is this your way of getting out of this relationship because of what is going on with us right now?"

"Melissa, sweetheart, I love you, but I have to do what is best for us. I feel that this will work out best for us at this time. You have to trust me. I love you and want nothing more than for you to be my wife one day. I will be home whenever I can", he explains. I am already in tears and have turned my back to him.

"Kalin, I really just can't believe all of this. Please tell me that I am dreaming and that I am going to wake up and this will all be over."

"Melissa, I didn't hurt my daughter, I simply spanked her bottom for not doing as she was told", he says with a long face. "I would never hurt a child."

"I am sure of it, Kalin. I believe in you and I know how you feel about our children. I have never doubted you. We will get through this."

"Thanks, honey", he responds. "I just want to take a hot shower right now. I will give Carl and Wendy a call just to let them know that I will need a place to crash for awhile."

"Yeah, but aren't these the same people who didn't agree with your being in a relationship with me because of Kayla?"

"That is old news."

"Yeah, right."

The following day, Kalin calls and speaks with Wendy and she speaks on behalf of her husband and agrees that it is okay with them that he moves in temporarily, until this matter is resolved. He will stay in their guest quarters.

Because of all this drama with the police and the report, it triggers, yet, another call to CCF that has to be generated. We find ourselves, once again, being visited by Children Come First.

When the investigator comes knocking on my door, I am somewhat relieved that I am already familiar with their processes and how they do things. I mute the volume on the television and answer the door.

"Hello Ms. Williams. My name is Leigh Bynum and I am the caseworker assigned to your case. There appears to be an allegation that Kalin, your boyfriend, spanked your daughter excessively and you stood there and did nothing about it", she explains. When I hear her read it this way, my mouth is dropped! *Did nothing? I didn't know that she was getting a spanking until it was all over.*

"Ms. Bynum, please come in and have a seat."

"Thanks."

"Kalin is my boyfriend. He spanked Sharell because she was writing all over the floor after she was told not to do it. He is not the biological father. She cried, but not for long. I was cooperative with the police when they asked me to take her to the hospital to make sure that she was okay. I did and she was, in fact, okay. There were red marks, but they were on her bottom. Now, that is the truth", I explain.

"Ms. Williams or Melissa, whichever you prefer, I understand that. I appreciate your honesty. I will have to see the child to see how she is doing. It is now 24 hours since this happened and I will be the judge of that. I can see that you take good care of your children. Your home is clean and the children are clean. I went by the school of your older children and have learned that they are doing well in school and that they always come to school clean. I have to say something to you if you don't mind", she goes on to say.

"Sure", I agree.

"Off the record, you understand", she says.

"Yeah."

"Regardless to whether I believe you are a good mother or the kids are clean or whatever the case may be, I will have to keep this case open because it clearly justifies Kalin being arrested. Personally, I don't think that these children are in any danger, but think about it. What would it look like if he got arrested and we drop your case? It would be somewhat contradictory. You understand what I am saying?"

"Yes, I understand. A blind man can see that this is all about this good ol' boy system. Sure, I understand. This is about protecting the police."

"I will make this as painless as possible. I will put together a case plan for you to follow with the children. I will set you up with weekly visits with one of our agencies, who will report to my office of his findings and when you have completed the case plan, we will be out of your life", she adds.

"Ma'am, I will do whatever I have to do to keep my children from being removed from our home. They are my life and I can't be without my babies. So, you go ahead and put together everything and I will completely cooperate with your organization."

As part of her procedure, she has to go through my cupboards to verify that there is food in the home. She has to walk through our entire apartment to make sure that the environment is safe for the children.

"Great! I am glad to see that you are willing to do what is necessary for the children. I will give you a call this afternoon with the therapist's name and I can then let you know where we have to go from here", she says.

"Thanks so much. I look forward to your call."

"Oh, and by the way. The information that I told you that was "off the record", don't mention that to anyone. They won't believe you anyway so don't make trouble for yourself", she says, as she closes the door behind her.

Is this for real? Can they do this? Can they force me to do these things and make these comments and just do this to people?

She gives me a call later in the afternoon with the name of the therapist who will pay the weekly visit. His name is Bob and he will be by the apartment every Wednesday at 8am, which is just an hour before my time to be at work.

Over the weekend, I decide to visit Kalin. He says that he has to get back because he and Carl have a business meeting to attend about getting some interior design work. I know that this is good for Kalin. He has an opportunity to do something that takes his mind off this little situation. He can really dive into his interior design work. He has already done some beautiful work at the model homes in the Miami area.

We agree to meet at the Downtown Inn off of 50th Street. We rush through our breakfast, and head back to the room for some much needed lovemaking. My body aches for him. He responds to my needs as if he really misses me too. I don't want to ruin our moment, but I have to give him the update on the children, simply because he wants to know. Once I tell him that I have agreed to do a Case Plan with CCF to keep my children in the home, he gives me his full support and tells me that his court date is coming up soon as well. He thinks that the parenting sessions are a joke. I didn't give it much thought but I agree.

"So, how are Carl and Wendy doing?"

"They are doing just fine. They told me to send my love to you and the children. Speaking of the children, I sure do miss them", he says.

"Oh, they miss you too. Sharell is always asking for you. Darren and Kameron told me to tell you that being that they are the men of the house now, they will take good care of me and you don't have to worry about a thing. And Christy is doing well also. She is always reading her books, playing video games, and stuff like that. And the little one just smiles when I mention your name. They love you so much. We all do."

"I miss all of you, too. We will all be together soon. I have to go now sweetheart. I don't want to miss out on getting this job. We need this money. Ok, sweetheart. I love you", he says.

"I love you too. Go ahead. Get out of here. Call me when the meeting is over."

"Of course I will." He drives off and waves goodbye and then vanishes into the middle of the day. He is out of sight, but certainly very close to my heart. Tomorrow is my first appointment with Bob and I can't sleep. I am rethinking my time with Kalin. Now I know why I love him so much.

CHAPTER 22

"Laura is What?"

Today is my first appointment with Bob. I wonder what he is like. Will he tell me all sorts of things "off the record"? I hope that this doesn't turn out to be a total waste of my time. But then again, I don't really care. I will do whatever I have to do to secure the home for my children. I don't really care what they have to say.

The doorbell rings. On the other side is a tall, somewhat handsome, man with spiked hair who claims to be from Narcoossee Mental Health.

"Good morning, ma'am. May I come in?"

"Of course! Please come in. Excuse my manners."

"Before we get started, I would like to go ahead and take a look around to see how the children are living and being cared for. All of this has to go in my report. You understand that, right?"

"Sure. Go ahead and do what you have to do."

Bob walks the entire apartment and returns with a facial expression that reads, "impressive". He explains that he will have to come by every week just to make sure that the children are still doing well and to make sure that there are no *further* incidents of abuse.

At these weekly visits, Bob speaks with the children to find out if they were spanked at all. He probes further just to make sure that Kalin is not in the home. We sit down and discuss his "parenting guidelines", of which do not include corporal punishment. It seems as if Mr. Bob gets annoyed when I factor the Bible as a source for corporal punishment. He becomes even more annoyed when I refer to Florida Statute to justify corporal punishment. He is interested in sharing with me the point of view from authors who do not believe in "corporal punishment". Their reasoning is that they believe that "spanking" teaches violence. Even after sharing my own experiences of receiving corporal punishment as a child, Mr. Bob still does not agree. This is all confusing to me because I read the

Florida Statute and it clearly states that anything *beyond* excessive corporal punishment is unlawful.

Our first visit is finally over and I have survived it. I can certainly tell that we are just not going to see things the same way. Under no circumstances does he believe in spanking a child.

Bob leaves and my first visit is officially over! As I am closing the door, the phone rings. It's my friend, Brittney Snow. *Can this be Brittney from Middleton? Where has she been?* I have not spoken to her in years. I hope that she isn't calling to read me the riot act for not keeping in touch with her.

"Hello."

"Well hello Meme! How are you doing sweetheart? How long has it been? I haven't spoken to you since you left here. I always ask your mother about you, but she never remembers your phone number. I finally got it from your brother. Are you okay?"

"Yeah, everything is going okay. Just a few bumps and bruises along the way, but all is okay."

"What about you?"

"I am doing okay. I don't know if you have heard about Laura or not, but I am calling you to give you some bad news about her", she says.

"Oh God! What has that crazy girl done now? " I can feel my heart starting to beat faster. I have to sit down.

"Meme, she died yesterday!" she says. "She's gone!"

"What are you saying? Are you telling me that Laura is dead? Don't tell me that! I don't want to hear that!!"

I let out such a loud cry that I am sure the neighbors can hear.

"What happened?"

"Apparently, she got herself pregnant by some guy who lived across the tracks and ---", she begins to say.

"And?"

"She found out he had AIDS and she didn't want to have the baby, so she went to Marin to get an abortion and something went wrong! There were some complications and she died right there on the table. She didn't tell anyone that she was going there. She didn't even come to me and talk to me about it. She died all alone. Her mother is so distraught over this."

"I can't believe this! I can't believe she did this and didn't tell anyone that she was going there! Why in the world would she not talk to someone? Were the two of you still talking? Why didn't she at least go to you?"

"Yes, we talked occasionally, but I have been very busy lately. I have been taking some classes to update my teaching certificate and I haven't been around much. I feel horrible about this!"

"Yeah, I know! I feel even more horrible for her daughter", she says.

"Daughter? Laura had a child?" I ask, sounding very surprised.

"Yes. She had a daughter named Princess. She is 8 years old and is so beautiful. Her mother will have to care for her because the father doesn't want to have anything to do with her. I called Laura's mother and told her that I would help out with Princess whenever I could. You need to give her mother a call. She was asking for you", Brittney continues.

"Oh my God! I can't believe this! I am so shocked over this news! Why didn't she let us be there for her? I am so mad at her right now! Oh, God, no!!! I don't know what to say! My heart is aching right now for my friend. "B", I have to go. I just can't take this right now. Besides, I was just on my way out. I need to get myself together first before going to work. I have to go, but I will call you later", I say, before hanging up the phone.

"Think you'll be able to make it to the funeral?" she asks.

"Of course I will be there."

"Good! You can stay at my house if you want. We have lots of catching up to do. I will see you then."

"Ok. Bye."

"Bye."

There is nothing in the world that could have prepared me for this call. I had no idea that Laura was in trouble. She was my friend for years and I didn't even know that she had a daughter. How would her mother take care of that baby? Her mother has to be at least 60 years old. This is horrible! I feel paralyzed and find myself sitting in the same spot for several minutes, just crying and praying, thinking that it could have been me on that abortion table, but I ended up not getting my abortions. I wish she would have let me be there for her in her time of need. Back in high school when I went to that same abortion clinic, Laura was right there with me. I should have been there with her!

I will have to give her mother a call when I return from work this evening. I can't talk to her right now. I just hope that I will find a way to get some work done.

It ends up being a quiet day at the office. The apartment occupancy is at 95% and the rent is 100% collected. When I make it to work, there are a few messages for me, but none are important enough to return the call right away. I have to find the words to speak with the mother of one of my closest friends. Laura was there with me when I attempted my abortion in high school. She spent several hours on the phone with me convincing me that everything was going to be alright. Even though she didn't exactly agree with my decision to have an abortion, she was right there with me. She even babysat for me on several occasions. She needed someone and none of us were there for her. Why in the world didn't she ask for help or talk to someone first? She went alone. That could have been me with those abortions, but both times, I was saved from getting them done. *God, why didn't you keep Laura from having hers done? Why didn't she have an intervention like I did?*

I make it through another long day. Before fixing myself something to eat, I decide that is time to go ahead and give Laura's mother a call. I have to go ahead and get it out of the way. I don't know what I will say or how I will explain that I didn't stay in contact with her daughter. I didn't even know that she had a child. I dial the number and hope that she isn't in and that I will end up just leaving a message. But, it's too late. She answers the phone.

"Hello."

"Hello Mrs. Walker."

"Well, hey baby, how you doing?" she asks. "I am so glad that you called."

"Yeah, me too. I am so sorry that it is under these conditions."

"Aw, it's alright baby, the Lord works in mysterious ways. That's what I always try to tell you young folks."

"Mrs. Walker, I am sorry about Laura. Brittney called me and told me what happened. I just can't believe that my friend is gone. I am so saddened by this news. And then I found out that she has a little girl. I didn't even know that."

"Yeah, that's my baby. She is one heck of a kid. My little princess is holding up just fine. She went in and put away her mother's things for me. They lived here with me."

"So, she never left Middleton?"

"Sure she did. She moved to Boston and was running her own greeting card business, but when she found out that I was sick, she sold her business and decided to come home to take care of me. She used her profit from selling the business for my medical treatments. That's my baby. She sho' did love her mama", she adds. "So, then once she got back, she started seeing some guy from the other side of town. She got herself pregnant and you know the rest."

"Wow! That is Laura for you. She is always full of love for everyone except herself. When is the funeral?"

"Next Saturday. Think you'll be able to make it?"

"Of course I will be there."

"Great. I want to make sure that you are at the reading of her Will, so plan on staying an extra day", she adds. *Why in the world would I need to stay for Laura's Will? I am not her real family. What could I possibly need to stay for?*

"Me? At the reading of The Will? Why?"

"I don't know baby. That is just what the attorney told me. I guess you will just have to wait and see. I really don't know."

"Are you doing okay Ms. Walters?"

"God is good, baby, all the time and all the time God is good. I'm gone be alright!"

"What about Princess? Do you need anything for you and her?"

"No. Laura was always so careful about everything, so she has already taken care of it. My baby even had her funeral paid for ahead of time. We have everything we need, but thanks for asking."

"Promise me that if you need anything that you will call me."

"I promise. So, I will see you next week, then."

"Yes you will. Goodbye."

"Goodbye."

****

Kalin is no longer in the home and my children need a babysitter when I am at work. I remember that Kalin's cousin, Jennifer, is in between jobs and may be interested in watching the children for me, so I decide to give her a call with my proposition and she seems thrilled about making some money again. She has three children to support and can use the money. She moves in and begins right away.

Jennifer loves to take the kids to the "castle park". Today, they are out at the park and will be out for hours. Kalin decides to take advantage of some quiet time with me and he drops by the house while the children are away. Kalin and I are so caught up into each other that, unbeknownst to us, the weather is bad outside and the children are walking through the door with Jennifer. They had to cut their time short at the park. Unfortunately, there is no time to warn her that Kalin is inside. Because Kalin is ordered to have no contact with Sharell, he can't be caught inside this house with her or he violates the Judge's direct order. The only way out at this time is to sneak out the back door. The kids are headed straight for my bedroom.

"Kalin, you have to go out the back, honey. The children will be knocking on my door any minute now."

"OK, hand me my pants off the floor."

Within seconds, Kalin is dressed and heading for the sliding glass door, that leads to the front.

"Goodbye, baby. I love you. Later!"

"I love you. Call me!"

I look out the window to make sure that he gets off safely. And what do I see! Scott is standing right outside watching it all go down. *What is my sister's son doing out there? Did he follow Kalin here or what?* Just as I figured he would do, Scott and his mother don't waste any time in reporting this incident to CCF. I am so sure that Kalin is on his way back to jail for violating the Judge's direct order!

Kalin's bond revoke hearing is scheduled for next week. I don't know what to expect. *Will he have to return to jail? Will he discover that he just can't take this relationship anymore? Can I blame him at this point?*

CHAPTER 23

"Not My Children!"

My visits continue with Bob. He is still telling me why different philosophers and professors disagree with corporal punishment. He can see that my mind hasn't changed at all on what I believe about corporal punishment. I have explained to him that I don't believe in it as a cure all, but just when it is necessary for a more harsh form of discipline.

On this particular visit with Bob, after speaking with the children, he has learned that Darren was disciplined by me and with a belt since our last visit.

"Ms. Williams, when I met with the children, Darren informed me that he got a spanking", he says, while looking down at his folder.

"Ok, did he tell you why he received that spanking?"

"You are not supposed to spank the children", he adds.

"Says who? I have the right to discipline my children if I need to do it. Darren stole money out of my friend's purse and then he tried to lie about it and blame someone else for it. If my son had been 18 or so when he did that, he would be sitting in someone's jail right now. He needs to understand that this behavior is not acceptable", I explain.

"Well, you know that I have to report this, right?"

"Of course you do. Do what you have to do."

He wastes no time to do it, either. The following day, while I am getting dressed for work, there is a knock on the door. On the other side of my door are a police officer of whom I am familiar, Madeline Serchay (the child protective investigator), the District Attorney, and another associate. Ms. Serchay starts out by explaining why they are all here.

"Ms. Williams, may we come in?" she asks.

"Sure. Come in."

"We are here today because I received a call from Mr. Bob informing me that Darren received a spanking. We just don't feel that you are learning anything from our instruction on corporal punishment and feel that it is time to shelter these children", she goes on to say.

"You feel that I am not learning anything? The last I read in your Florida Statutes, it states that only excessive corporal punishment is unlawful, so what are you talking about? I have the right as a parent to discipline my children!" I say, starting to get a little upset. "Darren stole $20 out of my friend's purse. Had he done that to you, he would probably be in Jail right now. I don't want my son to end up in Jail so I believe he needs to learn this lesson early."

Although she appears to be listening, she is not planning to walk out of this house without my children.

Right away, she begins to question Darren just to validate the report she has received.

"Darren, did your mother spank you?" she asks. He turns to me with a sad face as if he is seeking my help on how to answer the question.

"Son, tell her the truth. Tell her what happened."

He turns to Ms. Serchay and answers, "Yes."

Ms. Serchay continues, "Well, is that where you got those marks that are on you?"

I interrupt and criticize her for asking this question. "Why would you ask that question of my young son? How would he know where he got marks from?" I interrupt.

When Ms. Serchay finishes questioning Darren, she looks at me and announces her position on the matter. "Ms. Williams, please prepare clothes for your children as I will be removing them immediately from your care. I will go to the school to get Christy and Kameron. You will not have any visitation with the children until so ordered by the Court", she adds.

There aren't any tears in my eyes at this point. I am too angry to cry. My heart has stopped breathing. My life is my children and without them, I can't breathe. *Did she just say that she is taking all of my children? Not my children! Because I spanked my son! Is she serious? How will I survive this? How will I survive neither Kalin nor the children walking through these doors?*

Before I leave out of the room, I look into her eyes and say, "You just better make sure that you take care of my children because if anything happens to them, God help you! Believe me when I tell you that this is not the last you will hear of me. You have made a conscience decision to remove my children and I will not let this just slide by easily. You can believe that!"

"Sir, I want these children removed immediately", she instructs to the police officer.

"Ma'am, I am sorry. I will not be able to oblige you in this request. I am very familiar with this family. Ms. Williams works hand in hand with the sheriff's office and I have never known her or anyone in this family to be nothing but supportive not only to this community but to her children. I am sorry, but you will have to call someone else to carry out these instructions", he explains.

The officer walks away from her to come over to me to show his support. "Melissa, things are going to be okay. I will testify on your behalf if I need to do that for you and Kalin. Just let me know", he comforts.

This outburst from the Sheriff doesn't stop the child protective investigator from carrying out what she obviously has come here to do. She makes another phone call and within minutes, another police car pulls into my driveway. This female officer has no problem carrying out Ms. Serchay's orders. One by one, she places the children into the back of the government car. It feels as though my heart is no longer pumping. I feel as though my heart is gone. I can't cry and I won't cry right now. I have to be strong right now for my children, but how can I? My children are my life! I want to hit something or someone for this pain that I feel in my heart. It feels like a dagger is digging in so deep that after awhile, I can't feel anything.

"Ms. Serchay, will you please do me a favor?"

"Yes, Melissa, what can I do for you?" she asks.

"Being that you are picking my children up from school to remove them and place them in your custody, will you please bring them here so that I can tell them what is going on? For God's sake, I don't want them to be picked up by strangers and think that I have abandoned them. I want them to hear from me about what is going on."

"Sure, I can do that", she responds. "I don't mind helping you out."

Does this woman think that I really care what she cares about at this point? I could care less about her right now or the mule she rode in on to get here. Of course she doesn't mind because she knows that she is so wrong for taking my children.

This is unbelievable! Several minutes later, my children arrive and appear to be very confused. As I watch Christy and Kameron get out of the car, I am wondering just how to explain this to them and why they will not be sleeping in their beds tonight.

I can feel myself wanting to cry, but I have to maintain and be strong for them. I have to find the right words to bring comfort to them so that they will not be afraid.

"Hey guys. How was school?"

"It was good", they say in unison.

"Come closer so that I can explain something to the both of you."

"Yes, mommy."

"You see these nice people right here?"

"Yes mommy."

"You are going to go with them right now and when—", I say before the interruption.

"We don't want to go with them. We want to stay here with you", Kameron says as he is beginning to cry.

"I understand, but they are good people. You are safe with them. They just want to take some time to talk to Mommy and when we are all done talking, then you will be coming back home in no time."

"But why can't they just talk to you now?" Kameron asks.

"They think that it is better for you to be out of the house while we discuss everything. Trust me. You will be just fine." I reach over to comfort them both. The children nod their heads when I ask them if they understand what I am saying. Christy's eyes start to fill with tears, but I can tell that she doesn't want the tear to fall because she feels like she has to be strong. The more I talk, the harder this is getting. I reach out to give them both a hug.

"Christy, I want you to do me a favor and look out for your sisters and brothers. They will depend on you through this, okay."

"Yes ma'am", she agrees. "I will."

By this time, Ms. Serchay gives me a nod that it is time to go. I am not ready to let my children walk out of the door with the Department. I didn't do anything wrong. My children should stay right here with me.

I wave goodbye as she drives away with Christy and Kameron until they are no longer in sight. The second car that has Darren, Sharell, and Amber is now making its way out of the driveway.

The younger ones don't quite understand. They need their mother and CCF doesn't seem to care that they are crying and screaming to the top of their lungs. It doesn't seem to matter to anyone but me. As the younger ones are being taken, they begin to cry.

"Mommy, I want you", cries Sharell.

"You will be alright honey. Just go with these people and you will be home soon. It will be alright sweetheart."

Now that both cars are out of sight, I go back inside. Cindy has decided to shut down the office to be here for me through this. There is nothing that she can say that will take this pain away, and she realizes it, but wants to be here just to hold my hand. The tears are beginning to trickle down my face. I fall on my knees and look to God and ask, "Why?"

There is absolutely no way to describe the pain that I feel right now. My children are gone! I have decisions to make. I have to fight and keep doing what I know to do or I will choose to quit and let them win. My children believe that they are coming home soon and that is exactly what I have to do for them. *What will I do without my children? Why didn't I just run behind that car? Why didn't I yell at Ms. Serchay or somebody for removing my children?* I am so angry that it hurts.

The tears begin to roll down my face, tear after the next. Against Cindy's wishes, I still decided to go to work after all that just happened. I know that staying home will only make things worse. I am looking at these pages of this Agreement, but the words are running together. Cindy walks into my office with a situation.

"Melissa, I have a potential renter, but she has a problem. Under our normal guidelines, she doesn't qualify and when I told her that, she has requested to speak with the Manager."

"Ok. Let her in." She walks in and her children appear to be the same age as my children. "Good morning. Please come in and have a seat."

"Good morning, Ms. Williams. My name is Sharon and I really need to speak with you because my husband has left me. We have 3 children together and he is not offering any support to me. To be honest, I don't have anywhere to go. I don't have that much money saved right now, but I have secured a job and just haven't started yet. Ms. Manager, is there anything that you can do to help me get into an apartment? I don't have anywhere to go!" she begs.

Watching her with her children and how she is so desperate for a place to live makes me lose it. I can't control the tears now. I don't know if I am crying because of my situation or hers.

So that I will have the application in front of me as we discuss it, Cindy walks in to bring me the lady's application. She notices that I am crying.

"Ms. Melissa, why don't you just go home?"

"I am so sorry, ma'am. I didn't mean to upset you like this", says Sharon.

"It's not you. I am sorry to be so emotional. Please do me a favor and step outside so that I can consult with my assistant."

The lady gathers her things and leads her children to step outside.

"Cindy, I want to help this woman. I just feel that this is what my security "secret" funding is for. These are the types of situations that prompted me to put together this secret funding to help potential residents in this situation", I explain.

"But what about the monthly rent? Do you think she can afford it? Will she be able to maintain? She is just starting a job. We require that people are on the job at least a year", she says.

"That is the good thing about being the manager. I want to help this family and we are going to help her. How much money do we have in the "secret funding account"?"

"There is $5,865 in the account", she answers.

"Great! Call her in and we will tell them together."

"Yes ma'am", she says, as she walks to the door to let them back in.

Sharon and her children are now sitting in front of me again. "Ma'am, I have consulted with my assistant and we have agreed to help you. I will take care of the deposit and your first month. That will give you four weeks on your job to get organized with a budget. I have a friend at Miami Utilities who will assist me in getting your lights turned on at a discounted rate.

"Oh my God! Thank you so much! Thank you so much! How can I ever repay you?" she asks, while sobbing heavily.

"When you can, do it for the next person", I say, standing up to shake her hand. "My assistant, Cindy, will take care of all the paperwork. She will get you set up with all of your keys. The apartment is ready to go and you and your family should be able to move in this afternoon or first thing tomorrow morning. God bless you, ma'am."

"No, God bless you. I have never gone to an apartment community and people really care."

Sharon walks away and as she is leaving, I remember what my mother always used to sing. *"If I can help somebody as I go along, then my living shall not be in vain.."*

"I will be right there with you, Sharon. Please fill out the application. I will need a copy of your driver's license, social security card for you, and all the children. Make sure to fill out the portion titled, "Employer", and I will be right with you.

Cindy goes ahead of the renter and before she shuts the door, she looks back at me and says, "Melissa, please go home, sweetheart."

"Home? That is no longer a home for me. Kalin is gone and so are the girls. I just can't go home. Everything there reminds me of what I have lost. Kalin is not allowed in the home, and my children are removed. How will I be able to go on without my family?"

I feel a sudden urge to run and hide, but where will I go? I can't run away even if I wanted to because I have to work to keep the roof over my head. My children are depending on me, and so is Kalin. Everyone needs me and I am really trying to be there for them, but where will I get my strength? *Who will I rely on to be my best friend now? Who can I talk to that will understand? "God's got it all in control, He's got it all in control, He put that reassurance way down deep in my soul, God's got it all in control"*. . . Song from Shirley Caesar. When Kameron was having surgery, God had it, When Darren was born with a heart murmur, God had it all in control. When I had to struggle to care for my children while living in the Projects, God had it all in control – and He's got it now. To God be the Glory!

"I don't know the answer to that", she answers. "I do know that God loves you and will give you the strength to do this. I do know that I believe that you can do this. Trust God, Melissa, no matter what comes, just trust Him. With Him, all things are possible, if you just believe", she encourages. In my heart, I know that she is right about what she is saying to me. I can tell that Cindy is not going to let me feel sorry for myself.

"Maybe I will just go ahead and have my lunch now. I will go over and surprise Kalin and take him out for a picnic. I may or may not return."

"Now that is a great idea. Go and have lunch with Kalin!" she agrees. "Does he know about the children?"

"No, he doesn't know. I will tell him in my own way and in my own time."

"Alright, Melissa."

Cindy shuts the door and walks into the front room to take care of our renter. I agree with her and gather my things to leave and shut down my computer.

Because Carl and Wendy live just around the corner, I make it to their house within 15 minutes or so. I don't see any cars so it was easy to assume that nobody is in at the time. As I approach the door, I can see that there are two people inside talking, but their backs are turned away from me. I am not able to tell if that is Kalin or not. Out of curiosity, I stand behind the door out of their sight and once the gentleman gets up, I could clearly see that it *is* Kalin! It looks like he is in a heavy discussion with Wendy. *What the hell is that about? Why is he in a heavy discussion with her? What are they talking about? Why does she look mad?*

I need to knock on the door before someone calls the police thinking that I am a stalker or something. And besides, I am confident that Kalin will tell me what that conversation is all about. After the first knock, Wendy comes to the door.

"Hey, Wendy. How are you? Is my sweetheart here?"

"Sure come in."

Kalin walks from the back and grabs my hand and gives me a big hug and kiss on the cheek.

"Hey baby. How are you? What are you doing here?"

"I want to take my sweetheart on a picnic. Take the rest of the afternoon off and come with me."

"Ok, that is not a problem. I love being with my baby, so let me grab a few things and we will be on our way", he says, as he walks back to what I assume are his sleeping quarters.

"Great!"

Wendy walks back into the kitchen area and starts fumbling around with the dishes. We are both standing here in silence so I decide to make conversation with her while I am waiting on Kalin.

"So, how are you doing Wendy?"

"Well you know how it is. I am working everyday and just taking things one step at a time", she answers. Her answer almost seems as if she is having some kind of problem but I can't tell if she is having a problem with Carl or her job or what her problem is. She just doesn't seem happy at all.

"I am sure things will work out for the better." She doesn't look up at me to acknowledge my encouraging words.

"Sure. It's easy for you to say. You have a man who loves you unconditionally. He worships the ground you walk on. Believe me when I say that to you", she adds. Before she can finish, Kalin walks back into the room.

"Ok, honey. I am ready to go", he says as he approaches me. He grabs my hand and we head for the door.

"Goodbye, Wendy", he says to her, but she continues to fumble around with the dishes. She looks at him and gives him a half smile.

"You two have fun", she says.

We walk out to the car and drive off. I don't know whether to ask him about what happened or just wait. I don't want to ruin our picnic. This is the time that I get to spend with my boyfriend and just forget about anything and everybody. I will ask him later. I will tell him about the children later as well. I just can't talk about it right now.

Our picnic is over and I decide not to tell Kalin about the children. I am somewhat surprised that he has chosen *not* to discuss anything with me about his conversation with Wendy. I am sure if he knew that I had seen them talking, he would tell me. Fortunately for him, I don't have time to think about that right now.

****

I need to contact Ms. Serchay and find out about my children and to make sure that they are doing okay. When I finally get her on the phone, she is not willing to give me any information of the children's whereabouts. No matter how much I beg her to tell me more, she won't. I need to know something so I continue calling hoping to get someone who will give me some information. After several attempts, I end up getting a woman who can see how desperate I am for wanting to know about my children. Catherine informs me that she is not supposed to allow me time to speak with my children, but she will do it anyway.

"Sharell, hi honey, how are you?"

"I am fine, mommy, she answers. When do we get to come home?"

"I am not sure, honey. Just hang in there, okay and everything will be just fine. Did you all get something to eat?"

"Yes ma'am, we did."

"Are they treating you okay?"

"Yes ma'am, they are", she answers. "But I want to see you. I want to see daddy, too."

At this point, I am in tears but I do not want my daughter to hear me crying. I don't want her to think that there is a reason to be sad.

Just as I start to speak again to Sharell, the lady comes to the phone and informs me that our time is up. Although she was willing to let me speak with my children, she is hesitant about letting me know where they are now and where they will end up. She says that it's because they don't know if I will try to contact them without the court's approval. *It sounds to me like she thinks that I would go looking for them to hurt them.* But in the end, she finally tells me that they are all going to my sister's house.

Even though I am not thrilled about my family interfering in my life, I am grateful that they will be with someone that they know instead of being with strangers. *How can this happen? How do they know about my sister in the first place? How do they know that she is willing to take my children?* They must have known ahead of time. I don't understand, but it feels like everyone is against me.

God, I need you. I need your guidance, Lord. I know that you have not left me alone. God, I trust that you will get me through this. This, too, shall pass. I know that you say that you won't forsake me. Lord, please be with me as these storms get harder and harder.

****

I really need to speak with Kalin. It is time for me to tell him what has happened. I don't understand why it is taking him so long to come to the phone.

"Kalin, honey, I need you."

"Honey, what is wrong?" he asks. He can tell that I am crying by now.

"Will you please come over? I want to see you before I head off to work."

"Melissa, you know that I can't be there and have contact with the children. Are you trying to get me in trouble?" he asks, sounding very concerned.

"They are not here! I need you right now!", I plead with him.

"I will be there in 15 minutes", he says.

"Please hurry because I have to get to work soon."

Within 10 minutes, Kalin is knocking on the door. As soon as I answer the door, he is in my arms and stroking the back of my head telling me that he loves me and that everything will work out just fine.

"Melissa, you are scaring me. What is going on?" he asks.

"Kalin, they came and took all of the children on yesterday. That guy, Bob, turned me in because I spanked Darren for stealing money out of Cindy's purse. They said that his marks were from that spanking and they took the children away", I explain, as I am now fully sobbing.

"Yesterday? Why didn't you tell me? These people took my children away and you didn't tell me? That is why you came over, isn't it?" he asks.

"Yes, and I didn't want to ruin our picnic. We really needed that time together", I explain.

"Sweetheart, my children are very important to me. You should have told me. Don't cry, sweetheart. Don't cry. Everything will work out just fine. We have to just be patient, tell the truth, and I am sure that the Judge will see that we are great parents and that we take care of our kids. Come here. Let me hold you", he consoles.

Kalin and I take this time to hold each other and cry. He is hurt because he has his court date set up and the children have been removed. He is really trying to be there for me, but he is hurting himself.

"Kalin, I have to ask you something."

"What is it?" he asks.

"Please don't get mad when I say this, but it has been weighing very heavily on my mind and I just have to ask you about it."

"OK, shoot!"

"It's about the other day when I came over to get you for the picnic. Before I knocked on the door, I noticed that you and Wendy were deep in a conversation. She looked like she was upset. What was going on?"

"Melissa, I don't want to talk about that right now. We are going through enough stuff right now and I don't' want to complicate our life with other people's problems", he answers.

"Why is it that I feel that *this thing* is about us anyway? I need to know what is going on, Kalin."

"Sweetheart, please!" he blurts out. He let his arms down from holding me and walks over to the kitchen to get something to drink.

"Talk to me, Kalin!"

"Ok, you want to know what is going on?" he asks.

"Yes I do!"

"Ok, here I go. Several years ago, way before you, I had an affair", he begins to explain.

"With Wendy!" I shout.

"No. She wanted to sleep with me, but because we were friends, I would not sleep with her. She is my best friend's wife. I couldn't do that. In her mind, the true problem was that I had an affair with her sister. She told me that she was so hurt that I chose her sister over her. She thought I was trying to make some kind of statement by doing that. She couldn't understand that I just respected my friend too much. She never forgave me for that", he explains.

"And what does that have to do with the argument the other day?"

"She wants me *again*. Her husband won't make love to her and she just wants me for sex. Her sister shared our bedroom secrets. She told her about how well I was in bed and she wants to experience it for herself. I told her no! I told her that I was in love with you and that there is no other woman for me. She is torn over it", he explains.

"So, I am supposed to believe that you are not sleeping with her? You live in her house. The two of you are alone quite a bit and you haven't tried to sleep with her, right?"

"Either you believe me or you don't believe me, Melissa! You have to decide that for yourself!"

"That's just great, Kalin!"

"Listen, I thought that Carl and Wendy had mended their relationship and everything was going just fine. She suspects that he is seeing someone else and because of that, she needs to feel better. Since I have been at their house, she has been begging to me have sex with her", he explains. Kalin is careful in looking me directly in the eyes as he explains this to me.

I wonder if he can see the hurt in my eyes. Each time he speaks, my heart skips a beat.

"Are you serious?"

"Melissa, all of this happened before you and it was a long time ago. That is over! I am with you now. I love you now. I told her that I am in love with you and that I won't cheat on you! Of course, she is upset that I turned her down."

"So, that is why you wanted to stay at their house?"

"Melissa, don't you dare do this to us! I went there because they live close by here and it is convenient for me to come home when I need to get here quickly."

"Yeah, I bet it is convenient for you, isn't it Kalin? You have a woman there and one here. Please just go!" I shout. "I have to get to work and I really don't want to talk to you right now."

"Melissa, are you serious? I can't believe you. You know that I love you sweetheart. Our children are gone and all we have is each other. Let's stick together, baby. I need you right now. With this hearing coming up and everything, I don't want to fight with you. Let's spend this time loving on each other", he pleads.

Kalin has just walked out the door and for the first time since we have met, I feel that something changed between us. I start to feel very empty inside. *What just happened here? Did I just have an argument with the man that I love over someone who wanted to have an affair with him? Or am I mad because he is actually living in that someone's home? How do I know that they aren't currently being intimate with one another? Did he turn her down like he said that he did? All I know is that I have lost my children and it feels like I am losing my best friend, too.*

It is painfully clear that I am not allowed to have any contact with the children. I will; however, attend the Hearing today to find out if the Judge agrees with the action taken by Children's First. When we make it inside the courtroom, CCF presents a good case to the Judge and without any hesitation, she agrees with the State and the children remain in foster care. The children will remain with my sister and I am not allowed to visit them but can speak with them over the phone. I will attempt to call them when I get home tonight, but first, I need to call Kalin to see how he is doing. I don't like the way we left things between us in our last conversation. I agree with him. We need each other now more than ever.

On the day of the Bond Revoke Hearing, Kalin and I sit down to have a long talk before going to court. We talk about what happened the other day with our argument. He pulls me close to him and promises me that nothing has happened between him and Wendy. He assures me that he and I will get married as soon as all of this drama is over and the divorce is final. I believe him. I believe that he loves me. I know that he loves me. I trust him.

****

Today is Kalin's Bond Revoke Hearing. He is somewhat nervous about going to court, but is very concerned for me and the children's well being. He knows that I need him at home, but decides that this is something that we can't avoid. To make him more at ease, I assure him that everything is going to be okay. Before leaving, all of Kalin's witnesses gather at my office to pray for him. We decide to travel to the courthouse in two different cars. Kalin has quite a few supporters of people who believe in him and feel that this will all be over soon.

We finally make it to the courthouse. I start to feel the same butterflies in my stomach that I felt on the eve that we were waiting for the police officer to return to the apartment after going over to my sister's house to bring my daughter home. It seems as if time is passing by very slowly.

Why is he so peaceful over there? Is he not afraid that he will go back to jail or does he figure that the Judge will give him a break?

"If you are here for the State of Florida versus Kalin Thomas, please wait outside", commissions one of the bailiffs.

With Kalin still inside the courtroom, my stomach is in knots because we have no idea what is going on in there. *Why did we have to leave, I wonder. Why can't we be inside to hear what is going on?* The State and its witnesses are on one side and the Defendant's witnesses are on the other. While waiting in the hallway, I look over to the side where the State's witnesses are and notice my sister and her son, Scott. In my heart, I can't believe it! All I can think about is the pain that my family is causing me to feel. I am not proud of this anger in my heart. All I can think about at this very moment is the time that I lied to CCF to save my sister from this same pain that she is causing me right now. *Where would her kids have ended up had I not lied?*

Before we have an opportunity to go into the courtroom, I look over and notice that the State's witnesses are cheering and the attorneys are starting to leave the courtroom. When Kalin's public attorney walks out of the courtroom, he isn't concerned about speaking with me at all. In fact, he rushes out of the courtroom and heads for the courtroom next door. *What is going on, I wonder. Why isn't he saying anything to me? Where is Kalin? And why is the other side cheering?*

Kalin's witnesses are all baffled by the attorney's lack of concern. Our family friend, Baylor, runs behind the attorney for some answers. "Excuse me sir, but what happened in there? We didn't get an opportunity to go in and testify for Mr. Thomas", he says.

"Listen. On Monday, you need to get an attorney for him. They locked him up and took him into custody", the attorney says with little to no concern. My heart drops. He is back in jail! *Why didn't we get a chance to testify on his behalf?* We are all standing there baffled, not understanding this at all. My mind begins to wander. *Oh God! What went wrong? What in the world could we have done that was so wrong to deserve this? Am I a terrible mother? Did I fail my children? Did I fail Kalin? Did I fail you? How will I move forward from this? I don't understand.*

As soon as Baylor delivers this news to our group, I immediately run into the courtroom and Kalin is already taken away. The bailiff hands me an envelope with Kalin's belongings in it. My heart aches for him. As it stands, he will be in jail until the next hearing takes place. I stand up to walk out of the courtroom and the witnesses who came to support Kalin are very disappointed that they could not help us.

"Melissa, if you need anything at all, please don't hesitate to give me a call", says Carl, Wendy's husband.

"That's right. We are here to help", agrees Baylor.

Baylor ends up having to drive the car home because I can't drive a standard shift. I never learned how to drive it.

"Why don't you call Steve to see if he can assist you in any way to hire an attorney for Kalin?" Baylor suggests.

"Do you think he will?" I respond, fighting back the tears.

"You will never know until you try", he says. "What do you have to lose by asking?"

"True. I will give him a call when I make it back to the office."

"You know, Kalin knew that there was a chance that he would go back to jail", he comments.

"You think so?"

"Yes I do. Before we left for the courthouse this morning, he pulled me to the side and said that he knows that he is going back to jail. He knew that the odds were stacked against him. He felt it. Because of that, he asked me to look out for you because you would need it."

I don't know whether to cry or whether to be relieved right now. "Are you serious?"

"As a heart attack", Baylor comments.

"Yeah, and now he is not here and neither are my children. Can it get any worse?"

"You will be okay, Melissa, but you have to hang on and be strong."

"I know that I have to be strong but this is so hard." *What did I do to deserve this? Why is this happening to me? Please tell me what I should have done differently?*

Several days later, Kalin finally gets in touch with me to let me know that he is doing okay and that he so desperately needs me to come for a visit to see him at the County Jail. Waiting on that day to happen, I anticipate what it will be like. I have no idea what to expect as to how he is getting along inside. This is the second time that I will have visited someone in jail. I certainly didn't like it then and I don't think I will like it now.

With court and everything going on, I forgot to contact Laura's mother to get the address for the funeral home so that I can arrange flowers to be sent.

After a few rings, the phone is picked up. It isn't Laura's mother on the other end of the phone, but instead, it's a child's voice that I hear. "Hello there" the young child says on the other end.

"Well hello sweetheart, this must be Princess. How are you doing?"

"F-iiiiiiii-ne", she answers.

"Is your grandmother home?"

"Hold on", she responds. She places the phone down and I can hear her in the background calling for "granny".

"Hello", says Lorraine, Laura's mother. She sounds tired.

"Well hello, Ms. Lorraine. How are you doing? This is Melissa again. I forgot to get the address for the funeral home when I spoke with you the other day.

"Well hello there again. That was Princess that just answered the phone", she says.

"Yeah, I figured as much. She sounds like a little lady on the phone."

"Tell me about it. I don't know what I would do without my little angel", she comments.

"Well, I am glad that she is there with you. So, what's the address, dear?"

"Oh. Hold on for a moment." She puts down the phone and comes back within 30 seconds or so.

"The address is: 18741 Clausell Road, Middleton, AL 36145."

"Ok. Thanks so much. I will see you when I get there."

"Ok, baby. Drive carefully."

After a couple of days, I am finally on my way to the Jail to visit Kalin. I anticipate how he will react when he sees me. I wonder if he will feel the same or different towards me. *Will he still think I am beautiful? Will our love manage to hang on during this very tough time? Will I still be able to be faithful to him? How long will I have to go without him being at home with me?*

Now that I am here and I finally see the smile on his face, I feel so much more at peace. He is extremely happy to see me and begins to tell me how much he loves me and misses me and the children. During the visit, we are allowed to hold hands. Just this simple touch from him makes me feel better already. I look into his eyes and tell him how much I love and miss him and that I will stand by his side, no matter what. "Melissa, are you doing okay?" he asks.

"Yes, sweetheart, I am doing okay. He looks at me as if he doesn't believe me. I love you, honey."

"Honey, don't cry, it is going to be okay, I promise", he assures me. "I know that it looks ugly right now, but all of this will get cleared up real soon and we will be home and we will move on with our lives and will be able to pull all of this behind us", he says.

When the visit is over and I begin to leave, I notice that Kalin is forced to bend over and have the officer check him anally just to make sure that I didn't slip him any drugs or anything. *How humiliating for any one person to have to deal with! How inhumane is that!* Seeing this makes me not want to see him anymore because I don't want him to have to endure this.

I make several visits to the Jail to see Kalin. After each visit, it gets easier and easier. Being that the children are now residing with my sister, I am unable to visit with them, but I do get a chance to speak with them over the phone. Kalin worries about the children and often asks about them. I try my best to assure him that they are okay, even though I am not able to see them either.

After every single visit to Kalin at the Jail, I always go back home and crawl into bed and cry. I am so sad without him and my children at home. I have to face the painful fact that my family is torn apart. In my mind, it is still hard to imagine how we got here.

CHAPTER 24

"Back To Middleton"

*T*he phone rings and Ms. Serchay is on the other end of the phone. "Ms. Williams. We have a problem", she begins. "Oh God! What now?"

Right away, my heart sinks. *Are my children hurt, hungry, in trouble, what? Is my sister doing okay?*

"Melissa, the children are currently placed with your sister and her landlord is not allowing her to bring in 5 more children to the apartment. They are threatening to evict her unless your children move out. Do you have another family member that can take the children until this is resolved?" she asks. "Otherwise, we will move the children to separate homes because there is no one who can take all 5 children."

"I know what I have to do. I have to make a phone call and I will call you back in 10 minutes."

What the system tries to do is have the children be placed with a family member, as this allows for normalcy for the child so that they are able to cope. Even though my sister is doing all that she possibly can to destroy my family, I love my children more than I am mad at her.

"Okay", Ms. Serchay responds.

I know in my heart that the only person who will take all 5 of my children is my mother. I am not exactly proud of how she has responded to everything. I was actually hoping for a little bit more support from her but I know that this is not about me and I know that I have to do what is best and safest for my children.

In the middle of dialing my mother's number, I begin to feel at peace. Before I know it, she picks up the phone. "Hello."

"Hi Mom, how are you?"

"Fine, dear. Are you okay?" she asks.

"Looks like I am in a bind, Mother, and it looks like I really need you."

"What's wrong?" she asks.

"It is my children. I know that you are aware that they are living over to Diana's house. I just received a phone call from the caseworker who has informed me that the landlord has given Diana a warning about the children living in the apartment. They have told her that if she keeps the children, she will have to move out of the apartment. Before I call this woman back, I need to know if you can take my children temporarily until this matter is resolved", I explain. "They won't make it if they have to be separated from one another."

"Now you know that I can do that for you. You know that I will", she answers. "I heard about your friend Laura. Are you coming home to the funeral?"

"Yes, I will be home for the funeral. I will speak with Diana and see if we can't just bring the kids on this same trip."

"I am sorry about your friend. That child was in a lot of pain before she died. She was going through quite a bit. I never knew why you didn't keep in touch with her. She knew where you lived, but said that she didn't want to bother you", my mother continues. I can feel the tears coming.

After hanging up the phone, I immediately fall to my knees and pray.

Dear Lord, thank you for my mother's love to take in my children. I pray for her and her strength to take this on. I forgive my mother for whatever hurt she has caused because I know that I can't come to you with hatred in my heart. Forgive me Lord where I have fallen short and build me up where I am weak. My children need you now. I need you now. Kalin needs you now. Watch over my children while they sleep, while they eat, and while they go to and fro. Please Lord watch over Christy, Kameron, Darren, Sharell, and Amber. It is in Jesus' Name that I pray. Amen.

I decide to give Ms. Serchay a call to inform her that my mother in Alabama will take the children instead. We make the arrangements for the children to be transported to Alabama. Ms. Serchay comes to pick up more clothes for them because it now looks as if they will definitely spend the rest of the summer in Alabama. This is not a bad idea being that they normally spent summers with my mother in Alabama, so this won't be any different. She has no idea that we will actually be travelling together to Alabama, but I don't tell her any differently.

She finally arrives at my home to pick up more clothes for the children. When she comes inside, we sit down and begin to discuss what is going on with my family and this open CCF case. She goes through the spill of explaining to me that she doesn't really feel that I am doing a poor job with my children. She reiterates the fact that our home is clean, the children are always dressed appropriately and don't appear to be neglected at all. She basically gives me her personal approval of how I am raising my children. Unfortunately, this conversation is "off the record", which is how she oftentimes refer to our *private* conversations. She makes it very clear to me as to where all of this strife is really coming from. She feels as though my decision to be with Kalin is what's causing all of my problems. She goes on and on about how CCF just really wants to do away with him and get him away from the children once and for all.

"You know, Ms. Melissa, if you would just do what we tell you, this can be all over as far as we are concerned with *you*. Honestly, we just want Kalin", she says. "We just really want him in jail because we don't really think that you did anything wrong but we just want him away from these children", she admits. "Your family has told us all about him and how you just keep supporting him and they feel that if he is gone, you can have your life back. They say that you are so different since you have been with him."

"Who the hell are you or my family to decide what is best for me? How dare you be my judge and jury? That is just not right! How can you treat people like this? So, you are punishing me because I am still with him? That is ridiculous! You know who is really hurting in all of this? My children!"

She puts down her lemonade, picks up the children's belongings and head for the door. I continue to tell her how I feel as she is walking. "Honestly, Ms. Serchay, that is absolutely not fair. I am not going to say anything just to make you happy. I am not going to just do anything and everything to make you nor my family happy. It is my right to believe in what I believe and I will believe it until the day that I die. As far as Kalin is concerned, I know that he would never do anything to hurt my children and I don't care what you or my family say and that is just that."

As soon as these words leave my mouth, I already know that there will be consequences down the road. In her eyes and in my family's opinion of me, I am a parent who loves my man more than my children and a woman who decides to choose a man over her kids is not really a woman nor is she fit to be a parent.

After she leaves the apartment, I ponder over our conversation and play it all over again in my head.

The day has arrived for us to travel to Alabama. Because she has to come back on Sunday and I have to stay over for the reading of Laura's will, I will have to fly back to Florida.

My sister and kids have finally arrived. I am so happy to see them. They are all so neatly dressed, as usual. They don't waste time planting hugs and kisses on me. My sister gets out of the van and decides to stand in the corner with her arms folded. The children run inside and go straight to their rooms and start picking up some of their toys to take on the trip with them.

"Kameron, grab the snack bag for me, ok."

"Which one is it, Mommy? Is it the blue bag?" he asks.

"Yes sweetheart."

After a few minutes of our sweet reunion, I can tell that my sister is ready to get on the road. She doesn't like traveling too late. I decide to tell them that they are going to grandma's house for summer vacation. I believe this will work better than making them feel that they *have* to go. In a whisper, Sharell says, "I miss daddy too."

After several hours, we finally make it to Alabama. My mother is happy to see me. I have already made arrangements to bunk out at Brittney's. It is not that big of a deal being that Brittney lives just next door. Besides, she and I have lots of catching up to do.

Later that evening, I put the children to bed and decide to go on over to Brittney's. She is already waiting on me. She always goes all out when we get together. Tonight is no exception.

"Hey my friend", she says as she opens the door. "You look good girl!"

"What's up "B"? I have missed you so much!"

"Well get your butt on in here. We have lots of catching up to do."

"So, I see that you are still at home with mom", I say, giving her a hug.

"Hell, it is cheaper. I'm not crazy. I am teaching over at the elementary school and this gives me the opportunity to save up for my dream home that I want to build. And besides, Mom gets a chance to see her grandkids grow up", she adds.

"So how many children do you have?" I ask, as I begin to look around expecting to see them running around.

"I only have two. They are over to their friends' house tonight. It is just us. Mom is fast asleep."

"What about you?"

"Honey, my life is a long story. How much time do you have?"

"We got all night."

"I am finally in love with a man who is finally in love with me. I have 5 children and only 1 of them is his. We plan on getting married one day but he is still legally married. We live together. He makes me happy. I have a good job. I like my job, but I want to open up my own business one day. I love him. I love my babies. And that is pretty much it!"

"Sounds like you got it together?"

"Let's put it this way. Everybody has his or her very own cross to bear. Let's just say that I am wearing mine. But, I don't want to go into anything too negative right now. We are here for our girl."

"You're right. Doesn't it seem like we are too young to be burying our friend? She should not be dead right now. There is lots of speculation going around about whom Princess' father is. He is not really there for her but nobody really knows why or even who he is. She was very secretive about it. I don't know why though. She always told us everything! Everything except that! Her mother is so hurt over this. She is so angry about Laura's passing. Princess is doing just fine though. She is such an amazing little girl."

"The strangest thing happened. When I spoke with Laura's mother, she asks that I stay an extra day just so I could be there at the reading of Laura's Will. I have no idea why, though."

"Me either. I heard that she was loaded. Maybe she wants to leave you with some money. I mean, you two were the best of friends."

"I doubt that very seriously!"

The following day, Laura is buried at Beulah Baptist. The ceremony is beautiful. Many of our friends from high school have shown up to support the family. I am looking around the church and I recognize so many of the people here today. I see some of our old teachers. The church still looks the same way it did when we were all young. I can still see us standing up there in the junior choir in those green robes. I see Mr. Clay Wiggins at the piano playing like he is in some nightclub and how we thought that it was so hilarious. I can still see my Mother pinching our ears when we sat in church and talked. We were preparing what we would all wear that night to the Skating Rink. I have so many fond memories of being in Middleton.

Is that "Rock" sitting in the back with shades on? I wonder why he is here. He didn't really know Laura. She is way older than he is and she was my friend. I will see him later on. He is not a priority for me right now. Maybe I will get a chance to speak with him before I leave.

Laura is finally put to rest but my heart is not settled. I have so many questions for her, but it is too late. I wonder if she would have shared with me what was going on in her life if I had been here. I feel so sad for her mother. Brittney was right. Princess is beautiful!

Two days later.

The reading of the Will is about to begin.

"Please have a seat everyone. My name is Sean Wilkins and I was approached by Ms. Laura to bring all of you together for the reading of her Will so that her plans will be carried out. Sean begins to read.

"*Lorraine Walters.* Laura leaves behind to you the custody of Princess, stocks and bonds that she has, her home in Boston, her timeshare, and her boat."

"*Princess.* Your mother leaves behind to you all of her precious jewels and a bank account that has $20,000 in it that will mature over time that you can have access to when you turn 18. She furthermore states that after the passing of her mother, your grandmother, you will have everything that is being handed down to her.

"*Melissa Williams.* Laura leaves behind this envelope that will remain in the custody of Attorney Mike Richards that is to be opened *only* after the passing away of her mother, Lorraine Walters. *What in the world could be that secretive? Why won't she tell me now? Why do I have to wait until her mother dies?*

The Reading is over and I have no clue as to what could be in this envelope. I probably won't have to worry about it for quite some time because I will only get it after Laura's mother passes away.

The weekend is finally over and I have to get back to my own life in Miami. Before I head to the airport, I decide to drop by to see Laura's mother. It just seems to make sense, so I leave Princess some pictures of me and her mother during happier times. She needs to know just how close me and her mother were when we were growing up. I am one of her mother's closest friends and it is important to me that Princess knows that I am here for her, just as her mother would have wanted.

My flight back to Miami is a very peaceful one. Baylor is supposed to be there to pick me up when I land. I am ready to just go to bed and get some rest.

CHAPTER 25

"He Died. Why Should You?"

T he summer is off to a sad start for me. I just got back from Alabama where I had to lay one of my best friends to rest. My children are in Alabama. Kalin is back in jail. I spend most of my time working and trying to occupy my time to fill the void. I visit Kalin in jail as much as I can. There are days that I am unable to go see him because of my responsibilities with my very demanding job.

Today is a beautiful day outside. It is not too humid, which is quite unusual for Florida. I feel like eating some Ben & Jerry's chocolate ice cream. I have to call the kids to see what they are doing. And as usual, the conversations with the children are the highlight of my day. It looks like "Granny" took them swimming and they just returned when I called. They sound so happy on the phone and this pleases my heart. Their being in Alabama for the summer is actually turning out to be a blessing.

Our call is suddenly interrupted because of a knock at my door. It is Baylor! He begins to ask me a favor, but I interrupt him to inform him that I am on the phone.

"Christy, sweetheart, I will call you all back. There is someone at the door who needs me right now."

"Ok. Mommy! We love you!"

Baylor is already sitting at my dining table when I get off the phone. He begins to tell me that Alexander is at his apartment and is threatening to kill himself with his gun. He goes on to say that Alexander is a little down on his luck because he was just released from Prison and can't find a job and is just simply frustrated.

I don't think about anything but trying to save this man's life. I put on my shoes and head for the door. When I finally make it over to Baylor's apartment, Alexander is sitting at the dining room table with a beer in front of him. There is only Baylor and Alexander in the apartment. This is an uncomfortable situation for me because I am the only female in the apartment with two men who are completely wasted. *Oh Lord, I need you for this one!*

"Alexander, hey dude, what's going on?"

"Hey, lady, what are you doing here?" he says, not even looking up at me.

"Well, Baylor is concerned about you and thought I could help so he came over to get me to come talk to you", I respond.

"But, why, you are a busy lady?" he asks, while sipping out of his beer.

"Yes, that is true and yes, I should be home but I am here with you and I want to talk to you", I explain.

"What do you want to talk to me about?" he asks.

"Well, I hear that you are feeling a little down right now. Baylor tells me that you want to check out on us. I just can't let you do that you know. See, I want you to stick around because I care for you and so does Baylor", I say, as I put my hand on his shoulder.

I was afraid to get too close and say the wrong thing that could be misleading but I just know that I will do anything to keep this man from killing himself. Maybe I can call the police but that will probably make things worse.

"Ms. Lady, this doesn't concern you and why should you care anyway? You have your own life and Baylor has his life. I have just really missed out on mine. My time is over. Life is hard. People don't want to give you a chance. What am I supposed to do? I want to work just like everybody else and nobody will give me a chance and honestly, I am just tired of it", he explains. His words are starting to run together. I am sure that it is due largely to the quantity of alcohol that they have probably consumed.

Alexander gets up and pushes me out of the way to get to his truck. Baylor is starting to get agitated with Alexander and throws his hands up as if to say, 'oh well'. I decide to follow Alexander outside to his truck.

"Alexander, let me go with you."

"I want to be alone Ms. Lady. Please just mind your own business and go back inside. I want to be alone to go to the park", he says, as he reaches for his keys.

"I just can't let you do that". He is beginning to get frustrated with me, so he reaches underneath his seat and shows me his gun, as if he is admiring its design. He takes it out and puts it on the seat and looks at me as if to say that he really just wants to go and be alone. This is actually my first time ever seeing a gun right in front of my face.

"Alexander, please get out of the truck and talk to me."

At this point, I am almost in tears because the situation is getting more and more out of hand. He isn't listening to me at all! I am trying to talk to a highly intoxicated man who wants to kill himself. Baylor is inside and completely wasted. There is no time to call anyone. If I call anyone, it might end up being too late. I can't let him get out of my sight.

Will I die in the process? What if he kills us both? I wonder. *Lord, I need you. I can't walk away from this man. If it is my time to go, then I will see you shortly. Please be with me. Give me the right words to say to this man. In Jesus' name. Amen.*

Alexander is so much bigger than me so if he really wants to get away, he can. But there is something telling me that he doesn't really want to do this. After I beg and plead with him, he agrees to get out of the truck. He does, however, bring the gun with him. We sit down underneath a tree and continue to talk. He still has the gun on one side of him and I am on the other side. I start to tell him the story about Jesus hanging on the cross and why He did that.

"Alexander, why would you have to kill yourself? Jesus died on the cross and died for all of your sins and mine too. He doesn't need us to die. He wants us to have life and have it more abundantly."

The whole time I am speaking, he is holding his head down and shaking it back and forth. I am not sure if he is doing this because he doesn't want to hear it or if he just doesn't agree with what I am saying.

Then all of a sudden, it happens! My Spirit voice demands that I go home now. *Can't be! I am not done yet. I can't go home yet. What if he kills himself and I didn't stop him? I can't just leave him.* Although I begin to battle within myself to stay, it is time to go and God knows it. Again, it happens. That voice urges me to "go home".

I make my way into Baylor's apartment to speak to him and he is already out of it; he has passed out from being so drunk. Although I don't want to leave, I know that this is God's voice and instruction and I have to obey.

I go over by the tree where Alexander is still sitting and kiss him on the forehead and say, "Goodbye, Alexander, I have to go now. I will see you tomorrow. I love you dude, so go get some sleep okay."

"Ms. Lady, I won't be here tomorrow but I appreciate everything you have done. You are a God sent woman and that is why I love you", he says. "And I do mean that respectfully."

"I love you too", I say, with my back turned as I walk away.

Once I walk away, I don't know if he is going to go ahead and shoot himself and I will have to run back and see him sitting there with his brain splattered all over the tree. I don't know what will happen. In the back of my mind, I question whether I am doing the right thing or not. It isn't really up to me.

I get ready for bed. I can't sleep at all and don't understand why God made me leave. I didn't finish and it feels like I failed. If this man kills himself, it will be because I didn't do the right thing. In the middle of the thoughts going back and forth in my head, I manage to fall asleep.

The next morning, I am awakened because of the hard knock at my door. I don't know what news I will face now. I am somewhat afraid to find out. The knocking isn't stopping, but is actually getting harder and louder.

I open the door and it is Alexander! He is happy and doesn't look like the man from last night who was so down and out.

"Ms. Lady, may I come in?" he asks.

" Sure. Come in. How are you doing this morning?"

"I am doing just great. I just want to thank you for what you did last night for me. No one has ever cared that much for me. You risked your life for me and I appreciate that. As you can tell, I didn't kill myself. After you left last night, I saw a vision under that tree. I saw Jesus hanging on that cross like you were saying and I just knew then that I didn't have to die; He already did that for me", he explains.

I am already in tears at this point and reach over to give him the biggest hug. I thank God for this man's life and for revealing that to him. I can't wait to see Kalin to tell him about what happened.

After Alexander leaves the house, I begin to feel so proud to be able to be used by God. Baylor comes over later and we sit down and discuss what happened last night over some lemonade. I remind him just like I told Alexander that it wasn't me at all. God was in control of that situation the whole time.

****

Summer is coming to an end and I have to get the kids back home. I decide to call Ms. Serchay and share my concerns with her.

"Ms. Madeline, how are you today?"

"Fine, Ms. Williams. What can I do for you?" she asks.

"I am going to Alabama to pick up my children. I don't want to have any issues with my mother, so I need a document that says it is okay for them to return with me", I explain.

"There should not be a problem", she says.

"I know what should be, but that is seldom what happens. So, if you don't mind, I would like to have that letter to take with me just in case the police are involved. Please make sure that this letter is on State letterhead."

Days later, I pick up a van from Enterprise and I am finally on my way to Alabama to get my children. Arriving at my mother's house, I am not surprised that I am not welcomed with open arms when I walk into my mother's kitchen, where she is standing preparing dinner.

"Hello Mother."

"Hey! How was your trip?" she asks, not looking up to greet me.

"It was fine. I rested in Tallahassee for an hour or so, but I am here."

"Meme, I know that you are here to get your children but why don't you let Christy stay", she begs.

"Mom, I am taking all of my children back with me and that includes Christy too. She is going back home with me. Christy is my daughter and I love her and want her with me. Why can't you understand that?"

"Well, I just don't want her down there with him", she says.

"Mother, if you are concerned that the children will be hurt, why is that Christy is the only one that you care about? Come on. My children are not in any danger of being with Kalin. Don't let those people in Florida fool you. They are not giving you all of the facts. And for the record, I did not stand by while Kalin abused Sharell. She simply got spanked on her bottom and she was fine. Think about all the butt whippings we got growing up as kids. They didn't kill us, Mother. Just, please stop being so hard on him. He loves my children. I would not be with him for one moment if I thought any differently. You have to let me grow up and take care of my own affairs. I am out of your house and I have my own children. I want to raise them for myself. I want to learn how to be a better mother. You had your own children to raise and you did the best that you could do. Nobody is standing around and judging you for anything. None of us are perfect! You weren't perfect as a parent and I am not either. Let me learn from the mistakes that I will make on my own."

"I do care about all of them, but Christy wants to stay", she says.

"Well, Christy is not the adult; I am. She is going back with me and this is my final say-so on this matter."

My mother and I continue to talk and finally decide to disagree. It is at this moment that I begin to realize that none of their belongings are packed. I have to end up doing all of the packing myself. I don't mind because I am so happy to take them back with me that it doesn't matter at all.

When it is time to leave, my mother continues to whine about Christy staying in Middleton for the year. She wants her to go to school there. I am really starting to get frustrated because we have already discussed this matter more than I want to discuss it.

We finally leave Middleton! I can't wait to get back home with my children and start fresh with our life together.

CHAPTER 26

"Rita to the Rescue"

*A*ll is settled but there is one minor detail that has to be covered. I have to solidify a babysitter for Sharell, Darren, and Amber. I also need someone home when Christy and Kameron get home from school. Finding the right person to care for my children is not going to be a quick decision. I need time to seek out the right person.

After making some phone calls, I learn that Kalin's cousin, Jennifer, is still available so I invite her to move in with us, which will help me tremendously, which will also provide housing for her. She agrees and moves in, along with her 3 children.

For awhile, the situation is working well. All of the children play well together and can even share each other's clothes. As always, good things do come to an end. The relationship begins to deteriorate when Jennifer starts smoking marijuana. She starts staying out all night, which leads to her being gone for days at a time. With her not being home, I am stuck having to take mine and her kids to work with me. This starts to be too much for me to handle and I have to figure something else out. This has to change. This environment is becoming too unhealthy for my children. As much as I love her children, there is no way that I will continue to allow this type of behavior around my children. It doesn't matter to me that she is Kalin's cousin. As a matter of fact, I have already arrived at the conclusion that she will definitely have to move out of my house.

Right away, I start looking for a babysitter and remember that there is a nice older lady that I just recently approved for an apartment. I don't exactly know anything about her, but that she is much older and lives on the property.

One day on my lunch break, I decide to pay her a visit. After knocking a few times, I am beginning to wonder whether she is home or not. Just as I am about to walk away, her front door flies open.

"Well good morning Ms. Manager. Sorry about that, but I was in the back room and didn't hear you", she explains.

"Well, Good morning, Ms. Rita. I thought that maybe you weren't home."

"Is everything okay?" she asks.

"Ms. Rita, I have a business proposition for you. I was wondering if you are available during the day to watch my children for me."

"How many children do you have?" she asks.

"I have five children. Is that too big of a job?" I say, with a little bit of sarcasm.

"Oh come on now, she responds. That won't be a problem at all. Besides, I am not doing anything during the day, so I don't mind helping you out", she says.

"Great, thank God! Then, it is settled. I would like for you to watch them for me at my apartment", I say, as we shake hands to seal the deal. "I already have all of your background information, so I won't require anything more than what I already have. I forgot to ask. How much are you going to charge me?"

"Whatever you have to give me is fine for me", she answers.

This is great news to me! She is much older and more mature. I won't have the same concerns that I had with Jennifer. Ms. Rita will start watching my children for me while I work and she will watch them at my home. I am anxious to see how the children will react to her.

"Do you have plans for dinner tonight?"

"I sure don't", she responds.

"Great! Please join us tonight for dinner. We eat at 6:30pm. I live on Rogers Street."

"Oh, that big house on the corner?" she asks.

"Sure."

The children are excited to meet her as well. It makes my heart happy to see the children form a bond with her right away. She really does have a way with children. After witnessing this, I already know that this situation will work out just fine.

****

When I get home from work, the children have already eaten their dinner and ready for bed. She is fantastic with my children. I have always felt that a more mature woman would be the perfect fit to serve as a babysitter for them. Our pay agreement is that I can pay her what I can. And that is what I decide to do. She is happy on Fridays when I give her $150 for the week.

I have not had a chance to speak with Jennifer about her living arrangements because she is never here. Out of the goodness of her heart, Ms. Rita is also watching Jennifer's children as well. I give her extra for watching them.

It looks like Jennifer is pulling up now. I can hear the thumping noise of music coming from the car that is dropping her off.

"Jennifer, you know that I love you", I say to her as she makes her way into the doorway. I can tell that she is completely out of her mind.

"Yeah, yeah, yeah! You love me, right? What the hell eva!!! Nobody loves me. Don't even go there", she says, as she stumbles around trying to gain her balance.

"Jen, of course, I love you. But sweetheart, you have to get it together. You come in whenever you get ready. You neglect your children. You are always drunk and this is all unacceptable. Do you see me doing this?"

"I don't know what the hell you do!" she blurts out. "As a matter of fact, I think you cheating on my cousin. It's not normal for any woman to go this long without having a man up in her bedroom. I know you get it from somewhere!"

"Now, that is enough Jennifer! I am very faithful to Kalin. Don't go there with me!"

"It's like this, Jennifer. I don't do this around my children and I am sure as hell not going to allow you or anyone else to do it around my kids either. So, you got to go, honey!" I say as she stands up. She acts as if she is ready to pounce on me. "I need you to be out of here by this weekend."

She is not happy, but she knows that I am being very serious with her right now.

****

The day after I arrived back from Alabama with the children, Bob called to set up our appointment, but I was unable to do so at the time. He is just now calling me back.

"Ms. Williams, how are you today?" he asks.

"I am fine. I almost forgot that we have our appointment on tomorrow."

"Well, that is why I am calling. Although we need to meet, I was just informed by the Court that the Judge has ordered a Psychological Evaluation for you. We need to get this done first", he says.

"Ok, that is fine. What about next Tuesday?"

"That works just fine!"

"And for *our* next appointment?" he asks.

"Same time, same day, still works for me."

Bob shows up and his mindset is still stuck on his ideas about parenting and how *not* to spank children. This is just not going to happen in our household. Bob insists on alternate forms of discipline. I am open to any new ideas. He gives me the details about the upcoming psychological evaluation and what to expect of it. He goes on to say that it will take approximately 1 hour and that they will inform him of the results and that we'd discuss the results at our next appointment.

The days slowly pass by and nothing seems to matter to me at all. The psychological evaluation that I have to take has my focus and attention. From what I have heard, these tests are set up to always make you look like you are crazy. *What will my results be? Will they have an effect on my case?*

I begin to look around at my life and notice that it is moving forward every day, whether I like the direction it is going or not. My youngest child, Amber, is growing up without her father. *Will she recognize him when she sees him? Will she turn him away?*

As far as court is concerned, it seems as if nothing is working out in Kalin's favor. I haven't seen him in over 2 weeks and finally receive a letter from him today that he is not feeling well. Depression is starting to set in on him. This is very understandable because I am equally depressed. The holidays are approaching and Kalin isn't here to be part of the festivities.

I have to make it as fun for the children as I can. During the holidays, the networks show all of the 'oldie but goodie' Christmas cartoons. The kids and I sit down, with popcorn and candy in hand, to watch "Frosty the Snowman". But, there seems to be something a little bit more interesting blaring from the television.

During the commercial break, the news anchor, Kelly Williams, announces that there will be a report at 10 regarding a "Mother Distraught Over Child Abuse Charges". I can't miss this! I have to stay up to hear this. I am sure that Bob will have plenty to say about this story.

"Frosty the Snowman" finally comes to life again and the story is over. The children are all fast asleep anyway. As I expected, none of them make it to the end. The 10:00 o'clock news is next and I will finally get to hear the story.

Kelly Williams comes on the television screen and the voice over says the report is next. I listen very carefully as not to miss anything. She begins by naming the woman who is charged. Her name, Shonte Mallory, 22 years old, is being charged with child abuse because she left her children home with her boyfriend and when he wasn't able to get the children to eat their dinner, he put them in scalding hot water, leaving them with 2nd degree burns. Shonte was at work when it all happened. The boyfriend and she are both charged with abuse in this crime. I could never be with a man who would hurt my children on purpose. There is just no way!

I finally fall off to sleep with the television still on and the kids still in my bed. I wake up around 3 am and decide to just leave them there. Oh boy! Tomorrow is my psychological evaluation. *How do I prepare for this? Should I read something? Should I talk to someone who would know? Or do I just go in there and by myself?* I think that this is what I have to do. I decide to go ahead and flip off the switch and go to sleep and hope that I dream of Kalin and me and the happy times.

CHAPTER 27

"Don't Believe Him!"

I am finally sitting in the lobby at Dr. Roth's office waiting to get my appointment underway. *What will they speak to me about? Why am I here in the first place? I can only imagine what Bob has already told these people about me. Will they already have me figured out before I make it in the door?*

Sitting at the reception desk is a short, plump, white lady, with thick glasses on. She calls herself Patty. She is quite friendly but appears to be slightly uppity. I just thought about it. She didn't really greet me professionally when I walked in the door. Is this their way of making me "lose my cool"? Because I have it already figured out, I won't allow it to get the best of me. I have to remember that I am not here for her. I have to focus! I take a seat in the first chair I get to and pick up a "People" magazine that is already neatly placed on the end table. Tiger Woods is on the cover, with that million dollar smile. By the time I open the magazine to see if I can find his story, the receptionist calls me to the front desk.

"Ms. Williams, I need for you to take this packet and answer all of the questions truthfully. When you have completed this packet, please sign the last page and bring the paperwork back to me", she instructs.

"Sure. Not a problem."

I start answering all of the questions and at first, they are simple answers, but the second section is about the children and who does the parenting and who is the disciplinarian in the home. The third section throws me for a loop! This section is about the sexual behavior that I have with my partner. The questions are about who the aggressor is in the bedroom and who the submissive one is, who is on top, who takes lead, and questions of the sort. I don't know what this has to do with whether my children are safe with me or not. I answer all of the questions. At the end of the questioning, there is a page about questions pertaining to luck and whether I believe luck exists or if it just happens and questions of the sort. I don't care if they think I am crazy or not, but I am not answering questions about luck. I don't believe in luck! I cross an "x" over the entire page. I sign the last page and take the packet to Patty.

"Are you all done?" she asks.

"Yes ma'am, I am."

"Ok, have a seat."

Moments later, a short man with brown hair and dark rimmed glasses approaches me and asks me to come into his office. He offers me a seat and I take one right next to his desk. We talk about the weather, current events, children, husbands, and finally, the allegations that are placed against Kalin. He wants to know my opinion. He wants to know where I stand on discipline and the whole nine yards.

"Sir, I do not believe that Kalin meant to hurt my child, if that is what you are asking me. I don't know what all they have told you, but this man is very loving towards my children. I would not be with him if I didn't believe this", I say, without turning my eyes away.

"CCF seems to think---", he begins.

"With all due respect, I don't really care what they think. They took my children away, and for what! Kalin was arrested and is still in jail, and for what! I respect the organization and think that there are times when their intervention is necessary, but it just wasn't this time", I explain.

"It has really been wonderful speaking with you, but I will put together my thoughts and will submit it to the Judge", he says.

"Ok, sir, thanks so much. May I ask you a question?"

"Sure, go ahead."

"If the law clearly states that disciplining your child is your right, why is it that CCF teaches *against* corporal punishment? And to make matters worse, why will they punish you if you discipline your children?"

"Ma'am, that is outside of my jurisdiction to speak on those matters. These are matters of the judicial system and if you want answers, you will have to get it from them. Do you have any more questions for *me*?"

"No sir that will be it."

"Have a great day and my office will be in touch with you regarding the results of this evaluation."

"Thanks."

I am finally done with the appointment! It wasn't too bad. I survived the questions and I managed to keep my cool.

Ms. Williams, the evaluation will be ready for you to pick up in a few days and there will be a charge of $50 to get the results. We will give you a call when it is ready", she says.

I didn't know that I would have to pay for the results of the evaluation. What are they talking about? The Judge is the one who wanted this evaluation. I think that she should pay for it! I don't have money for this.

"Ok, thanks."

I know that I am not paying for this but I just don't want to get into it with this lady.

On the way home, I replay the visit with Dr. Roth over and over in my head. *What could I have said differently? How did I do? I wonder.*

I finally make it home and I am quite relieved. It is such a beautiful day. It reminds me of one of those days back in Middleton when we would all have to get up, get dressed, and get outside to help Momma in the yard. We would burn the trash and that smell of burnt trash is a good memory growing up. I would love to just wake up and have a different life. This is the one I have, though. Walking in the door, the phone is ringing and it is Curtis, Wendy's husband. He asks about the children and about Kalin and says that he has some disturbing news to give me.

"Melissa, are you sitting down?" he asks.

"No, but should I be?"

"Yes. I will just come on out with it. Kayla is dying. This is a shock to all of us. She didn't tell anyone about this. Apparently she knew about it but kept it to herself because she didn't want anyone to worry. She was recently diagnosed over 2 weeks ago with Leukemia and it is in its final stage and is causing her organs to shut down. The doctors don't believe that there is anything that they can do for her. They said that they can make her comfortable but that was about it", he explains.

I am speechless! I can't feel anything. I don't know what my next words will or should be.

"How is her son, Phillip?"

My tears are starting to flow down my cheeks. I still have the car keys in my hand and just start pounding them on the table. Phillip is Kayla's son who just recently graduated from high school and entered into Penn State on a full scholarship.

"He is fine. He got in today. He is at the hospital and hasn't left his mother's bedside. As soon as we told him, he packed his things and flew to Florida. He is staying at our house but is asking for Kalin. He just wants to see him", he says.

"Of course he is. Did you tell him about Kalin's situation?"

"Yes I did and he understood. I was hoping that you could get the word to Kalin and let him know what is going on."

"I would love to go to Kayla. Do you think that she will see me?"

"I really don't think it is a good idea. You can call her. I think this would be better", he says.

"Ok, I will contact the Jail to get this news to Kalin and I will also give Kayla a call."

"Thanks for letting me know. Will you please tell Phillip that we are so sorry?"

"Of course I will."

I had no idea that Karen was ill! *Did she know that she was dying? Did Kalin know that his ex-wife was ill? Would he have stayed if she had told him?* I feel horrible for Phillip. He is her only child. Kalin raised him as his own child. I know that Kalin would want to be here for his son. I have to get in touch with him and give him the news.

After several phone calls to the Jail, I am finally successful in getting the word to Kalin about his ex-wife. Because there is a death in the family, he is afforded the opportunity to make a phone call. He calls me to ask me to contact Kayla and to see if there is anything that we can do for her. By now, the doctors decide to release her home. I don't have time to waste. I need to give her a call now, before it is too late. She picks up the phone on the first ring.

"Kayla? Good morning sweetheart."

"Good morning to you, Melissa", she responds. "How did she know it was me?

"Hey, I hear that you are a little under the weather. Is there anything that you need me to bring you?"

"If you don't mind, I would love some juice. I am a little thirsty and that would be just fine", she answers.

"Great! Is there any particular flavor?"

"Whatever you choose is fine with me", she answers. "Melissa, thanks", she mumbles.

I feel so sorry for her at this very moment. She is only 36 years old and her life is almost over. Just like Dana and Laura; it just doesn't seem fair. I feel so privileged to see another day. Just as I am about to say goodbye, Kayla begins to speak.

"Melissa, I wish you the best with Kalin. I know that he really loves you. Just so you know, he told me when he came to see me one day. But there is something that I want to say to you before I leave this world", she begins.

"What is it?"

"Don't trust him. He is going to try to tell you that he never slept with Wendy. He probably told you that he slept with her sister. It is just not true. He *did* sleep with Wendy and I personally know it to true. I walked in on them myself! Wendy's husband was away on a trip and Kalin went over there to supposedly fix something in her kitchen. I followed him because my woman's intuition said that something just wasn't right. Be careful. I am obviously not saying this to you for my personal gain. You seem like a nice woman and I just think you should know", she continues.

"I appreciate that. I will bring you the juice this afternoon."

How in the world could he lie to me about this? Why did he lie to me about this? He slept with her. He may have slept with her sister, but he did fool around with Wendy and he was staying at her house! I am so pissed right now!!!

Little do I know that the next time I see Kayla will be at her funeral. I was never able to take her the juice she wanted because later on this evening, she passes on quietly in her bed at home. Her son is the only person next to her when she takes her final breath.

I have to tell Kalin! I have to let him know that she is gone! The tears are falling down my face non-stop! I am hurting for the family. I can only imagine what this woman went through during her last minutes. It is just so painful to think of this. *How will Kalin react to this news? Will he blame himself for pushing the divorce? Will he blame me or what? Should I tell him what Kayla said to me about Wendy? Maybe not now, but one day I must!*

Kalin is devastated when he finally gets the news. Due to these circumstances, I am afforded an appointment to see Kalin right away for a visit.

"I should have been there for her", he says at my visit with him. "Why didn't she tell me that she was sick? I could have done something about it. And now, my son has lost his mother. I won't ever forgive myself for this."

"Kalin, you could not have done anything. She was way too gone. Why are you blaming yourself for this? You sound like you should have remained with her", I say with tears in my eyes.

"How can you be so selfish at a time like this? My son's mother has died and this is all you can say!" he yells.

"I don't mean it like that. How do you think I feel right now? Listen to what you are saying! How do you expect me to feel?" I ask, crying softly.

"Baby, I am so sorry. I didn't think about that at all. Let's calm down. I am just hurt right now", he explains.

"I understand that completely."

During our conversation, Kalin speaks non-stop about Phillip. He keeps mumbling something about the divorce. I start realizing that I just have to let him grieve. The thing that gets my attention is when Kalin says, "I want to take the plea and get out of here. My son needs me and I won't let him down."

"Let *him* down! You are letting *me* down! We have sat here for 7 months or so saying that you are innocent and you are going to plead guilty to these charges just to get out of here for Phillip. I can be there for Phillip! How are you going to do this to *us*?"

"There you go being selfish again!" he shouts.

"Is that what you want? Is that really what you want? You want to walk in that courtroom and tell the Judge that you have sat in Jail for 7 months and now you want to say that you are guilty!"

"Listen. I don't really care what you think about my decision. You will never be able to understand this. I need for you to call my attorney when you walk out these doors and tell her that I want to cop a plea and get out of here!" he instructs.

"Kalin, do you realize that your trial is set for next week? It is almost over and you want to take a plea?"

I let go of his hands and turn away from him.

"Honey, this is nothing more than I am just hurt right now. I am so crushed right now", he says.

"What? Are you still in love with this woman or something?"

I recognize that I am acting like a jealous woman but I can't stop thinking about what Kayla said to me when we last talked. *What she said reminds me that Kalin does have secrets. And just maybe, he is not telling me the truth about how he feels about his wife.*

"Are you serious right now?" he asks, starting to get angry.

"I mean, you are very upset. You probably regret ever leaving her, right? Now, you wish you had stayed with her? Did you know that she was ill?"

Kalin is now the one looking away. He seems to be annoyed with my questions. I think I may have struck a nerve. "Listen, I love you. I have loved you since the day I first met you. I will always love you, Melissa Williams. You are the woman that I want to spend the rest of my life with.

If you don't know that by now, you never will. I didn't know that she was ill. I don't have regrets for divorcing her. I never should have married her. I am not in love with her, but yes, I love her. I love her like I love everyone. I love my son and I need to be there for him. All I can think about is what he must be going through. He needs his father right now."

"I will contact your attorney for you. Kalin, I will do that only because I love you, but I have to admit to you that I do not agree with you on this. We are your family now! Taking this plea can, perhaps, change *our* lives together."

Now that Kayla has passed away, I am sure that Phillip needs Kalin more than ever. But in all honesty, Kalin needs him too. Kalin knows that I don't agree with him about his decision, but his mind is made up and it doesn't seem like he is going to change it anytime soon.

Just as Kalin wants, I call Carolyn at her office to tell her what Kalin has decided. Although she is surprised of his decision, she knows that it is just that. It is his decision. "Melissa, what brought this on?"

"His ex-wife passed away and he wants to get out of Jail to be there for his son, Phillip."

"This is *her* son, right?" she asks.

"Yes, but Kalin raised him since he was 9 and he will not change his mind about this", I respond.

"Well, it is his decision and if he wants this, I have to oblige", she says. "Bring all of the children to the courthouse tomorrow morning around 10 am. I will see you then."

The following day, we all show up for court. As instructed by the attorney, I bring the children to court as well. When Kalin looks up and sees the children walk into the courtroom, his eyes fill with tears and he begins to shake his head. He looks so lifeless standing there crying.

When his name is called, we all approach the bench and the attorney begins to explain that Kalin has decided to accept the State's offer and has agreed to plea nola contendre. The Judge goes through the normal questioning about whether he is sure and if he has been promised anything and if he understands what his punishment could end up being if he decides to go in that direction. After each answer, weird thoughts begin to race through my head. *Would this Judge decide to give him the maximum penalty? Does Kalin know what he is doing? Will the Judge consider the fact that the children are in the courtroom?*

"Mr. Thomas, based on the questions answered, I now sentence you to a punishment of 3 years probation, with an opportunity for early termination with cooperation", she says. "You may now be released."

Even though I am happy that Kalin is getting out, I am also very concerned about him and how he will handle being out after all these months of being locked away. I begin to wonder. *Will things go back to the way they were? Will he still want to spend his life with me or will he want to just move on to escape all of the drama that our life shares together?*

Today, Kalin will walk into our home for the first time. Because of my recent promotion, I moved the family to a new home. There are beautiful orange trees in the backyard and the children have more than enough room to run around and play. I turn the fifth bedroom into my office space. Going to the new property also means that I will have an entirely new staff, but one of my conditions is that I am allowed to bring Cindy with me to the new property.

Kalin and I finally enter into the house. After giving him the tour of the house, we end up in the bedroom and just stand there looking into each other's eyes. We begin to slowly undress each another and begin to make passionate love together over and over and over. I can't get enough of him and he can't get enough of me. We are so drawn into one another that I forget that I have to pick up the children from school. One of Kalin's conditions for his release is that he is not allowed around any of the children until he is cleared through CCF. Although we are glad that he is out, he still can't come and live inside the house with us.

Kalin has heard so much about Ms. Rita and he is now going to meet her. And after all of these months, she will also get to meet the man that she has heard me talk about so much.

"Well, who is this good looking young man?" asks Ms. Rita, as she comes into the living room where we are sitting.

"I have heard so much about you. Thank you so much for taking care of my family while I have been away", Kalin says as he gives her a hug.

"You are quite welcome. It has truly been my pleasure. And Mr. Kalin, don't worry about anything. It will all work out just fine. God will work it out for you. Believe me! I know. So just enjoy this time with your family."

"Thanks for saying that. I need to hear it. It is hard being in there knowing that you didn't do what they are saying that you did. I would never hurt my children and it pisses me the hell off to be looked at that way. It just doesn't seem like anyone wants to hear the truth", Kalin says.

Instead of going to live with someone else, Kalin decides to sleep in the car at night and come inside during the day while the children are at school. Leaving him out in the cold in the car is extremely hard to do. It takes several hours for me to fall asleep because I stand in the window and watch the car all night. He doesn't know that I am watching but I am watching and praying over him that the angels keep him warm during these cold months.

Kalin and I find out that Kayla's body will be put to rest on Thursday. We are pondering over whether or not to attend her funeral service. I think that Kalin should be there because this woman was his wife for 6 years or so. More than anything, I want Kalin to be there for Phillip, but he is very adamant about not attending if I am not with him.

"Kalin, I really do think that you should go alone to the funeral. If I am there with you, it will only complicate things and will upset everyone. Honey, I understand and I trust you. Please go alone", I plead with him. "This is why you said that you copped a plea, remember? So go and be there for your son!"

Kayla's family recently visited Florida to check on Kayla. When the divorce was final, she was so upset that they had to come see about her. According to Kalin, their marriage was over way before I became involved? *Is this true or not?*

"Melissa, listen, sweetheart. I love you more than anything in this world. Don't get me wrong. I love my son. I raised him up to be a very good young man and he will understand why I won't show up at the funeral without you. The bottom line is this. If you don't go, I don't go! This is final and I won't say another word about it!"

"Ok, stop yelling! I will go with you!"

We just stand there looking into each other's eyes until we both stop crying.

"Melissa Williams, you know that I love you."

"Kalin, yes, I do know that and I love you too", I respond.

"It is time for you to become Mrs. Melissa Thomas", he says. "You have always been my wife in my heart and I believe that we said "I do" a long time ago, but I want to make it official", he says, while gazing into my eyes.

"What do you mean Kalin?"

"We will go downtown and make it official", he announces. "I want the whole wide world to know that you are my woman."

We stand there hugging and kissing like it is our very first time. Kalin is kissing me with such passion that I can almost feel his tongue at the back of my throat. I can feel my heart rate speeding up. I have never felt in my life the way I feel at this very moment. We have already gone through so much together. I love him so much and I can't wait to be his wife. But it is Kayla's viewing tomorrow as well. This doesn't stop us from calling around to other family members and friends and sharing our news with them. It is no shock to most people because they always thought that we were married anyway.

Today, I get up with a very peculiar feeling. I don't know whether to be sad or happy. On one note, Kalin's first wife is having a viewing of her body where she will be put to rest on tomorrow. Kalin is sad about that. He did spend 6 years of his life with this woman. I know that they had some happy times that he may even think about today. On the other hand, I am making my own history. I am marrying the man of my dreams. I am going to stand before an official of some sort and he or she will ask me if I am sure that I want to marry this gorgeous man who has put this huge smile on my face and this melodious song in my heart. He is the same man who loves me for everything I am. He is also the man that my family thinks wants to hurt my children. He is the same man who they treat with so much disrespect. I love him, but I also love them, but because he will be my husband, I love him more. My children love him and respect him. They think of him as "dad". That is all that matters to me. As far as I am concerned, I am marrying the right man. Ms. Rita just got the kids out of the house and Kalin walks in and finds me in the bathroom.

"Melissa, are you okay?" Kalin asks with concern. He can tell that something is wrong because I am slouched over while sitting on the toilet.

"I am fine, honey. Don't worry."

"We can put this off for another day if you want", he says.

"Are you kidding? I have wanted to officially be your wife for the longest and nothing is going to stop me from being your wife on this day."

"Meme, are you kidding?" he asks. "You have always been my wife."

After getting some lunch, Kalin and I go our separate ways to get dressed for our ceremony. Even though I know that he is excited about becoming my husband, I know that deep down inside, he aches for Phillip and Kayla's family. Amazingly so, I am not jealous at all. I know that Kalin has loved this woman at some point and I can't take that away from him. Now is not the time to be a jealous girlfriend. I am very confident in my relationship with Kalin and was never threatened by Kayla. I know that this man loves me and I know that because I love him, and I will stand by him through anything.

Kalin spends the first part of the day doing my hair making sure that I will be the beautiful bride that he imagines for me to be. Even though this is not the vision I had for my wedding day, this is the day that I will become Mrs. Melissa Thomas and that is all that matters!

On the way to the courthouse, Kalin and I don't say a word to each other. I am looking out the windows as if this is my first trip downtown. It is almost as if I am noticing things that I have never seen before today. My mind starts to wonder. *Am I ready for this? Does he love me or does he just miss her? Why was I sick this morning? Was that a sign that I should not marry Kalin or what? What is he thinking? Is he thinking that we should just turn this car around and go home? Am I ready to give up the I for us? How prepared am I really to be his wife?*

We are rushing and very careful not to offend one another so we just don't talk at all. When we finally make it to the courthouse, we can't find a parking spot anywhere! We follow the elevator up to the fourth floor and sign in. *Who would have thought it would be this impersonal?*

I am wearing a dress that shows off my figure. It is a black dress with lots of bright pretty colors. It is Kalin's favorite dress. He says that the colors really show off the highlights in my face. He loves the shape of my legs and says that I am actually very sexy to him. Kalin wears a nice pair of trousers with a tie. He is dashingly handsome, to say the least. I often peek over at him while we are waiting to be called. He will often look up and catch me looking at him. We look like a couple of teenagers who are just so in love. It is such a shame that our families aren't here to witness the ceremony.

"Melissa Williams, Kalin Thomas", the receptionist calls, looking over her glasses. Kalin and I walk over to the "Wedding Ceremony" line. We end up behind this younger guy and his much older bride. I start thinking about the challenges that they will, no doubt, be exposed to during their marriage. They look so happy, though. He looks into her eyes like she is the only woman around.

When it is our turn, the presiding official asks if we agree to meet the terms of marriage. We both agree and they say, "you are now married."

"Is that it?" I am very surprised that the ceremony is over so quickly.

"Yes ma'am, that is all there is to it. What do you think you get for $150?" she asks.

"I would have loved to have heard a song, at least."

"A song? Please! Next!"

From the time we are called until the end, the ceremony altogether lasts 20 minutes. I walk away from the courthouse, attached to Kalin Thomas for eternity. We can't keep our hands off one another. There is no turning back now. He is my husband and I am his wife and I will never allow anyone to come between this marriage. I will always choose him first.

While most people gather with friends and family and watch them eat piles and piles of food that they spend the rest of their lives paying for, Kalin and I share our reception over a value meal at McDonald's. Everyone in McDonald's is now aware that we are newly married. They break out in a cheer for us, congratulating us as we eat our food. We are having our very own little reception at McDonald's with a bunch of strangers. This is certainly not what I planned for my wedding reception but it is the man that I care the most about anyway.

We finally leave McDonald's and decide to stop by the funeral home to view Kayla's body. I am not prepared for what I am about to see. Her body is still bloated. She does not look anything like the woman I remembered. *I start thinking to myself that they did a terrible job on her. She doesn't even look like herself. What is Kalin thinking, I wondered. How is he feeling? We just shared a beautiful moment, is it overshadowed with this wake or what?*

As we walk outside to leave, Kalin grabs my hand, looks into my eyes, and says, "Mrs. Thomas, I want to spend the rest of my life with you. I know that we will go through things, but it doesn't matter because not only are you my wife, but you are also my best friend."

"Thanks, baby. I am honored to be your wife."

Ms. Rita has taken the children away for the evening so we can spend our wedding night in our bed. Candles are lit all around our bedroom. The soft music is playing. Kalin takes me into his arms and pleasures me in a way that makes me totally surrender to him. We continue to pleasure each other throughout the evening. We decide to leave everything behind us. I still can't get the thought of Wendy nor Kayla out of my mind. *Somehow, I feel that there is still something else that he isn't telling me about Wendy, but this is certainly not the time to discuss it.*

CHAPTER 28

"Keep Your Nose Clean!"

*T*he phone rings and the caller ID reads "Roth Office". "May I please speak with Mrs. Williams?" the person on the other end asks. It sounds like the receptionist. She did say that she would call in a few days.

"This is she."

"Mrs. Williams, this is Patty from Dr. Roth's office with the results of your evaluation. It is ready for you to pick it up. The fee is $50. Will you be coming in today?"

"No, Patty. I will not be able to come in today to get that, but I will let you know when I will be in."

"Ok, not a problem. Have a fantastic day!" she says.

"You do the same."

I can't believe this! I am not paying $50 for something that I don't think that I need. If the Judge wants the results, then she will have to pay for it. I decide to give a call to the one person I trust with CCF to see if she can work her magic and get me the results. I am sure they will tell her. She is the one assigned to my case.

I dial the number, hoping that she will pick up the phone.

"May I please speak with Leigh Bynum?"

"She is no longer with us. Is there anyone else who can help you?"

"What happened to Leigh? She is the person assigned to my case."

"What is your name and I will give you the name of your new caseworker?"

"My name was Melissa Williams, but is now Melissa Thomas."

"Hold on and let me check it out for you. May I place you on hold?"

"Sure."

What happened to Leigh? Did she finally break one of the "Department's" rules? Should I ask this person on the phone why they re-assigned my case? What if I do? It is not like they are going to tell me the truth anyway!

"Ms. Williams, your case is re-assigned to Daniel Todd. He will contact you later today. What is your new phone number?"

"My new number is 555-0185."

I wonder if I should still try to reach Leigh and see what happened. Leigh gave me her cell phone number back when she was the one visiting me. I am curious to see what happened to her. I don't really care to try to reach Bob. I put her number in my stack of information associated with CCF. I hope that it is still there. I found it!

"Leigh, is that you?"

"Yes, who is this?" she responds.

"I don't know if you remember me or not but this is Melissa Williams. I am actually Thomas, now, though. You came by my hou—"

"Yes, I remember you", she interrupts. "I remember you Melissa! How can I forget? How are you?"

"I'm fine. I tried reaching your office but they said that you no longer work there. What happened?"

"That is correct. They fired me. I haven't been on your case for a couple of months now. Can we meet for coffee or something so we can talk?" she asks.

"Sure. What about right now? I am not doing anything."

I know that I have to get to work but I am very curious about what she wants to tell me.

"Ok, I am not either. Let's meet at Starbuck's on the corner of 17th and Dolphin Parkway."

"Sure, I will see you in about 30 minutes or so."

What in the world does she want to see me for? Is she going to tell me why she lost her job? Can I trust her at this point? Should I tell anyone where I am going? Is she trying to set me up or something?

Kalin is not so sure that I should meet with her. He tells me that I shouldn't trust her. Although I know that he is right, I need some information right now and I just have to take a chance. He wants to follow me to Starbuck's, but I convince him that it is not a good idea for him to go. He finally agrees with me and sends me on my way.

I arrive at Starbuck's right on schedule. The place is packed with the morning people who are on their way to work. I have already called my job to let them know that I will be a little late getting to work. I have to because I am very curious as to what she wants to speak to me about. Leigh is already there and waiting at a table for me. She looks very sad.

"Good morning Leigh. How are you?"

"I am fine. I just want to see you in person to talk to you and explain exactly what happened. I know that you told me you called the office looking for me, but I was also called by the person you spoke to. She is a friend of mine."

"Oh, I see. So, what happened?"

"Can you believe this? They conspired against me to get me fired. They didn't want me there because I was beginning to figure out what they were doing. I was noticing how they were starting to remove children from their homes for no reason. I was starting to see how they were putting children in foster care that should have been home with their families. One thing about them is this. They do not like people who fight them back. They will take your children away from you just because they *can*. And there is no need to try to fight them because they will always win. The Judge will always side with CCF", she explains.

"And let me guess, you found out something and questioned them on it, right?"

"You got it! Remember when I visited you the first time and I told you how I felt that you were doing a great job with your family? I didn't see anything wrong with how you cared for your children. Hell, they were all neat, your home was clean and I just didn't see what the problem was. Well, I went to my supervisor and told him what I witnessed and he basically told me that they didn't care about that. She told me that Ms. Madeline Serchay called the shots and she wanted your kids out of your house. She is the one behind this whole thing because she doesn't like you", she explains. "When she came to speak with you one day, she was hoping that you would turn against Kalin. She thought that by removing your kids, it would make you do *anything* to get them back. But you didn't!"

"And why are you telling me all of this?"

"Because I like you and I think that what they are doing is wrong", she responds.

"Is it *really* because they fired you?"

"Hell yes, it is because they fired me. Someone needs to complain about them and put some fire behind them. They are so wrong, Melissa. They don't care about those children. It is all about money", she says.

"How so?"

"When they take a child out of the household and places it in foster care, there is money exchanged. The State makes money for this. They don't even have to have a good enough reason and nobody is going to stop them. They will even get people to lie on you if that is what it takes. But if they don't like you, you are toast! I am trying to help you and to warn you to 'watch your back'!"

"So what should I do now?"

"Do nothing right now but what they tell you. Keep your nose clean. Don't let them catch you slipping. If they tell you to jump, ask how high. I am not saying not to fight for your rights. I am just advising you to keep your nose clean", she instructs.

"I have a question for you, but you may not know the answer."

"Try me."

"Remember the psychological evaluation that I took 2 or 3 weeks ago?"

"Yes, I do remember that. Bob put it in the file. You met with a Dr. Roth", she answers.

"I need to know the results of that evaluation. His secretary called me and told me that it was ready, but that I have to pay $50 for it. I don't have any money for that. Hell, they were the ones who thought I needed it. Why should I have to pay for it?"

"I agree. I saw the evaluation. Don't pay for it. I couldn't get a copy of it but I can tell you what it says. Give me a moment", she says. She picks up her cell phone and calls someone. She is writing down some information and at this point, I am assuming that it is from the evaluation. She finally hangs up the phone.

"It is always good to have people on the inside that can help you. I just spoke to my friend over there and she looked it up for me. I thought I remembered what it said, but I wanted to make sure before I told you."

"OK, so tell me, what did it say?" I ask in anticipation of hearing what the good doctor has to say about me.

"The report is completed, but in a "borderline" status", she says, in a matter of fact kind of way.

"What the hell does that mean?"

"It means that he can't say that you have issues but he can't say that you don't", she explains. "The report does say that your expectations of your children are not realistic and that you want them to do better than perhaps they are capable of doing."

I can't believe what I am hearing. "My expectation of my children is not realistic". I want my children to be the best that they can be. I don't want them to grow up thinking that they can't achieve all that they want. It doesn't matter where they grew up or how they lived. I want my children to live in a clean

home. I don't want them to steal. I want them to grow up to be good citizens.
Is there anything wrong with that?

"Wow!"

"Melissa, how much did you tell Bob about your past?" she asks.

"A lot."

"Yeah, I saw in his report that you tried to kill yourself when you were younger. He knows about how promiscuous you were. He put in his report that you often spoke on and on without stopping and how you changed the subject quite a bit. The evaluation was all about what he thought of you as well as Dr. Roth. Honey, you can't always be so open about everything."

"So, I was being honest with the guy and he used it against me?"

"I would say so, Melissa. Listen, I have to go now. It is a pleasure seeing you again. I wish you the best of luck with CCF. You are going to need it! They are not fair. Just remember that! They are not always thinking about you. Just be careful and keep your nose clean", she instructs, as she is getting up from the table. "Melissa, trust no one!"

Leigh gets up, walks from the table and into the parking lot. I am still sitting down trying to gather my thoughts and my next plan of action. She just gave me some valuable information but what I am going to do with it? Who will believe me? I will do one thing and that is to keep my nose clean and continue to do as they tell me to do. The time will come when I will have to use this information. I need to get to work so I finish my coffee and bagel and head to the parking lot. Hopefully, I will be able to keep my focus at work today. I am proud of where we are so far this month. The vacancies are down, the rent is collected, and the property looks amazing!

Now that Leigh is no longer on our case, we finally get to meet the new caseworker. He is scheduled to come to the house for a visit. Now that Kalin is out of jail, CCF is making regular visits to the home to make sure that Kalin is not living inside the house with the children and to make sure that there are no *further* incidents of abuse.

The new caseworker has arrived and is right on schedule. Standing on the other side of the door is a man who appears to be in his late 50's, wearing dark rimmed glasses, with knit pants on, who looks very unfriendly.

"Good morning, Mr. Todd, please come in."

"Good morning, Ms. Williams. Thanks!", he says, as he walks in and begins to take a look around. "I am sure that you are aware that I am your new social worker and I look forward to working with you and the children so that we can finally bring your family back together", he explains.

"Now that is the best news I have heard in a long time."

"So, you just recently moved, right?"

"Yes sir, we did. I didn't like living on the property anymore. It was beginning to be too much of a hassle. I want my kids to have a backyard and be at peace. The big promotion and bonus helped out a little too."

"I agree. The place looks nice. Do you mind if I take a look around?" he asks.

"Sure. Be my guest." Mr. Todd walks every inch of the house checking out the bedrooms, the kitchen and the backyard. He even takes a peek inside the kitchen cabinets to make sure that we have an adequate amount of food for the children.

"You have a lovely home, Ms. Williams", he compliments. "Now let's talk about other things. Is Kalin residing in the home?"

"No, sir. He isn't residing in the home. He is not allowed to live inside just yet. He sleeps out in the car at night."

"He lives on the premises but outside in the car?"

"Yes. He lives outside in the car."

"OK, is he having any contact with the children at all?"

"No sir. He is not having any contact with the children. He is not allowed to and he is very careful about this. He would like to and I think that it would be healthy for the children if we can work out a visit for him."

"I agree. Are there any adults who will offer their time to supervise Mr. Thomas as he visits his children?" he asks.

"Ms. Rita lives here with us. She is my live in babysitter and she takes care of the children when I am away at work. She can be one of the people who can supervise", I suggest.

"Ok, who else?"

"My father in law can do it also."

"Are they both willing to show up in court so that the Judge can see who they are so that she can make a ruling on it?" he asks.

"Of course."

"Ok, what are their names and dates of birth?"

"My father in law is James Thomas and his date of birth is March 15, 1943. The babysitter's name is Rita Gardner and her date of birth is July 17th, 1940."

"Wonderful! I will run their names through our databases and if there is a problem with these people who you have given me, I will let you know. Otherwise, we will just go with these."

"Sounds like a plan! So, if the Judge agrees, Kalin will be able to visit with the children?"

"Sure, I don't see why not", he answers. *These guys are not as bad as what Leigh told me. Could she be wrong about them? Should I dismiss what she said. Perhaps I should just hold on to it. As for today, they are being nice.*

After several court hearings, the Judge finally decides to assign Rita and my father in law, James, as being the responsible adults who will supervise visits with Kalin and the children. As long as either of them is around, Kalin is allowed to be around the kids. When the children come home from school, Kalin will be right here waiting to see them, while Ms. Rita prepares dinner.

Daniel still comes around to check on things. We have already made several court appearances. The Judge finally agrees that Kalin can move back into the house. The kids are so happy that daddy is finally going to move back into the home and come out of the car. I am very happy too. It is not easy trying to make love in the backseat all the time. It is only fun after so many times.

Since this nightmare began, it feels like something is going right for once! This is progress for us. Everything is finally starting to go as planned and it feels like we are getting our life back on track. Kalin and I are following through with the case plan. We are taking parenting classes and have successfully completed several hours of community service together. These requirements are part of Kalin's probation but I decide to take the classes and do the community service with my husband.

CHAPTER 29

"What A Pitiful Sight!"

Today is one of those days when you want to stay inside and watch Life Time TV. It has been raining all day. The kids are so hyper and happy because Kalin is home with them. Ms. Rita is also home with them. She fixes their favorite meals for breakfast and lunch. We must not be as organized as I think we are because we all forget that Ms. Rita has a doctor's appointment and she has to leave the house, which means that she will have to leave Kalin alone with the kids unless we are able to get JT to come over. Hopefully, he is not busy. Kalin gives him a call.

"Hello Dad. How are you?"

"I'm good. Is everything okay?" TJ asks.

"I really need a big favor. Are you busy right now?" Kalin asks.

"Tell me what you need."

"I am here at the house with the children and Ms. Rita has to leave. Without you or her here with me, I can't be here with the children", Kalin explains.

"I will be there in about 15 minutes or so. I don't want to see you get in trouble for being there like that and you are not supposed to be."

JT heads over to the house and arrives right before Ms. Rita's taxi makes it to the house.

In the meantime, I am at work and getting ready to leave when my car stalls. I don't know if it's the battery or what it is. I need to call the house to see if Kalin can instruct me on what to do.

"Hello", said one of the kids. It sounds like Christy.

"Hello sweetheart. It is Mommy; how are you?"

"Yeah, mommy, it's mommy!" she yells. "We are having fun with daddy. He is playing games with us!"

"Ah, that is wonderful. May I speak with daddy?"

"OK", she says.

"Yes, dear", Kalin says.

"Honey, is JT there? I was hoping that he could pick me up because the car is stalling and won't start."

"Yes, he is here, but Ms. Rita had to leave because she had an appointment that she couldn't reschedule", he explains.

"Oh, I see. If he leaves, that puts you home with the children without supervision."

"That is correct. We can't take any chances."

"It won't take long. He will be right back. Let me speak with JT."

"OK, if you think so."

"Hey, JT!"

"Hey Meme, how are you? What's up?"

"I went outside to get into the car and it won't start. It acts like it wants to crank up but it won't. The rain is coming down hard and it is starting to thunder outside. Do you think that you could come and pick me up?"

"I don't mind but that will leave Kalin here with the children by themselves", he responds.

"It will be just for a minute. We will be back in no time."

"Ok, if you want me to. I will be right there."

Unbeknownst to us, Daniel is on his way to the house to pay a surprise visit. As soon as my father in law pulls away from the house, the child protective investigator pulls into the driveway. He knocks on the door and finds that Kalin is home with the children without supervision. He becomes very concerned because we have not broken any of the rules thus far. He decides to come inside and wait for me and my father in law to return.

JT and I decide to stop by McDonald's to get dinner for the children. But, when we pull into the driveway, I notice that there is a car already parked in our driveway. The car has yellow tags, so this is my clue that this must be an agency's car. I have to walk in here and explain to this man why Kalin is home without supervision. I know that we are in trouble but I have to face the music and hope that he will understand.

"Mommy! Mommy is home and she has McDonald's!"

I can see far into the family room that Kalin is sitting with Daniel and it looks like they are in a deep conversation. Daniel looks up and sees me handing the kids their individual Happy Meals. He walks towards me.

"Mr. Todd, I know what you must be thinking but it was only for a few minutes that my father in law left the house and it was only to pick me up from work", I explain. "I went outside to start my car and it wouldn't."

"Don't worry about it. I won't say anything, but just please try not to do this again", he says. "Besides, I was having a good conversation with Mr. Thomas."

****

A couple of weeks later, we are at our regularly scheduled appointment in children's court. As always, it is still the most humiliating experience. When you walk into the sitting area where everyone is waiting for their case to be called, you sit there looking around at everyone else wondering what landed them on this fourth floor. You look around and see attorneys sitting with their clients, of whom many of them just met that day. Then, they walk into the courtroom as if they have this good working relationship with the client who was assigned to them just because they can't afford a private attorney.

I am sitting here watching this young mother who is sitting next to me in her short skirt, dressed like she is getting ready to go to the club. She looks scared. I don't know if I should say something to her or not. I am sure that she can use some encouraging words. Just as I am about to speak to her, she gets up because her name was just called and she follows the bailiff down the hallway.

This is such a negative experience. It is so easy to second guess yourself in this type of situation. You have to know and believe in who you are to survive this type of humiliating experience. I can see the bailiff escorting in some young boys, who just came in from the Juvenile Detention Center. They are all shackled together. What a pitiful sight! And then, there is me. I walk around here in my nice business suit, which means nothing in this place. I am still being investigated by CCF, just like they are. *Is this real? Is this how I am supposed to be spending my life? This is certainly not how I pictured my life.*

All of the other players in the game finally arrive and we are called into the courtroom. The Judge, dressed in her black robe, enters into the courtroom and takes her seat. She addresses all the players and everyone identifies himself and offers their title or position in the matter. She begins by asking if there is any new information on the case. I am relieved that Daniel did not expose our little secret about what happened the other day.

Right before the Hearing is over, Daniel Todd speaks up.

"Judge, there is some new information that I must share with the court", he begins. I start feeling myself tense up as he begins to talk. He can't even look over at me as he is speaking.

"Yes, Mr. Todd", she responds.

"I would just like to make the court aware that on my last visit to the home, Mr. Thomas was found at home with the children without either of the adult supervisors that were appointed by the court", he says.

I can't believe he did this to us. He said that he would not mention this to the Judge and that it would just be between all of us. He just told us not to do it again. What a snake!

"Ms.Williams, is this true?" the Judge asks.

"It is now Mrs. Thomas, but yes, your Honor, it is true and I am extremely sorry. It was only for a brief moment. My father in law was there, along with Ms. Rita, but Ms. Rita had to go to an appointment. I called the house to have my father in law pick me up because I went out to start my car and it didn't. It was storming outside and I asked my father in law to come and get me. We returned home as soon as possible. Before coming home, I stopped by McDonald's to get the children something to eat", I explain.

"Mr. Todd, how were the children when you made the visit and found them home with Mr. Thomas alone?" the Judge asks, not even looking up from looking in the folder in front of her.

"The children were fine. They were happy and didn't seem like they had any problems being alone with Mr. Thomas. When the mother arrived with the father in law, the children ran to her and were very happy", he answers.

"So, congratulations are in order on your marriage. Congratulations! Don't do it again, Mr. And Mrs. Thomas", the Judge orders.

"Yes ma'am", Kalin and I both say in unison.

I hate to admit it but I am having some very unkind thoughts. *How could this man lie to me? Why did he say he wouldn't say anything and then come to court and do the opposite? Honestly, what did I expect? Did I think that he really cared for us or what? Another lesson learned!*

The Judge decides that the children are progressing as they should with Kalin back in the home. She is pleased with the progress of the Case Plan that was adopted and equally as impressed with the fact that we both took the parenting class. It is now time to address the results of the Psychological Evaluation that the court ordered for me to take. She turns her attention to CCF's attorney, David Mitchell, who seems to be very articulate and thorough.

"Mr. Mitchell, what is the status on the Psychological Evaluation that Mrs. Thomas was ordered to have with Dr. Roth?" she questions.

"His secretary faxed it over to me just yesterday, so I haven't really had a chance to look it over", he answers. Our attorney, Maggie Peters, speaks up.

"Your Honor, it is not the Court's fault that Mr. Mitchell did not review this evaluation. The Court should know that Dr. Roth does not feel that the children are in danger of being with their mother", he interjects.

"I would really like to review it for myself", Mr. Mitchell says.

"Listen, Your Honor, this family has done everything asked of them. I would like to suggest that we put it on the books to meet in 3 months and at that time, we can begin the "reunification" for this family", he explains.

"Aren't the children already home?" she asks.

"Yes, they are, but the reunification will mean that we are completely gone out of this family's life, giving them the opportunity to have a normal life and enjoy their kids", Maggie explains.

"So be it. We will meet again on August 18th to see about closing out this case. Dismissed."

CHAPTER 30

"Hurt My Baby and It's Over!"

*I*t is beautiful outside and Kalin and I decide to take the children to the park. I am not really feeling well, but decide that it is wise to spend as much quality family time as possible. As we are walking out the door, the phone rings. *Who in the world can this be? I wonder.* Kalin walks over and picks up the phone and it is Stuart. Stuart worked for me at one time as a maintenance technician. He missed too many days from work, which ultimately led to his termination as one of my employees. He was too busy paying for sex with women and selling drugs.

"Hello", Kalin says.

"Hey man, this is Stuart. Did I catch ya'll at a bad time? I can call back if you want", he says.

"Of course not! Don't worry about that. How are you doing?"

"I need help man. I really do. When I try to do right, it always haunts me. Do you all have room for me in your home?" he asks. "I am sorry to be so blunt, but I need help, man."

"Listen, brother, you need our help and it is done", Kalin offers.

"I just need to lay my head at your crib for about 2 months or so", he suggests.

"Stuart, this is what friends are for. We love you and believe in you and want to see you beat this thing and anything that we can do, we will do."

Besides, the children will leave for North Carolina next week once school lets out and will be gone for the entire summer. I hope that we will be able to help Stuart kick his drug habits. He is such a nice guy. He really wants to do better.

With court taking me away from work so much and Kalin not landing too many interior design assignments, our finances are starting to slip away from us. I don't know how much money we have left in our savings, but

I am sure that it isn't enough to live off for too long. I don't want to have to get another loan to get us by. Kalin and I will have to put our heads together to figure it out, especially now that we are taking someone into our home.

The kids are finally off to North Carolina with Kalin's mother. She is on the phone with Kalin now telling him how happy she is going to be when they make it in. It sounds like she has so much planned for them.

Stuart moves in and appears to be pretty comfortable. He looks like he is truly having a rough time. He needs a good haircut and a shave and I am sure that by the time Kalin is done with him, he will look like a million bucks. He smells like he hasn't bathed in a few weeks. He reeks of alcohol. Kalin and I love him, though. It doesn't matter what he is doing, has done, or will do. We love him and will be there for him.

"Hey guys, I just want to thank you both for letting me stay here with you for the summer. This is exactly what I need right now. When my wife died, Kalin, I just didn't know what to do and I ended up turning to drugs. You just never know what you will do when that time comes when it feels like all hell has broken out in your life", he begins to say.

"Stuart, say no more about that. This is how love goes, brother! You are our brother and we love you. I don't ever want to think about living without Melissa, so I can only imagine the hurt that you feel for your sweetheart", Kalin responds.

"I tell you what. People are always complaining about this and about that, but never stop to see God's best that is right there in front of them. Don't take anything for granted. Tomorrow is promised to no one. I never thought that the love of my life would ever leave me. When she died, I felt so empty inside. I just couldn't go on. I just wanted the pain to go away and drugs would do that for me. Deep down inside, I know that it isn't right for me to do them, but I just need to figure this thing out", he explains.

"So, what is your plan for shaking the habit? Are you planning to get into a drug rehabilitation program or something? I have a friend who can get you in. What do you think? Are you ready?"

"Yeah, can we do that tomorrow? I would love to meet him and get it started. I need to do this and I need to do it now!"

"Well alright then. It is on. I will give Harry a call tomorrow and see about getting you started. We will pay for everything", Kalin adds.

Is my husband living in the same household that I am living in? He knows that we can't afford to take on anything at this time. Maybe he knows something that I don't know.

"Hey man, are you hungry?"

"Heck yeah", he responds.

"Let's go get some barbeque over to Big Al's. It's the best in town", Kalin suggests.

"Do you mind, Melissa? Kalin asks.

"Of course not. Please go and enjoy yourself! Show Stuart around our neighborhood. I am going to take a hot shower and go to bed. Just drive carefully!"

****

I am awakened by a loud noise only to find out that it is actually coming from the television. Now that I am up, I decide to get out of bed and walk downstairs to see if Kalin and Stuart have made it back in. I must have overslept because they have returned and have gone again. He has left a note on the refrigerator and it reads,

> *"Honey, Stuart and I have already eaten breakfast. You were sleeping so peacefully and I just didn't want to wake you up. We are meeting with Harry today to see about getting Stuart into the rehab program. I will see you when we get back. Love, K."*

It looks like I have a little time to myself today, which is just fine with me. Besides, I need to call Mom and make sure that the kids have made it safely to North Carolina. She picks up on the first ring, which means that she probably has caller ID.

"Hello", she answers. I can hear the kids in the background.

"Hey Mom. How are you? Are those the kids that I hear in the background?"

"It sure is. They got me up first thing this morning to let me know that they want some pancakes grandma style", she answers.

"That's great!"

"Did you need to speak with them?" she asks.

"Yes, please. I will be brief."

"Hello Mommy", says Christy.

"Hey honey! How are my precious babies? I know that you all are happy to be there with Grandma. I hear that she is getting ready to make you some pancakes "grandma style". I don't want much. I am just checking to make sure that you all made it there okay and to tell you all that I love you and already miss you."

"Ah Mommy, we love you and miss you too" she says, sounding like she is ready to jump into her summer full speed ahead. "Ok, let me speak back with your grandmother?"

"Ok, I am back", she says.

"OK, Mom, I love you and thanks for taking the kids this summer. If you need anything, please give us a call, ok."

"You bet sweetie. And tell that son of mine that I love him too. Is he in?"

"No, Mom. He is out with one of our friends. He won't be back until much later, but I will give him the message."

"OK, I will talk with you later, honey."

"Yes ma'am. Goodbye."

It looks like I have the whole day ahead of me. Without Kalin around, this is a good time to take my pregnancy test. I might as well find out the truth and deal with it. It's Saturday and this is my jeans day, so I grab my Dolphins' hat and off to Walgreen's I go. For some reason, I am not excited at all about finding out these results and it shows in my stride. I walk sluggishly to the isle where there are rows and rows of pregnancy tests and grab the one that will give me the quickest results. By the time I make it to the cashier, I see someone that I know in the corner of my eye. *It's Mr. Daniel Todd, our CCF caseworker. What in the world is he doing in here?* I don't want him to see me because this may be a little awkward for the both of us. Who knows? Maybe he has another client on this side that he has to see. *But, why does he look so upset?* It is not my business and I won't interfere because he it can be almost anything!

"That will be $22.68", the clerks says. I am trying my best not to be noticed by Mr. Todd. I hand the clerk the money and head for the door to make it to my car without being noticed.

On the way home, the thought of what I am about to do runs through my mind. I don't know how I am going to feel when I get these results. *Will I be happy if I am pregnant? Will I be sad when I get these results?* I don't think that I want to be pregnant at this time. We already have five kids and I just don't think that my body can take anymore. *Why in the world was Mr. Todd on our side of town in Walgreen's looking upset? And who was that woman with him?*

I am pulling into my driveway and in no time, I will have the results of this pregnancy test. I carefully follow the steps outlined in the instructions.

The mixed emotions that I am starting to have is getting the best of me. It will be another 20 minutes for the results, so I might as well walk downstairs and get something to drink. There is a note on my refrigerator. I wonder what Kalin has left behind now. But, this time, the note is from Rita. She stopped by. Ms. Rita's note reads:

"Mrs. Thomas, Kalin called and said that you haven't been feeling too well lately so I figured I would stop by and get something good for you that will help settle your stomach a little. The lemonade is in the refrigerator. Enjoy!

Love, Ms. Rita."

Because of her, I am getting ready to eat a Crisper's salad, with some lemonade from Chic-Fil-A and a piece of cornbread from Boston Market. What a pleasant surprise! I am so blessed to have Ms. Rita. She is still doing for me even though the kids aren't here. She doesn't have to do this but I am so glad that she did. My results should be done by now, but I am no longer in a hurry to see them. So, I will just sit here and enjoy my lunch and when I am done, that is when I will go upstairs to get the results. Before I finish, Kalin and Stuart return.

"Hey guys, how are you? How did it go with Harry?" I ask, as Kalin puts the keys on the counter and Stuart sits at the dining table.

"It was quite successful. Harry got him in and he will begin his rehab this Saturday. I have to drop him off. They just have to get his bed approved and everything", Kalin explains.

"That is great news Stuart! How do you feel about that?"

"I am so excited. I know that Heather would be so proud of me if she were here. Today is the anniversary of her death", he says, sounding happy but disappointed.

"So, let's have dinner tonight in her honor. I might as well tell you now", I say, standing up to face Kalin.

"What is it?"

"I am not sure if we will have another reason to celebrate or not."

"What are you saying, sweetheart?" he asks.

"Right up those stairs is a pregnancy test that I just took that has the results. I don't know what the results are, but we can find out together."

"OK, let's go". Kalin and I rush up the stairs with Stuart right behind us. We make it to the bedroom and Kalin decides to go into the bathroom first. Before I have a chance to look at the stick, he is already screaming that he is going to be a father!

"Congratulations, man! Stuart says, giving a nice man hug to Kalin.

Kalin walks over to me and gives me the biggest kiss right there in our bedroom with Stuart watching. "You have made me the happiest man alive today, Mrs. Thomas. I am so happy that we are having another baby", he exclaims.

I have to admit that I am faking everything from this moment on. I just decided that I am not happy about being pregnant. I am tired. I just can't do this anymore.

"That is great honey!"

It looks like we are celebrating in remembrance of Heather, Stuart's wife, and my pregnancy, except I don't share the enthusiasm with Kalin. Being that Ms. Rita is a mother figure in my life at the time, I decide to give her a call and talk to her about what I am feeling.

"Ms. Rita, thanks for the lunch. I thoroughly enjoyed it. Do you have a moment?"

"Of course. Is everything okay?" she asks, sounding very concerned.

"I just found out that I am pregnant again and I am so unhappy about it. I don't want to have another baby", I admit.

"Well what does your husband say about this?" she asks.

"My husband is thrilled about it but my husband is not the one who has to carry this baby", I respond. "I just don't think I can do it again."

"Ms. Melissa, you have to honor your husband on this one. You have to just get used to the idea that you are going to have another baby and that is just it", she says.

Is this dejavu or what? I don't want to hear this. I want her to tell me to go against my husband and do what I want to do because it is my body. I should feel ashamed of myself for not wanting to have a baby that was conceived in love with my husband. I know that I should be happy, but I'm not!

Because I don't share in his enthusiasm, I soon become very depressed and oftentimes back myself into a corner almost daily. As much as I have always enjoyed having sex with Kalin, I now find excuses not to have sex. The last thing I want to talk about is God's goodness. If I hear that again, I am going to scream! I am just angry because I just don't think that I have the strength to have this baby and maintain my sanity.

With this new thing now, Ms. Rita and I talk almost every day. When she sees that I am never going to agree with accepting this baby, she informs me that she knows where I can get a pill that will make me cramp and the baby will pass through the toilet. Are you serious? I didn't even know that they made stuff like this. I am excited that I can simply take a pill and this can all be over.

The following day, she and I decide to go to the pharmacy to pick up the pill, but they are out of them. They don't have any in stock and not really sure when they will get some in. So, as a substitute, Ms. Rita learns that I can take this liquid medication and it will do the same thing. She pays for the product, gives it to me, and I take down the entire amount. I do it without even thinking once about what my actions would do to my husband. He is excited about this baby and I am about to crush that dream of his.

"Ms. Melissa, are you sure about this?" asks Ms. Rita.

"Yeah, I am ok. I am just a little hungry. Other than that, I am doing okay."

"Ok. I am just trying to help you. I can't say that I agree, but I care about you", she says.

After taking down my Whopper at Burger King, I start feeling even more nauseous than I normally do. I don't know why. I thought this stuff was supposed to make me cramp and then bleed. I am just sick to my stomach right now. We give it up for the day and I take Ms. Rita home and head home to my husband and Stuart. I hope that they have already gotten something to eat because I *do not* feel like cooking.

I walk into the house after a long day and my husband, with his gorgeous smile, greets me at the door with a wrapped gift. I can see the candles burning as I get closer inside the house.

"Well, hello, Mrs. Thomas", he says. He reaches for me and pulls me in closely and gives me a very passionate kiss. He puts his hands in mine and leads me to the family room that he has already set up with the massage table in the middle of the floor. There are flowers and candles everywhere. The jazz music is on and my husband is looking quite tasty with his linen shorts on. He is not wearing a shirt, which leaves his sexy chest exposed. "I know that you have not been feeling too well lately and I thought that you could use a nice massage. I love you baby and ----"

Before he can continue, I ask him, "Where is Stuart?"

"He is out sweetheart. I told him that I wanted to spend some alone time with you and he said he'd hang out at Keith's to give us some privacy for the evening", he answers.

My husband and I share a very special evening together. He gives the world's best massages. Kalin starts with my toes, one by one, and makes sure to touch and massage every inch of my body, all the way up to the top of my head. By the time he is finished, I am so relaxed. He gets up to fix us some grape juice. He gathers me in his arms and takes me to our bedroom and makes passionate love to me, over and over again. We take our time taking care of each other. I am exhausted! I eventually fall asleep in my husband's arms and nothing else matters at this moment. Nothing!

****

The following morning.

My husband asks me what my plans are for today and I lie to him. He thinks that I am going to the Mall to do some early school shopping. The truth is that I plan to pick up Ms. Rita so that we can go back to the pharmacy to see if they have any other suggestions for me to abort this baby. *I can't believe that last night wasn't enough for me to let this thing go about trying to abort our child! I just can't though, I just can't.*

When we walk into the pharmacy, the guy behind the counter looks at us as if we have good news to tell him, but instead, we need to know if he has any other suggestions for aborting the baby because nothing that he told us to do is working.

"Hey ladies, I don't know why any of the stuff that I told you to do didn't work. This stuff has worked before", he says, surprised that the potions aren't working.

"I don't either", Ms. Rita responds.

"I have one last thing to suggest to you and if this doesn't work, I don't know what else to tell you", he says. "Get some turpentine and sugar together and drink that. This will definitely cause you to abort the baby."

"OK, I will try that and see what happens." *Where in the world am I going to get some turpentine? I wonder if Kalin has some out in the garage. I won't know what it looks like but I can't really ask him for it, but at the same time, I don't want to take the wrong stuff either. I want it to work this time. I am going to ask him for it and then just lie to him about what I need it for. He won't know the difference.*

When we make it back to the house, Kalin and Stuart are hanging out in the garage, painting the dresser for me. "Kalin, honey, do we have any turpentine out here?"

"Sweetheart, what do you need turpentine for?" he asks. My silence tells him exactly why I need the turpentine. Before I can say another word, Kalin's eyes fill with tears.

Stuart and Rita can tell that we are about to get into a serious conversation, so they both decide to go into the house. Rita announces that she will begin dinner. I have to tell him the truth. I might as well confess to Kalin what I have been doing since I found out I was pregnant. Once I am done telling him everything, he becomes so upset and crying. Kalin turns his eyes away from me.

"Meme, how could you do this to our child?" he asks. "Don't you love me and love the baby that we made together?"

"Kalin, this has nothing to do with that. You know that I love you. This is not about my love for you. I just can't do it anymore. I am so tired and I don't think that I can go through it again – the morning sickness, the doctor visits. For crying out loud, our savings are almost gone. I know that I got the promotion, but you have to figure that I won't work as much being pregnant. I will have to adjust my job, which means that my salary will be adjusted. You are not doing that much interior design work these days. I just can't do it again, honey. Please understand", I explain. *How can I hurt the man of my dreams? This is a man that I have shared my bed with in good times and in bad times. I love him so much and what is preventing me from loving our precious baby?*

"Mrs. Thomas, I love you more than any woman I have ever loved, but I promise you that if you hurt my baby, you and I are done", he says, with tears in his eyes. "How can you hurt my baby? I will never be able to forgive you for that."

Kalin, no doubt, shares the news with Stuart because Stuart starts sharing scriptures with me every time he sees me. It has become an "after dinner ritual" almost every night. There is a revival coming up at New Destiny Church and Stuart comes up with this great idea that we should go to the Revival. God knows that I don't want to go, but I will agree to it anyway. I have only been to the location in Orlando, but not the one here yet.

All day, I try to get out of going, but nothing works! We all get dressed and decide to leave the house in enough time to beat the traffic. We finally pull into the parking lot and the place is packed! This almost feels like all of Miami is here to hear what Dr. Zachary Tims has to say.

We take our seats and shortly afterwards, the choir starts to sing one of my favorite songs, "I Won't Complain". God's words are working on me right now. I look over at my husband and he has tears freely flowing down his face. Stuart is enjoying it as well. *Why can't I just get it? Why can't I understand that God doesn't make mistakes and this baby is a gift and not a curse?*

The service is finally over and Dr. Tims' sermon, *Give It To God,* is a success with the audience. I know that I have to learn how to give all my problems, all my misunderstandings, all my heartaches, all my grief, all my financial problems, and anything that I don't understand, all to God. I think I can get this. I need to go home and study over the scriptures that he has mentioned in his sermon.

The line to the parking lot is moving rather slowly, which gives lots of time for anyone to notice me. I look to my right and notice a sweet couple that was once my tenants at the apartment community. I am really hoping that I can get out of here without either of them recognizing me. But it's too late! The wife, Patricia, notices me and is heading my way.

"Ms. Melissa, is that you?" Patricia asks, as she approaches me. Her husband follows.

"Oh, hi there! How are you two? I didn't know that you all went to this church."

"Well, yes, and wasn't that sermon wonderful?" Patricia asks.

"Yes, it was fantastic. I can't wait to listen to the tape again." I wonder if she notices that I am looking for the closest exit out of here.

"Well, Ms. Melissa, are we pregnant? You didn't tell anyone. Congratulations to you and Kalin!" she says, as she reaches over to pat my stomach. *I just want to die because I am not thrilled about this at all. How can she say that? I want to punch her for being happy. Before I know it, the thoughts that I am having just seem to creep into our conversation.*

"I am not happy about it", I say, with almost a very angry tone.

"What do you mean you are not happy about it?" she asks, with a huge frown on her face. "Don't you know that that baby inside of you is a precious gift from God?" *I thought to myself that she had some nerve telling me what I should be happy about. How dare her chastise me like a child?*

"I'm not saying that it is not a gift but what I am saying is that we didn't plan this and it has come at the wrong time. I just don't know if I can do this", I respond.

"Ms. Melissa, you have been blessed with this baby inside of you and I would give anything for God to bless my womb with a child. You are very fortunate. You need to pick yourself up and accept this and be happy", she says in the same kind of voice as my mother back in 1987 when I was pregnant with my first born child.

On the ride back home, Stuart and Kalin both notice that I am very quiet, but they dare not say a word to me about the service. I can only imagine what they would say if I told them about my conversation that I had with Patricia and her husband. They would probably start telling me that God had something to do with it, so I will keep it to myself. But now that I think about it, is there any truth to what she was saying? *Should I just finally put an end to this madness and accept that I am carrying a precious baby that my husband and I created during passionate lovemaking?*

I get home and go straight to my bedroom. I am so ashamed of how I have handled this situation that I decide to lock myself into our bedroom and sit in total darkness. I am so angry at myself for what I put everyone through lately with my moody tones, my low performance in the bedroom with my husband, and my short-tempered attitude towards everything and everyone. This has to be the night that I put this to rest, send this problem to Hell and trust God.

> *Dear God, thank you for life, health, and strength. You are worthy to be praised. God, please forgive me for trying to kill my baby. Please bless this womb that carries my child. Give it health and wipe away anything that I may have caused to happen to my unborn child. Forgive me for what I have done. Show me how to be a better mother, wife, and friend. I need you, Lord. I can't do this without you. You have always been right here with me. You brought me through 5 other children and you can bring me through this as well. You are a good God and I trust you, no matter what comes my way. Just knowing you are here with me is really all I need, Lord. I give this child to you and I thank you for every single one of my children that you have given me. Thank you for my husband. Thank you for the friends who have come into my life with your Word. I thank you Lord. In Jesus' name. Amen.*

I feel whole again and completely free of stress and worry. In my closet tonight, I have found peace with God and feel strong enough to move on from this.

CHAPTER 31

"Liberty and 'JUSTICE' For All"

*M*y belly is starting to get bigger. This is no different than the others when it comes to the morning sickness. With this pregnancy, looking at eggs makes me want to throw up and lemons have become my favorite snack. The problem with the lemons is that I add salt to them when I eat them. Kalin is once again the very loving husband throughout the pregnancy. He makes me walk, strokes my ego, gives me lots of massages, facilitates my late night cravings, attends all of my doctor's appointments, and is the most supportive husband a woman who is pregnant can ever want.

The summer is finally coming to an end, which means that the children will be arriving from North Carolina soon. Stuart is in the Rehabilitation Program and is making great progress. While in there, he is studying Florida Law. I didn't know that he was interested in practicing law. He is, apparently, getting the help he needs so that when he is released, he will be able to take care of himself. Kalin and I agree that it is better for him to take Stuart to the Rehab Center because I don't do too well with goodbyes and emotional things like this. I guess I have gotten used to having him around. He is like another brother to us. I am still sad for what happened to the love of his life. I just pray that he will learn how to live with her not being here. I can't imagine ever living without Kalin.

The phone is ringing and it's Kalin's mother calling.

"Hello."

"Melissa? It's Mom. How are you?"

"Fine, Sweetie. And you?"

"Good! We are about 2 hours away from Florida. We should be there by Noon."

"Great! Drive carefully and we will see you when you get here."

Ken's mother and his stepfather are bringing the kids back because we don't feel comfortable putting them on a plane. Until they get here, I will

204 | TORN: The Melissa Williams Story

just straighten their rooms out as much as I can and wash their sheets. For some reason, I feel like a Blimp today! This baby is kicking like crazy and moving around as if she has someplace to go. The funny thing is that I can actually see her foot when she kicks. Kalin can't believe that I have decided to continue working until my baby arrives, as opposed to taking some time off. The truth of the matter is that I enjoy working and it takes my mind off the fact that I am about to have my sixth child. Just as I am putting the bed linens in the dryer, Kalin walks into the laundry room.

"Honey, do you have any idea what we should name the baby?" Kalin asks.

"I have no idea. I am running out of names, with this being the sixth one and all. I tell you one thing though, baby, I am ready for us to finally get some justice. I am tired of this mess with CCF. I just want them to all leave us alone. I am tired of all of this mess with the Case Plan and Judges and everything!

"Yeah, I know baby. It will be over s—"

"Wait a minute! That's it! That's her name if it is a girl!"

"What is her name? What are you saying?"

"Justice! We will name our daughter, "Justice"!"

"It has a nice ring to it. I love it!"

I finally make it to work, but for some reason, I am cramping just a little bit today. I go to the bathroom to make sure that I am not bleeding. I am in "labor".

"Ms. Melissa, are you okay over there?" my assistant, Cindy, asks.

"Yes, honey, I am okay."

"What was that moan for?" she asks. "It sounds like someone is in labor."

"OK, so maybe I am, but I know what to do. I am not going to have this baby in this office. I know when it is time to go. If it gets too intense for me, I promise you that I will contact my husband to pick me up."

"Alright, Melissa. I don't agree with it, but I have to trust you to do what you say you will do", she concedes.

"Thanks." Little does she know but I have gone back and forth to the restroom all day today suffering with diarrhea, but there is no way I was going to miss work today. We have our annual inspection with Florida State Inspector Thomas Gray, which is the most important inspection for a Tax Credit Property. I had to be here today to make sure that everything went according to plan. As usual, we pass the inspection with flying colors and the staff is relieved.

The labor pains are coming a little stronger so I have to call Kalin to pick me up now. When he arrives, I confess to him about how I have been feeling today. "Honey, I have a confession to make. I was actually in labor all day, but I didn't call you because I feel as if I just needed to work today. I figured it was better to be here than to lie around in a hospital bed all day", I confess. "So, when we get home, I am going to take a warm bath and wait for the time for us to go to the hospital."

"Are you serious, Mrs. Thomas?"

"Yep, honey, I am serious. I was okay, though. It is not like I don't know what it is going to feel like. This is certainly not the first one, but it is, for sure, the very last one", I say, with just a little huff in my voice.

I finish with my bath and everyone is in the family room watching "Martin". Kalin has already packed my bag for me and we are sitting around waiting for me to say "when".

"OK, honey, let's go, it's time now."

"Mommy, can I go with you?" asks Christy.

"Well, they may not let you in there with us, sweetie." I look over at Kalin to see what he thinks about it and he gives me his approval. I know that I am taking a chance by letting her go but I eventually say, "OK, you can go".

After giving hugs and kisses to the other kids, we are finally on our way to the hospital, with Christy sitting in the back with the car seat that is already prepared to bring our little one home. Christy must have asked thousands of questions or it at least seems that way. It also seems like Kalin is driving extremely slow and that the hospital is miles and miles away. When we finally make it to the hospital, I am able to walk up to the labor and delivery area. When we make it to the nurses' station, I have to explain to the nurses that Christy is already aware of what to expect. Surprisingly so, they agree to let her into the labor and delivery room with us. We are so relieved that she is going to be allowed into the room. We know that this will be a memorable experience for her.

After several hours, our newest addition makes her entrance into the world. We name her just as planned, Justice Thomas, the last of the Mohicans. Unfortunately, Christy has fallen asleep and misses the entire event. She does; however, get up in enough time to cut her sister's umbilical cord.

After six babies, I finally agree to have a tubal ligation. I actually wanted it after the birth of Sharell, but the hospital wanted me to go before a Board of Directors to get it done. But it is time now! I am ready to let this be the last one. The doctors waste no time in getting me over to the Operating Room to perform the procedure. Holding tightly to my hand, my husband kisses my forehead and says, "I love you, sweetheart."

When I awake from my deep sleep, Kalin is standing over me. My mouth is dry, but I manage to speak.

"Honey, where's Christy?"

"In the waiting area", he answers. "She says hello."

After just 48 hours in the hospital, I am finally on my way home.

As soon as I walk in the door, Sharell hands me a list of messages that came in while I was in the hospital. One by one, I read them. They are from Daniel Todd, a couple of letters from bill collectors, and Brittney! *I wonder what is going on now. It seems like the only time I talk to Brittney is when something is wrong. I am a little nervous to return her call.*

"Hi Mommy", all the kids say in unison.

"Hello to all of my precious children. How is everyone?"

"Mommy, we want to see the baby! Let us see the baby!"

Kalin lowers the baby so they can get a glimpse of our newest addition. Justice's sisters and brothers are in awe of her. They all beg to hold her. I am tired. I just want to find the bed and get in it. I am exhausted. The surgery has me a little sore. I need to take my pain pill and get some rest.

"Honey, do you need anything?" Kalin asks.

"Yes, baby. Please get me a pain pill and fluff the pillows for me, sweetheart."

"Ok, coming right up", he says.

With all of the attention that Justice is getting, she is going to be just fine. Her grandfather, uncle, and several cousins have shown up to see her, but I have to get some rest.

****

The kids are off to school and my pain pill is working. I think I will return my calls now. I am not returning calls to the bill collectors because I have already sent in their payments, but I will call Daniel's number instead.

"Hello", Daniel says, answering the phone.

"Hello, Daniel. This is Melissa Thomas. You called?"

"Yes ma'am. I need to come out for another visit. I just need to see what is convenient for you. I want to discuss results of the Psychological Evaluation before we go back to court. I have some recommendations that

I would like to make and I just want to discuss them with you and Kalin first", he says.

"Well I just got home from the hospital. Can this wait?"

"Congratulations on the new baby, but this can't wait, Mrs. Thomas. If you want to wrap up this case plan and everything, I would suggest that we get this meeting over with before we go to court", he suggests.

"Fine. What about tomorrow? Say around 10:30 am?"

"Ok, tomorrow it is."

I have one more call to return and then I can assist Uncle Juney in the kitchen with tonight's dinner. He makes the best Lasagna in the world so he has come to my rescue. I really want Kalin's meal to be special for him tonight. I just remembered that I need to call Brittney, but I can't find her number. Just as I am looking for the number, the phone rings.

"Hello", Uncle Juney says from the kitchen. He is able to get to the phone sooner than I can. I hear him say, "hold on". He walks into the room and says, "Meme, Brittney is on the phone for you. She sounds like she is crying", he announces.

"Hello Britt, you ok?" I ask as I pick up the phone.

"Hello Meme. I hear you are a new mommy, congratulations!" she says, as she is sobbing.

"Honey, thanks, but what is wrong?"

"Laura's mother died this afternoon. When I called you the other day, she was still alive. She was trying to help these kids that were outside her house and they killed her. A bunch of kids, can you believe that?"

"What happened?"

"I don't know why, but they choked her. She was on her way home one day and the kids were outside the house. She was asking if they wanted food, but they were more interested in getting what was in her purse. They knocked her down, grabbed her purse, and killed her. She would have given those kids anything that they wanted, but they killed her!

"I can't believe this! I just really can't believe this! So, what is going on with Princess? Is she okay right now?"

"The foster care people came and took her away. There is no other family so they took her until they figure out what to do with her."

"I have to go Britt. I can't take this news right now. I don't want to get too upset. My prayers are with them. But, I have to go now. But I am so happy that you called to give me the news. You know, I care about what is going on in Middleton."

"You bet. I will call you when I find out more."

"Thanks dear, Goodbye."

"Oh my God! I can't believe this! Poor baby! What is this world coming to?" I yell. Uncle Juney rushes into the room.

"Is everything okay?" he asks.

"No! Remember when I had to go to Alabama to bury one of my best friends? Well, now some kids have killed her mother. This is just horrible! I have to get up there to do something!"

"You need to get yourself better, Meme! You can't do anything right now. Just relax. Everything will be alright", he consoles.

Right away, I remember that I am supposed to contact the attorney in Middleton to find out what Laura has in the letter that she left behind for me to read once her mother passes. I will have to wait for the death certificate before I can even contact the attorney. I will wait for Britt to call me back with more information. I will have to use her to get the death certificate for me.

In light of what I have just found out, I am not looking forward to a good time tonight when Kalin gets home. I know that we have planned Lasagna, but I am not in the mood now. All I can think about is Princess and what she must be thinking to now lose her grandmother. My heart is aching for Princess. Poor child! *Who will take care of Princess now, I wonder.*

Although I am no longer excited about tonight's dinner, Kalin walks in and is very happy to see all the trouble that I have gone through to make tonight's dinner special. When I give him the news of Laura's mother's death, he becomes disheartened. We sit down to have our dinner, but Kalin can certainly tell that there is something else on my mind.

"Honey, I think that I am ready to go back to work. I think I really need to get back to work. What do you think?"

"If you feel up to it, then that is okay with me", he responds. "You don't have to if you don't want to because we are bringing in enough to get the bills paid right now."

"I know. I just want to, ok."

"Hey, have you heard anything about Stuart at the rehab? Is he doing okay?"

"As a matter of fact, he is doing just fine. I stopped over to the Rehab Center before coming home today. He said to tell everyone hello. He is doing just fine."

"That is just wonderful! I am so proud of him."

CHAPTER 32

"He's Gone!"

*M*y first day back at work is a bit hectic for me. They have so much going on and I am trying to figure it all out again. I am not surprised, but the place is in good shape, even in my absence. I guess that is the sign of good leadership. They don't really need me anymore.

"Cindy, I am going to go ahead and leave now. It seems as though you have everything under control here", I say to Cindy as she is making changes to the "rental board". "I have an appointment at 10:30. I may come back in the afternoon."

"Ok, sweetie. You didn't have to come in at all. Go to your appointment and just get some rest. You trained us well. We got this!"

"I see that!"

As soon as I walk in the house, I am drawn to the mail that is sitting on the countertop. I have received a letter from lawn care solicitors, a postcard for the new dental facility that just opened up around the corner, a birthday wish for Kalin from his mother, and a letter addressed to me that doesn't have a return address. Right away, I open the one addressed to me and inside is a piece of paper titled, "Death Certificate". It's Lorraine's Death Certificate! And who sent this to me? And how do they know that I need this? This is exactly what I need to finally get the contents of Laura's letter. When we are done with Daniel, I will contact the attorney in Alabama.

Just as I am taking the last bite of my bagel, the doorbell rings. Daniel is here! "Good morning Daniel", I say, as I open the door. He looks like he has aged quite a bit. He looks like he has quite a few things on his mind. I dare not ask him about what I saw. I haven't even told Kalin that I saw him that day.

"Good morning, Mr. and Mrs. Thomas", he says, walking in and wiping his feet off at the door mat.

"Mr. Todd, would you like some coffee or juice or something?"

"No thanks. I just had some. Let's just get through everything if you don't mind. I have another appointment on this side that I have to get to before I get back to the office." *No doubt, it's his Walgreens friend. Let it go Melissa!*

"Fine. Let's sit here."

"Ok, what I want to talk to you both about is the fact that I have reviewed the Psychological Evaluation in detail and have broken it down piece by piece. I want to make a recommendation to the court that your family be reunited because you have successfully completed the Case Plan. You are meeting the requirements for the supervised visits. I think that your family has had enough. What do you say?"

"Are you for real? Are you saying that you want to close this case and let our family live a normal life? That is excellent news! But why couldn't you tell us this over the phone? I think this is fabulous!"

"Yes, I could have, but I wanted to see you in person, because I need to ask a favor of you", he goes on to say. "Melissa, I know that you saw me that day at Walgreen's. I didn't approach you because I didn't want to deal with it there. I am closing your case because I want you to forget what you saw", he adds. Kalin is staring at me because he doesn't have any idea what is going on.

"Kalin, I never told you about this. Several months ago, I went to Walgreen's to get the pregnancy test and ended up seeing Daniel in there with this lady, but I didn't approach him. I didn't think anything about it, to tell you the truth. *OK, so I lied about that part because I have done nothing but think about it since I saw him with this woman, who looked like she was sad. He looked annoyed.*

"Ok, what does that have to do with us?" Kalin asks.

"It wouldn't look good if your wife started talking about that. The woman that I was with is not my wife and I just don't want issues", he continues. *I wonder why he was with her in a pharmacy. Can't be! Were they in there getting a pregnancy test? Can't be!*

"Look, Mr. Todd. What you do is your business; we don't have anything to do with that", Kalin says.

"Fine. I will petition the court to terminate this case and allow you all full reigns with your family", he says. "You will get a letter in the mail with the date of the hearing and I will see you there."

Mr. Todd leaves and Kalin and I just stand there shaking our heads. We agree not to discuss this anymore. We will show up at court and take the blessing. At least, we will have CCF out of our life and can move on with our family and be somewhat normal again.

Summer is approaching and as always, Kalin and I agree to allow the children to go to Alabama for the summer to be with my mother this time. Everyone except Justice! She is too young. She has to stay with Mommy and Daddy.

****

Days pass. It is Fourth of July and is extremely hot outside! It certainly looks like rain. I wonder what the weather man has to say about it. Justice and I have plans to go over to Carl and Wendy's house for a barbeque later on. But, we have to wait for Kalin to get home first. He has to work today. I wonder how Ms. Rita is doing today. I am sure that she is busy cooking some ribs, greens, potato salad, lemon and apple pies. When I call her number, she picks up the phone right away.

"Good morning, Ms. Melissa. How are you today?"

"I am fine and how are you?"

"Busy in the kitchen cooking for the holiday!"

"I bet you are!"

"I am glad that you have called. Do you mind giving me a ride to the grocery store? I need to pick up a few things that I forgot", she says.

"Sure. I don't mind. Justice and I are sitting here doing nothing. I just need to get dressed and then we will be right over."

"OK, I will be ready."

Within 30 minutes or so, Justice and I are pulling up to Ms. Rita's apartment. She is outside waiting on her porch for me. She comes right on out to the car. She looks like she has been cooking all night. Knowing Ms. Rita, she is having all of her family members over to celebrate the holiday. She gets in the car and right away, she starts playing with Justice, who is placed snugly in her car seat and playing with her little bear. We make it to Publix and it looks like there are a lot of people who are also picking up last minute items. Right in the middle of the parking lot is a guy with his truck selling watermelons. What a deal! He is selling them at a 2 for 1 price. This is too good of a deal. I have to pull over and get a few. Ms. Rita jumps out and runs into the store.

By the time I park, she is already coming out!

"Wow! That was fast", I comment.

"Yeah, it's like that when you know what you need", she responds.

I drop her off and since the Rehab Center is on the way, I decide to stop by to see Stuart. *I hope that he is not too startled when I show up. It is 4th of July and there is no reason he should be alone. I will just be a minute.*

I pull up to the Rehab Center and it looks so deserted. I don't know if I should go in or what. Maybe I should just call him instead and talk to him that way. Oh well! I am here now. I get Justice out of the car seat and walk to the front entrance. At the front desk is a middle-aged woman who looks like *I* disturbed *her* from doing something else that she would rather be doing.

"Good morning, ma'am. I am here to see Stuart Peters, please", I say to the receptionist sitting behind the desk. Her nametag reads "Belinda". Belinda must really hate her job.

"Ok, let me see here", she says, as she takes her pen and goes down the folder sitting in front of her. She looks puzzled. "Ma'am, I do not see a Stuart Peters on the list. Are you sure you have the right name? I am not finding his name anywhere on the list", she says.

"There must be a mistake. My husband dropped him off here and he spoke with him the other day right here. Please get someone else because I know that he is here." Belinda picks up the phone and calls a supervisor to assist her. Within a few seconds, a man walks through the door wearing a long white coat. His nametag reads, "Dr. Nichols".

"Sir, there must be a mistake. Stuart Peters is not on your list. I know that he is here. Please tell me what is going on."

"Ma'am, there is no mistake. He was discharged out of here and has been gone for about a week. He left against my wishes. He felt as if he didn't need the program anymore, so he checked himself out. We couldn't stop him, being that he was here on a voluntary status", he goes on to say.

"Are you sure?"

"Yes ma'am. Check with your husband because he is the one who picked him up. I distinctly remember because I met with them both before he left. He said that he had some important matters that he had to take care of and if he needed to return, he would."

"Ok, I am sure that there is a good explanation. I am so sorry to have bothered you."

"No problem", the doctor says.

Leaving the Center, I feel very sick inside. *Why didn't Kalin tell me about this? Why did he tell me that Stuart was doing fine when he is not even here anymore?* This is getting crazy! I need to speak to my dear husband. My mind is so cloudy right now, so I put in Yolanda Adams' CD and let the words to her song, "I Gotta Believe", just take me away. I love this woman's music. She is truly the best in gospel right now. I still love the old school gospel though. I get caught up in the moment and forget all about what just happened at the Rehab Center. Justice looks so peaceful, just sitting there in her car seat.

Kalin better have a good explanation for what I just discovered! How is he going to sit there and look me directly in the face and lie to me about Stuart being at the Rehab Center? We finally make it home and as soon as I walk in the door, the phone starts ringing. I rush over to the phone and it is my sister in Middleton.

"Melissa, I have horrible news. Spanky just got shot! He is at the hospital and I don't know what is going on with him!" she says, breathing fast, without taking any breaks in between. Spanky is my nephew who was just released from jail, trying to get his life back together. *Who would want to shoot him?*

"Oh my God! Is he okay?!"

"I don't know dear. I am on my way to the hospital. I couldn't get anyone else on the phone. Everyone here is going crazy. I don't know anything. I heard it on the scanner and I am rushing to the hospital. I will call you when I know more!" she exclaims.

"Ok, please call me back! I am going to sit right by the phone until you call!"

I can't believe this. My nephew is trying to do the right things with his life. *Why in the world did this happen to him? Who did this?* I have to call someone and let them know what is going on, but I need to call Kalin first. I am not sure if he is still at work or not. I can wait until he gets here. I have to calm down. My nephew is going to be just fine. There is no need to worry. I have to calm down now. I can't lose it. I will call Diana and at least let her know something.

Diana must be home doing nothing because she picks up on the first ring.

"Hello."

"Hello dear. It is Meme. I just got off the phone with Stacey and she told me that Spanky got shot! She said that she is on the way to the hospital to get more information and when she finds out, she will give me a call. I will sit right here until I hear something."

"Oh my God, Meme! I can't believe this! I can't believe that this is happening. Did she say anything about Momma? How is Momma doing?"

"She didn't go into any detail. She said that everyone is going crazy down there, understandably so. She will call me b—", I say, looking at the phone that just beeped. "Hold on, this is a call from Alabama."

"Hello."

"He is gone ya'll! He is gone! His body just couldn't take it anymore. He is gone! It happened so fast, Meme! Let everybody know!" Stacey shouts.

"How is Momma?" I ask, sobbing into the phone.

"She is a complete wreck right now", she answers. "Meme, please pray. We need God's help right now."

I click back over to Diana.

"He is gone "D"! That was Stacey. She says that he passed!! Oh my God! She says that Momma is a mess! Oh Lord, please help us! I have to call Nikki and tell her about what happened to her brother. I don't know how to break this news to her. We have to stick together on this one. You and I are the older ones here and we have to support the younger ones. They are looking up to us. Are you with me?"

"Sure. Let's just go over to her house. I will pick you up", Diana says.

As soon as Diana hangs up, Kalin walks in the door. I am so upset about Spanky that I don't have time to focus on Kalin's lie.

"Hi honey! Are you ready to go to the barbeque? I am ready to eat. I am so hungry", he says, without even looking my way to see that I am on the floor crying. He finally notices.

"Kalin."

"Honey, what is wrong and why are you down there? How are the children? How is the baby? Why are you crying?" he asks.

"My nephew, Spanky, was shot and killed today. I am sick inside. Oh my God! Diana is coming over and we are going to go over together to tell his sister, Nikki. She is going to be so distraught over this. She loves her brother so much. Oh God, Kalin!"

"Honey, get up. You are a strong woman. You have withstood so much in your life. You stand strong and remember that God doesn't make mistakes. Go ahead and cry, but you need to be strong for the rest of the family. I know it hurts, sweetheart. You can do this."

"Kalin, and you know what else? I went to the Rehab Center to see Stuart and he wasn't there. What is going on? I thought you went over to see him the other day? Why did you say that, knowing all along, that he wasn't even there?" Before he can answer, Diana has pulled up into the driveway and is knocking on my door.

"I will tell you all about it later. Go ahead and take care of this right now. Do you want me to go with you? I can have somebody watch Justice", he offers.

"No, Diana and I have to do this together. We have to do what Momma would expect us to do", I respond.

"Ok, honey, I love you."

I jump in Diana's car and head for Nikki's apartment to deliver this horrible news to her. Diana is smoking cigarettes like crazy, one after another. I am sitting with a blank look on my face, practicing in my head how we will deliver this. I say a short prayer in my head, *"Lord, please give me the right words to say to my niece. Please send your Comforter dear Lord. Please look over my Mother".*

We pull into the complex and I can already see that Nikki is home. At least, her car is parked in the parking lot. I look at my sister before we get out of the car and notice that she is still very upset over this news.

"D, I know that this is hard but we have to be strong right now. We have our work cut out for us with Nikki. Please pull yourself together, ok. I need you right now."

"Ok, Meme, you will have to do all the talking", she says. *No, sister, God will do all the talking. I am in pain, too!*

We knock on the door and Nikki's oldest daughter comes to the door. "Hey Auntie Meme", she says. I can see that they are just about to leave.

Nikki comes to the front and sees that Diana has been crying and right away, she can sense that something is wrong. She already looks like she wants to cry.

"Sweetheart, have a seat. I have to tell you something", I begin. She grabs my hand and looks me directly in the eyes. Her husband has his eyes directly on me, as well as the children. It feels like time is standing still. *Oh Lord, don't fail me now!* "Nikki, Spanky is gone, sweetie. He was shot and killed this afternoon. His body couldn't handle it and he passed on peacefully."

"NOOOOOOOOOOOOOOOOOOOOOOO!!!!!" she shouts. She jumps up out of her seat and starts running through the apartment. Her husband grabs her and when she starts crying, Diana starts crying and so do the kids. Nikki's screams could wake a dead person. She cries so loud and hard that she eventually just pass out. I take over and slap her in the face until she opens her eyes. She looks me directly in the face and says, "Why, Auntie? Why did they kill my brother? Why did they do this to my brother? Why did God let them kill my brother?" she asks.

"Sweetheart, I don't know why these things happen. I can tell you this. God doesn't make mistakes. Spanky will always be with you. Nobody can kill that", I say, comforting her and rubbing her forehead. I feel so bad for her. I wish that I could wake up and this just be a bad dream, but it is really happening.

We finally get Nikki calm. I get up to fix her some tea with chamomile to calm her down. When she dozes off to sleep, Diana and I leave for home. We don't really say much during the drive. We are both dealing with what has just happened. She drops me off and drives off.

I walk into my house a totally different person. Kalin is up waiting for me. I drop my purse and run right into his arms. "You ok, honey?" he asks.

"Yeah, I am now. Thanks for waiting up for me. Where is Justice?"

"She is asleep. Are you hungry?"

"I am, but I don't want to eat right now. I just want to go to bed. Before I do, I want to give Stacey a call to see just what really went down in Middleton with my nephew."

"It is late, sweetheart. Don't you want to just deal with this in the morning?" Kalin asks.

"No, I really need to know now." I am sure that Stacey has been taking calls all night because she picks up on the first ring.

"Hello."

"Hello Stacey. It's Melissa. I just called to let you know that me and Diana went over and gave the news to Nikki. She didn't take it too well. Can you tell me exactly what happened up there?"

"This is what I know so far. Spanky left from Momma's house and went over to one of his friends' house where they were having a barbeque. Apparently, there was a drive by shooting and when the guys in the car started to fire their weapons, he jumped in front of a bunch of kids that were playing by the street. He saved their lives. When he made it to the hospital, he had so many bullets in him, his body just couldn't survive it. All of his organs had shut down and he just closed his eyes", she explains.

"Wow! Unbelievable!"

"Momma was in the room with him when he passed. He stayed with us long enough to tell her that he loved her. This is hard but we can make it if we stay together. You take care of the group down there and I got Momma."

"Alright, sis. Goodnight. I will talk to you later. Love ya."

"Goodnight. I love you, too."

I crawl in bed next to Kalin and hold him close. He is not sleep yet. "Honey, everything will be alright."

"I know." Before I close my eyes, I have a conversation with God. *Okay Lord. I won't question you because you do not make mistakes. I won't ask you why you allowed my nephew to leave us when he was finally starting to get his life back together. Lord, I just want to know that my nephew accepted you into his life. I just want to know if my nephew is with you or not. Please forgive the young man who killed my nephew. Forgive him because he has no idea what he just did.*

CHAPTER 33

"As Long As He's With You"

*A*fter careful preparations, we are on our way to Middleton to bury my nephew. If I don't forget, I will also give Attorney Richards a call to finally get the contents of the envelope from Laura, since I mysteriously received the death certificate. The ride to Middleton is not all bad. We start to reminisce about all the fun times that we share as a family. I even bring up the funny things that Spanky did. This had everyone in stitches. It didn't last too long. With everyone in the car, it is fun reminding everyone of the good times. Just as there is laughter in the car, there is also a period where no one speaks a word. My sister is reading "Ebony", while I am doing some work on my laptop. The kids are just sitting still and watching the cars go by.

When we pull into Mom's driveway, Nikki jumps out of the van and runs directly to Mom. They stand there holding each other and crying for what seems like 25 minutes. Everyone can tell that our Mother really wants to break down but she is much too strong for that. At least, she needs everyone to think that she is strong. I know that her heart is piercing with pain.

I step out of the van and notice that Brittney is heading towards the van. She runs to me with open arms.

"I am so sorry about your nephew, Meme", she begins. "He was such a good kid. I was the one who gave him a ride over to that party. I am so sorry for ya'll."

"Thanks dear", I say, moving toward the house.

"Hey, did you get the death certificate that I sent you?" she asks. I am puzzled because she didn't have a return address on the envelope. *Why didn't she put her address on it so that I will know that it came from her? How did Brittney know that I needed the death certificate? I never told her about what happened at the reading of the Will.* I don't have time to think about this right now. I am here for something different. I will, however, give the attorney a call while I am in town.

"Yes, I received it. Thanks."

Watching my mother and niece embrace each other takes me back to when I was a little kid and my oldest brother died. I was very young but I remember the events just like it all happened yesterday. This moment quickly took me back as a child when my oldest brother died. His name was Albert Lee and he was Spanky and Nikki's father. He was a diabetic and died at a very young age. As a matter of fact, Nikki and Spanky were very young kids. Although I was very young, I remember the details of his death as if it were yesterday. I remember watching my mother's face when the news of his death was delivered to her. I remember all of the strange events that happened after my brother's death. I remember how my mother cried and cried at his funeral.

"Hey everybody", I say, as I was walk into my mother's house. My brother, Theo, is here, with his family. My sister and her husband are here. They are eating some of Mom's Sweet Potato Pie. "Let me get a piece of pie!" I say, making my way to the table where my mother has at least 6 of them lined up neatly. Brittney gives me a hug and politely leaves.

"Hey Meme, I will catch up with you later, honey. Spend the time with your family", she says as she heads for the door.

"Thanks dear. I will see you later."

The day of the funeral is here and everyone is getting dressed up for the occasion. I decide to leave Justice with Brittney's mom since she is so young and Ms. Leslie isn't going to the funeral anyway.

"Mom, are you okay?" I ask, as she is in her bedroom getting dressed.

"Yes, honey, I am fine. God has this thing all in His hands. I don't have to worry about a thing. I am glad that you all made it here, though", she says. My mother is a strong woman and this is the response that I expected her to give, but deep down inside, I know that this is very hard for her and I know that she blames herself. When my brother died, my mother adopted all 4 of his children because their mother left them. Spanky is my brother's oldest son and now *he* is dead.

"You know, Mom, I think that Spanky did a good thing by sacrificing his life for those young kids. I will forever look at that as his contribution to this World. I am proud of him, aren't you?"

"Yes, I am, actually", she answers. "I heard about your friend's Mother. That is a shame and a pity what those young folks did to that woman, raping her and *then* killing her. Lord have mercy! That poor woman has never done anything to anybody. And the sad part about it is that those same children that hurt her like that, she used to take care of them and their mothers when they were all "cracked" out. I just don't know what this world is coming to", she continues.

"I didn't know that the kids also raped her. Britt didn't tell me that part", I say, with a puzzled look on my face. "Ok, Mom, let's get you finished. Come here and let me put a little makeup on you."

"OK, let's hurry, though. I don't want to have anybody waiting on us. We need to get out of here and put all of this past us", she says. When I bend down to get my makeup case, she says, "Oh, and Meme, I am glad that you are here. I heard how you handled things in Miami when the news came in and thanks for keeping it together and making sure that the family made it here", she comments. At this point, I have tears forming in the corner of my eyes. I don't think I remember ever feeling this appreciated by my mother.

The funeral service is beautiful. The church is decorated with white roses throughout. The procession is beginning and I am not too far behind my Mother. I won't take my eyes off of her. I want to make sure that she makes it through this. I can see that several of my high school classmates showed up to the funeral. That means a lot. I walk by and I see my high school sweetheart, Brian, sitting between his parents. Brittney is sitting with one of our other friends, Pam. They did a great job on my nephew. He looks so handsome in his NY Yankees' jersey. I bend down and give him a kiss. He is so cold. He looks like he is just sleeping. I can't lose it because I have to stay strong. *Lord, thank you. Thank you for getting us here. Thanks for giving me an opportunity to say goodbye to my nephew. Thank you for using him to help someone else. And Lord, I know now that he is with you and I thank you for receiving him into your bosom. In Jesus' name, Amen.*

I finally get to my seat, still holding Kalin's hands. I came into this not thinking I could make it through this part, but I have. I hold it together until Brittney's cousin walks up to the podium to sing one of my favorite songs, "I Won't Complain". The tears are flowing down my face non-stop. My husband grabs my hand tighter to let me know that it is alright. The entire family is in tears at this point. *Lord, please help us through this funeral. Please comfort my family. We still trust you and love you because you don't make mistakes. In Jesus' name, Amen.*

The service is finally over. The family is gathered in the reception hall to have dinner. I decide to excuse myself to spend my final moments with my nephew, at his gravesite. I have to say goodbye to him in my own way.

"Honey, will you please make sure that the children make it back to the house and get changed? I have something that I have to do and I want to be alone, if that is okay with you."

"Sure, honey. Are you okay? Are you sure that you don't need me?" he asks.

"I am sure. I will be back soon."

I finally make it down the hill to my nephew's gravesite and sit in one of the chairs that are still there. I am looking at his coffin and admiring how beautiful it looks. I have never done anything like this, but I remember my mother used to always tell me that there is no need to be afraid of dead people. She said that it is the people that are walking around that you need to worry about. I have to make peace right now so I begin to speak to Spanky.

> "Nephew, I love you. I feel that you are with God so I know that you are finally at peace. I am so proud of you for giving your life for other children to live. I love you so much for that. I am sorry that your life was cut short and that you didn't really have a chance to see what you could do with yours. The family is hurting right now. Momma is in so much pain and thinks that she is hiding it, but I know better. I know what she is feeling in her heart. Your sister is not handling this thing too good either. She will learn to be okay. I love you so much. I will miss you for the rest of my life. Thanks for being an inspiration to your cousins. I love you now and forever. Goodbye."

I really feel that I have made my peace with the passing of my nephew. I have to let him go now and let him be at peace. I get up from the green chair and begin to walk away. The clouds are starting to darken and a light drizzle lets out. My tears begin to flow, but not from sadness. When I make it to the top of the hill, I turn back and blow a kiss in the air to my nephew. I must have been down there for a while because everyone is already gone from the church.

I get back in the car and pull out my Palm Pilot to get Attorney Richards' number.

"Hello, Richards and Associates, how may I help you?" the lady on the other end says.

"Yes, my name is Melissa Thomas and I need to speak with Attorney Richards, please."

"Hold on for one second, please. He is on another line right now." After a minute or so, he picks up the phone.

"Hello. Richards, here. How may I help you?"

"Yes sir. This is Melissa Thomas. I was instructed ---", I say, before he interrupts.

"Yes, I know. You are Melissa Thomas, Laura Walters' friend. I was expecting a call from you. I am sorry about your nephew. I read about it in the Middleton Journal. I figured you'd be calling me at some point."

"Thanks for your concern, sir. The reason that I am calling is because of the letter that I am to retrieve from you that Laura left behind for me. According to the Last Will & Testament, I am supposed to get it from you after her mother passes, I explain.

"That is correct. I know that you just buried your nephew, but can you come by my office this afternoon? I will be here until 3pm", he says.

That is only 45 minutes away. I wonder if I can make it. "Sure, I will be right over."

I am very familiar with where his office is so if I take the 250 Expressway, I can make it on time. I have to give my husband a call to let him know when I will make it back to the house. I don't want him to worry.

"Hello", says Kalin when he answers the phone. There is a hint of sadness in his voice.

"Honey, it's me, your sweet wife", I say, trying to interject some humor. "I am on my way to the attorney's office to pick up the letter that Laura left for me." He sounds like he doesn't have a clue what I am talking about so I have to remind him. "Remember, the letter that Laura left for me that I was to get *only* after the passing of her mother?"

"Oh yeah, that's right. I am sorry sweetheart. My mind is half gone right now", he says.

"How are things back at the house?"

"They are quite good, honey. Everyone is sitting around laughing and having a good time. You know how your family is when there is a fresh gallon of moonshine. Believe me. They are all doing just fine right now", he says. "But you take it easy out there and hurry home as soon as you can."

The 250 Expressway didn't fail me this time. I am pulling into the attorney's parking lot right now. The trip has taken approximately 30 minutes.

"OK, honey, I am pulling in now. I will call you back when I am done."

"Goodbye, sweetheart."

Attorney Richards' office is immaculate. I would not be surprised if his wife decorated the place. Standing in the doorway is a very handsome man who stands approximately 6 feet tall with striking features. He is walking towards me as if he is expecting me.

"Hello, and you must be Melissa", he says, as he extends out his hand to me.

"Yes, I am. And you are Attorney Richards?"

"Here it is, Mrs. Thomas", he says, as he hands me the envelope, along with a confirmation of receipt of the document.

"But I didn't give you the death certificate. I have it right here", I say, patting the folder in my hand.

"No problem. I already have it", he says. *Now how did he get the death certificate? Who sent it to him? I didn't know that anyone else even knew that I needed to get it to him? Oh well, I am sure that I will find out soon enough.*

"Oh, okay, then. Thanks Mr. Richards."

"Ma'am, if there is nothing else, I want to get out of here and get home to my wife and kids who are waiting for me to show up so that we can go for a picnic", he says, as he stands to lock the office door.

"Thank you. If I have any questions, is it okay for me to call you?"

"Of course you can. Drive safely back to Miami."

I don't want to open the envelope yet, because I don't want to see anything horrible at this moment. I have enough going on right now dealing with my family's loss. I will read it once I make it back to Miami. *What can be in this letter so important that it can't wait?*

I finally get back to the house and Kalin is right! Everyone is in good spirits. It doesn't seem like we just buried my nephew just hours ago. It could be because everyone is drinking Budweisers and homemade Moonshine. This is typical after a funeral.

We finally wrap up the weekend and head back to Miami. I was so busy that I didn't speak to Brittney before I left. I will call her when I make it home. She will understand. *I am still puzzled as to how she knew to send me the death certificate and how the attorney got it. My guess is that the same person who sent it to him is the same person who sent it to me. But what is Brittney's involvement in this matter?*

The ride back home is not as bad as coming. It seems like we make it back in record time. Everyone is dropped off and we head for home.

We pull into the driveway and I pick up the mail before going inside. There is a letter from the courts. No doubt this is probably our court hearing date. I tear open the envelope and it reads:

ORDER SETTING CASE FOR DISMISSAL. The Court hereby sets this Action for August 8, 1999....

This is it! Daniel Todd did just like he said that he would do. He is asking the Judge to dismiss our supervision and end this nightmare. The other mail in the pile didn't matter at all. There is; however, one piece of meal that grabs my attention and it is from Stuart Peters. In the middle of everything else, I forgot that I was supposed to pick a fight with my husband about Stuart and why he didn't tell me that the was no longer in the Rehab Center and that my husband is the one who took him away without telling me anything about it.

"Honey, there is a letter here from Stuart. It is addressed to you. Do you want me to open it?"

Kalin looks at me as if I have a third eye, "No, Mrs. Thomas. It is addressed to me. Thank you very much", he says, as he takes the letter from my hand. Kalin drives me nuts when he does that. He just finished reading the letter and is walking into the kitchen without saying a word. He knows that I want to know what is in the letter.

I follow him into the kitchen. "So, what did he say?"

"He checked himself back into the Program. When he went to take care of the business he had to take care of, he relapsed, but he checked himself back in. He thanked me for understanding and being his friend through it all. He did give me some news that I didn't know about. He gives a meaningful explanation as to why he relapsed. Here you go! Read it for yourself", he says as he hands me the letter.

Dear Kalin, How are you doing my friend? I just want to thank you for being a good friend to me during the hardest time in my life. After losing my wife, it seemed as though I just didn't have anything to live for. Taking the drugs took away the pain I felt. I have to be honest with you and I have to be honest with myself. I didn't take those drugs just because I lost my sweet wife. I took those drugs to also hide the shame and guilt that I was carrying. The night my wife died, I was there. I was riding along in the car with her. She was driving. My wife had just told me that she was pregnant and I told her that my mistress was pregnant. The look in her eyes is one that I will never forget. She took her eyes off the road and looked at me like I had just ripped her heart out. A truck was heading in our direction and hit us. I survived the accident but she and our unborn child died in that accident. Now that I am back in Rehab, I had to send a letter to someone to tell the truth to and I couldn't think of anyone who deserved to hear the truth more than you. Tell Melissa hello. I know that she came to see me on the Fourth of July. Tell her that I appreciate it. I have to go now my friend. I am doing well and should be completed with my Program by the end of the year. I love you and thanks again for everything.

Love, Stuart P.

I am crying so hard now that Kalin grabs me and holds me tightly. With everything that is going on, I need this good cry. We just stand in silence for a few minutes without saying a word. We finally let go of each other and start taking things out of the car to bring them into the house. The kids are already in their rooms playing their video games. They don't waste any time getting back to the things that they like to do!

CHAPTER 34

"Back In Court For The Finale"

Kalin and I prepare ourselves for our upcoming court hearing in a couple of days. Kalin is off to work and the kids are in school. "Uncle Juney" and I just finished our morning coffee.

"Meme, if you don't need anything else, I am going to go for my morning jog", he says, getting up from the table.

"Fine, no problem. I have some things to do myself. I will see you when you get back. Have a nice jog."

The house is quiet. Justice is asleep. Kalin is gone to work. The kids are at school and "Uncle Juney" is gone for a jog. I decide to finally open up the letter that Laura left behind for me.

> *To my dearest friend, Melissa Thomas.*
>
> *I am going to now tell you something that I could never tell you when I was alive. My daughter, Princess, is your son's sister. Her father is "Rock". I am so sorry that you had to hear it this way. I am only telling you now because I am gone and my mother is gone and she has nobody left. I want you to do me a favor. I want you to raise her as if she is your child so that she can be with her brother and hopefully get to know her father. I am very sorry about the "Rock" thing. It was a one night stand that we had together. He always loved you, Melissa. I was extremely jealous of that. From that one night together, I got pregnant. Please take my daughter. I have left behind everything that she will need. I know that you will make sure that she goes to college and become a very successful woman. I want her to grow up with a good family. Please remind her*

everyday just how much I love her. You will always be my best friend. I love you forever.
  Friends always, Laura Walters.

I drop the letter like it is a hot potato! I don't know whether to scream or cry. I don't know whether to be angry with "Rock" that he had a fling with one of my best friends. I don't know what I am to think right now. Now it makes sense why he was at the funeral service. All I do know is that there is a little girl out there who doesn't have any family and is alone sitting in some foster family. I have to do something. I can't believe this! I have to wait until my husband gets home to give his the latest bombshell. I am sure that he will see it my way that we have to raise Princess as our daughter.

I need to clear my head, so I put on one of my favorite songs from back in the day, "Jesus is Love", by the Commodores. *"Father, help your children..don't let them fall by the side of the road....teach them to love one another...that Heaven might find a place in their hearts...Jesus is love!"* I get so caught up in the song that I almost forget that the kids will be home in a couple of hours from school and I haven't gotten their dinner started yet. Besides, "Uncle Juney" will be back soon. This is too much to deal with right now.

Kalin gets in from work and after dinner and he's finally settled in, I figure there is no time like the present to tell him about the contents of the letter. I am not quite sure of the mood he's in, but we have to talk about it eventually.

"Honey, I never told you what was in the letter from Laura. Feel like talking about it?"

"Oh yeah! With everything going on, I completely forgot about it. So, what did she say in the letter?"

"Sweetheart, you might want to sit down for this one. In the letter she left behind for me, she explained about who her daughter really is. She wants me to raise her daughter because she is Darren's sister. Apparently, she had a one night stand with Rock and Princess was conceived. She wants me to raise her daughter right along with her brother. I have to admit that I am in shock about this. Rock had a fling with my best friend and neither one of them told me about it. She has made it very clear that money is not an option. She went so far as to give me the account numbers for all of the bank accounts. She has put me in charge of those accounts. She has done a very fine job of making sure that her daughter's college is paid in full.

Taking on Princess will not be a liability for us. She just needs to be with family. I can't believe this! What do you think?"

"Whoooooooa! How much can one person take?" he asks, not really expecting an answer from me.

"I know, honey. I understand if you tell me that we can't do this. But, honestly, I have to do something. I can't just leave this child out there. It is not her fault. I won't feel right if I don't honor Laura's wishes. This is not about you. This is not about me. This is about the child."

"I support you. If this is what you want to do, let's do it", he says, grabbing my hands and looking into my eyes. *I love this man! What a great person he is. I just love him so much for being so understanding.*

"Thanks so much, sweetheart. I will be in touch with the attorneys next week. Let's finish up our thing with the courts first", I suggest.

"Ok, sweetheart, I love you."

****

Kalin and I are on our way to the courthouse. After going back and forth to court for several months, the case is finally closed! The Judge listens carefully to every word that Daniel Todd has to say about the progress that we made with our parenting and how happy the children are. He mentions how the children are excelling in school and are on the honor roll. He didn't stop at anything to get the Judge to see it his way. What a relief! After two years, the case is finally closed and we are once again living in our home with our children free from the watchful eye of Children Come First.

CHAPTER 35

Why Did I Do That?"

Now that this court ordeal is behind us, I think it is time to share the news about Princess to the other children. So, Kalin and I come up with this bright idea to call a Family Meeting to discuss it.

"Hey guys, Mommy and Daddy need to tell you something." The kids all gather in front of us next to the fireplace.

"Remember my friend who died last year and how said I was when she died?"

"Yes!"

"Well, before she died, she wrote up this letter to the attorney for her daughter to come live with me after her grandmother passes away. She wanted her to come live with us because she is actually Darren's sister." I don't think they quite get it. I feel like maybe Christy understands what I am saying and maybe Kameron, but the rest of the children look like they have no clue as to what this announcement means. And Darren, himself, looks shocked right now. His mouth is wide open. He looks very confused. "I know this is hard to believe, but sometimes, it happens that two people get together and don't intend on making a baby, but they do. Regardless to how Princess got here, she is here now and she doesn't have her Mommy to make things better for her. Do you all remember how it felt when you didn't have your Mommy?"

"Yes ma'am. We were sad!" they shout.

"And then to make it even better, we are going to go ahead and move into a much bigger home since our family is growing. Dad and I have already picked out a house. It has 6 bedrooms, 3 ½ baths, a pool, and a huge backyard. So, do you all agree with me that she should come live with us?"

"Yes! It is okay. Look at it this way. We will have another girl around" shouts Sharell.

"Well, it sounds like we all agree and - - -", I say before being interrupted.

Right away, Christy makes it very clear how she feels about the whole thing. She is not happy. That is for sure.

"I can't believe this! You guys are always finding a way to bring more and more people around and spending less time with us. This is not fair! I don't want to leave now! I just got used to being here at this school and now we have to leave. Please, let's not move!" she pleads.

"Christy, it is a bigger house, more things to do for ya'll and the schools are just as good as the one you are in right now. You can make new friends over there in the new district.

"I am not happy about this", she says.

"Sweetheart, I promise you that you will do fine in the new place. We are moving and that is just that!" Kalin says, getting up and walking away.

Neither Kameron nor Darren has any issues with our announcement. Sharell, Amber, and Justice are too young to understand what is going on. "Hey guys, I am going to give Ms. Rita a call because we want her to make this move with us. Right?"

"I guess so", mumbles Kameron. By now, the other kids are back to doing what they were doing before the announcement. It is not long after this announcement that Christy starts to withdraw from us. She doesn't seem to have fun with us anymore. When she does come around, she always seems angry. I won't address it with her because I am sure that she *will* get used to the idea. And once we move to the new house and she starts meeting new kids, she will be just fine. This is not like her to be this way and for this long, though. *Why can't she just get used to the idea like everyone else?*

The kids' birthdays are coming up. I will throw the biggest birthday celebration and hopefully, this will make Christy a little happier. I end up getting her all of her favorite things. I invite all of her friends that she will be leaving behind. The party is a huge success. I let her have a sleepover with her friends, hoping that she will lighten up just a little. I don't know what she is feeling right now, but I know that her birthday celebration ends up being the talk of the town. Her friends seem to have really enjoyed themselves.

When we finally catch up with Ms. Rita at her sister's house, she gladly accepts our offer and agrees to move into our new home, right along with us. She has agreed to live with us during the week and go home on the weekends.

****

It's moving day! There are boxes everywhere! The kids are excited about the move. Christy is still very unsure and uneasy about this move. I don't know why she is sulking because the house is absolutely fantastic. It is big enough so that Christy has her own room, the boys have their room together, Kalin and I have our room, Ms. Rita has her own room. Sharell and Amber will have their room, and Justice and Princess will have their room together. Christy's room is right across from Ms. Rita's room. After adding my special touch to it, the house is quite comfortable, decorated in red, black and white. I am always buying nice things for the house. It is important to me that my children understand that this house is theirs too, so I let them decide how they want their rooms to be decorated. Because it is so much easier to shop online, we visit the websites of Target and Bed, Bath & Beyond to find just the right bed sets. And tomorrow, we will stop by the stores and pick up our items.

Right in the middle of our internet surfing, the phone rings. The caller ID reads, CARL AND WENDY. I wonder which one is calling so I pick up the phone and say, "Hello."

"Hello Melissa. How are you? How is the family?"

"Everyone is doing just fine. How are you?"

"I am holding on. Is your husband home?" she asks.

"Yes, he is. Hold on!"

Ken is upstairs putting up shelves in the kids' room so I decide to send Kameron up to tell him to pick up the phone. *I really want to listen in on this call. But, how can I? Kalin will not forgive me if he knows that I am listening on the call. I just have to trust him to tell me what their conversation is about.*

"Honey, I got the phone. Thanks!" he yells from upstairs.

I put down the receiver. The kids and I resume our search on the internet for their bedroom themes. Christy is not interested in looking right now. Kameron and Darren decide on Superman. Sharell and Amber will go with *Bratz*. Justice decides for her and Princess to decorate their room with Dora the Explorer. The kids can tell that I am a little pre-occupied. I am trying to figure out why Wendy would call my house looking for my husband and why he doesn't have a problem taking the call. It has been 15 minutes! *What are they talking about?*

After 25 minutes upstairs, Kalin finally comes downstairs and kisses me. "Honey, I have to go out for awhile because I need to run an errand", he says, in a matter of fact kind of way.

"Really? What errand do you have to run at 9:30pm?"

"I need to get something for the shelving that I am doing. Home Depot is 24 hours!" he says.

"Yes, but I am not 24 hours. I want you home with me. You can get that when you go to work tomorrow. Well, let me get my jacket. I want to go with you."

"Sweetheart, that is not necessary. Stay here with the kids. I will be back shortly."

Before I have a chance to say anything else, Kalin has grabbed the keys and has slipped out the door. I can't concentrate on Dora the Explorer or anything else right now. I want to run behind him, but I know that I can't do it. But there is one thing that I can do. Without Kalin's knowledge, I had a tracking device put in the car when I purchased it. I never thought I would need it. But, for some reason, I never felt like he was telling me everything there is to know about Wendy. In just a few minutes, I will know exactly where Kalin is headed and where he ends up. As the computer is searching, my stomach is in knots. I can't believe that I am tracking the GPS system in my car to find out where my husband is. I should just trust that he went to Home Depot.

The computer has stopped searching and gives me the results of my car. Kalin lied to me! He did not go to Home Depot. He went over to Wendy's house! There must be some type of explanation about this. But, why did he tell me that he was going to Home Depot if he knew all along that he was going to Wendy. So, I figure this much. Whatever she called him for, he is going for it. I trust Kalin! He is my husband and I love him and I know that he loves me. I will just ask him when he gets home. *My mind is starting to wonder. For the first time since Kayla's death, I am reminded of the conversation about how she caught Kalin and Wendy making out at Wendy's house after she followed him.*

It has been an hour since Kalin left the house. I am just starting to get a little pissed. Because I don't want any distractions when he comes home, I decide to go ahead and put the kids down to bed and take a nice warm bath. When the door opens to my bedroom, Kalin walks in with a Home Depot bag. My heart drops. The tracking device read that he was at Wendy's house. How could I have missed this? I should have trusted my husband. I just never should have done that!

CHAPTER 36

Ms. Rita Brings Trouble"

S pring Break is approaching and we don't have any definite plans for the children other than for them to be home for the entire week. Ms. Rita has been discussing with me the problems that her family is starting to have with her grandson, Tim. I always listen with an open heart, hoping to have the opportunity to help out one day. After thinking about it for a moment, it just seems like a no-brainer to me to have him to come and spend the week of Spring Break with us. It will give him a pleasant change.

"Kalin, Ms. Rita's family is starting to have serious issues with her grandson. He is always walking the streets and getting in trouble, so we thought it would be good for him to get away for the week", I explain. What do you think?"

"I don't have a problem with it", he responds.

Rita calls her sister to have him ready for us to pick him up.

It is settled. We set up the boys' room so that he can bunk out in there with them. The kids are happy when we tell them that he is coming. From what I know of him, Tim is 16 years old, challenged in school, and often gets in trouble in his neighborhood. For some reason, Ms. Rita's sister, Linda, has custody. Ms. Rita's daughter, Dee, is unable to care for her son because she has Down's Syndrome.

Most of the week has passed and there have been not one sign of trouble. Tim has been on his best behavior thus far. I am quite shocked when I get a frantic call passed to me from Ms. Rita.

"Ms. Melissa. You might want to come home. The police are at the house", she says, sounding very upset.

"What's going on? Are the children okay?"

"The children are fine. It's Tim!"

"What happened?"

"The police followed him here because he was seen selling drugs down the street. They traced him back to the house and he admitted to them that he has more, here in the house", she explains.

"Are you serious with me right now?" I yell.

"I am so sorry, Ms. Melissa. I can't be----", Rita says, and the phone hangs up.

I drop everything and head home. On my way home, I call Kalin and when I mention that the police are at the house, he immediately becomes upset and doesn't hear anything else that I have to say.

Kalin and I make it to the house around the same time. By the time we show up, the police are already escorting Tim out of the house in handcuffs. He can't even look me in the face. He is scared to death of Kalin and what he will do or say to him. The kids know that this is something serious, but they are not sure what exactly it is that Tim did.

"Why, son? Why do you feel like you have to do this? You don't have to be some drug dealer out in these streets", he says to him.

"Easy for you to say! Look at where you live!"

"Son, we work very hard for this. You have to work for what you want in this life. It is not going to be easy."

"Well, I appreciate ya'll for letting me stay here this week. I have enjoyed it."

"You disrespected this household in the worse way possible, son. You bought drugs around my family and that is a big no-no."

I am so upset right now! We let this boy into our home and this is how he repays us. I can't believe that Ms. Rita didn't tell us more about him and what he is up to. I thought that she would have been a little more responsible than that.

"Mr. Kalin and Ms. Melissa, I am so sorry about what Tim has done", says Ms. Rita.

"No, Ms. Rita, this is not your fault, nor is it your responsibility. We don't blame you for what he did."

CHAPTER 37

"I Don't Understand Teenagers"

Christy is now entering 7th grade and will be attending McShuster Middle School. She has already established her friendship base because she spent the last part of her sixth grade year at this school. She is learning quite a bit about herself and so are we. She is becoming of age and is becoming interested in boys. This is one thing that I dread more than anything. She is going through this phase where she'll rather talk to her friends instead of spend time with her family. She never wants to attend family functions with us and whenever there is an opportunity to do so, she would rather stay home. I think I will give Brittney a call to see how she handles her daughter who is only a year or so younger than Christy. She picks up the phone on the first ring, almost as if she is expecting someone else.

"Hello, Britt", I say, as she picks up.

"Oh, hello Meme. I thought that you were someone else", she says.

"Who else could you be expecting from this area code, crazy girl", I respond. "I have something to ask you."

"About?" she asks.

"Your daughter, Felicia. She is about the same age as Christy. Are you noticing anything differently with her? Is she sometimes anti-social with the family? Does she seem withdrawn at times? Is she starting to like boys? Please help me out with this one."

"Melissa, calm down. It is normal. Girl, sometimes it seems like Felicia is the devil. She gets quiet sometimes and acts like she is mad at the world. If I didn't make her come out of her room, she never would. Don't worry about it. She will snap out of it eventually", she says. "Just give it some time. Keep loving her and supporting her and it will be fine."

"Ok, I was just wondering. I am not used to her being this way. She is starting to act up in school and everything. I just want my sweet daughter back."

"I promise you. This is just a phase."

"Were we like this?"

"I am sure that we were, so don't worry about it."

"Since I have you on the phone, I might as well ask you what I am thinking", she comments.

"What is it?"

"There is some talk going around here about Laura's daughter", she states.

"Oh, yeah. What are you hearing?"

"That her father is "Rock". I don't believe it but that is what I am hearing."

"Don't believe everything you hear. And besides, what difference does it make? Laura is dead and her daughter needs her father, even if it is Rock. So, where did you hear this from?"

"I can't reveal my resources. You know that!"

"Well, I have to go now, dear, but thanks so much for the advice."

"Anytime, my friend. I love you."

"Love you too."

I wonder if Ms. Rita notices a change in Christy. It is really bothering me. I hope that this is just a teenager thing and that she will snap out of it. Ms. Rita admits that she, too, sees a difference in Christy, but feels that she will soon snap out of it, just like Brittney suggests.

While we are in the middle of our discussion, Kalin walks in to see how long I will be before I come to bed. That sounds like one of those, 'I really want to have sex, so please hurry up' questions. I guess I will go to bed and discuss this at some later date.

"Meme, I am starting to worry about our daughter", Kalin says.

"What do you mean?"

"I have been reading her diary and she is talking about this one boy that she is infatuated with named Calvin. She also talks in her diary about how she hates this boring a** house and how she never gets to do anything", he went on to describe. "Maybe we should start talking to her about boy/girl stuff, what do you think?"

"Maybe it will go away, Kalin", I respond. "Maybe we are overreacting."

"Maybe so, honey", he agrees. "We will just wait and see what happens."

And that is exactly what we do. We wait and wait to see if either her attitude about boys change or either her attitude towards her family changes. Her attitude towards her family remains the same but we don't hear anything about boys for a while. She continues to treat us like the plague. She does; however, start to spend lots of time with Ms. Rita.

CHAPTER 38

"Go Buccaneers!"

"Children, hurry up! It is time to walk out the door for church. You all have had more than enough time to get dressed. We will be leaving in 10 minutes", I announce to everyone, while putting the final touches to my makeup.

"Mommy, I really don't want to go. Can I please stay here with Daddy to help him finish up everything for our Super Bowl Party? Please! Please! I will go next week", Christy asks, pleading her case.

"Honey, why not? I will make sure that she gets some work done", Kalin argues for her.

"See Mommy. Daddy agrees that I can stay home", she says.

"Ok, Christy. You may stay home, but you will be going next week. I need you all to be in church. Do you understand me?"

"Yes ma'am. I will go next week. Thanks Mom", she says, while throwing her arms around my neck and planting a kiss on my cheek.

So, we leave the house without Kalin or Christy. However, Ms. Rita, me, Kameron, Darren, Amber, and Justice jump in the car and head to New Destiny, where Greg Powe from Revealing Truth Ministries, is visiting from Tampa and is delivering today's message. We have to hurry up to make sure that we get a park that is not five miles from the church. There are thousands of people expected at church today. I have heard great things about this minister.

"The Lord knows just how much we can bear. He won't put more on you than you can stand. He will be right there! He won't leave you nor forsake you. Just trust Him in all things. Let Him lead you. Let Him be your guide. Don't put your trust in people, money, or the things of the world. Put all your trust in the Lord. He won't lead you wrong!" Greg Powe shouts from the pulpit. The crowd is really feeling this guy. I have to admit that he is preaching a word that I truly need to hear today. I sure wish that Kalin would have come to hear this. This Word has set me free today! I will get the tape and take it home to share with Kalin.

Because there is so much traffic, it takes about 35 minutes just to get out of the parking lot and onto the interstate. Everybody agrees with me that the service was absolutely wonderful. I think that I will visit his church the next time I go to Tampa.

We finally make it into the house and Kalin and Christy have decorated the house with Super Bowl favors. We have at least 20 people coming over to the house for our Super Bowl Party. Christy is so proud of the work they have done decorating the house.

"Mommy, isn't the house beautiful? Daddy and I did a great job, right?" she asks.

"Yes, you did. But you missed a good sermon today. They had these kids dancing to that music that you all love."

"Cool! she says, pointing to the beautifully decorated table.

"It looks nice. Everything looks nice. I love it!"

Even though Ms. Rita normally goes home on the weekends, she decided to stay with us this weekend to join in on the Super Bowl festivities. We are excited because a Florida team is playing in the game. It's the Tampa Bay Buccaneers against the Oakland Raiders. Everybody knows that Tampa Bay is going to win this game!

We are all gearing up for the game, when our first guest arrives. This group is a mixture of our friends and Ms. Rita's friends. Ms. Rita's grandson, Tim, is the first one to show up. Today is a fun day, so we aren't concerned about what happened with Tim. Everybody deserves a second chance. Ms. Rita opens the door for him, but I do take special notice that Ms. Rita, Tim and Christy are talking as if they are in a deep conversation. *What is that all about, I wonder. Why is Ms. Rita having such a deep conversation with Christy? I will ask her about it later.*

All of our guests finally show up and the game begins. The room is half divided. There are people cheering for the Bucs and the rest for the Raiders. This makes the room more exciting. We run out of snacks, so I have to make a run to Publix to pick up more snacks. *Boy, can these folks eat!*

The game is finally over and the Tampa Bay Buccaneers pulls it off! They win the game, 37-21. The Raiders' fans decide to leave before the team is honored with the trophy. I can't say that I blame them. We are putting it on a little thick, rubbing it in and all.

"Goodnight, everyone!" I say, as I finally put out the last guest.

We all retire to our rooms and Ms. Rita and I vow to clean up all of the mess the following morning. It is time to go to sleep.

"Hey, Ms. Rita, is everything okay with Christy? I saw you and Tim talking to her quite intensively this afternoon. Is there anything that I need to know about?"

"Oh no!" she answers. "She was just talking to us about school and sports."

"Okay, I am just checking. If there was anything that I needed to know about my daughter, I am so sure that you would tell me."

"Of course, I would, Mrs. Thomas."

It has been a long day, so we all retire to our rooms to get some sleep.

CHAPTER 39

"Why Are You Saying These Things?"

I have so many things going on in my head right now. I have learned about Princess' situation and the fact that Laura claims that she is Rock's baby. Dana just died recently and Mark hates me. Stuart is feeling really down because of his guilty conscience of how his wife died. I try my best to tell him to get a grip on it. The kids are doing fine, though, with the exception of Christy going through her pre-teens stage. I am curious as to what Ms. Rita keeps whispering about with Christy and then telling me that nothing is going on. I don't know what to think of it all. Why does life have to be so hard sometimes? Why can't everyone just get along and make life easier for the next person?

"Momma, the phone is for you?" yells Ms. Rita from the other room.

"Who is it?"

"Leigh Bynum. At least I think that this is what she said."

"Ok, I will pick it up". I wonder why she is calling me. *Was I supposed to call her for something and just forgot to do so?*

"Hello."

"Mrs. Thomas, how are you doing today?" she asks.

"I am fine. How are you doing?"

"I am doing okay. I need to speak with you about something. Do you have a minute?"

"Sure, what's up?"

"I have some disturbing news to share with you", she begins. "I just found out through the grapevine that your daughter is saying some things to some school counselors that you might need to know about. She is telling them that your husband has been doing some inappropriate things to her. I don't know all of the particulars, but I came across this information with some people that I know. I don't want it to just hit you on the top of the head, so I thought I would give you a call to warn you of the storm that is coming your way", she explains.

"I can't believe this. Are you sure that you heard this right?"

"Yes, honey. I heard it right. Of course, I don't know the truth of it, but it is out there, so I just want you to know."

"No, thanks so much for calling me. I don't know what to do with this information. I need to go in here right now and question my daughter", I say, sounding panicked.

So now, I guess I see what all the whispering was about. Apparently Christy has been saying these things to Ms. Rita also. Why in the world is she saying these things?

I walk into the kitchen, where Ms. Rita is fixing lunch for the kids.

"Ms. Rita, may I please speak with you?" I ask. She puts down the sandwich bread and walks towards me.

"Yes ma'am. Is anything wrong?" she asks, looking puzzled.

"Yes, there is. I just received a disturbing phone call from a former caseworker with CCF who informs me that Christy has been saying some things about inappropriate behavior by Kalin. Have you heard this at all?"

Because she is unable to make eye contact with me, I am starting to believe that Ms. Rita is aware of these accusations.

"She did tell me something like that, Mrs. Thomas. She came to me about a month ago and said that he touched her inappropriately and was doing it since she was 11 years old", she answers.

"What! Are you serious with me that she told you this about a month ago? You have been in my house and all the time knowing that my daughter is saying these things and you didn't care to come to me and speak to me about it? Why didn't you come to me, Ms. Rita? She has been staying here with him alone when we go to church, but yet, you said nothing to me. Please answer this for me. Why didn't you say something to me?" Ms. Rita is speechless. She can tell that I am very upset about what I am hearing. She is just standing here with her head lowered. "And then, I have to hear about it like this. This is wrong, Ms. Rita, and you know it is."

"I am so sorry, Ms. Melissa. I just felt that she should be the one to tell you. I didn't think that it was my place to come to you with this information", she responds.

"Ms. Rita, you are the adult! This is not about who should tell who. You had knowledge of this information and you said nothing! You know that Christy is always here with him and still you said nothing! This makes no sense to me at all. She is accusing Kalin of this inappropriate behavior, but she doesn't mind staying here alone with him. Did you know on Super Bowl Sunday that Christy was making this allegation towards Kalin?"

"Yes, I knew then", she says, looking as if she is ready to cry.

"And you did and said nothing?"

"Since you put it that way, I guess I did nothing. I am terribly sorry, Ms. Melissa."

My heart is broken. I am so angry, but who am I angry with? Am I mad at Christy for saying it? Am I mad at Ms. Rita because she withheld this information from me about my child? Am I mad with Kalin that he has done something to make my daughter say these things about him? How in the world will I ever be able to deal with this? I don't know if I can handle something like this? I love my husband, God knows I do, but I love my daughter also. I can't turn my back on my child? Isn't it true that men come and go? God, please give me the strength to deal with this.

Ms. Rita and I are deep in our conversation and the door to the front family room opens. It is Kalin and he is coming this way. He opens up the kitchen door and Ms. Rita walks out without even acknowledging his presence. Christy walks out as well.

"Honey, what is wrong? Why are you crying?" he asks.

"Kalin, we need to talk", I say, putting my hand over my mouth.

"What about? What is wrong honey?" he asks, sounding almost panicked.

"Kalin, Christy has been telling counselors at school and Ms. Rita that you have been touching her inappropriately since she was 11 years old and—", I say, before he interrupts me.

"Are you fucking kidding me? Touching her inappropriately? I don't believe this shit! I have NEVER touched this child like that. Ain't no way in hell I could be that stupid! Why in the world is this child saying this about me? I have never done this, Melissa. You have to believe me! I would NEVER do anything like this to hurt my child. Oh my God!! This can't be happening right now", he continues to say.

The entire time Kalin and I are talking, my head is hanging down. I can't look him in the eyes. I don't know what I will think I see if I look into his eyes. To be honest, I don't think I really want to hear what he is saying right now. I don't think I can feel my very own tongue. I am in so much mental pain right now that I can't cry.

"Meme, what are we going to do now?" he asks.

I don't have an answer for him. How do I answer this question? I think that if I have to answer this question right now, I don't think that Kalin will like what I have to say. Because of my lack of response, Kalin starts to feel that I no longer want a life with him. Without saying a word, he gets up and gathers his things to prepare to leave the house. I don't even ask where he is going or anything. I just let him walk out. Nearby in the other room, Amber and Justice notice that he is getting ready to leave and start crying for him. I don't see him, but I can hear that he is sobbing unstoppably. Justice cries to go with him. He is trying to tell her to go to her room and go to sleep but she is refusing. She is screaming, "Daddy, please don't go!"

I don't move from the spot that I am in. I can't move. I am sitting in my favorite chair rocking back and forth. No one comes to me to see why daddy is leaving the house. The boys are still in their room and don't come out at all. Christy is in the room with Ms. Rita while all of this is unfolding.

I finally get out of my chair to see if Ms. Rita has any pain medication that I can take.

"Ms. Rita, do you have anything to help me sleep?"

"Let me see, Ms. Melissa", she says. She walks to her closet and comes out with a bottle of pills. "Here you go. Just take one now and you will be sleep in no time. These are very powerful sleeping pills", she says, handing one to me.

"Where is Justice?"

"She left with your husband. She was crying so hard that he just took her with him."

"Ok. Please take care of things for me. I have to go lie down. Thanks for the pill." I can tell that Christy is not bothered at all with what just took place. I walk over to her and give her a hug and tell her that I love her.

I decide to go to my room to let the sleeping pill do its magic because I need to fall asleep right now. Before I know it, I am in a deep sleep having a very vivid dream.

In my dream, I can clearly see myself and Christy. We are in this wide open room that has nothing in it, other than its 4 walls. Christy and I look up at the ceiling and notice that there is a red stain in the ceiling and red colored droppings on the carpet. As we approach it, it looks more and more like it is blood. I tell Christy that we need to call the cops because someone must have been murdered. Christy agrees and gives the cops a call. The next day, I decided to go to this same room, but by myself this time. I decide to look further into the red stain, so I get on top of the house. Once I get up there, I clearly see that the red stain is actually from a red crayon that has melted on top of the house. I immediately pick up the phone and call the cops to tell them that there is a mistake and that there really isn't a murder. The dream is over and I wake up in a sweat.

I jump out of the bed and immediately recognize that Kalin is not next to me and I start to worry about him. Sharell comes into my room and starts whining that Kalin is not here and she is beginning to worry about him. She looks up at me as if I should be worried about him as well. She picks up the phone and dials Grandpa "JT" and he answers on the third ring.

"Grandpa, have you seen daddy?" she asks. He must have told her yes, because Sharell is now speaking with Kalin. She hangs up the phone and gives me a hug and tells me that he is okay and that he is at grandpa's house. She makes sure that I am aware that he was just crying on the phone.

"Mommy, what is going to happen with daddy?" she asks.

"Baby, I don't know", I respond, hugging her close to me. "This thing is in God's hands now."

Sharell and I lay in the bed for a little while longer until it is time for me to get up and get dressed for work.

How in the world can I make it through the day with all that went on last night? Lord, I truly need you. I still have to go to work and do a good job. I can't allow Satan to win. I have to stay strong.

CHAPTER 40

"Why Did He Run?"

I muster up the strength to go to work. My eyes are still puffy from last night. I hope that the staff won't be able to tell that something is wrong.

Did I remember to give Christy a hug before I left the house? I need to make sure that she knows that I love her, but that Mommy is really hurt and confused right now. I will make sure to talk with her tonight, just me and her. I want to get to the bottom of this right now. I wonder how Kalin is doing. How did he sleep last night? What is he thinking right now? I need him to know that I love him too, but that I am hurt and confused right now.

I pick up the phone to dial my father in law's number, but I get a call first. It looks like Ms. Rita is calling me from the house.

"Hello Ms. Rita, how are you?"

"I am fine, Ms. Melissa. I am sorry to bother you at work but I thought that I would give you a call to let you know that CCF came by and they want to see you. They said that they will come back this afternoon being that you are at work right now. The lady's name is Melinda Wooten. She will be back at 5", she continues.

"Fine, I will be there. Thanks."

I proceed to call JT and this time, he picks up the phone.

"Hey JT, how are you? It's Melissa."

"Yes, I know. I have your hubby here and I am glad that you called because he is sitting here talking crazy about how he is going to kill himself because of this mess. He keeps saying that he didn't do anything to Christy. And Melissa, I believe my son. I might as well tell you that up front. I know that my son didn't do what Christy is saying that he did. I don't know why she is saying it, but he is just absolutely devastated. I am going to let him talk to you now", he said, handing the phone over to Kalin.

"Honey, I love you", Kalin says before anything else.

"Kalin, I love you too. How are you doing sweetheart? What is JT talking about?"

"I can't go on with anyone thinking that I could ever hurt my child or anyone's child. I am so hurt that this child is saying this about me. I can't believe it! I don't want to lose you, Melissa. I love you more than anything in this world. I can't lose my family over this. I don't have anything else!" he says, sobbing through the phone.

"Kalin, slow down. There has to be some type of explanation for all of this. Why in the world would Christy say this about you?"

"I don't know Melissa. I really don't know. I haven't touched our daughter inappropriately at all. I have done nothing but try to be a good father to her and –", he says without taking a breath.

I interrupt him. "Listen, we will have to speak about this later. I will come over and we can talk then. I can't deal with this right now. I have to concentrate on work and then later, I have to be home to deal with CCF. They have already showed up at the house. They don't waste any time, do they?"

"Melissa, I wanted to die last night. When I left our home, I went to the Williamson Bridge, stopped the car and wanted to jump. The only reason I didn't is because Justice was in the car with me and I didn't know if she would try to jump after me or what. I couldn't do it, but I sure as hell wanted to. How do a man cope with shit like this when they know they didn't do anything wrong?"

"I don't know. I really hope that we can work this out. I love you Kalin *and* I love my daughter."

"I know that you do Melissa. I know that you do. Have a good day at work honey."

I want to tell Kalin about my dream but I am still trying to figure the dream out myself. *Does it mean that things aren't always what they seem* to mean that my marriage looks good, but it really isn't? *Or could it mean that Christy may say something but when you really look at it, it isn't what she claims?*

It isn't until 4:30 that I finally look up realize that the day has pretty much passed me by. I am going to finish signing these bonus checks and head for home. As soon as I pull into my driveway, I am forced to remember about the white government car with the yellow tag. *Oh Lord, please give me the right words to say to these people. We need you Lord. I need you Lord. Please show us mercy in this process. In Jesus' name. Amen.*

The closer I get to the front door, I can see that there are two investigators waiting for me on my porch.

"Hello, my name is Melissa. I am so sorry that you are sitting out here. Why didn't you knock on the door and Ms. Rita would have gladly let you in?"

"It is okay. We are fine out there just enjoying this beautiful Florida weather", I say, trying to make small talk. "My name is Denise Woods and my partner's name is William Moss."

"Great, please come in."

We all walk into the house and are greeted by the children. They are all very happy to see me, so much so that Ms. Woods comments about it.

"Boy, are they excited to see Mommy!"

"Yeah, I know. May I offer either of you something to drink?" I ask, trying to sound polite.

"No thanks. Where may we go to talk in private?" asks Ms. Woods.

"Here in my office", I say, directing them to my office nicely decorated with all of my Mary Kay ribbons and Kalin's "Designer of the Year" awards. I have to admit that we are both doing quite well in our careers at the present moment.

Denise pulls out a folder and picks up her pen and explains that she will be taking notes as we talk and that William will only interject as he sees it necessary.

"So, Mrs. Thomas, you must know why we are here", she begins.

"Yes, I know that you are here because of Christy's allegations against my husband."

"Correct. We were informed of this by school counselors and just need to check on things to make sure that everyone is doing okay. Where is Mr. Thomas currently staying right now?"

"He left last night and went to stay at his father's house."

"Don't you think that this is the one thing that admits his guilt? Why did he run?" she asks, not looking up from her folder.

"He left the house because it was just an understood thing to do. I didn't ask him to leave. He just knew that he had to leave. He denies the allegations and clearly says that he didn't do anything inappropriately with my child."

"And you believe him?" she asks.

"I don't know what to believe right now, Ms. Woods. This news is devastating to my family. I love my daughter, but I love my husband also. I don't know what to think at this point. It is all very hard to believe because I have lived in this household and have never noticed anything out of line between Kalin and Christy. Ms. Rita is our live in babysitter and she is the one who is with the children more than anyone", I explain.

"And now, about Ms. Rita. I understand that your daughter confided in her about these allegations", she says, waiting on my response.

"Yes, I learned just recently that she spoke to Ms. Rita about it. According to Ms. Rita, she has been aware of these allegations for at least a month. I have spoken to her about this and I even questioned her about why she didn't at least inform me of this. She simply said that she didn't feel as though it was her responsibility to divulge the information to me. She knows how I feel about this. I completely disagree with her because she, herself, knows that Christy is around my husband alone and if she knows that my daughter is always around my husband alone, why would she agree for them to be together? She should have spoken up sooner."

"So, you are trying to hold everyone else responsible other than your husband?" she asks, looking at me as if I am the one on trial.

"No, I am not!" I say. She is really starting to get me upset because I can clearly see where this is headed. She must have gone through all of the previous complaints and think that she has all of the answers about my family.

"Ma'am, there is no need to get upset", she comments.

"And there is no need for you to judge me or anyone in my household. You don't know what is going on here. You are here to investigate the facts. Please don't judge me or my family. I would appreciate that", I say to her, while standing up now at my seat.

"I am sorry, Mrs. Thomas. I know that this must be hard for you", she says.

"You damn right it is hard and I am tired of people judging me on this."

"Well, we will need to speak with the children and Ms. Rita before we leave", she announces.

"And I have absolutely no problem with that, Ms. Woods. I will add that just last month, we had CCF in here because Sharell went to school with a mark on her wrist and one of the teachers reported it. Your department was in our home for 5 long weeks talking to us about alternative forms of discipline. When that counselor came, she spoke with each child individually. You might want to refer to those notes as well. This will give you an idea of what was going on in the house before the allegation and even how Christy was coping with everything."

"I will remember that. Thanks. Do you have anything to add, Mr. Moss?"

"I have one question for Mrs. Thomas. Will Mr. Thomas come back to the home to reside?" he asks.

"Not until this is all cleared up", I respond.

"So then, you are telling me that you are still interested in having a relationship with someone who hurt your child?" he asks, looking over his glasses.

"Sir, it is alleged, which means it is not proven. I would not even consider having any type of relationship with Mr. Thomas if I even thought for one second he hurt my daughter. There is just no way!"

Ms. Woods and Mr. Moss stay in the office and one after another, the children go in to speak with them. They leave Ms. Rita for last. Ms. Rita comes out of the office, along with the two investigators.

"Mrs. Thomas. We will review all of our notes and we will be in touch with you", says Ms. Woods as she makes it to the front door. I get up to follow her out and she says, "No, please, sit down. We will let ourselves out." They are gone, but I know that my new nightmare has just begun.

CHAPTER 41

"Stuart's New Friend"

The rest of the evening goes well and after dinner, I decide to finally have a talk with my daughter. I don't want to upset her any more than she already is right now, but I need to talk to her to find out exactly what Kalin did to her. I need to get to the bottom of this. I need to get my own answers.

"Christy, are you done with your dinner, honey?" I ask, as she is playing around with her peas on her plate.

"Yes Mommy. I don't really want to eat anymore. It was good, Ms. Rita", she says, as she is getting up from the table.

"Ms. Rita, I will take care of the dishes tonight. I want to spend some time talking to Christy."

We decide to speak in her bedroom because it is her comforting space. She has pictures of her friends all neatly placed on the wall. She has tons of honor roll certificates and track ribbons. I am looking at a giant poster board of Charles Barkley, her favorite basketball player. She says that she wants to be a pediatrician one day because of her love for animals. But, she also talks about being an engineer one day, as well.

"So honey, how are you doing with all of this going on around us?" I ask, as she stares at the ceiling.

"With what going on?" she asks.

"You know. The thing with the CCF coming around and the thing about Daddy", I answer. "This must be so hard for you."

"It is hard. I told Ms. Rita and told her not to say anything about it", she says.

"But why not tell Mommy? Why didn't the two of you come to me and tell me about it? I love you so much honey", I say, as she is now looking at the floor. It is almost as if there is a bug down there that she is concentrating on and hoping to squash.

"I didn't think you would care or would believe me", she answers. "I just needed to tell somebody about it."

"Well, that is what I want to talk about. I want to know what happened to you. I want to know what Kalin did to you, sweetheart. I want to know when and where. Where was I when all of this was going on?"

"Mom, listen, he just did it, okay! He just did it", she says.

"I hear you honey. But what did he do? Where did he touch you? Where was I when he did these things to you? I am not trying to upset you, but talk to me now. Tell me what happened to my baby. I love you sweetheart and I need to know what happened", I plead with her.

Christy doesn't give me anything else to go on. She doesn't give me any pertinent information as to what took place when Kalin inappropriately touched her. I don't want to question her anymore because she is starting to get a little upset.

"Alright baby, I love you. Please brush your teeth and get back in bed. I love you Christy. I always will love you no matter what. You are *my* baby and I love you. But, Christy, I love Daddy too and that is why it seems so confusing, but don't let anyone tell you that I don't love you because I love you so much." Christy is looking deep into my eyes as if she is hoping to see the truth in them.

I can tell that she is ready to go to sleep, so I give her a hug and tuck her in bed. It sounds like the other children are just getting into their beds so I decide to tuck them in as well. I don't know what to think about my conversation with Christy. I don't feel like I know anything more right now than I knew before we had our talk. Maybe I can get more information out of Kalin. I need to get to the bottom of this and I don't really care what I find out, but I can't move on in life without knowing why my daughter is saying these things.

I need to talk to Kalin *now*. Hopefully, he picks up the phone. I did tell him that we would talk later. That is why I am not surprised when he picks up the phone on the first ring..

"Hey honey, I am so glad you called", he says.

"Yeah, me too. I am ready to talk now."

"Ok, let's talk. What do you want to ask me first?" he asks.

"Why is this happening to us? Please tell me why after all of these years of peace in our home that we have to now deal with something so serious? I don't get it honey. I feel like someone is out to punish me for something that I did in another life or something", I begin to say.

"Imagine if you were the one they were saying it about", he says. "I will always be looked at as the man who "messed" with his wife's daughter. People don't care whether you are innocent or not. The fact that our child is saying this, is enough for people to believe her. I don't care about any of them. I do care if my wife believes it or not. Do you believe I did this to her, Melissa?" he asks.

There is silence on the phone before I answer the question. I hesitate as if the phone is bugged or something.

"Kalin, I have been with you for over 12 years. I have slept in the bed with you every single day of those 12 years, with the exception of the 6 months you spent in jail and the 2 months sleeping in the car and the other 2 months that you stayed at Carl and Wendy's house. I have NEVER seen you do anything inappropriate as it relates to the children or to any other woman for that matter. I truly believe that you didn't do this, but I want to know why Christy is saying it. I need to know where it is coming from. You can't imagine how it feels to have your daughter say something like this about your husband and feel like you have to choose. It is like being caught in the middle. I am caught between you and between her. I love you both and I won't choose sides. I will always stay on the side of truth, whichever way that falls", I explain.

"I have no problem with this. You are right to believe that I didn't do it because I didn't. I would never do anything like this to a child. This reminds me of the young lady who made an accusation against me when I was teaching that I was inappropriate with her. Although the truth came out later that she was just infatuated with me, the damage was already done. And because of it, I never wanted to teach again. At the time, I was married to Kayla and this false accusation almost destroyed my marriage", he says.

"I can only imagine what she felt."

"Listen, let's take one day at a time and see what happens", he suggests.

"Sounds good to me. I have to get some sleep. I have a long day tomorrow. I have to contact the attorney regarding the letter that Laura left for me. I have tons of questions for him."

We both decide it is time for bed and hang up the phone. I only chose to get off the phone because I don't really know what else I can say to him. I don't want to come across as if I think that he is a monster, but my daughter must be hurting deep down inside to make this kind of accusation against Kalin.

We get up the next morning and Ms. Rita seems a little agitated, but I am not going to ask her about it. Something has truly upset her. I have my own issues right now, or I would ask her what is bothering her. There is quite a bit of stress in this house right now. I am doing as best as I can to keep it moving along normally. Ms. Rita usually wakes up and makes sure to say good morning but not this morning. She makes breakfast for the children and walks right past me in the kitchen while I am preparing my coffee.

"Ms. Rita, is everything alright this morning?"

"Yes ma'am. Everything is fine. Why do you ask?" she responds.

"You seem a little agitated about something. You walked right past me and didn't say good morning or anything."

"No, I am fine, but thanks for asking. Good morning."

"Good morning. I have a phone conference tonight with an attorney in Middleton, so I will be late getting home from work. I also have to do some shopping before I get on the plane this weekend for Texas. So, don't wait up for me. Just feed the kids and I will see you in the morning."

"Okay. That is fine. I am so sorry if I offended you, Ms. Melissa. I just have lots of things on my mind right now. Is there anything else?" she asks.

"No, that is all. Get some rest, okay."

Something is not right with this picture. There is more going on here than I know about, but I just don't have time to try to figure it out.

As soon as I make it into the office, Cindy gives me my messages. The one from Stuart Peters is marked "Urgent". I haven't heard from him in quite a while so I need to give him a call to make sure that he is okay. I might as well call him before I get my day started. When I dial his number, a lady answers the phone.

"Hello, may I speak with Stuart Peters, please."

"Oh, okay. Hold on. He will be on in just a second", she politely says.

"Hello, Stuart Peters."

"Stuart, Melissa here. It's been a long time since we talked. I received an urgent message from you. Is everything okay?"

"Oh honey. Everything is better than okay. I just wanted to give you all a call and give you some good news. First of all, I will be in Miami this weekend and would love to stop by and second of all to let you know that I am finally clean. I am free of drugs for over a year now and I am finally getting remarried", he says.

"And let me guess, that was her who answered the phone?"

"Yes, her name is Phyllis. She is wonderful. She is everything a man could ever want in a woman. She and I just opened up our very own law firm. We are both lawyers. She is an amazing cook and has 2 sons. I just wanted to share my good news with my family and introduce her to you", he says.

"Well, I have some news for you, but my news is not so good. Kalin is not living at the house right now. My daughter is alleging that he touched her inappropriately so he left the house and is staying with his father. I take the kids over there to visit with him every weekend. We are taking one day at a time to see what happens with this", I begin to explain.

"Kalin could never do anything like this", he interjects. "I don't believe that for one moment. Not Kalin!"

"I know. I don't believe it either, but I do want to know what is behind what she is saying. I need to know for my sanity, Stuart. How can a woman ever choose between her daughter and her husband? We are not just talking about any husband. We are talking about a husband who came in and raised 4 kids like they were his own. We are talking about a man, who unselfishly named these children as his own. That is just not something you walk away from without trying to at least get to the bottom of it", I say.

"It's like you are actually caught in the middle! Did you talk to your daughter?" Stuart asks.

"Yes, of course. She didn't give me any detail. She just said that it happened and that was that. She refused to go into anymore detail about it."

"Let me take this case for you. I might as well tell you that Kalin will definitely be charged and you will need good representation. Let me do this for you. I don't know anyone who would have taken me in. I was a druggie and homeless and had nothing. And the two of you took me in and loved on me and believed in me when no one else could find the strength or the time to do it. I will never forget it. You won't have to pay me. Let me help my friends through this mess", he pleads.

"Do you think he will be arrested?"

"Yes, dear. I am sure that he will be arrested. With everything going on in the media right now, the police and judges are all panicked right now. Did you hear about the woman who was seeing this guy and he raped her daughter and got her pregnant?"

"Oh my goodness!"

"And that's not the worst part. He got the girl pregnant and after she got pregnant, he started messing with his girlfriend's son. The boy got sick behind it because the damn man had AIDS! And guess what the Mother did? She took him back and put the children in foster homes. When she came to me for representation, I just turned her down cold. She should be ashamed of herself. I am very picky about the cases that I take. Because I know Kalin and believe in his innocence, I will take your case", he says.

"Give Kalin a call. I am sure that he will love to hear from you right about now. He can tell you yes or no. I don't see why he won't go for it, but I can't answer for him. To be honest with you, I don't see where he really has too many choices."

"Alright sweetheart. I just wanted my family to meet Phyllis. We will get together at a later time. I will substitute this weekend and just take her on a cruise or something", he says.

"Yeah, because this weekend, Kalin and I are flying out to Texas. We already had plans before all of this happened, so we thought that getting away won't be so bad right now."

"I agree. I will give him a call now. It will all be alright, Melissa. You know that right?"

"I do. Thanks for reminding me, though."

I manage to make it through the rest of the day without going crazy. My conversation with Stuart is quite refreshing. It is really good to hear from him. I am so happy that he met someone and it sounds like she makes him very happy. That name, Phyllis, sounds familiar to me. Maybe I will meet her and will be reminded of where I know her from. The clock is ticking away and it looks like I am on schedule to have my phone conference with Attorney Richards from Middleton.

"Cindy, I am expecting a call from Attorney Richards. Please put him through when the call comes in."

"Of course, dear. My kids can't wait to hang out at your house this weekend while you and Kalin are away in Texas", she says.

"I know. My children are really looking forward to it, also."

By the time I make it back to my office, Cindy is buzzing in Mr. Richards. "Mr. Richards, on line 1."

"Hello Mr. Richards, how are you this evening?"

"I am fine, Mrs. Thomas. How is the weather in Florida?"

"It is a very beautiful day. It was like 70 degrees today."

"Great, let's get down to business, shall we?"

"That sounds good to me because I have to get out of here and go shopping. Kalin and I have a big trip to Texas planned for the weekend."

"Late honeymoon or something?" he asks.

"No, it is actually a business trip, but we are turning it into pleasure", I answer, with a slight grin on my face that I am sure he is able to tell.

"Great", he says. "Now, I understand that you opened your letter that you received from Laura Walters, your deceased friend. Thanks for sending me a copy of it. How do you feel about hearing about this child this way?"

"It is all very surprising because to be honest with you, I had no idea that "Rock" was having a thing with Laura. Nonetheless, the child is here now and is without a parent. I spoke to my husband about this and we are more than willing to take Princess into our home. The only condition is that I will decide if and when the time is right to tell her about who her father is. I just don't think it is relevant at this point. If he wanted to be involved, he would have been. From what I understand, he was told that he was the father and rejected her", I explain.

"The child has a right to know who her father is, whether he accepts it or not", he states.

"But why? Why should we put her through all of that just to get her heart broken?"

"This is something that will be addressed at a later date."

"Next question, would you take this child even if there was no money involved?" he asks.

"Of course I would. I have loved her mother for many years. We were the closest of friends. I remember when we were young and I needed someone to do something very important with me that even my mother didn't know about it. Laura was right there with me. She kept all of my secrets and everything. We were so close. I will love her daughter just as much as I loved her. I will raise her to know about her mother. I will make sure that she knows all about her mother. I will most certainly do that."

"Mrs. Thomas, I am convinced that you will do right by Alexandria Walters, and I will recommend to the Courts that you be named as her legal guardian and will ultimately gain full custody. Are you ready for this?" he asks.

"Of course, I am. Just draw up the paperwork and send it to my office. I will look over everything and I will be in touch."

"Ok, and Mrs. Thomas?" he asks.

"Don't hurt your husband too bad while in Texas. Let him breathe a little bit", he says and afterwards laughs.

"I will take very good care of Mr. Thomas."

"What a lucky man he is!" he says. It almost sounds like Mr. Richards is flirting with me a little. He is a gorgeous man. I am sure that the women in Middleton love going into his office just to catch his eye.

"Well, thank you", I respond, as if he isn't flirting.

"Goodbye."

Our meeting finishes up a little sooner than expected so I think I will go ahead and get home and do my shopping before I get in to work tomorrow. I am sure the kids will be surprised to see me. I pull into the driveway and notice that there are a couple of cars in my driveway. *Who can this be? Was Ms. Rita having guests over to the house? I don't recognize any of these cars. Should I go in? Will I interrupt anything? Does she have a boyfriend or something that she has been hiding from me?*

I decide to go in through the side door so that I won't disturb anyone. As soon as I open the door, I can hear someone yelling in the background. *I think I should just let Ms. Rita handle it because I am sure that she is involved in whatever is going on in here.* I peep around the corner just to listen and see if I recognize any of the voices. I think I have caught the very end of the conversation. Ms. Rita is having an argument with her sister. *I hope everything is okay with them. Should I get involved or should I just go past the den and into my bedroom?*

"Rita, I can't believe your sorry ass! You come into these folks' house with this mess. You ought to be ashamed of yourself. Now, what you gone do when they find out you smoking crack in they house around they children? These folks trust you with they kids. And then you sit around here like you care about them. I have a mind to tell them what you been up to. They seem like such nice people and they took you in. They even took your bad ass grandchild into their home and you let him mess them up too!" she says. "And then you go and let yo own grandson get arrested knowing those were your drugs that he was caught wit. You need to be ashamed of yo'self."

So, Tim went to jail for Ms. Rita? Those drugs were hers! Wow!!

It doesn't seem like Ms. Rita is in the room at all because I can't hear her voice at all. I finally hear her mumble words but I can't quite make out what she is saying.

I can hardly make out what Ms. Rita is saying, but it sound like she is saying, "Fuck you Lois! Fuck you and the mule you rode in on. I'm gone keep working with that girl up there and get me mine. These folks here got a good life. What I got? Not a damn thang, so there you go. I ain't thinking about nobody. What dey don't know won't hurt dem", she says, as she walks to the refrigerator and pops open what sounds like a soda. *Working with that girl up there? What is she talking about? What girl?*

"God don't like ugly, Rita! That's all I got to say. You keep on doing what you doing and I promise you that it will all come out one day and I just might help them do it. You wrong, girl! You wrong as hell and I hope they find out about who you really are", she continues.

The phone rings and it interrupts their conversation. I can hear Lois saying that she needs to go, so it is time for me to go back out and come back in as if I just got here. I don't want her to go outside and see that I have her blocked in.

I walk back outside and put the key in the door and walk in making an announcement, "I'm home everyone!"

The kids rush to the back room and give me lots of hugs and kisses. Ms. Rita and her sister make their presence known.

"Ms. Melissa, this is my sister Lois. Lois, this is Ms. Melissa", she says.

"So nice to meet you, Lois. I am glad to finally meet you."

"Nice to meet you, too", she responds.

Rita looks a little upset right now. She looks like she is mad at the world. This is exactly how she was this morning before I left for work.

"Ms. Rita, are you okay honey?"

"Yes, I am fine. Why do you ask?"

"It just looks like you are upset about something?" Before I can get an answer from her, Lois decides that it is time for her to get going. She excuses herself.

"Okay, Rita. We will talk later honey. Enjoy the soup!" she says, as she makes her way to the front door.

"How did your meeting go, Ms. Melissa?" she asks.

"It was fine."

"So, what happened with it?" she asks. *Why is she asking me so many questions about my meeting with the Attorney? She knows that I am not going to divulge that information just yet until it is settled in court. Is she worrying about whether I will pay her more to care for another child or what?*

"It is being worked out with the attorney. I am waiting on paperwork", I say, leaving it at that. I make it over to the kitchen to get a bottle of Aquafina Water.

"Did you finish all of your shopping for your trip?" she asks.

"No, I will take care of that tomorrow, though."

"So, will Mr. Thomas still accompany you on the trip?" she asks.

"Of course he will. We had these plans for several months and the trip is all paid in full. We have business to take care of for this trip. We are trying to break into a new business and we have potential investors to meet with out there", I explain. "Cindy, from the office, said that her kids are really looking forward to coming over for their play date this weekend. I appreciate you for staying over this weekend with the kids for me. Thanks a bunch. Did anyone call?"

"No, just your friend from Middleton, but she said that you didn't have to call her back. I told her that you were going to be late getting in and she said that she will just talk with you at a later time."

"Ok, well I am going to bed. Goodnight." *Why is it that I feel that something is just not right with Ms. Rita? There is something that she is not telling me. And that conversation with her sister, what was that all about? Who is the girl that she is working with? What is going on? I am too tired to think about it right now. I don't feel like talking to Kalin either. I am going to bed now.*

Tomorrow is another day.

CHAPTER 42

"Is There A Problem?"

*I*t is 2 days away from my trip to Texas, which includes a weekend with my husband. I still have to get my shopping done. This is definitely one of those last minute shopping moments that my husband always accuses me of having. I have been busy though. Thank goodness that I can actually do all of my shopping online and just stop into the store and pick up everything.

Macy's is having a great sale on cocktail dresses and I need to get a couple of them for the trip. All done! I need to see if Kalin needs anything, but he is at work right now, or at least he should be at work. I don't know why I decide to call him, but he answers the phone on the first ring.

"Hey honey, what are you doing home?"

"I am going in a little late. What's going on honey?"

"I just need to make sure that you are all packed and to see if I need to pick up anything for you for the trip."

"I will need you to pick up some more cologne for me. I ran out a couple of days ago. Other than that, I am pretty packed. I almost forgot. You will also need to get my tuxedo and put it in the cleaners. But that is it! Are you excited that we will be getting away from everything for a few days?" he asks.

"Yes, I am very glad about that. I am looking forward to spending some quiet and alone time with my husband. We need to spend this trip talking and confirming our love and commitment to one another."

"Yeah, that is right. I will pick you up. Please be ready, Mrs. Thomas. How are the kids?" he asks.

"They are all doing just fine, sweetheart."

"OK, see you then."

The rest of my day is spent doing tons and tons of paperwork. I am going to go ahead and head home early so that I can spend some time with my children before I leave. This is really not a good time to leave, but the trip is already paid for.

I make it home and find the kids and Ms. Rita just getting ready to sit down for dinner. It seems like I made it home right on schedule. They are so excited to see me home for dinner.

"Hey guys, how is everyone?"

They all start yelling, "good, and awesome". I even heard one of them shout, "Marvelous!" Those are certainly Kalin's words. He is always "marvelous".

"Hey guys, I have a great idea. When we finish dinner, let's go get some ice cream. What do you say?"

"Yeah!!" they all shout in unison.

When dinner is over, I pack the kids in the SUV and head to Ben & Jerry's over at South Beach for some after dinner dessert. They seem to really enjoy this time with me. Christy seems to be uplifted a little. She gets to ride in the front with me. She always likes that.

"Hey guys. I want to talk to you all for just a second. You know that I am taking a trip to Texas, but I will be back in a few days. Ms. Rita is going to be here with you. And of course, your friends are coming over this weekend to play with you. Your weekend is pretty full so you won't even miss me."

"Will you come back?" Justice says, reaching over to give me a hug.

"Of course, sweetheart. Mommy will be home in a few days", I say. "I will remember to bring you all something back from Texas, ok."

"Ok, Mommy! We will miss you", says Kameron.

"I will miss ya'll too."

"OK, let's get some ice cream! Tell the lady what you want, one at a time, please."

Before we make it to the house, I tell the kids to mind their manners and listen to Ms. Rita while I am away.

"Yes ma'am!"

We make it inside and Ms. Rita has already cleaned the kitchen so we are able to walk in and get ready for bed. I take all the kids in the den and read a bible story to them. The story tonight is about Joseph. *This is actually my favorite character in the Bible.*

I put my head down on my pillow and start thinking about all the fun times that this family has seen. I remember the first time we took Ms. Rita to Middleton with us. She had a blast! She always talks about that trip. She says that it was like being around the family she wishes she had. We traveled to Middleton for a special birthday celebration for my oldest brother. While on the trip, Ms. Rita was with me when I spoke to my father on his death bed. She and I would sit and talk about this trip for hours before it happened. She always told me to love my father and to forgive him even though he was never around in my life. We stopped in Mission Hills to see Kalin's family also. So, Ms. Rita got to meet them as well. However, I also remember when we were getting ready to leave and my niece, Nikki, started asking these questions about Christy staying in Middleton. I remember thinking, *here we go again!* That sparked a small argument and I left saying, "see, this is why I don't like coming home. All of you think that you can run my household! Take care of your own kids!" Kalin constantly reminds me that this was the last time he will ever travel to Middleton to visit my family.

I am sitting here thinking about the fun or maybe not-so-fun that we have had, but, *how much do I really know about my babysitter? Has she been truthful with me about her life and where she is from? Why is someone else taking care of her daughter and her grandchild? What is it with this woman? She does a good job with my children, but is that enough? Can I really trust her?*

I finally fall off to sleep and wake up with my alarm clock blaring in my ears. I set it for 2:30 am because Kalin will be here at 3:30 to pick me up for the airport. My father in law has agreed to drop us off so that we don't have to pay for parking at the airport.

I walk into the kids' rooms and give them all a kiss before leaving out. Ms. Rita got up with me to fix me some coffee for the road. "Here, Ms. Melissa, this cup is for Mr. Kalin. Isn't he going with you?" she asks.

"Yes, my husband will accompany me on this trip. We have some business to take care of. Thanks again for staying here with the children."

I reach over to give her a hug and I am truly awakened when I hear the horn blowing outside. Kalin is here! I grab my two suitcases and overnight bag and head for the door. Kalin is waiting outside to take my things to the car. He looks in, sees Ms. Rita and says "good morning" to her.

"Good morning sir. Ya'll have a nice trip. Everything here is under control."

"Ms. Rita, here is the number for the hotel. We are in room 2346. We will arrive in Texas in approximately 2 hours. I will call as soon as we land. Please let the kids know that I stopped in their rooms and gave them kisses before leaving."

"Ok, Ms. Melissa. Get out of here before you are late getting to the airport. The children are in good hands."

Me, Kalin, and JT head for the airport. Our flight is on schedule and we leave Miami on schedule heading for Dallas, Texas. We make it to Texas and I get to the phone right away to let Ms. Rita know that we have made it safely. The kids are all up getting dressed for school, so I get a chance to tell each of them to have a good day.

****

"Ok, Ms. Rita. We are here. If you need anything at all, please give me a call here at the hotel. We are scheduled to meet up with the investors for lunch, but until then, we will be in the room", I explain to her.

"Ok, not a problem. Everything is fine here."

Kalin and I head to our room and decide to have breakfast in our room. We are both so exhausted that after we finish eating, we decide to take a small nap before heading to our lunch with the potential investors. I am finally getting into my room and the phone rings. *Is Ms. Rita calling me already?*

"Hello."

"Melissa?" the lady on the other end asks.

"Yes, it's Melissa. Who is this?"

"Melissa, it is Leigh Bynum. I am so sorry to call you there but I have some very interesting news to give you sweetheart. As soon as you get back to Miami, you really need to speak with your babysitter", she instructs.

"What happened?"

"Your babysitter has been talking to CCF against you. She is telling them all sorts of things going on in your household. She told them about a conversation that you had with your daughter after your husband left the house. She told them that you were trying to get your daughter to change her story. She told them that you have been taking the kids over to Kalin's father's house to see him. She even told them that you are there right now on that trip with your husband. She is not in your corner sweetheart. For some reason, she is working overtime to get your kids in foster care. I don't understand, why though.

`"Oh my God! Ms. Rita said what!" I shout. Kalin must hear me because he jumps up and sits up in the bed, looking at me with a puzzled look on his face. "I can't believe this is happening to me. What in the world did I do to deserve this, huh?"

"Honey, I am so sorry to tell you. Like I told you before, I have connections and anything that concerns you and your family I want to try to help you. They have it in for you, Melissa. You are not a typical CCF client. They don't know what to do with you. They figure that the best way to get to you is to go through your family and for whatever reason, they are all talking to CCF and now they have Ms. Rita", she continues.

I knew it! I felt that something wasn't right with this woman. How can she do this to me after all we have gone through together? I let this woman bring her grandson into my home and he stole from me. I let her bring her daughter to live with us for awhile when the family she was with grew tired of her. I trust her with my precious children, my family. And now I am all the way here in Texas and she has my children, probably poisoning their minds for sure. I knew that something was wrong!

"Melissa, what's wrong?" Kalin finally asks. I throw my hand up to let him know that I will speak with him when I get off the phone.

"Ok, Leigh. Thanks so much for calling me. Thanks for having my back."

"No problem, anytime!"

"Leigh, how did you get the number to the hotel?"

"I called the house and told *your babysitter* that I was with CCF and needed to speak with you. She probably thinks that I am calling you to get you in trouble or something. I knew that she would be more than happy to give it to me."

"Alright, thanks again!"

"Try to enjoy yourself, ok?"

"Yeah, right! Like that is going to happen", I say sarcastically. "Goodbye."

I have a lump in my throat the size of a watermelon. I don't know what to think right now. This woman has been with me for so many years and has become a part of my family. This nightmare is getting harder and harder to deal with.

"Kalin, there is a problem", I announce, as I sit him down to explain. "I believe that it will be a matter of time and CCF will be coming for the children again. And you won't believe who is helping to nail the coffin on us?"

"Who?"

"Ms. Rita. She has been talking to CCF feeding lies to them about our family", I begin to explain. "She has been working with my family off and on since this nightmare began. They are even working to see who will take my kids when CCF gets them. Can you believe this?"

"Honestly, I believe that your family will do anything to get rid of me and make me perish", he says. "They believe that I hurt my daughter. They have tried from the beginning of our relationship to make me go away and they finally think they have a good chance now. So, no, I am not surprised at all.

Let's try our best to have a fun time here. We need to get ourselves prepared mentally for this meeting at 1 o'clock. We can do it honey."

For lunch, Kalin and I meet with our potential investors in the Hotel Restaurant. They show up and seem to be enjoying Kalin's conversations about Florida. I just want to hop on the plane and head for home right now. I don't care about this business venture anymore. All I can think about right now are my children and what must be going on with them right now.

Back at the Hotel Restaurant.

"Mr. Thomas, I love your proposal. It looks pretty promising. I like the ideas that you have presented here. I like the numbers that you have also given. They seem to be pretty realistic. All I want to know is how many of these boarding houses would you like to have?" Mr. Wilmington says, as he looks at Kalin over his glasses.

"As many as the Lord will allow, sir", he says.

We wrap up the meeting and say our goodbyes to these two gentlemen.

"Honey, I am so glad that you were all over it because my mind is not here at all."

"I know that it isn't. Let's go upstairs and take a long shower and sit on the balcony and have a couple of glasses of wine", he suggests.

"That sounds good, but I need to call the kids first."

"Of course, honey."

I pick up the phone to call the house while Kalin takes his shower. Ms. Rita answers the phone.

"Hello", she says.

"Hello Ms. Rita. How are you and the kids doing?"

"Everyone is doing just fine sweetheart. You sound sad", she says.

"No. I am just tired. We had a great business lunch today. It all sounds promising. The investors were impressed with our offer. Are the kids up?"

"Yes, they are sitting in the den watching television. They all had a good day at school. Kameron made a "B" on the Science test that he was worried about. Christy had some friends from her club at the house today."

"Great! May I please speak with Christy?"

"Sure."

She yells to them that I am on the phone and I can hear their little feet pattering away to get to the phone.

"Hello, Mommy", Christy says when she picks up the phone.

"So, how did your meeting go with your friends?"

"It was good. We came up with some really good ideas about what we want to do for the homecoming dance that is only 3 or 4 weeks away", she says.

"Wow, awesome! That sounds good. I hope they all work out. How are your other sisters and brothers doing?"

"I will let them tell you."

Darren grabs the phone. "Mommy, when are you getting home?" he whispers. "I hate being here with this lady. She is being so mean to us. She is so different to us when you are here and when you are not here. I don't like her anymore", he admits.

"Son, what is going on?"

"She is always cursing at us. She makes me go outside to take out the trash when it is dark. And Ma, she is always talking on the phone to Auntie Diana about what is going on in the house. She was telling those people about you being over there in Texas. She is always talking about you to people on the phone", he continues to say.

"Sweetheart, everything will be alright. I promise you that it will. Mommy will take care of everything when she gets in, ok?"

"Yes ma'am. Just please hurry home!" he exclaims.

"How are Kameron, Amber, and Justice doing?"

"They are fine. She is not mean to them. She is just mean to me and Kameron. She lets Christy get away with everything. She never has to do her chores anymore. Auntie Diana and all of them were over here today just hanging out. They left the house in a mess!"

"It is okay, son. Everything will be better when I get home, ok?"

"I love you Mommy!"

"I love you too, but put the others on the phone so I can speak to them too."

I have finally spoken to all of the children. Now that I know they are fine, I can get some rest and enjoy this beautiful Hotel in Texas. But before I leave the phone, Ms. Rita picks up the phone.

"Ok, we will be shutting down our trip a little early. I need to get home to take care of some things. I will let you know when we get in."

"Ok, not a problem. Did that lady from CCF call you over there? She said it was important so I gave her your number. I hope that this was okay", she explains.

"It is fine. Thanks for letting me know, though."

I hang up the phone with her. Kalin is just getting out of the shower.

"How are the kids?" he asks.

"They are fine. I have to go home, sweetheart. Can you please finish up the business here?"

"Sweetheart, I will take care of everything. You're not leaving tonight, are you?"

"No, of course not."

"Well, jump in the shower and I will have that glass of wine waiting on you when you get out. The water feels great!"

I jump in the shower and Kalin is right. It feels so relaxing. I love the special touch they put on the room with the waterfall lamps that light up the room. It is so romantic. It is such a shame that I am here in Texas, in this romantic hotel room, and can only think of getting back to Miami.

Kalin and I sit on the balcony for a couple of hours just talking about the current events of our life. He mentions to me that Wendy called him and before he can tell me what she wanted, I stop him in mid-sentence because hearing her name just makes my stomach sour. I don't want to know anything about a woman right now who has slept with my husband at some point, especially knowing that she would have him again if she could.

"Sweetheart, it was nothing. She called to invite us to the surprise birthday party that she has put together for *her husband*", he explains. "I think it will be fun! I told her that we will be there, Mrs. Thomas", he says. "Sweetheart, you are my wife and I love you and it will always be Melissa and Kalin. Nothing will come between us. Deal?"

"Deal!"

We finish off our night with my husband giving me a much needed massage. It is so magical that my underwear seems to have disappeared into thin air. Before I know it, Kalin is hiding under the covers.

I get up the following morning and see if I can get a flight out, but there aren't any going to Miami. It looks like I will have to wait it out and fly out tomorrow right along with my husband. *I might as well enjoy the rest of the trip and take care of these issues when I return home.*

CHAPTER 43

"Fire Her Or I Will!"

Our plane lands right on schedule back into Miami. Urban Legend is the newest airline and they are so efficient with their flights arriving on time. I am quite pleased with them so far. I will try them out a few more times and see if I *still* like them.

I think I see my father in law. He is just as punctual as can be. He always says that he doesn't like to be late, but he is always telling me that I will be late for my own funeral.

"Hey Dad!" Kalin says as he approaches his father. They give each other a manly hug. My husband looks just like his father. I think that he will grow old gracefully just like JT.

"Hey son, how was your trip?" he asks.

"It was fine. We got a little rest. I tell you what. The investors really like our idea and before we left, we met with a few more of their closest friends so that we can eventually pitch them our idea as well. It was a huge success. They said that they will be in touch by the end of the week with their decision", Kalin says.

"That is just wonderful!"

"Oh, and you remember that guy Stuart that used to live with us? Well he is now an attorney and he wants to represent me in this case. He feels that they will eventually charge me with something and he wants to help", Kalin explains.

"That is great honey. So, I guess he did call you? I spoke to him and gave him the number and he told me that he would call you. So, what do you think about him representing you?"

"Heck yeah. I trust him and I believe that he will fight for me because he knows me too", Kalin says to me and JT.

"And how are you young lady?" he asks, looking at me wondering why I am looking out the window.

"I am fine, dad. Thanks for asking. I just have lots on my mind."

"What's wrong now?" he asks.

"JT, how much do you know about Ms. Rita?"

"Why, what did she do? Did she do anything to my grandkids?"

"No, nothing like that. I just want to know how much you know about her", I repeat.

"I know that she is a slimy, crack headed, thieving woman", he answers.

"What?!"

"Yeah. She is really good with the children, but she has issues. The best thing you did was to let her move in with you just so you can keep your eyes on her. I would never let her take the kids back to her house and in her neighborhood. She can't really be trusted that well", he continues.

"So, why didn't you tell me this before?"

"I tried to tell you. Remember you said that you believe in giving people second chances?"

"Oh yeah. Well, I still believe that. But, I am going to have to let her go. I can't allow this woman to be around my children anymore. I don't trust her and I want her out of my house", I finally open up to JT and say.

"Why, what happened, Melissa? You aren't saying anything", he says.

"I found out that she has been calling CCF and telling them all sorts of stuff about our household and that she has even been speaking with my family about me too", I reluctantly answer.

"Yeah, get her the hell out of your house! Fire her or I will and I mean it and I won't be nice about it at all!"

"I will take care of that as soon as I get home."

"Melissa, I think it is the right thing to do, but be gentle. Ms. Rita is like family to us. You don't have to go in there with guns blazing or anything. Just keep it business. Don't attack her personally. Say what needs to be said and let it go", he advises.

"Ok, got it!"

Kalin and I arrive at the house and they let me out. Kalin takes my bags to the door and waves to the family so that he can go on his way. The kids bombard the door when they realize that I just entered the house. Ms. Rita is standing in the kitchen and it smells like she is baking chocolate chip cookies.

"I'm home!"

"Hello, Ms. Melissa. How was your flight?" she asks.

"It was fine. We made it back right on schedule. Texas was hot. We have gifts for everyone!"

One by one, each child gets his special gift from Texas. We even purchased a set of pajamas for Ms. Rita's daughter and a house coat, with the Texas Cowboys emblem on back, for Ms. Rita. She loves it!

"Sweetheart, I really need to speak with you", I say, before she has a chance to get away.

"Is everything okay?" she asks.

"We just need to talk, just you and me. I want to talk to you tonight right after we put the children down for bed."

"Ok, sounds good. Is it okay for me to get a shower first? It has been a long day", she says.

"Sure, that is fine." Ms. Rita walks away and heads for her bathroom to get a shower. Waiting for her to return is making me very tired. I know we need to talk, but it will have to wait until tomorrow. I am exhausted!

"Ms. Rita, we will talk tomorrow. I am tired and I am going to bed!" I yell to her from the hallway.

CHAPTER 44

"Dejavu Or What?"

I wake up the next morning and realize that me and Rita did not have our talk. She is still here and is in the kitchen right now fixing breakfast for me and the kids. *How can this woman be so kind and loving, but yet so evil all at the same time?*

I don't have time to speak with her before going to work. I guess we will have to have our talk this evening when I get home from work.

"Ms. Melissa, CCF called you yesterday. I forgot to tell you last night. We were all so hyped up about your returning that I forgot to tell you.

"Who was it that called?"

"Denise Woods. She is the lady who was here with that guy that time that came right out after the accusation."

"Yes, how can I forget?"

"She called and said to please get in touch with her."

"Ok, I will call her when I get to work. Did she leave her number?"

"Oh Lord, I don't know where I wrote her number down at", she says, as she starts looking around in her purse for the number.

"Don't worry about it. I will look through my things to see if I can find her card that she left", I say, putting the finishing touches on my makeup. "I almost forgot to tell you. I am taking the kids out to a movie tonight. I promised them some quality time when I got back. They said that they want to talk to me about something. So, being that we will be out, just cook enough for you and your daughter. We won't be here."

"Ok, that sounds good. Have fun!"

She walks me to the door and hands me my briefcase as I am walking through the front door to get into my car.

I finally make it to work and get to see all of the paperwork waiting on me, as well as the messages. I go through the messages and see that Denise Woods tried to call me at work. I need to give her a call seeing that she left an urgent message. *I guess everything that Leigh called me is about to unfold. But why does it have to be so soon?*

I dial her number and she answers on the first ring.

"Hello", she says.

"Hello Ms. Woods. This is Melissa Thomas. I understand that you have been trying to reach me."

"Yes, I need to speak with you briefly. I know that you are at work, but I will try my best to be brief", she says.

"Go ahead."

"We have been informed that you have been taking your kids to see your husband while he is at his father's house", she says. "Is that true?"

"Yes, it is true. What is the problem?"

"Your husband is being accused of raping your daughter and you want to know what the problem is?"

"I am at the house with him when the children are there. His father is there, as well. What is the problem with that?"

"The problem is that your husband raped your daughter!"

"Listen, Denise. You are not in a position to say this. How can you call me on my job with this? That is not your place to say that. This is something that will be decided upon by a court of law. Where do you get off calling me and making these kinds of statements?" I say angrily. My assistant manager rises from her desk and notices that I am getting upset. She puts her hands up as if she wants to know if all is okay. I mouth the words to her, "I'm okay". She closes my door so that I can continue my conversation.

"So, do you want me to come to your house right now and remove your children from your house? Is that what you want?" she responds.

Her voice is becoming elevated right along with mine.

"Listen, you do what you feel that you need to do. I didn't do anything wrong. My children are not in any danger of being around their father nor are they in any danger of being with me. I thought you people were all about trying to do your best to keep families together instead of always trying to tear them apart. Listen, I am sorry. I don't mean to yell at you. It is just that this whole thing has really taken its toll on my family and I don't think that my children can handle any more separations right now. Ms. Woods, I really have to go now because you are completely out of line right now and I am not going to sit here and listen to you speak to me in this way. You should have more respect for people than this. Has my husband been convicted of raping my daughter? Did you perform a rape test on her? No, right? I have to go."

"We will be in touch, Mrs. Thomas", she says before hanging up the phone.

"What in the world was that all about?" Cindy says.

She makes her way into my office now that I am off the phone.

"CCF called me wanting to know why I am allowing my children to see their father. She acts like he has been tried and convicted in a court of law and everything. I just told her that the kids are not in danger of being around their father. She said that she would be in touch. I won't be surprised if they try to come and get my kids again."

"Take it easy. Don't get yourself upset over nothing. Calm down and look over these reports from last month. These are our numbers. We didn't do too badly. We did great on our budget. Corporate always likes that", she says.

"Yeah, I know. I am always thrilled to see these kinds of numbers, too. I will have to take my staff out to lunch before the week is over", I say, starting to calm down and move on past my conversation I just had with Denise.

"Now you know that we like that!" she exclaims. "I almost forgot. There was a detective by the name of Lewis Pettigrew who called while you were on the phone. He said to make sure you give him a call as soon as you are done. He sounded like it was urgent." *I don't know if I have anymore energy to call this guy. This woman from CCF has sapped all of my energy and patience for today. I will call him back later.*

The next couple of days pass and I finally get a visit from Detective Pettigrew from the Miami Police Department. I see his police car when he pulls up in front of the community, but I have no idea that he is here to see me. He gets out and walks inside.

"I am here to see Melissa Thomas. Is she in?" he asks looking around.

"Sure, hold on," Cindy says as she gets up from her desk and starts walking toward my office.

"Mrs. Thomas, Detective Pettigrew is here to see you", she announces to me as I am hanging up the phone.

"Sure, send him in." *I forgot to call this man back. Now that is going to make me look like I am avoiding him. I really don't know what to expect. Why is he here to see me? What is he going to ask me?* Within seconds, he is already in my office.

"Good morning, Mrs. Thomas. I am sorry to bother you here at work but I called a couple of days ago and left a message for you, and ---", he says.

I interrupt him, "Yes, I know. I do apologize for that. It has been somewhat hectic, but I am glad that you stopped by."

"I hate to have to see you here at work, but I –", he begins to say.

"It's okay. Don't worry about it", I say, as I throw my hands up to let him know that it is okay. "How may I help you?"

"We are doing an investigation regarding your husband. Are you aware of the allegations being made against your husband by your daughter?" he asks.

"Yes, I am aware."

"We want to speak with you, we want to speak with him, and then your daughter", he states.

"That won't be a problem at all."

"Is it okay for me to speak with you here at your office?" he asks.

"Sure, just let me inform my assistant that I will be tied up and not to disturb us", I respond. I get up from behind my desk and walk out to the front to tell Cindy that I will be in a meeting if anyone calls or comes by. I return to my office and close the blinds with the understanding that this will only take a moment.

"Ok, now where were we?"

"I would like to ask you some questions regarding what has or is taking place in your household", he begins.

"OK."

"Now, your daughter claims that your husband has been touching her inappropriately since she was 11 years old. Have you ever seen anything like this?" he asks.

"Absolutely not."

"Has she ever said anything to you about your husband touching her inappropriately?"

"Not before July 12th of this year."

"So, she never came to you about him doing anything to her at all?" he asks.

"No, she did not."

"I understand that your daughter disclosed this information to your babysitter. Is that correct?"

"That is correct."

"Any idea why she told her and didn't tell you?"

"No sir. I have no idea why."

"Did you ask your daughter about her allegation?"

"Yes, I did."

"And what did she tell you?"

"I went to her and asked her what he did to her. I wanted to know the specifics of what took place, but she never disclosed any of that to me. I still don't know what she is saying that he did to her. When I saw that she was getting upset with my questioning, I stopped talking to her about it."

"Let's talk about the babysitter. Are you aware that she contacted our office?"

"No, I am not."

"She contacted our office and let me refer to my notes for a moment here. She said, and I quote "Mrs. Thomas' daughter is alleging that her stepfather touched her inappropriately and her mother is trying to get her to change her story. Mrs. Thomas is still seeing him and is actually in Texas with him right now. She takes the kids to see him and tries to get her daughter to go see him…" he states, reading from his notebook pad.

"Wow. I am shocked that she would contact your office with such untruths. I don't know why she is saying these things. I did take the other children to see him, but I never forced Christy to go. I never even mentioned that to her. And yes, I just returned from Texas with my husband. We had some business that was arranged some time ago, so we kept our plans. As far as me trying to get my daughter to change her story, that is just untruthful. I had a conversation with my daughter and I was simply trying to get more information from her. I wanted to know what he did to her. I didn't go at it like I didn't believe her. I just wanted some information about what he did. I don't understand why she was able to be descriptive with Ms. Rita, but she didn't have any words when it was time to talk to me about it. I really don't understand this", I explain.

"Is Mr. Thomas out of the home?"

"Yes he is. He has been out since the night I was made aware of my daughter's allegation. I confronted my husband and he denied it. All I know is that I have never seen my husband do anything inappropriate to my daughter. Ms. Rita watches the children every single day and she has never said anything to me about her seeing my husband doing anything inappropriate."

"Has she ever been home with him alone?" the Detective asks.

"Of course she has. There was never a reason that she should not have been", I respond.

"Well now the CCF Department is involved and they are very concerned for your other children. I believe that they will be running their own investigation. As for ours, I will need to speak with your husband. Do you know the number where he can be reached?" he asks.

"Yes, the number is 555-4544. This is his father's house", I respond.

"We will come by the house tomorrow afternoon to speak with your daughter. Are you okay with that?" he asks.

"Yes, that is fine with me."

"And as far as your husband is concerned, we will go out and meet with him also."

The Detective is done questioning me at this time. He gets up and leaves my office. Once he is out of the office, Cindy rushes to my side.

"Is everything okay, Mrs. Thomas?" she asks.

"Yes, everything is fine". She can look at my face and see that I am simply saying this because I don't want to talk about what just happened.

"Please let me know if you need me for anything. I want to be here for you as a friend. I know that I work here for you, but we are also good friends. I know that this must be hard for you, honey. Please find the strength to hang in there. The children really need you to hang in there. With your husband now gone out of the house, you have to hold it all together. I know that you can do it", she says, rubbing my hand.

I know that if I hold up my head, I am going to cry. I grab her hand and mouth the words, "thank you". Cindy rushes back to her desk because the phones are ringing off the hook.

After Cindy leaves my office, I get up to close the vertical blinds. The sunlight coming in is blinding me. *I don't wish this hurt that I feel in my heart to happen to anyone. This pain won't even give me a moment to breathe or anything. I love my daughter. I love her so much and I can't imagine what she must be feeling or thinking right now. She is my first born. But I love my husband too. People are telling me that I can't love them both. People are telling me that I have to choose my daughter or my husband. Why can't I just choose to love them both? Why can't I just wake up from this nightmare and be at one of our fun Sunday afternoon outings?*

"Cindy, I am going home", I say as I walk past her as she was counseling one of the residents about their increase of rent. "Call me if you need me".

"Yes ma'am. Take it easy. I will call you later", she says, without looking up.

I am taking my time to get home on purpose. I always enjoy the quiet time that I get while driving along in the car. I need to hear my uplifting music right now. "The battle is not yours, it's the Lord's", sings Yolanda Adams so beautifully. I start to wonder, *whose battle is it then? Why am I going through this Lord? What did I do that was so wrong? Why me Lord? Why did you let me live just to have to go through this heartache? I wish I would have died when I wanted to die. Is this what you have saved me for? This is so unbearable!*

I finally make it home. The kids are already working on their homework. Christy is sitting at the dining room table, along with Kameron and Darren. They look so peaceful. They don't have a clue what is really going on in our lives right now. I want to take them away from all of this. I want to bring their father back into the house and make our life normal again. Ms. Rita is busy doing something in her room. I start thinking about how she and I were supposed to speak together a few nights ago. I never followed up on our meeting. Maybe it is best that I not get rid of her just yet because I need to find out what she is trying to do. I will not confront her about calling the police, *just yet*. If I let her go, I will not find out anything at all. My mother always said to "keep your friends close and your enemies closer". I think I will give her sister a call to see if she will talk to me about Ms. Rita and see if she has any idea why she is trying to destroy my family after all we have done for her.

"Hey guys!" I say. They all jump up to greet me at the door. I decide that it is best that I start spending more time with them now more than ever. "Are ya'll ready to go to the movies? I have already ordered the tickets online and we are good to go! We have to stop by Walgreen's to get our movie snacks", I say, putting down my briefcase. "I just have to change clothes and then we are out!"

Ms. Rita is sitting in the den area and she looks pre-occupied.

"Ms. Rita, we will be leaving for the movies shortly. We will get dinner while we are out", I tell her.

"That is fine. Dee and I will fix us something to eat. Ya'll have fun, ok", she says, walking back into the kitchen.

"Ok. Come on guys! We don't want to be late for our movie!"

The children are all dressed and ready to go. We say our goodbyes to Ms. Rita and Dee and head for the car. It seems as if the children are very eager to have me alone. From the moment I get out of the driveway, they start telling me how they feel about having Ms. Rita at the house now. I am really shocked to hear my children say that they do not want her to watch them anymore. For crying out loud, she has been with us several years. She is part of our family.

"Momma, we know that you love Ms. Rita and we love her too, but she has changed a lot! She is mean. She curses all the time. She lets her daughter listen to all that rap music and it is just not as fun having her in our house as it used to be", admits Darren, as he is playing with his new toy that Kalin and I just purchased for him. *This might have something to do with her allegedly being on drugs. That is certainly something that I have to get to the bottom of as soon as I can catch up with her sister.*

"Really? I thought that we were all getting along just fine", I respond.

"Well you thought wrong", the kids all say in unison.

"How about we do this? Let me talk to her and see if we can't get a better understanding of how things should be around the house", I suggest. "Will that work?"

"Oh yeah, she needs to stop talking bad about our daddy, too", says Kameron.

They all agreed. "Yeah, that's right!"

We finally make it to the AMC Theatre in South Hills and we are right on schedule for the movie. I have already put the snacks down in my purse and we head for our show, "You Got Served". Darren is really looking forward to this movie so that he can catch some new dance moves. He is my little dancer in the group. He wants to dance his way in to the end zone, he says. He always talks about how he wants to buy his Mother a brand new house, with all of the clothes I could ever want. That boy's a dreamer! He said he is going to make it to the NFL one day.

I know that they are not concerned about Ms. Rita right now, but I am. I wonder if she is planning her next big thing to try to hurt us. *Why in the world did she tell those lies to the detective? What is her motivation to bring our family down?*

We head for home. I am pulling into the driveway and when I turn on the interior lights to my car, I see 5 sleeping children, with the exception of Christy, who is just looking out the window, staring at no particular object.

She helps me get her sisters and brothers inside and we head for their bedrooms. It was a long night. When we get inside, Ms. Rita and Dee are already gone to bed.

CHAPTER 45

"Is There Probable Cause?"

I wake up the following morning and the dream that I had last night is so vivid. I feel like crying but I don't exactly know why. I need to call my husband and make sure that he is doing okay. I quickly grab the phone from the nightstand and dial my father in law's number. Kalin picks up on the third or fourth ring.

"Hello", he says, sounding very groggy.

"Honey, hey, it's me. I was—", I say before being interrupted.

"The kids okay?" he asks, before I can finish.

"Yeah, the kids are okay, but I had a crazy dream last night and I just needed to make sure that you were okay", I explain.

"Yes, baby, I am fine. I was asleep, though", he says.

"I know, but I was worried. You know how it feels when you can just feel like something is going to happen. That is how I feel. Maybe I am just paranoid or something. Did a Detective Pettigrew call you?"

"Yes, he did. I spoke with him at length when I got home yesterday. He told me that he had already spoken to you."

"Yes, he did."

"That is fine, honey. He said that he is going to meet with Christy today at some point. Who knows? Maybe this will all get cleared up and we will be a family again", he says.

"I know. I just don't understand everything. I don't know why Ms. Rita is telling lies to the police. I don't understand why she is being so secretive about everything. And I still don't understand what is going on with my baby. Why did she say those things about you? I really don't get this."

"Honey, I promise you on my life and my kids' life, that I did not do anything inappropriate to our daughter. I just don't know how many more times or how many more ways I can say this to you. I know that this is extremely hard for you. I know that it is hard for her. I don't know why either, but I know that I didn't do anything wrong to her. That is what I *do* know", he continues.

"Well, I just wanted to call and make sure that you were okay. Please give me a call this evening when you get in from work, okay?"

"Okay, sweetheart. I promise to give you a call. Don't worry. The truth has to come out", he says, before hanging up the phone.

"Have a great day."

"You too!"

Knowing that Kalin is safe and sound, I decide to go ahead and get my day started. Everyone is still asleep and it is 3am in the morning. I can't go back to sleep so I might as well get up and use this time to talk to God.

> *Dear God, Father of our Lord and Savior Jesus Christ. I thank you for waking me up this morning. Thank you that I woke up in my right mind. Lord, I pray that you will watch over the Thomas family this morning. Please protect my children. Please watch over Christy, Kameron, Darren, Sharell, Amber, and Justice. Please keep my babies safe from hurt, harm, and danger. Be with them at the school, on the playground, and even as they sleep. Send your angels to always be around them and to protect them. Lord, whatever this thing is that has me feeling this way, please guide me through it. Lord, you told me that I could come boldly before you and make my requests known. Lord, I need you to show up in this "thing". I need your presence to be made known. I pray that the truth be revealed in this situation. Lord, forgive those who are working very hard to destroy me. Lord, your Word says that "no weapon formed against me shall prosper and every tongue that rises against me in judgment shall be condemned". Please direct my steps. I love you, Lord. Amen.*

Prayer changes things. It may not come when you want it but my momma always said that it comes when you need it. I get up off my knees feeling much better than I did when I got on them. The kids are starting to get up now and I have to get dressed. I walk into Christy's room to let her know that the Detective will be here today and I just want her to tell him the truth.

"Christy, are you up sweetheart?" I ask, with her back turned against me. She hears my voice and rolls over.

"I am up now, Momma. What's wrong?"

"Oh, nothing sweetheart. I just want to let you know that a Detective Pettigrew will be here today at some point to speak with you. I spoke with him on yesterday and he said that he will come and speak to you today. I am letting you know because I don't want you to be surprised when he comes. I may not be here. Just tell him the truth, okay", I advise.

"Yes ma'am", she says.

"Mommy loves you sweetheart. Don't ever let anyone tell you that I don't. I know that this is a crazy time right now, but they don't write books on how to deal with this kind of stuff when it happens in your family. I do know that I love you."

"I love you too, Mommy."

Christy gets up and gets dressed. I can hear the other children starting to move around. It smells like Ms. Rita just put on my Folger's coffee. *It is such a shame that this woman has to be so evil because she really does take good care of me and the children.*

When I walk past the kitchen, Ms. Rita catches a glimpse of me coming out of Christy's room. "So, Ms. Melissa, how is Christy?" she asks.

"She is fine. I was just saying good morning to her. Oh, by the way, Detective Pettigrew will be here today to speak with her. I was just letting her know that. I just simply told her to tell the truth. I may not be here when he comes because I have tons of work to do today. I am glad that I won't be here because no one can say that I told her to say one thing or the other." *I hope that she takes this as a hint that I know what she has been saying to people. How dare she say that I tried to get Christy to change her story?*

"Oh, okay, I see. So you spoke to him?" she asks, looking as if she wants me to clear her conscience.

"Yes I spoke to him", I say, without giving her any indication that he said anything to me about her allegations. "Well, let me get dressed and get out of here. I have so much to do today."

"Is there anything special that you would like for dinner, Ms. Melissa?" she asks.

"No, just whatever you cook is always good", I respond. *The truth is that I can't eat her cooking anymore. Everything that she cooks lately makes my stomach hurt.*

I finish getting dressed for work and still remember the look on Christy's face as I spoke with her. It was as if she wants to tell me something, but she is caught in mid-sentence with a voice that keeps her from talking to me.

I finish getting dressed, drink a cup of coffee, and finally leave for work.

After a twenty minute drive, I pull up to the Clubhouse. As soon as I walk through the door, Cindy has my messages in hand, ready to hand them to me.

"Here you are sweetheart. These are your messages and here is a package that was delivered for you on yesterday after you left. The outside of the envelope reads, **Attorney Richards, Middleton, AL.**

"Finally! I was waiting on this package to arrive", I say, sounding very excited. I decide to wait before opening it. Cindy hands me my messages and the first one is from "Stuart Peters" and he says that it is urgent. I pick up the phone and immediately dial his cell phone. "Let's talk a little later. I really need to make this call."

She closes the door behind her and I dial Stuart's number. He picks up on the first ring.

"Hey, Stuart, what's wrong?"

"Melissa, Kalin has been arrested. He is okay! He called me from the police station. He told me to tell you not to worry. He said that he is hanging in there. Apparently, the police showed up on his job and escorted him out of there. The car is still there, so have somebody take you over there to get the car", he explains.

"Do you think you will be able to get him out?"

"We will have to find out tomorrow when he goes before the Judge to see if he will allow a bond. If he does, we will work on it from there", he explains.

"What if he doesn't?" I ask.

"Then, he will remain in jail until there is a trial", he answers.

"What happened? Did the police send out a warrant for his arrest? He met with the police on yesterday. What went wrong? They are meeting with Christy today."

"Melissa. Calm down. Let me explain. Kalin did meet with Detective Pettigrew. I was actually there with him when he was questioned. This arrest didn't come from the police. The Judge who deals with CCF is the one who pushed this arrest. The social workers presented a situation to the Civil Judge, who pitched a fit to the Criminal Judge and all of this is what led to Kalin's arrest. Don't worry. Let's see what the Judge says tomorrow morning. Try not to worry too much! I will see you tomorrow morning. Don't worry. He is actually in good spirits."

"How can I not worry? It is my job to worry for him. Oh my God! I don't know how much more of this I can take? I just don't know!" I say, as I begin to cry.

"Melissa, don't do that! Don't you fall apart on me now! Kalin is going to be fine. You have to hold it together for the children. He can't do that for you. He is a strong man and he will do what he has to do to survive in there. I am sure of it. I want to tell you this but I don't want you to freak out on me", he begins.

"Ok, tell me. What is it?"

"After the detective left on yesterday, Kalin and I went out for some coffee and we had a little talk. *Is he going to tell me that Kalin confessed to something because if he does, I am going to throw up?* He had lots of things on his mind", he says.

"OK, what did he say to you?"

"He explained to me why he thinks Christy is saying these things. He told me that he didn't touch her and I believe him. Trust me when I say this. I would not be representing him if I didn't believe him. He thinks that your babysitter is behind all of this. He explained to me that the two of them had a disagreement one day about something very small. There was something that had to do with the children and he sided with his children on it. It was something as insignificant as agreeing with the children that they didn't have to eat all of the food that she put on their plates. He said that it went from there with little things that they would have disagreements about. He even told me about how she talked against you and your parenting habits and how she felt like you should do more for your children and just all kinds of stuff. From the sound of it, the babysitter is not in your corner like you want to believe. He thinks that she encourages your daughter to say these things. He told me that one of his buddies knows her from the 'hood' and said that she is a crack addict. *I want to admit to Stuart what I overheard that day between Rita and her sister, Lois, but I just can't tell him what I overheard them saying to each other.* He mentioned to me that the hammer that nailed the coffin was when he told her that they might have to reconsider having her as the babysitter", he explains.

I am listening to every word but I am in shock. I don't understand how I can live in the house and trust a woman with my children who hates my guts and will do anything to ruin this family. *Why am I still letting her live in my house? Why is she still here?*

"Ok, I hear all of this. So, now what do I do? Why is it that CCF felt it necessary to get involved on the criminal side of things to see my husband go to jail?"

"Unfortunately, they do this all the time. If there is someone that they want to see arrested, it is a done deal. When the Judge found out that your daughter made this allegation and CCF is involved and your husband wasn't arrested, well, let's just say that she raised holy hell to the prosecutors' office", he answers.

"But what about probable cause? Don't they have to have a reason to arrest you?"

"Are you kidding me? This is Florida. They don't need a reason to arrest you or at least they don't think that they do", he answers.

"There is no evidence at all except my daughter's allegation, right?"

"That is all I see so far. I am going to be at the Bond Hearing in the morning and I will call you as soon as I find out what is going on. Ok?"

"OK, and thanks so much Stuart. I don't know what we would do without you."

"It is my pleasure. You and Kalin are good people and I thank God for the two of you because I don't know where I would have been had you two not taken me in and showed me love", he says.

"OK, I will wait to hear from you on tomorrow."

Stuart and I hang up and I just have this sick feeling in the pit of my stomach. I don't know whether to cry or what I feel right now. What I do know is that my husband was just arrested. My daughter says that he did inappropriate things to her. My babysitter is living in my house while I make it easy for her to betray me. CCF is starting to be another pain in the behind and I want to die right here and right now. I want to change places with Laura. This is too hard. This is not what I wanted to be here in this world to have to live with from day to day. Aren't the people who have passed this life in a much better situation than I am? What is my reason for being here? What is it that God wants from me? Am I being punished for something that I should not have done? *Lord, I am so sorry for whatever I did to be in this much pain! I am sorry! Please forgive me!*

Cindy must hear me crying because she walks into my office and picks me up from the floor.

"Mrs. Thomas, please hold it together. I know that this is hard. I know that you want to hit something. Please talk to me sweetheart. Don't hold it in. Let your true feelings come out. Tell me what you want to say that you can't say to anyone. I am your friend. I am here for you. I wish I could do more for you. Get up off the floor and go into the restroom and wash your face. There are residents and potential customers coming into the office. Let's get some work done, ok?" she says while holding my hands.

"Ok, you are right. God's got it, right?"

"That is right sweetie!"

"Kalin was just arrested", I blurt out.

"What!"

"Yeah, Stuart just told me. They went to his job and arrested him right there like a common criminal. How embarrassing that whole thing must have been for him! I will need for you to give me a ride to his job to pick up the car."

"Not a problem. Just let me know when you are ready to go."

Cindy goes back out front to take care of the residents who just walked in. I close my door and turn on my computer. My attention is suddenly drawn to the picture that is sitting on my desk of me and Kalin at our last anniversary party. He was so romantic that day. He showed up here on the job dressed in a tuxedo and walked right into my office and sang me a song. The entire staff was in on it with him. That was a very happy day for us. Cindy is right. I have to get some work done and take my mind off of this for awhile. I have to hold it together for my children. *Should I tell them about their father? It will devastate them for sure.*

While the computer is still starting up, I decide to open the paperwork that arrived from Attorney Richards. With everything going on, I have not had any time to think about the legal issue that I have to deal with regarding Princess, Laura's daughter, who is in foster care. I open the package and the first thing that I notice is her picture that is taped to the front side of the document labeled, **Details Surrounding Adoption for Alexandria Walters.** I can't believe how much she looks like her mother when Laura was younger. She is so beautiful. I am looking at the picture to see if I can see "Rock" in this baby. *I guess she looks like him.* The paperwork is pretty basic in that it reiterates what Laura's request is. She wants her daughter to be raised by me and Kalin, right along with Darren, her brother. She didn't want me to know about it until after her mother had passed.

The paperwork looks pretty basic. I scan through it quickly, but when I turn it over on the backside, this is when it gets complicated. The paperwork reads, "In the event of demise, incarceration, or anything of the sort of Melissa and/or Kalin Thomas, Alexandria will be placed with longtime friend, Brittney Snow and all funds will be transferred into Brittney's account, until Alexandria becomes of age and is competent enough to handle her own affairs."

What in the world is this all about? Why didn't Brittney say anything to me and why didn't Attorney Richards say something about this during our phone conference. I can't think about this right now. I will have to call him later about this new information.

CHAPTER 46

"Tell It To The Judge!"

"**M**rs. Thomas, you have a call on line 1. It is Denise Woods", she says in her professional tone.

"Hello, Ms. Woods, this is Mrs. Thomas. How may I help you?"

"I am calling to inform you that there is a hearing on tomorrow morning in Judge Karen Stowers' courtroom. The meeting is for both you and your husband to attend. You should be there by 10 a.m.", she states.

"What is this meeting for?"

"It is up to the Judge to decide whether or not you get to keep your children in your home", she says coldly.

"What do you mean?"

"CCF will present the evidence to the Judge to convince her that your children are better off in Foster Care as opposed to living with you", she begins before I interrupt.

"Hold on, what are you saying? Are you telling me that you agree that my children should be removed?"

"Well, you don't see anything wrong with letting your children go visit a child molester? And if you are okay with that, then I am not okay with you", she says.

"This is so unfair that you can just treat people the way that you do. He has not been found guilty of anything and you are already treating him like this", I begin.

"Mrs. Thomas, tell it to the Judge. I just called to let you know to be in the Judge's courtroom tomorrow at 10am", she concludes.

"Fine! Thanks for calling."

I hang up the phone with her and dial Stuart's number. The phone goes to voice mail so I leave a message for him to return my call.

I have to get some work done. I have to approve next month's specials. Our occupancy rate is at 94%, with less than $1,000 in delinquent accounts.

Most of this balance is due to late fees and unrelated charges. Because our occupancy rate is pretty good, I will put together a nice little bonus for my leasing staff. I am sure that this will be a nice surprise for them. They work really hard to make me look good to the Corporate Office. For the last five years, my staff has been named "Best in Collections" for the entire company. The secret to this success is that the residents are so happy with our management team that they are excited about paying their rent. They don't want to leave the community. It doesn't hurt to be a strict manager either. They know that I have no tolerance for residents who don't pay their rent. We have lots of fun here too. The holidays are approaching and I am sure that we will start preparing for the Annual Christmas Party soon.

Time is getting away from me. *Why hasn't Stuart called yet?* I have to get out of here soon. I get the work all wrapped up and decide that it is time to take it home.

"Cindy, I am out. I will see you tomorrow. I have to be in court by 10 am and I will be in when I am done there, ok?"

"Ok, Mrs. Thomas. Take it easy."

I finally get home and all of the children ambush me at the door.

"Mommy, we are so glad that you are home!" shouts Amber.

"Mommy is glad to be home. I love you all so much! Don't you ever forget it! Where is Ms. Rita?"

"Oh, she stepped out for a moment. She told us that she had to go down to the corner store. *Corner store? Why is she having to go down to the corner store? We just finished picking up groceries and I thought that we had everything that we needed.*

"Hey, Ms. Melissa!!" shouts Ms. Rita's daughter, Dee.

"Hey, sweetheart. How are you doing?"

"Fi-i-i-i-nnne", she slurs. Because she is Down's Syndrome, it is hard to understand some of the words that she says at times.

"Good!"

"Hey Ms. Melissa, yo kids said you taking dem to see a movie", she says.

"I am", I respond.

"I wanna go, please!"

"Ok, honey. Not a problem". *I really don't want her to go because I want to talk to the kids about what happened to their father. I also need to tell them about the court hearing on tomorrow morning regarding their placement.*

"Ok, kids. Go ahead and use the bathroom so that we can get out of here."

They all go their separate ways to get ready for us to depart and in walks Ms. Rita.

"Ms. Rita. I am taking the kids to a movie."

"Ok, that sounds like fun. I hope that ---", she says before I interrupt.

"Yes, we will have fun. There is something else, though. Your daughter is going with us."

"Oh, she is?" she asks, sounding surprised.

"Yeah, it is no problem with me. She is welcomed to join us."

"Ok, thanks, Ms. Melissa", she says.

We are all settled in the car and on our way to AMC off of 23rd. The radio is on and the kids are singing along with Ciara, with her song, "1-2 Step". I have to admit it but the song has a nice beat to it. It reminds me of the high school dances that we used to have that lasted in the wee hours of the morning. The children are not too fond of *my* dancing.

Our movie finishes and we get back in the car and head for home. I have to turn down the music so that I can hear myself talk.

"Kids, I have to talk to you before we get home", I begin.

"Mommy, I am sleepy and tired!" exclaims Kameron.

"Guys, sit up. I really need to tell you something", I begin. "Daddy was taken to Jail this morning", I explain. "He is okay!" I say before anyone can say another word.

"What! Why, Mommy?" the kids ask. I notice that Christy is not showing any emotion as I deliver this news.

"The police just want to talk to him about something that is going on right now. That is all! Before you know it, this thing will be handled and we will be a family like we used to be", I say trying to reassure them.

"Oh no, Mommy! I don't like hearing this", Kameron, says, followed by Darren and Sharell.

"I know, but it will all be okay. We have to be strong for him, okay?"

"Okay, Mommy!"

"Ms. Melissa, my mommy told lie, she did, she tell lie", Dee says, without anyone saying anything to her.

"What did you say honey?"

"My m-o-m-m-y told lie", she says again.

I have no idea what she is trying to say to me. What is saying that her mommy lied about? I don't even know how to communicate with her about this.

"Ok, sweetheart." Because I can't understand what she is trying to say, I basically dismiss her comments.

"Told her it was bad thing to do", she continues.

I don't know what happened but whatever it is, Ms. Rita's daughter is trying to tell me all about it.

We finally make it home. Everyone is already sleeping in the car. I open the car doors for the children to get out. It is quite difficult because they are all sleeping. By the time I open the door, they start waking up because of the chill in the air. When we finally make it inside, Ms. Rita is sitting in the family room watching Lifetime.

"Hey, Ms. Melissa, so you guys are back, huh? How was your movie?"

"The movie was fine. The children had a blast. So did Dee! She just really enjoyed herself. I can hardly wait to take her to Disneyworld in Orlando. She is really going to love it. Her eyes just lit up when we were watching the intro to the movie and she saw Mickey Mouse."

Dee is actually 30 years old physically, but only 11 or 12 years old mentally. She loves her coloring books and crayons. She enjoys watching cartoons with the children. I just really feel sorry for her to have a mother like Ms. Rita. She deserves so much better. To everyone's surprise, she really loves Kalin. She *still* asks about him and every time she says his name, it brings tears to my eyes. Kalin was always going outside with the kids and playing with them. She seemed to really enjoy this attention. We always made her feel special because she didn't really get to live a normal life.

"Really?" she asks.

"Really! I didn't mind at all either. She is a joy to be around", I continue.

"So how is everything going Ms. Melissa? You have really been acting differently. You and I don't talk like we used to talk. I know it is hard, but you have to know that I love you and these kids more than anything. We are a family, right?"

I can't believe that she just said that. Does she know that I no longer trust her at all anymore? I certainly don't consider her part of my family anymore. She has betrayed me and for what? We have been there for her more than anyone. I specifically remember a time when she called me and begged for me and Kalin to take her back into our home and how she not only asked for her to come back, but she also asked for us to allow her daughter to live with us too. We didn't have to think about it. In our minds, she is family to us. It didn't matter what she had done or who she did it with. We loved her. And now she sits on my couch and has the nerve to say that we are a family! I am going to pretend that I don't hear this.

"I am just tired these days. We have lots of stuff coming up at work and I have been strategizing with the staff. My husband not living in the same household is also a bit strenuous for me as well", I lie.

"I know that it is. That is why I am here. I am here to help you get through this, Ms. Melissa. Everything will be just fine", she says.

"Well, I have to get to bed now. I have a long day tomorrow. I have court tomorrow morning."

"Really, for what?" she asks.

"I don't want to get into it right now. We will talk tomorrow. OK?"

"Ok, Ms. Melissa, goodnight dear."

I need to get out of here before I break down in front of her. Deep down inside, my heart is so heavy right now. I close the door behind me and I just want to scream! I am so hurt right now. I don't want to sleep, *until Kalin is released.* I don't want to eat, *until Kalin is released.* I don't want to do anything as long as my best friend is locked away like a common criminal. I don't understand all of this. I don't know why so much is coming at me all at once. And now I have to find out whether my husband will bond out or not. And then I have to go into this courtroom and face the Judge regarding the children. I didn't have the heart to tell them about that. I just pray and hope that I will walk into the courtroom and the Judge will see that I have not caused any harm to my children. I have my proof for her to see. I have testimonies from their teachers and I have their grades, all to show the Judge that they are not in any danger of being with me. I need to talk to God right now. This pain hurts deep in my heart. I would not wish them upon anyone.

Dear Father in Heaven. Lord, I come to you as humbly as I know how to come to you. I come to you with a forgiving heart for all those who are trying to bring harm into my life. Lord, forgive them! They don't know what they are doing. Lord, I pray a special blessing for my husband who is locked away in a jail cell tonight. Please watch over him and keep him safe. Send your angels all around his bedside tonight. Watch over him and in your arms, let him rest. Watch over this family as we sleep tonight. Keep us safe from hurt, harm, and danger. Lord, I ask that you be with us tomorrow as we walk into the courtrooms. Please show us favor, Lord. But all in all, your Will be done. Please give me the strength to deal with whatever happens. In Jesus' name, Amen.

What happened to my life? Where did it go? Why is it being taken away from me? I don't know what I did that was so wrong to deserve all of this.

Lord, you said that trouble doesn't last always, but this surely is or so it seems. The same Lord said that He won't put any more on a person than they can bear. But this hurts! I can't explain it. I wish that I had someone I could talk to, but my best friend is not here and I can't trust Ms. Rita.

I finally make peace with myself and fall asleep. I have to attend two court hearings on tomorrow. Kalin's hearing is at 8:30 and the children's hearing is at 10. I won't have any problems being able to make it to both of them.

CHAPTER 47

"Nothing Else Matters"

*T*he day starts like a normal day. The kids get up and start dressing themselves. Ms. Rita is busy in the kitchen getting my coffee started. I am sitting in my bedroom listening to Joel Osteen's CD that gets me pumped up when there is something very important to deal with. I know that I can't do this on my own. I need God's help, for sure!

"I believe I can fly, I believe I can touch the sky, I think about it every night and day, spread my wings and fly away...I believe I can soar, see me running through that open door....I believe I can fly...", sang Yolanda Adams on her CD. I love when this woman sings. She lifts me up like you don't know. I repeat the song over and over until I get it down deep in my spirit.

I finish listening to the last part of Joel's CD and walk into the kitchen.

"Ms. Rita, I have an appointment at the courthouse. I will check in when I can."

"So, what's going on at the courthouse?" she asks.

I have already told her last night that I didn't want to get into it. I just don't want her to know that her lies are actually being considered so much so that it actually got Kalin arrested and it has me fighting to keep my children in my household.

"Oh, it's nothing; just small stuff."

"Oh, okay", she responds.

Before heading over to the courthouse, I decide to stop by the office first to see if I received any messages. Cindy is already at work when I walk into the office. She is preparing the office for our residents. She is putting out the food for the monthly continental breakfast. The office looks so amazing! *I do not pay this woman enough money for all that she does for this community.*

She seems so happy to see me. "I thought you were already gone to the courthouse", she says.

"I am on my way there", I answer.

"Ok, do you need me to go with you?" she asks.

"Aaah honey, that is so sweet! Who would watch the office if you left with me?"

"That is true!"

"I appreciate it, but just please be here for me when I return. Did I receive any messages?"

"Oh, I almost forgot. The attorney from Middleton called right after you left on yesterday", she begins. "He said that he would call you back."

"Ok, thanks dear. Well, I am going to go now. I don't want to be late."

"Ok, I will see you when you get back in this afternoon."

I leave the office and decide to pick up JT to go to court with me. He is so emotional about all of this with Kalin. On the way to the courthouse, for the first time, he breaks down and starts crying because he is so torn about the allegation against his son. Kalin's brother, Kenneth, is not happy with me right now. He just flat out told me that his brother is crazy for not divorcing me and that he would have left me the first time he went to jail.

We finally get to the courthouse, park in the garage and head inside to look for Courtroom 4B. Kalin will learn whether or not he will get a bond or if he will have to stay in jail until his trial. Walking through the crowded halls in a courthouse is very stressful. I know that my eyes play certain tricks on me but it looks like I see Ms. Rita's sister standing at the end of the hall, with her arms folded.

"JT, is that Ms. Rita's sister over there in that white shirt and blue jeans? She is standing right next to the guy with the Bucs hat on?"

"I think it is", he responds.

"What is she doing here?" I ask in a very accusatory tone.

"I don't know", he answers. "Knowing Ms. Rita the way I do, she is probably up to something", he comments.

The courtroom area is packed. There are several inmates waiting to hear their fate regarding whether they will receive a bond or not. The inmates are all behind this plexiglass window, except that they are on the television monitor. Their family members are in the room across from the Judge with hardly enough seating for everyone. You have to sit here and just wait to hear them call your family member's name.

"JT, do you see Kalin's attorney anywhere? He said that he would be here."

"Then, I am sure that he w---", JT begins to say, before being tapped on his shoulder.

"I am here. Nice to meet you sir. I am Stuart Peters, Kalin's attorney and friend of the family", he says, as he extends his hand to my father in law.

"Nice to meet you sir", he says.

"Kalin is doing just fine. I went by the jail to see him this morning. He said that he had a rough night but not to worry. He said to make sure to tell you that he loves you so much, Melissa. The man is really missing you girl", he states.

"I am missing him, too."

One by one, they are called. JT, Stuart and I sit patiently waiting to hear Kalin's name. The camera appears to be panning the room at the Jail. I can hardly wait to see my husband. I am sitting here looking around this room and still don't understand how I got here. I am living someone else's life. This doesn't feel as if this is part of God's plan at all.

"Kalin Thomas", the Judge says. I can clearly hear this as I am deep in thought. "Please stand". Stuarts walks behind the plexiglass window to stand with the other attorneys.

"He looks so scared, right JT?"

"Well, this is very hard for him, Melissa. He cried all night after he came home from being out with his attorney after the Detectives left", he adds.

"Really?"

"Yes, really!"

"Mr. Thomas, you are being charged with seven counts, all felony charges regarding a minor. How do you plea?" he asks, not even looking up from his folder.

"Not guilty, your honor", he answers. Kalin nods at the Judge when he speaks.

"Very well, then. Count 1-$20,000, Count 2-$15,000, Count 3-$15,000, Count 4-$70,000, Count 5-$15,000, Count 6-$25,000, and Count 7- no bond. So, being that out of these 7 charges, there is one that holds "no bond", you are not given a bond at this time. Next!"

"NO BOND! DID I HEAR HIM CORRECTLY?" I say softly to JT.

Stuart speaks up to the Judge to plead Kalin's case. "Your Honor, Mr. Thomas is no flight risk or anything. He needs to be out to be able to provide for his children", he begins to say.

"Sir, I don't care. This man has 7 counts and one of them does not offer a bond. As a matter of fact, the penalty, if he is found guilty, is life in prison. No can do!"

"Thank you, Your Honor", Stuart accepts. He looks to Kalin and pats him on the shoulder. Kalin doesn't get upset at all.

Stuart walks back to where we are and says, "Well, it looks like we begin to fight now. There is no bond offered. That means that Kalin will now have to start building his defense. He will not be released at this time, Melissa. He expected that this would happen. I prepared him for it. So, don't you fall apart, sweetheart. The system is what it is. It is not always fair, but we have to learn to work within this system", states Stuart.

"Ok, I know all of that. I just have to mentally prepare myself for this next hearing now."

"What hearing?" he asks.

"The one on the 4th floor", I respond. "That is why I left a message for you. I want you to accompany me to this hearing as well."

"That is the Civil Division, isn't it?" he asks. "Why do you have to be there? What is this hearing about?"

"Well, now they want to take my children because all of this. Do you have time to accompany me to this hearing?"

"Oh my goodness! I wish I had known beforehand. I have another appointment, Melissa", he answers.

"I understand."

"No, I can't leave you hanging. Let me make a phone call", he states. Stuart walks away and returns shortly, "Let's do it."

"That was quick! How did you manage that?"

"My girl, Phyllis, is going to take care of my appointment. We really do make a good team, you know?"

"OK, let's do it."

"We have a little bit of time before the next appointment, so let's go to the Cafeteria and get some coffee", I suggest.

"OK, fine with me", Stuart and JT both agree.

All I can think about is how my husband is sitting in some cold room, with hard seating, waiting to get a piece of bread and a cup of water, while we are enjoying our freedom. I am so proud of how he handles it.

"Melissa, what's on your mind sweetheart?" he asks, as we are getting on the elevator.

"Just thinking about Kalin and how he is being so strong through this."

"Well, I spoke with him right before the hearing this morning and he already accepted that he probably would not be offered a bond. He told me that he would keep his head on strong and try his best not to fall apart. You got one strong man there! " he says.

"That is good. I just wish that I could be as strong as he is. I feel like I am falling apart. For crying out loud, my husband is in jail with no bond and now I am walking to the 4th floor to see if a Judge agrees that I should be able to keep my children", I respond.

"We will hold this thing together, sweetheart. I am not going anywhere. I will be with you all through this, ok."

When I finally get my coffee, it doesn't feel as hot to me. I feel like I am numb. I have to admit that I wish I weren't going through this right now. I can't wait until this is all over. *I wonder why Ms. Rita's sister is here at the courthouse. Is it a coincidence or what?*

Right in the middle of thought, I look up and see her sister approaching our table. *Is she coming to me or does she see someone else? Did she, perhaps, have a court hearing of her own?* Within seconds, she has made it to our table.

"Ms. Melissa, how you doing suga?" she asks, putting one hand on her hips and the other on my shoulder.

"I am fine, dear. How are you?" I respond.

"Girrrl, I sho' need to talk to you", she says. "Hey JT, how you been? I ain't seen you in a long time. You don't come around our side of town no more", she continues.

Stuart gives me this strange look, but I just throw up my hand to let him know that it is okay.

"Just busy", JT answers. "I still come around, though. You just haven't seen me."

"So, what do you need to talk to me about?" I say, directing my attention to Rita's sister.

"My sister, yo babysitter", she responds. "Now, I know you don't want me to tell yo' business 'round everybody", she states.

"It's okay to speak to me in front of them. To be honest, your timing couldn't be more perfect. I don't have anything to hide and this man here is my attorney. Stuart Peters, please meet Lois and Lois, please meet Stuart Peters."

"Nice to me you, Lois", Stuart says. Like a gentleman, he stands up to greet her properly. "Lois, would you like something to drink?" he asks.

"Nah, I'm good", she responds.

She pulls up her chair and joins us. It looks like we have at least 30 minutes to get to the 4th floor, so we might as well take advantage of this moment to get some information from Ms. Rita's sister. *I am not quite sure how creditable her information will be.*

"So, Lois, you were saying?"

"Well, I know I ain't supposed to say nothing about this because my sister made me promise, but I can't see her do this to ya'll good folks. Lord knows, you ain't been nothing but good to my sister and she should be ashamed of herself for trying to hurt ya'll", she begins.

"OK, and how is she hurting me?"

"She been backstabbing you bad. She been talking to the police. She been talking to CCF. She even been talking to yo family. She still on 'dem damn drugs, you know? You need to watch yo back. I knew she was no good when she let her own grandson take the wrap for her drugs. That was her drugs in yo house the day when the police arrested Tim. She ain't what or who you thank she is. Trust...", she explains.

"Really?" I ask, sounding as if I haven't heard this before today.

"Well, let me ask you dis. Why you thank I'm here? You thank I like hanging 'round this muthafucka? I got tickets out there I haven't paid yet", she states.

"But, that doesn't explain why you are here", I say to her.

"She told me to come just to see what happens. She been knew 'bout 'dis. Who you thank gave that cracker yo niece's number? She the one been helping CCF. I knew they was gone take 'dem chirren. You betta wake the hell up! She told me how you been walking 'round there not wanting to tell her what's going on, but she already knows everything! She said you been trying to be all secretive and shit but CCF already told her what was going down", she continues. "Believe me, if they take yo kids today, you can thank my sister and yo family for it. And besides, yo family ain't innocent either. They got it in for yo husband. They can't stand his ass!" she continues.

"Wow! I can't believe she is doing this to me! But let me ask you something. Why are you betraying your sister and telling me all this stuff?"

"Let's just say that I know what it's like to lose yo kids over some bullshit!" she exclaims. "And I think you a real nice lady. I remember that time when you let Tim live at yo house that week. But now you know she is the nasty wench. She is evil honey. And Tim, I saw what that boy looked like when he came from yo house. Your husband gave him a hair cut and I ain't seen him smile like that since. I don't like to see people get mistreated. I hate bullshit like that, even if it is my sister."

I am sure that my mouth is opened wide enough for flies to make their way into it. I can't believe what I have just heard. *Is this woman for real? Is this information true or what?*

"Are you sure of this information?" Stuart asks.

"Hell yeah, I'm fo' sho' about all this shit. I ain't bullshitting wit you now. My sister ain't 'bout nothing. She is a trip! That's why we don't get along! That's why she can't even have custody of her own child or her grandson. That's why he's with me", she answers.

"But wait a minute! Her daughter is in my house with her", I respond with a puzzled look on my face.

"Yeah, but she ain't supposed to be. She just got that child to get that child's money. It is such a shame", she responds. "She used to sell her own daughter to dem crack heads."

"Well, we have to go now. May I call you later?" I ask.

"Hell, I don't care. My number is 555-1244. I am home by 8 every day", she responds.

Lois walks away and takes pieces of my broken heart with her. I can't believe what I just heard. *How can I be so wrong about Rita? How could I have allowed this woman into my family's life? It is like I opened my door for the devil and he came into my home and took over and now I may lose my entire family because of it?*

"Melissa, I know that this is quite a bit of information. We need to go now. Let's knock this out and then we will talk later on, ok?"

"See, I knew that woman was up to something. I can't believe this! I am so mad at you Melissa because you should have fired that bitch. And now she is there with my grandkids and doing all of this to my son", he says as he begins to cry. JT shakes his head and walks away. *I can't tell him of my plans. I don't want to let her go because I want to be close enough to see what she is really doing. Now I know!*

We jump on the elevator and head to the 4th floor. When we finally get there, the waiting area is packed. All of the seats are filled. There are a few bailiffs in the room just to keep the peace. I have heard that these areas tend to get a little out of hand. Over in the corner, I see a group of men dressed in orange with shackles around their waists and feet.

"Boy, is this place crowded or what?" Stuart asks while I sign us all in.

"I'm telling you!" JT agrees.

We finally find a seat in the back. We wait patiently for the bailiff to call our name. This crowd looks mostly like a group of women who have decided to show up after the nightclub closed down. The women are not dressed in professional attire at all. They are dressed in short skirts, big earrings, and tons of makeup. The truth of the matter is this! I am here just like they are here. What did they do to get a ticket to the 4th floor? They are probably wondering the same thing about me.

While we are waiting, I can overhear some of the conversations. I hear one young lady talking about how she is missing time off from work to deal with something that wasn't her fault. I hear another young lady talk about how CCF took her baby because she couldn't afford to live in a better neighborhood. *Can they do that? I didn't know that they can take your kids if you live in a neighborhood that is not so safe.*

"Melissa, we didn't get a chance to talk about this hearing. What exactly is this for and what is the allegation?" Stuart asks.

"I received a phone call on yesterday from Denise Woods, the child protective investigator, and she informed me of this meeting. Apparently, they have new information that they want to present to the Judge to see if she will allow CCF to remove the children from my custody. They believe that the children are not safe living with me anymore", I explain.

"Now that is crazy! Why do they say that?" he asks.

"I don't know. That is what I am about to find out. The only thing I know is that they have information that I was allowing Kalin to still see the kids after he left the house."

"And, did you?" he asks.

"Yes I did. I would take them over to JT's house. They loved seeing their father. I didn't think there was anything wrong with it", I admit.

"Neither do I, but they think differently than we do. Hell, they are wired way differently than we are. I can't make you any promises, sweetheart. I won't do that to you. I have to be honest and tell you that there may be a chance that they *will* remove your children from your custody. Most times when people show up in this courtroom, the State will take the kids regardless of what is said", he explains.

"Oh Lord no!" my father in law shouts.

"Let's just walk in here and see what happens", Stuart comforts.

It seems like an eternity before we are called, but we are so happy when we hear the bailiff say, "Everyone here on the Thomas case, please come forward."

We finally make our way into the second waiting area. This is where you see the clients, who have attorneys. Some of the clients have their own private attorneys and some will get court appointed attorneys when they get inside to see the Judge. I see Denise Woods, who is refusing to make any type of eye contact with me. She is busy talking to a guy in a suit, who I will assume is the attorney for CCF. They look to be in a deep in conversation. I am sure that they are busy preparing for the hearing. *I can only imagine what she is telling him about her encounter with me.*

"Go ahead and come inside, please", the bailiff announces. We all step up and head toward Judge Karen Stowers' courtroom. When we make it inside, there are several people already waiting inside the room. I have no idea who all of these people are. I don't recognize any of them. Behind us is the CCF crew. Denise, and a guy dressed in a dark blue suit, that I am assuming at this point is CCF's attorney. "Please sit here", said the bailiff as he directs us to the "Defendant" section. We are all sworn in.

The Judge enters the room and all stand at attention. The bailiff announces, "Judge Karen Stowers, now presiding."

"Thanks Michael", she says, nodding toward the bailiff.

"Ok, let's get started. We are way off schedule today for some reason so let's go through this as quickly as possible. The case brought before me today is the Children Come First Protective Services versus Melissa & Kalin Thomas, in the interest of the children, Christy Williams, Kameron Williams, Darren Williams, Sharell Williams, Amber Thomas, and Justice Thomas. Based on what I have read, the child, Christy Williams is alleging that her stepfather, Kalin Thomas, touched her inappropriately and has been doing so since she was 11 years old. She is now 13 years old. Is Mr. Thomas in the courtroom today?" she asks, looking directly at me.

"No, your Honor. He was arrested on yesterday", Stuart answers. The Judge looks somewhat relieved to hear this. It looks like she rolled her eyes when she received this answer from Stuart. *Is it true that she really had something to do with causing his arrest?*

"Well, good", she comments. *Did she just say 'good'? What has this world come to? He hasn't been tried and convicted yet and these people act like he has!*

"So, Mr. Peoples, what is the recommendation of the State regarding this case?" she asks.

"We recommend that these children be placed with a family member who has already agreed to take in the children. The background checks were done and have come back with no issues and we would like for you to place them with this family. We feel that this placement is a safer environment for the children. There is enough space for the children, with us accommodating the family with 2 sets of bunk beds.

So, it looks like Lois was right! She knew that a family member would be getting my children. The family member is either Nikki or her sister, Neicy. Safer environment? What the hell are they talking about? I haven't mistreated my children. I have provided for them even without Kalin being in the household. Stuart, please say something?

"Your Honor, I object. The State has not presented any type of evidence as to why their environment is unsafe", Stuart interjects. "These children are being very well cared for by their mother and there really is no need for these children to be removed from this home."

"If it pleases the Court, I will get to that at this time. Christy Williams contacted our office and informed us that she wanted to be removed from the home. We were also informed by the babysitter that Mrs. Thomas was taking the children to see their father and stepfather and she also took off for a few days to Texas with him. The babysitter also informed us that Mrs. Thomas is always in her daughter's room trying to convince her to change her story regarding her allegation. So, we believe that ---", he states before getting interrupted. *Oh Ms. Rita! How could you lie like that? I haven't tried to get Christy to change her mind about anything! All I did was question her about it? Why is it that they can all talk to my daughter about this but I can't without there being some type of suspicion?*

"Your Honor, isn't it the objective for this Department to keep the families together? Mrs. Thomas is a very hard working woman, who has always provided for her children. Their grades are impeccable, she keeps a nice home, and there are no issues with the children in the community. As a matter of fact, Mrs. Thomas has served on several community boards and has always been a big supporter of the Children's Society", he explains.

"Sir, I don't care about all of what Mrs. Thomas has done. This is about her daughter who is apparently accusing her husband of being inappropriate with her. I don't care about evidence. This is not a criminal courtroom. They will handle the criminal side of it downstairs. In my courtroom, all I care about is the fact that the child stated that this happened to her and that is enough for me. I will find in favor of CCF in that the children will be removed from their home with their mother and placed into foster care, effective immediately", she says, with her voice sounding as if there isn't anything he can say to change her mind.

"But, Your Honor..", Stuart begins again.

"Sir, this is my final decision. If there is any information that your client needs the court to be made aware of, she can present that at the next hearing. My ruling is final", she states.

"Thank you Judge", says Mr. Peoples, giving a nod to Denise Woods, who is sitting next to him. *Did this just happen? Did this Judge just say that she is removing all of my children from my home because she is placing them in a safer environment? I would never hurt a single hair on their heads! Now, I know what all of the secret talks were about between Ms. Rita and my family. That bitch knew all along that she was working with CCF to get my children taken and she knew that she needed to work with my family to make sure that there was somebody who would take them in. I am so numb! I can't move from this chair. I want to scream! I want to hurt someone the way I am being hurt. How can you care for someone as much as me and Kalin do for Ms. Rita just to have her hurt us this way? Why, Lord, Why? I just don't get it! What will she gain by doing this to us? And then, she sat there this morning like she didn't already know about this hearing today? Oh God, please forgive me for what I am thinking?*

"Melissa, don't panic. Don't give them what they want. We will discuss this later. I will get you in to visit with the children as soon as I can, ok", he comments. I know that he is talking to me, but my brain is not registering all of this. "They are still your children. They can't take that away from you. Be strong, my friend."

"This is messed up how they coming in to get my grandkids. This is just wrong", JT mumbles.

"Your Honor, the mother would like to know if and when she will be able to visit with the children once they are removed", he asks.

"We will discuss that at our next hearing. We will reconvene in 2 more weeks to review this case. Hearing adjourned", she states, before getting up to leave.

I look around the room and it feels like all eyes are on me. I can only imagine what these people must be thinking. Sure, everyone just knows what they will do if this were happening to them. You never really know! It is easy if there are very clear suspicions. It is very easy to choose to believe your child. This is not that type of situation. Ms. Rita is the one who is always with our children. She has resided in my home all these years and she has never seen anything going on in our home. She would have told me. My children go home to my mother's in Alabama every summer and she never felt it either. *Why is everyone surprised that I am reacting the same way?*

Denise looks so happy sitting over there. She knows that she removed my children because she could. She didn't come to my house and find a pigsty. My children's rooms were all nice and neat, my home was immaculate, and there was plenty of food for them. She knows that when she went to the schools, she received good information there, too. She has talked to my neighbors, but she still had them to remove my children. Why doesn't she tell them the truth? What I am learning is that nobody really cares about the truth. I need to call Leigh and let her know that what she predicted has come to pass.

We finally leave the courtroom and standing outside is Ms. Rita's sister, Lois. She rises up as she sees us exit the courtroom. It isn't me that she approaches. She goes right over to Denise Woods. They are talking like they are good buddies. How in the world does Denise know Lois? Is Lois *really* in on Ms. Rita's game? Their conversation doesn't last long because CCF's attorney approaches Denise and Lois walks away.

"JT, look over there. Did you see that? Why was Lois over there talking to Denise Woods? And how do they know each other? Isn't that weird to you?" I ask.

"It is weird, but nothing surprises me. Melissa, believe me when I tell you. That Rita is something else! She is so evil", JT responds.

Lois finally walks off and Stuart and I agree to speak in his office instead of discussing the case out in the open in the courthouse.

"We have quite a bit to go over before our next hearing", Stuart mentions. "Let's get out of here."

"So, now that the Judge has signed the order for the children to be picked up, but when will it happen? How long do I get with my children? Where will they live? What is the next step in this process?" I ask, starting to cry.

My father in law reaches out to give me a hug. We make it to the elevator to go downstairs but I honestly don't know how I am able to put one front in the front of the other one. In this moment right here and right now, nothing else matters to me. My husband is in jail with no bond and my children will be taken away from me any day now. I might as well be dead because nothing means more to me than my husband and my children. Without them, I am nothing!

"Melissa, are you okay, honey?" Stuart asks.

"I am not going to pretend with you because you are just like my brother, Stuart. I am hurting right now. I want to be mad at the world. I feel like they are all against me. Please tell me how to feel. Please tell me that this will be alright. Please tell me that there is some type of misunderstanding and that they aren't coming to get my children, please tell me—", I say, before JT interrupts me.

"Meme, my son loves you like there is no love. If I know anything about him, I do know this one thing. He would never hurt a child. I know that for a fact. From the moment my son met you, he has loved you and those kids. He doesn't care that they aren't his. I know this for a fact and to see him up there in that orange being treated like a—", he says, until the sobbing overtakes him.

"JT, I know that you are hurting, man. Kalin needs you two to be strong out here for him. I am going to put my all into this entire case, you hear? You two are like family and I know that they got it wrong, but I need all of your strength to prove it. We will be victorious. Look at it this way. At least the children will be staying with family members and not some strangers", Stuart interjects. Let's plan to meet on Friday at my office so that I can go over everything with you. We need to start building Kalin's case. Being that there are transcripts and court documents from the Children's Court, we have a place to get started. What about 2 pm?"

"2pm it is. See you in a couple of days!" I respond.

"Ok, see you then."

We finally get back to our cars and go our separate ways. The ride back home with me and JT is a very quiet one. We are both crying hysterically. He is apologizing for not being stronger and so am I. I know what I have to do to make it through this. I know one thing! I won't make it without the Lord, from where all of my help comes.

I can't wait to call Leigh. She will know exactly what I should do at this point.

We finally reach my father in law's house.

"I have to go now, JT. I have to get back to work. We are right in the middle of preparation of our budgets for 2003 and I have to be there. The sooner I get to work, the sooner I can leave to go home. I want to tell my children in my own way about what happened today", I explain.

"OK, but if you need me, you know where to reach me?"

"Yes, I know. To be honest with you, I don't want to see Ms. Rita's face right now. I want her out of my house! I don't care where she has to go, either."

"I hear you and I truly can't blame you for feeling this way", he responds.

My father in law heads into his house so that he can get his day started. He has this big construction gig going on that will keep him busy for quite a while. He has agreed to pay Kalin's attorneys fees. Kalin's father is a very generous man. He helped me and Kalin get our first car. He has already tucked some money aside for the children's college fees. All of the children call him "grandpa". That includes Sharell, Darren, Kameron, and Christy. When Kalin and I began to date, JT accepted my children as his grandchildren. He doesn't treat them any differently than Amber and Justice, who are his actual grandkids.

CHAPTER 48

"Nothing to Live For Anymore"

*D*riving away from his house, I start seriously thinking about running away from everything and everybody. It doesn't matter to me whether I go home or not. There is nothing for me there. My time is limited with my children and then they will all have to leave the house. My husband is suffering more than he ever has. Christy is hurting right now as well. She needs her mother and I am empty. I don't know what to say to her. She has so many people in her ears right now. I don't know if she will even want to talk to me. It has been very difficult to get close to her with Ms. Rita in the way. This is so hard that even Yolanda Adams' voice sounds cold to me. I remember those very encouraging words from Tyler Perry when he said that, *"when all hell is breaking out in your life, this is the time to praise God!"*

Lord, I need you right now. I don't even know what to say. I don't know where to put this hurt but right in your hands. I don't know what will come of all of this. I don't understand it. I don't know why people have to be untruthful. I give you all the praise, Lord. I know that you will protect my family. I won't lie though. This hurts so badly. I want to cry, but can't! I want to hate everyone, but I can't! Lord, please help me deal with this pain. In Jesus' name, Amen.

All I can think about is how my children will react to this news. I want so badly to call Denise and let her know that I know what she is trying to do. I seriously want to rip out Ms. Rita's heart and then I want to shove it in the Judge's mouth. I am an angry woman right now. If I have to speak with someone right now with the way I feel, I will probably say almost anything.

I finally make it back to the office and head for my office. Cindy didn't notice that I had made it in because she was very busy with one of the residents. I am actually glad that she is busy so that I don't have to relive what just happened at the courthouse. I know that she means well. It's just that I don't like talking about it with everyone, over and over again. I just want to get some work done and hurriedly get out of here so that I can go home and prepare my children for what is to happen next.

"Well?" Cindy asks. I didn't notice that she was standing at my door.

"Well, I am truly being tested. Kalin did not receive a bond and the children are being removed within the next 24 hours or maybe even before", I say, without making eye contact with her. "I don't see where I really have anything to live for."

"Oh my God!" she exclaims. "Mrs. Thomas, I am so . . .", she begins.

"Honey, don't say it. I know. Believe me, I know. I really can't talk about this—", I say, right as the tears start flowing down my face. Cindy closes the door and walks inside.

"Melissa, I know it hurts. But, honey, God is able. He will walk you through this", she says.

"This is, by far, the hardest thing that I have ever had to go through in my entire life. I don't understand it", I say, sobbing heavily at this point.

"God won't put more on you than you can bear, Melissa", she says.

"Well, He must really think highly of me", I say in a sarcastic tone. "I will be fine. I promise. This is just another thing. This is just another opportunity to be used by God. Now, go back to your desk and finish doing what you have to do. I want us to have our meeting in a couple of hours regarding the budget for next year. The sooner we finish that, I can get home."

"Do the children know anything yet?" she asks.

"No, I want to tell them myself. I will let them know tonight", I respond.

"I almost forgot. Your babysitter came by earlier today. I got a chance to meet her daughter. She said that she was moving out and wanted to make sure that her mail still came here", Cindy states, looking puzzled.

"Really?" I ask. *So she already found out that the children are being removed and she is already gone? And the nerve of her to want me to still be responsible for her mail!*

"Is everything okay?" Cindy asks.

"Yes, everything is fine. She knows that the children are being removed so she won't have a reason to stick around."

"OK, Melissa. Enjoy your children tonight, hold them, and let them know that you love them. Your children are very strong. They will be okay", she assures me.

"I know. Thanks."

When Cindy turns to walk away, I have to give my father in law a call to give him this information. He picks up his phone on the first ring.

"Melissa, you okay?" he asks, before I can say anything.

"Yeah, I am fine. I am still at work. Well guess what?"

"What?" he asks.

"Ms. Rita has already come by the office to let my assistant manager know that she is moving out and wants to make sure that her mail will continue coming to my address. Can you believe that? She has already moved out! She found out, either from Denise, or her sister, that the children would be removed, so she figured out that there is no reason for her to stay."

"See, I told you. I can't stand that woman and she better hope that I don't see her around anywhere. I hate her for what she is doing to my son", he says angrily.

"I know, JT. Let's just keep trusting God. I just wanted you to know."

"Do you want me to come over when you have to talk to the kids?" he asks.

"No. I want to spend that time alone with them. Don't get me wrong. I appreciate you for wanting to be there for me, but this is something that I have to do by myself."

"Ok, I will talk to you tomorrow", he says.

"Yeah. Love you Pops!"

"Love you too!"

****

"Cindy, are you ready for our brief meeting?"

"Yes, I will be there shortly. I will turn on the special greeting, lock the door, and put a note on the door. We should be done in about 30 minutes, right?"

"Yes, especially if you have all the answers for me that I gave to you", I respond.

"Of course, I do."

Cindy and I sit down and go over the current contractual vendors one by one to verify what they will charge the following year. For the most part, the vendors are all still giving me the same monthly price, with the exception of the carpet cleaning company. *That won't be hard to keep my regular price. This guy gets all of my carpet cleaning work, even my emergency service work. He will keep his numbers the same or I will just go somewhere else, or I will divide the work and I will only use him whenever the other guy isn't available. What is he thinking? This is a low budget property. The last thing we can do here is go up.*

"So what's this with Tim's Carpet Cleaning?" I ask.

"Well, he believes that he needs to go up on his prices a little. He says that he has been at the same price for too long", she answers.

"I will give him a call. It looks like everyone else stayed the same. That is good. This will be easy. I will get my numbers right and we will be ready to turn in our Budget Proposal by Friday", I say. "How is everything else going? Are there any issues with any of the residents?"

"No, none. The residents are happy and the renewal letter responses are coming in everyday. It doesn't look like we will have but one or two apartments to rent after it is all said and done", she says.

"Great. Pull out the visitor cards and go to work. I haven't put out an ad and I am not going to start now."

"You bet!" she says.

"Now, that is what I'm talking about! I just love this property! Anything else?"

"No. Personally, Attorney Richards has called a couple of times. He really needs you to give him a call."

"I really don't want to talk to this guy."

"He sounds like he really needs to talk to you, though. When he calls here and I tell him that you are not in, he sounds like he doesn't believe me or something."

"I will call him tomorrow. If we are done here, I really would like to go ahead and get home."

"OK, take it easy. I will see you tomorrow."

****

"Mommy, you're home!" shouts Amber as I open the door. The rest of the kids follow behind her. By the time I make it through the foyer, they are all standing in front of me except Christy.

"Ms. Rita is gone! She is finally out of our house, Mommy!" shouts Darren.

"I know. I heard. How do you know that she is gone?"

"Because I can see that all of her stuff is gone out of her bedroom", he answers. "She didn't clean up her room, though. I am so glad! Now, we can finally be a family with her gone", he adds.

"Where's Christy?"

"In her room. Where else would she be?" Kameron answers.

"Let me go in and speak with her. I will be out in a minute, ok?"

"OK, Mommy!" both Kameron and Darren shout.

Christy's door is shut so I knock on it. She invites me to come in. It has been awhile since I came into her bedroom. She has all of her pictures of her pet friends on the wall. I forgot how much she really likes sports, too.

"Hey honey, are you busy?" I say as I take a seat on her bed.

"No, Mommy, I am not busy. I am just listening to some music", she answers.

"What are you listening to?"

"Missy Elliott. Her music reminds me of your old school music that you like to listen to", she answers.

"Yeah, I know. I love her music because of that reason. I really like the song that she does with Ciara."

"Me too!"

"Do you have a moment to talk with your momma?"

"Sure, Ma, what's up?"

"I need to talk with everyone, but since you are the oldest, I would rather speak with you first", I begin.

"Ok."

"There was a court hearing today and Daddy is not coming home any time soon. The Judge would not give him a Bond to get out of jail, so he will stay there until the trial is over."

Christy does not react to the news. She does not make a comment about Daddy at all. She mumbles one word.

"Ok", she says.

"There was *also* a hearing today in Children's Court and the Judge decided to grant your wish to be moved out of our home. You will go live with a family member as you suggested", I say to her.

Christy does not look up when I tell her the results of the hearing. *Is she upset? Is she happy about the Judge's decision? She acts almost as if she already knows.* Seconds pass and not a word out of her. She finally mumbles something.

"I told them no", she says.

"You told who no?"

"Ms. Rita. I told her that I didn't want to leave my house. She said that it is the best thing to make sure that we are safe. She did all the talking. She talked to Auntie Diana and Nikki. She is always talking to those people who would come by to see us. Let me guess, we are going to Nikki's house, right?"

"To be honest with you, I don't know. They didn't tell me where you would be going. They just said that it was a family member who has agreed to take you all in."

"That's it! I already know. I know because she asked us one day if we would like to come live at her house sometimes. We didn't know it would be for good."

"It's not for good! I will fight for my babies! I just really need to make sure that you will stay strong for me and that you will look out for your younger siblings. They will need you. Be patient with them and make sure that you always let them know that I love them very much. Can you do that for me?"

"Of course, I will. Don't worry. We will be just fine at Nikki's house."

"Christy, I love you sweetheart. You know that, right?"

"Yes. I do know that."

"Don't leave this house thinking that I don't love you. Don't ever let anyone tell you that I don't love you. Don't let them tell you that I love Kalin over you. You are my daughter and I love you very much. I won't lie to you because I respect you too much. I love Kalin, too."

"Ok."

My daughter and I continue our conversation for at least 30 more minutes before I realize that I need to give dinner to them. But first, I need to have my "talk" with the other children now.

"Who wants pizza for dinner?" I ask, walking into the den, where the kids are watching *High School Musical*. I have to admit it but the kids that are picked to play in this movie are very talented. I hope that, for my kids' sake, the director will come out with a sequel to this movie. The kids really enjoy it.

"I do!!" they all shout. *I am so glad because I do not feel like cooking and this will give me some time to speak with them about CCF coming by on tomorrow to remove them from the home.*

"OK, I need for everyone to gather around", I announce.

The kids are all sitting at my feet waiting to hear why I have called them together in the den.

"I have some good news and then I have some not-so-good news. Which would you prefer to have first?"

"I want the good news first", states Kameron.

"OK, here we go. The good news is that you all will be spending some time over at Stacey and Tatum's house. The not-so-good news is that you will be moving out on tomorrow and I don't know exactly when you will be coming home", I explain.

Each of the children has a puzzled look on their face. They are looking around at one another to see if they are just as confused. Christy decides to help make this go over smoother.

"Guys, we will have fun. We will just have more kids to play with", she says.

"Yeah, but are you coming too, Mommy?" asks Sharell.

"No, sweetheart. I have to stay here. Remember the lady who came by to make sure that ya'll was all doing okay?"

"Yeah, how could we not? She was always here talking to Ms. Rita. Did she say something to make them take us away?" asks Kameron, standing on his feet at this point.

"No, she just feels like it would be safer if you lived somewhere else", I continue to explain.

"I don't want to leave you, Mommy!" Justice shouts.

"Me neither. Please don't let them take us away!" shouts Kameron.

"Daddy's gone and now we have to leave?" asks Darren. "What is going on here? Why is this happening to our family? We didn't do anything wrong. I hate to say this, but I hate that lady. I hate Ms. Rita too. I wish she had never come here. I knew this would happen. Her and Auntie Nikki and Auntie Diana been talking about this for awhile. They always get together and talk when you are at work. It is not fair! This is not fair!" he says, starting to cry loudly.

"Son, I know it hurts. Just because you will be in a different household doesn't mean we are not still a family. We will always be a family. They can't take that away from us. Darren, son, hate is not the answer! Hating Ms. Rita or Auntie Nikki or Auntie Diana is not the answer. God teaches us to love, even our enemies. They haven't won just because you will be living in another household. Now, give your Mommy a hug!" I say, as I embrace them all in a group hug.

Within seconds, we are all standing in that same spot, giving our love and support one to the other. Christy reminds me that she will look out for her brothers and sisters while they are at Nikki's house.

"OK, now I don't know when I will be able to visit, but as soon as they give me the go ahead, I will be right there", I tell them.

"OK, Mommy!" they all shout.

"I love you", Darren says, and they all follow. I make sure that Christy knows that I love her too. This is very important because I don't want her to feel like we are being separated because of her.

The doorbell rings. For a moment, I actually thought that they had forgotten about the pizza being delivered. "The pizza's here!" shouts Sharell.

We finish our evening watching *High School Musical*, eating pizza and drinking Mountain Dew. After dinner, the kids rush upstairs to take their baths. We all gather in my bedroom to pray together and say why we are thankful. It is important that my children not go to bed with anger in their hearts as that they know that it is with God's help that we will get through this.

"I am thankful for Mommy and Daddy and that they both love us", Justice says.

"I am thankful for food to eat and a nice house to live in", Amber confesses.

"I am thankful that I have two daddies who love me and my favorite mommy", says Darren.

"She's your only Mommy, boy!" shouts Kameron.

"Oh yeah, to my only Mommy and the best Daddy", Darren re-states.

"I am thankful for my Mother who will do anything to make sure that we are happy", says Christy. *There is something about the way she says this that makes me so sad in my heart. It is true. I love my children more than I love myself and there isn't anything I wouldn't do for them.*

"Aaah, Christy, I love that! I love you", I say, giving her a hug and putting a big kiss right on her cheek.

"OK, Ok, don't get all sentimental on me", she says, laughing.

"I love my mommy and my daddy who is in jail and I hope he is safe", says Sharell. *It is so amazing to me how thoughtful my children have become. I want to make sure that they stay that way!*

"OK, everyone has said what they are thankful for. So, let's pray and head upstairs to bed. Who wants to lead us in prayer tonight?"

"I will!" shouts Kameron first.

Dear God, thank you for the food we just ate. Thank you for our home. Thank you for Mommy, for Daddy, for Christy, for Darren, for Sharell, for

Amber, for Justice and for me. Please watch our house tonight. Please watch over the place where Daddy is staying. And please watch over Grandpa. We love everybody and please forgive them for making us leave our Mommy. We love you God and Goodnight.

"Kameron, that is the best prayer, son. That was just wonderful and God just answered you for everything you asked Him for. You just have to believe it!"

"OK, time for bed, my precious children."

One by one, I tuck them into their beds. Shortly afterwards, they are all asleep. From their bedroom door, I watch them sleep and tears are starting to fill my eyes. I don't know what time they are coming to get my children, but there will never be a right time. But for tonight, they are here with me and I thank God for that.

To ease my nerves, I think I will put in one of my favorite movies. Let's see if Denzel can put a smile on my face. This is one good-looking man! I hope my husband doesn't get too jealous because I know that I have lusted over him probably way too many times.

I put in *Remember the Titans,* which is my favorite movie of all times. I love the part when Campbell and Bertier are communicating about the issues that they are facing on the team and Campbell days, "Nah see, I'm gonna look out for myself and I'm gonna get mine."

"See man, that's the worst attitude I ever heard", Bertere responds.

"Yeah, attitude reflects leadership, captain!" Campbell says.

The music fades and another scene begins. This is my favorite scene in the entire movie. The next thing I remember is that I am waking up to the phone ringing in my ear.

"Hello", I say, coming out of a deep sleep.

"Hello, sweetheart", the voice says.

"Who is this?"

"It's your husband. What? You forgot about me already, huh?"

"Oh hey! I love you so much. How are you? I miss you, Kalin. I miss you so much. I can't do this. I can't go through this without you here. I need to—", I say, before he interrupts me.

"Mrs. Thomas", he says. "Slow down, baby. Listen, I am calling you to tell you that I love you and I need you to be strong. Remember the song, "I need you to survive"? When you get off the phone, put in the CD and meditate on the words. We are going to make it, baby. I am not afraid of what lies ahead. I love you and I love our children. We won't go through this hating anyone. It may get very hard, but we will survive this", he says.

"Kalin, we went to the children's court after your bond hearing and --", I begin, before he interrupts me again.

"I already know. The children are being removed. I found out from Stuart. He came to see me and he told me all about it. That is the main reason I am calling, so please let the children know that I called just so I can tell them I love them because once they are removed, I won't have any communication with them and just really want them to know that their Daddy is thinking about them."

"OK, honey, I will do just that. I don't know what I am going to do with my children gone. They are handling it pretty well, though."

"Of course they are! They are very brilliant and resilient children. I am very proud of them, too", he responds. "My time is up, sweetheart. Be strong and be encouraged. I am depending on it. Either I will call or Stuart will call to let you know when you will be set up for a visit. I love you, baby."

"I love you, too."

I can hardly wait for morning to let the kids know that their father called to say goodbye to them. *Either this will make them happy or more sad.*

CHAPTER 49

'Please Don't Take Them!'

The alarm is going off in Christy's room. That means that she is either still asleep or just being too lazy to turn it off. I head towards her room and the closer I get, I can hear muffled voices. I wait to see if I can hear it again. *Is there someone in the room with her?*

I slowly open the door and see her sitting on her bed and Kameron sitting in the bean bag next to her bed.

"Oh Mommy", Christy says, sounding surprised that I have entered the room. "Did the alarm wake you up?"

"Well, yeah, sorta! What are you two in here talking about so early in the morning?"

"Nothing, Mommy. We are just talking about how much we are going to miss you when we leave. None of us want to leave you, but we know that we don't have a say in the matter, or do we?" she asks.

"The Judge has made her decision, but you make sure to tell all of the people involved exactly how you feel. It should be your true feelings and not anyone else's."

"That is right, Mommy! I am so sorry about all of this. I didn't mean for any of this to happen to our family. I don't want to leave home. I love being with you and my sisters and brothers", she says, sounding as if she is holding back her tears.

"Christy, listen to me, sweetheart. This is not your fault. There are definitely people to blame in this situation, but it is not you. I want you to throw that out of your mind right now! I don't want you thinking like that. You leave this house knowing that. Do you understand me?"

"Yes ma'am."

"Well, alright then. Let's finish getting you all dressed for school. I will prepare your things. Just go to school and have a good day. Let me worry about the rest", I say, comforting her and giving her a big hug. Kameron joins in on the hug as well.

With all of the early morning commotion, the rest of the kids find their way into Christy's room.

"Being that you are all here, I might as well tell you. Your father called last night to tell each of you goodbye and to tell you that he loves you and wants you to be big girls and big boys over to your Auntie's house. He said that you all should know that he is praying for us every single day. He said that he is doing okay and is still safe. He also said to ----", I say, before being interrupted.

"They better not mess with my daddy in there. Mommy, please tell him that we love him too", exclaims Sharell. She grabs me around the waist and starts crying. "I love my daddy and I miss him so much."

"I know, baby. Your father is one tough cookie and he will be out in no time and things will go back to being the way they were. We will be a family all over again without all of the stress added to it."

"Hopefully, you won't bring Ms. Rita back", Darren interjects.

"Oh son, why is it that you hate this woman so much?"

"Because she tore our family apart and we were still being kind to her while she was ripping us apart. I hate her, Mommy!! I really do!"

"I don't want you to hate anyone, son. The Bible says that we should love those who do us wrong. Please find it in your heart to forgive her, ok".

"Mmmmhhh", Darren mumbles.

"Ok, is everyone done?"

"Yes!"

"Give me a hug and get on out to your bus stop."

They each grab their book bags and head for the front door. I stand in the doorway until they are out of sight and after they are gone, I fall on my knees and cry out to God.

Oh God, no! Why so much pain? Lord, please help me through this. I don't feel like I can go through this without you. I know that I can't go through this without you. I need you Lord. My heart hurts right now. Lord, please give me the strength to do this. My children need you. My husband needs you Lord. I pray especially for Christy. I pray that she understands that she is not at fault for this. Please give her peace of mind. I especially pray for Darren, too. He is building hatred in his heart and I don't want that to happen. I truly believe you for a miracle with this situation. In Jesus' name, Amen.

The tears are now unstoppable. I don't want to go to work. I want to crawl back into bed and feel sorry for myself. I really don't want to live in this world without my children and my husband. They are my family and they are all gone from here. Listen to that sound, nothing!

I know what I can do. I can just take all of the pills in the medicine cabinet and end all of my pain and all of my fears right now. Who would miss me anyway? My family already thinks that I am useless. My children will be better without me. Look at what I have allowed to happen to them. I have allowed them to be taken by the State once again. What will they go through over there? What will they remember from this experience?

The phone rings and interrupts my deep thought. It is Cindy on the other end of the phone sounding panicked.

"Melissa, I have bad news, honey. The police came by here looking for you. They tried to ask me some questions about you and your husband. It looks like *your babysitter* has really been trying to make you look bad. She is really trying to nail you and your family to the wall, but why?" she begins to explain.

"Oh my God, what did they ask you?" I ask, wiping the tears away from my eyes.

"He asked if you ever told me that your husband was abusive. He asked about the children and what type of child Christy is. I don't know how they know this, but they even asked me about what I know about the conversation between Christy and her friend, Latrice. They finally wanted to know if you would be in today", she explains.

"So what did you tell them?" I ask, not wanting to sound as if I didn't trust her. *To be honest, I can't really trust anyone right now.*

"I told them that you and Kalin are the best parents to your children. I told him about how the two of you would tutor children who were falling behind in school and how you did that for free after the county refused funding of the Program. I told them how you encourage the children here at our community and the respect that everyone here has for you. I told them that there are no issues with Christy and that she is a good kid, who follows the rules and does great in school. About the Latrice situation; I told the Detective that I was not present when Christy and Latrice talked, but I told them what Latrice said to me *after* her conversation with Christy. Latrice told me that Christy admitted that "the truth was stretched a little" about her stepfather, but that she "didn't care because she just wanted him out of the house because he was so strict."

"How long did he stay there?"

"About 45 minutes or so."

"Ok, I will be in. I was just having an emotional moment after sending my kids off to school."

"And how was your evening with them?" she asks.

"It was awesome! We ate pizza and stayed up watching *High School Musical* until everyone fell asleep. Kalin surprised us and called last night. He found out that they were being removed and he called to say goodbye."

"Sounds like loads of fun. Before I forget, please go ahead and contact that attorney in Middleton. He has called here twice already", she reminds me.

"Oh yeah! I keep forgetting to call him. I will call him right now. Let me pull myself together, get dressed, and I will be in as soon as I can."

"Ok, I will see you when you get here. Drive carefully."

****

"Hello, may I please speak with Attorney Richards?" I say to the receptionist.

"May I tell him who is calling?" she asks.

"Yes, tell him that it is Melissa Thomas."

"Ok, hold on please." *I can only imagine what the emergency is. What could have happened?*

"Mrs. Thomas, how are you?" Attorney Richards says.

"I am fine, how are you?"

"Personally, I am doing just fine", he answers. *Why do I feel like there is a 'but coming?* "But we do have a problem with this situation regarding Princess. It has come to my attention that you are experiencing some problems in Miami regarding Children's First. Is that accurate?"

"Oh my goodness, Mr. Richards! What are you talking about? What does what I am going through down here have to do with Middleton?" I ask, starting to get upset.

"Mrs. Thomas, your friend, Laura Walker, has given you full custody of her daughter now that her mother is dead and there is no way that we can legally move this child to an environment where the State Department is frequent. That smells to me like trouble. This is why I made the revision in the agreement", he explains.

"So, that is why you put in there about Brittney getting full custody if something happens to me or Kalin? And how do you even know Brittney

Snow? Did you just pull her name out of a hat? Come on, now! Be real with me. What is this all about?"

"Mrs. Thomas, I spoke with Ms. Snow and asked her if she would be willing to take Princess if anything happened to either you or Kalin and she agreed. She made me aware that the three of you were such good friends and that it is what Laura would have wanted", he continues.

"Excuse me, but Laura made her requests known and she did it very clearly. If she had any intentions of Brittney having custody of her daughter, she would have said it", I argue.

"So are you saying that Brittney is not good enough to care for Princess?" he asks.

"No, that is not what I am saying."

"OK, then, let's see what happens, but a decision has to be made pretty quickly because Princess is currently in a foster home, awaiting the completion of our paperwork. I will be in touch with you soon."

"Is it possible for me to be in contact with her while she is in foster care?"

"Sure. I will make a phone call and set something up for you", he answers.

"Great, because she has already lost her mother and her grandmother and she needs to know that we are here for her. The sooner this happens, the better it will be for her."

"Ok, that is fine. I will be in touch with you soon. Goodbye".

"Goodbye." *Did my ears just hear correctly? How do Attorney Richards know about Brittney? How convenient it is that this was added into the paperwork and all of a sudden, my children and husband are gone? Should I call Brittney or what? Am I thinking too hard? How in the world could Brittney have anything to do with this? What kind of friend am I to sit here thinking that my longtime friend would do anything to hurt me?*

On the way to work, I start building a "To Do" list in my head. I need to hear "Joel Osteen" tell me that the best is yet to come. I need to hear from someone that the last part of my life will definitely be better than this part. This is the part that should be called, "HELL". I mean, isn't this what "hell on earth" is? It must be! I remember back in the day when my mother and her missionary lady friends from church would get together. I would oftentimes hear them say that "somebody's always got it worse". *That is definitely one way of looking at this.*

Joel Osteen has managed to get me to where I can at least think positively around this. He said that I have to have faith. I have to believe that God can solve this "thing" in my life. He was there when I was deep in the clubs; he was there when I didn't know how I would feed my children; he was there when my son had to have open heart surgery at such a young age; he was there when Darren was diagnosed with a heart problem but was later healed and if he can be there for all of these things, he can be here now. I just have to believe it. I don't have to tell anyone that it isn't that easy, but I just have to choose to believe His word.

I have finally made it to work and it is business as usual. It is time to get back to work and not focus so much on my pain. Attorney Richards, Stuart, CCF, or anything else will matter today. I need a serious break right now. I have to just ease into this day and trust that it is going to be a good one. No stress! I have plenty of work awaiting me to keep my mind off my troubles.

"Good morning Cynthia!" I say, which leaves her puzzled.

"Cynthia? You never call me that! What is up with you?" she asks.

"Nothing. I am putting all my cares in a box and giving them to God. I can't fix this thing, honey! I am moving on so that God can fix it all. That is just where I am today", I say, sounding very enthusiastic.

"Well, I like that. That sounds awesome. Well, great, we have lots of work to do today", she says.

"Yes, I know. That is why I want to just relax and get some work done to take my mind off things for a change". *Am I crazy or what? Now, I know that my children are being removed today. What am I thinking? This is technically the worst day of my life. Why in the world am I so happy? I don't have anything to be happy about to be honest with you. But I know that deep down inside, I have to be enthusiastic. I have to act like this thing is already fixed, even if I am faking it.*

"Has it been slow this morning as far as the phones are concerned?"

"Yeah, why?" Cindy asks.

"Because I want to go over some of the reports with you and get updated on everything."

"Sure. Not a problem. As a matter of fact, I will call next door and have them send over one of their leasing agents to handle the front for us for the first part of the morning", she offers.

"That is thinking ahead. Great! Let's do that. Things are pretty slow over there and I am sure that Anna won't mind. If she has any questions, just send her over to me."

Cindy rushes off to make her call to the office next door. In the meantime, I need to get a cup of coffee and doughnut. I just realize that I left home without eating this morning. I forgot because I was getting the kids' clothes packed, which was extremely emotional for me. I feel like I am sending them off to boarding school or something.

"OK, done!" Cindy says, as she meets me in the kitchen to pour herself a cup of coffee.

"Did Anna have any issues?"

"No, none at all. They are not that busy over there and her leasing agent is glad to do it", she answers.

"What is her name again?"

"Her name is Brianna."

"Ok, great. When will she get here?"

"Within the hour."

"Cindy, let me ask you a question. What exactly did Christy's friend say about her conversation with Christy?"

"Aah, Melissa, I thought you weren't going to deal with any of that today. Let's keep it all business. I don't want you to stress yourself out today", she says.

"Come on. I need to know. Don't you think?"

"Ok, and then will you move on to something else?"

"Yes, I promise."

"OK, she told me that she talked to your daughter and she told her that your husband is super strict and that she didn't really like him in the house. She told her that Ms. Rita despised him so much and she ----", she is explaining when I interrupt her.

"But, why? Why does she hate my husband so much?"

"Let me finish, honey! She said something about how he is always trying to speak up for the kids whenever she would tell them something to do. She said that she has to get what is hers and she would do whatever she has to do. The woman claims that she is just tired of not having."

"But I don't quite make the connection between her and Christy. How do they fit together?"

"Melissa! That's enough. It sounds like I hear Brianna coming. No more talking about this, ok?"

"OK! Let's go to work."

Brianna walks in. She is such a cutey. I remember the days of being that petite. She is a thin girl, with very distinct features. She can be a model for sure. That bone structure that she has is just to die for. I would love to have her working over here for me, but I know how Anna is. She loves having the pretty girls working in her office.

"Good morning, Brianna. Thank you so much for coming over to help us out", I say, extending my hand out to her.

"Good morning to you, Mrs. Thomas. It is my pleasure to help out. We are a team, aren't we?" *Anna better look out because I may have to come up with a great incentive in pay to get this girl in my office.*

"Well, I like the sound of that. Welcome! Cindy and I will be in my office for the better part of the day because there are several things that we have to go over to prepare for our budgets, and the upcoming festivities. Would you like some coffee or something?"

"Oh, no thanks. I don't like coffee, but I will get some water and then I will be ready to go", she says.

"Wonderful. Thanks again!

Cindy and I head for my office to get started on our great plan for the day. I open up my file on my desktop labeled, "Melissa's Agenda". This is where I keep all of the items that I have to cover. This keeps me on track so that I don't miss anything. Cindy is the only person who has access to this file because she keeps me on track with all of my appointments. As soon as I open the file, I am snapped right back into reality when I see a note that she left for me here that reads, "Kids off today". *Oh no! Not now! Not here! I can't just lose it right here. I have my assistant manager here and another young lady in the office. Suck it up Melissa! You can do this. It is okay. You have made your peace. It is all good!*

Cindy can tell that something is wrong because I stopped talking in mid sentence. "Melissa, what's wrong? You act like you saw a ghost", she says.

"I will be right back".

I get up to leave as if I am rushing to throw up and I am right at the edge. I fly right by Cindy before she has a chance to say another word. As I am rushing out of the office, I notice that she moves behind my computer to see what I am reading. I don't exactly get a chance to see her reaction because I am already over the toilet putting down my doughnut and coffee.

When I make it back to my desk, Cindy walks up to me and gives me a hug. She whispers in my ear, "It will be alright, sweetheart. You can do this. You were born to do this. I got you, ok."

When we release from our embrace, I have a feeling that everything will work out just fine. It is almost as if God placed her in this spot just for me. I mouth the words, "Thanks" and we begin our agenda meeting.

"OK, first order of business. I spoke with Tim the other day regarding the carpet cleaning contract and he re-issued the contract with the same prices as before", I begin.

"Oh, wow! How did you do that?"

"I told you that I would. Let's just say that we understand each other. So, with that said, we are good with our budget plans. All of the other numbers are in place. I will prepare this and "interoffice" it with the package this Friday. Next item on the agenda is "FESTIVITIES". Every year, we have the Christmas Party for the children and ----", I say, before Cindy interrupts me.

"And I understand if you don't want to do that this year with your children being ---", she begins to say. She notices that I put my hand up to signal for her to stop speaking.

"And we are going to have an even bigger one this year!" I continue. "There is no way in hell that I am going to make these residents pay the price. Because my children are being taken away, I will win because I am going to go out of my way to help the children here at the property. Kapeesh!"

"Kapeesh, you *are* the boss!" she responds, with a big smile on her face.

"As a matter of fact, I want us to not only do a Christmas Party for the children at this property, but I want us to do a Party for the kids at the property next door. For crying out loud, they haven't had one for years. Nobody has taken the time to have one for them. That will change this year! So, draft me a letter for the vendors to donate money for the event, but word it in a way so that they will understand that I need them to give even more this year because we are having two parties. The vendors that we use are the same ones that they use next door so this shouldn't be a problem", I continue.

"But what about your children?" Cindy asks.

"What about them?"

"How will that make you feel by having a party for the children and yours aren't even here?" *I never thought of it this way. I know my children will miss being here, but they are not selfish children. They will be very happy for the kids.*

"I feel just fine. I love my children and their not being here means that they are just going to miss the party, but these children will not feel that pain. I am sure that the holidays won't be the same for me, but the reason for the season is to give, share, and to bless others. So, there you go. So, get my letter drafted for me to review this afternoon. I want to get the letters out of here by tomorrow."

"OK."

"Next item, do me a work order for maintenance to bring out all of the Christmas decorations. I need to see what we have so that I will know if I need to go out and purchase more."

"Ok, that one is easy."

"Next item on the list. What do you want to do for Thanksgiving this year? Do you have any ideas?"

"Well, what about a Pot Luck for the employees?"

"That sounds nice, but I was thinking more of what we will do for our residents? The season is not all about us. I would love to do the Pot Luck for the employees, but we can do that anytime. The holidays are about others. So, what do you think?"

"Well, we could put a Food Drive here in the office and donate it to a charity?"

"I have one better than that. Let's have the Food Drive, but turn around and donate it to a family here at the property. Let's do something for our own", I suggest.

"Now, that sounds like a plan."

"There is one problem. In the past, we have had Food Drives here and people don't donate", she says.

"They will donate this year. I want it everywhere! Order a stamp from OFFICE DEPOT and have it read, "Give to the Food Drive at the Leasing Office to help your neighbor" or something like that. Stamp the work orders, receipts, or anything that leaves this office. I want you to make a note to have it mentioned in the Monthly Newsletter, as well. Remember, this is about helping other people. We will make them remember. You will see!"

Our meeting is going so well until my phone rings. *I know that I told Brianna not to disturb me unless it is important.*

"Hello."

"Mrs. Thomas, I know that you don't want to be disturbed, but there is someone here to see you and she says that it is very important. She says that you will know what it is about. She has a police officer with her". *Is it happening right now? You can't be real. Is this going down now!! They are here to remove my children. Oh my God!*

"It's okay, Brianna. Thanks. Tell them that I will be out shortly."

Cindy already knows what is going on so she grabs my hand and looks me directly in the eyes. "Don't you do it! Don't you fall apart. You knew that this would happen today. Hold it together. I will walk out this door with you. Be strong. God's got it, baby! I know it hurts, but you show them who God is!"

I know that she is right and like she said, I knew that this would happen today, but it just caught me off guard. I was hoping that I had a little more time.

Cindy and I walk out of the office together and she heads toward Brianna to let her know that she doesn't need her anymore. I know that she is doing this to protect my privacy. Hopefully, Brianna will think that this is about a resident or something.

"Good morning, Ms. Woods", I say, as I extend my hand to her.

She doesn't act like she wants to take my hand, but she does anyway. I guess she doesn't want to look anything less than professional.

"Can we speak with you in your office?" she asks, showing no emotion at all for what she is about to do.

"Sure, we can talk in my office."

I give Cindy the look to assure her that I am okay and that I notice how she got rid of Brianna. She holds up a set of praying hands, which helps me remember who I am. The police officer, Ms. Woods, and myself head for my office and close my blinds. When I make it to my desk, I close the application that I was in so that I can focus on our conversation. I put aside the notes that I had already taken during my meeting with Cindy.

"Ok, please have a seat."

"Mrs. Thomas, are you aware why we are here today?" she asks.

"Yes, you are here to rip out my heart and take my children out of my home for no reason." I can tell that she does not like that answer. She wants to respond to it, but she decides against it. The police officer; however, gives me a puzzled look.

"I am here to let you know that I will be at your house by 5:00 pm to remove the children. Please make sure to have all of their belongings ready. I am on a tight schedule and will leave your house and take them directly to their foster home. Your niece is expecting them by 6:00 pm. By letting you know ahead of time, you should have them ready to go", she states. At this point, I have zoned out of the room. I am sitting here. I see these two people here in my office, but my body is somewhere else and I am just looking in on this meeting. In my vision, I can already see my children's faces as they are being carried away in the white car.

"Yes, I will have them ready. I have already packed their things for them."

"Great. One more thing. Is it necessary for me to bring the police officer along or will this be a peaceful transfer of the children?" she asks.

"It will be a peaceful transfer. I have always taught my children to accept things with dignity and I won't go back on that word for you and nobody else."

"Well, if you had made better decisions, I wouldn't have to take your kids, now would I?" *Oh no she didn't! Did she just say what I thought she said? Calm down, Melissa! Don't let the devil win now! He is trying you. Let it slide.*

"Ms. Woods, there is nothing more important to me than my children. I don't care if you don't believe that. They believe that! This thing that you are doing, I am at peace with it. This is a job for you. I know that you don't love my children. Your job is to pretend to love them and protect them but it is a way of life for me. When this allegation was made, I spoke to every single one of my children about whether my husband had touched them in any way and one by one, they said "no, no, no" and I believe them. So, you go ahead and remove them because that is your job. But, just be careful about judging me, ok?"

"But, there is one who says that he did", she remarks.

When I am done speaking, she has this look on her face as if she wants to "fix me" for speaking to her that way. At this point, I don't care what she does. She has already given the green light to remove my children and honestly, there is nothing else she can do that will compare to this pain that I am feeling right now.

"I will be at your house by 5. Just please be there and have them ready", she says as she stands up to leave.

My eyes remain fixed on them until they are out of my view. I put my face in my hands and begin to sigh heavily. I have made up in my mind that I can't cry anymore. I have to be strong for them because my children will do what they see me do. If I cry, they cry. If I am strong, they are stronger.

Cindy walks in. "What did they want?" she asks.

"Oh, just to let me know that they will be at my house by 5 to remove the children".

"Well, you knew it was coming. It is not a surprise. You will be okay. Be strong and get out of here in enough time to spend a little more time with them", she encourages.

"You bet I will. Cindy, why are you so supportive to me?"

"You are like the sister that I never had, Melissa. I remember when we first met and how mean I was to you. You didn't bat an eye on being kind to me. When my father first laid eyes on you, he could see right past your exterior and saw God in your eyes. I will never forget what he said to me about you. I have learned that he is right. I believe that God put us here to help each other. When I was being mean to you, I was just hurting because my mother had recently passed away. I was angry at the world. This is a hard time for you and I promised God that if he forgave me for being mean to you that I would serve Him until the day I die. He wants me to walk you through this. So, I guess you can say, we are appointed one to the other."

By the time she finishes explaining herself, I am already in tears. Her answer touches me so much. All I can say is "Thank you Jesus for loving me this much."

"Now you go and do this thing tonight and I will be at your house around 6 with dinner. How does Chinese sound?" she asks.

"Yeah, that's fine."

There is no sense in kidding myself. I am no good for the rest of the day. Let me go through my emails and get out of here as soon as possible.

****

I finally make it into my driveway with at least an hour or so to spend with the children before Ms. Woods arrives to remove them from the house. I walk up to the door and wipe the tears away. I don't want them to think that I was crying. I pull out the Visine and put a few drops in my eyes so that they will look fresh.

"Hello gang! How are you?" I say, announcing my entrance.

"Mommy! You're home! We are so glad to see you", Darren says, as he runs out of his room to give me a hug.

"How was school everyone?"

"It was fine! I told my teacher that we are leaving the school because we have to move", he says.

"Well, what did she say?"

"She said that she is sorry to hear that."

"Where's everyone else?" I ask.

"Christy is in her room. Kameron is playing on the Playstation. Justice is in the den and I don't know where Sharell is", he answers.

"What do you mean? Didn't she come home?" I ask, in a panic tone of voice.

"She got off the bus, but when she got home, she left", he explains.

What in the world is going on here? Did my child run away or what?

"Christy, where is Sharell, honey?" I ask, while Christy removes the earphones from her head.

"I don't know. She just left out and hasn't come back yet."

"Is everything okay, Mommy?" she asks.

"I am sure everything is fine. Let me go outside and see if anyone has seen her. Stay here. Christy, make sure the kids stay in the house", I instruct.

I don't know what is going on here, but I am soon to find out. Sharell may be over to her friends' house playing or something. She has never done anything like this. That is all I need is for CCF to show up and one of the children are missing. She will think that I did it on purpose. The first door I knock on is one of Sharell's closest friends, Renae. I am sure that she is here. After the first two knocks, no one answers, but before I knock the third time, I see that someone is peeping through the curtains. There is a slight hesitation and then the door opens.

"Hello, Mrs. Thomas", the frail kid who answers the door says.

"Hey sweetheart, is your mother here?"

"No ma'am", he answers. I almost want to give up, but I get this strange feeling that Sharell is actually hiding in their house. Moments later, Renae's mother comes to the door. She steps outside and speaks to me about Sharell.

"Hey, Melissa. How are you? I know this looks weird, but I am going to tell you the truth. Sharell is inside. She came home from school today and came right over and she was in tears. She said that these people were coming to pick them up and take them away and that they won't be able to see you again. She was very upset so I told her to stay here until you got home and I would talk to you. She made me promise to hide her here until after the people leave", she explains.

Even though she doesn't offer it, I start crying and end up with my head on Renae's shoulders. I feel so helpless right now.

"Sweetheart, is everything okay?" she asks, grabbing me by my shoulders.

"No, it isn't alright. CCF is coming by at 5 to remove all of my children out of the house. I don't really want to talk about all of the particulars right now, but that is why she is running away. I need to see her right now, please."

"Sure, come on inside."

Renae and I walk through the living room and she points to the room where Sharell is.

"I walk up to the door and I can already hear Sharell passionately crying about how she doesn't want to leave the house. I walk in on her.

"Renae, may I speak with Sharell alone?"

"Yes ma'am". She gets up to leave, but gives Sharell a hug first before exiting the room

"Momma, I don't want to leave! I don't want to go over to Auntie Nikki's house. I want to stay home with you. I won't go! They can't make me go. Mommy, please tell them that I can't go!" she pleads.

For a brief second, I have thoughts of picking up all of my children and just running away. How far will we get before the cops track us down? Her pleas for help have me so drained, but I am snapped back into reality when I look down and realize that it is 15 minutes until 5 and Denise will be at the house shortly to pick them up.

"Sweetheart, I know that this is hard for you. This is not a permanent thing. I promise you that you will come back home. I am not going to lie to you. I don't know when that will be or how long it will be. I just don't know. But please do this for me and Daddy. We both need for you to be strong. Mommy and Daddy love you so much. If it were up to me, you would not be leaving the house right now. But, there are some people who think that you will be better off with someone else for a little while", I explain.

She is starting to calm down a little. I notice that she has stopped crying and has loosened her grip from around my neck.

"So, come on and go home with me. They should be there now."

"No, Mommy, I don't want to go! Please Mommy, no!"

Renae's mother must have sensed that things aren't going well because she walks into the room to offer her assistance.

"Sharell, baby, it will be okay. Just go with them today and things will be better and you will be back with Mommy in no time. Okay?"

She guides Sharell to stand up and she does. While walking us to the door, Sharell is still holding her around her waist. She walks us out onto her porch and hands Sharell over to me. I thank her so much for watching over my daughter and we head for our house. As soon as we open the door, I can see headlights shining through my front room, which means that someone is outside.

"Mommy, you are back! Where was Sharell?" Darren asks.

"She was over to Renae's house", I answer. "She is going to be fine. You are all going to be fine. Guys, the people are here so let's get ready to go."

"Mommy, I don't want to go and leave you here", Darren says. The others join in and this reluctance to leave by Darren makes Sharell cry even harder than she did at Renae's house.

Oh Lord, I need you now! Lord, please comfort my children. They are hurting right now. I don't know the right words to say to them. But you do! Please bring calm to this situation right now. I can't do this by myself! Please walk me through this part of this process. In Jesus' name, Amen.

There is a knock at the door and it seems like panic enters the room. All of the kids start crying because they know what that knock means. I walk over to the door and there stands Ms. Woods, but instead of having the police officer with her, she brought along another co-worker, who, in my opinion, is the worst possible person who could have walked into my home, Ms. Madeline Serchay!

"Well, it is nice to see you again, Mrs. Thomas", she says, with much sarcasm in her voice.

"I wish I could say the same", I respond, not even looking her way.

"Are the children ready to go, Mrs. Thomas?" Ms. Woods asks, as if she can't see that they are already balling their eyes out.

"They will be in a few minutes. I have their things ready to go."

I don't know where I got the strength to walk into the room to gather their luggage, but I did. Darren and Kameron, being the big boys that they are, pick up some of the smaller items and head towards the front door with the bags. Sharell, Justice, and Amber, being the youngest children are still clinging to my waist, with no effort of trying to let me go. Christy comes from the back, with her headphones still clamped onto her ears, with her luggage across her shoulders. Darren and Kameron take the bags that they have out to the car. Christy comes closer to give me a hug. "I love you Mommy and I will do as I promised to you. I will look out for my sisters and brothers. I will make you proud."

"That's great, baby! Thanks for that. I appreciate it!"

"Ok, guys, it is time to go", I say as I pat the three clinging to me. "Ms. Woods has to get you guys out of here so that she can be on time for her other appointments."

Neither one of them looks up, but they are still crying. Darren walks up to me and grabs his youngest sister, Justice, and holds her in his arms. Kameron reaches for Sharell and Amber and lead them to the door. *How did my boys get to be so mature? It is as if they grew up overnight while I was sleeping. My kids can tell that I am drained and just have nothing else to give. How did they get to be so smart?*

"Mommy, we love you!" Sharell shouts, as she is being led into the van. Justice looks back and waves goodbye to me. Amber wipes the tears away and tells me that she will be a big girl for me. My sons give me one final hug before getting into the van. "Mommy, I promise you that we will stick together and will do everything you taught us to do", Darren says. Kameron looks so helpless. He looks about as drained as I do. "I love you Mommy", Kameron says, as he is buckling his seatbelt. "Bye Mommy!" Christy says, as she leans in to put on her seatbelt.

"Mommy loves all of you. Goodbye! I will see you as soon as these folks tell me I can come see you. Until then, say your prayers every night and know that Mommy and Daddy love all of you, ok", I say, right before the van door is shut.

The white van drives off and it feels as if some stranger came like a thief in the night and took away everything that meant anything to me. I would give up my beautiful home and my nice car just to have my children back here with me. It feels like there is nothing else to live for. I wish that I could have stood in front of the van as it pulled off and let it run over me. I am sure that the pain of the car hitting me would feel better than the dagger that is going through my heart right now. Everything that is the most important to me is gone! My husband is in jail and my children are on their way to live at my niece's house.

Once the van is completely out of sight, I run back into my empty house, a house that once housed seven of the most important things to me. They are gone. They are gone into the night and have taken my heart with them. I walk into the house knowing that from this moment moving forward, there will be a war. *I guess I am getting ready to learn what it means to "fight the good fight of faith".*

Before I have a chance to run and hide from the world, my doorbell rings. I really don't want to answer the door. I don't want to see anyone right now. Maybe if I just let it ring, they will think that I am not here. *Oh silly me! My car is in the driveway. That is a dead giveaway that I am home! Oh, I almost forgot that Cindy said that she will be coming over tonight.*

I hurry to the front door and open it up. There, on the other side is my best friend, Cindy, with Chinese dinner, just like she promised. Are my eyes deceiving me? She has someone else with her. It's Leigh Bynum!

CHAPTER 50

"Cry If You Need To!"

"**O**h my goodness! What are you doing here Leigh?" "I am sorry to intrude, but I called your office today and spoke to Cindy and she informed me of what was to happen today. I am so glad that she trusted me enough and opened up and let me know what was going on with you. Now, I see why you were on my mind so strongly. How are you?" she asks.

"I have been better. They just left here with my children and it feels like my world is over!" I say, fighting the tears.

"Oh, it is not over and we are going to help you through this. You are not alone! Cry if that is what you have to do. You are here with us. Do whatever you feel like doing! We are not here to judge you, but to help you to get through this night because we know how tough this is for you", she explains.

"You should have seen them. When I got home today, Sharell had run away to her friends' house. She was hiding because she didn't want to leave here with CCF. It was so sad! Poor child just wants to be home with her Mommy! What is so wrong about that? I don't understand! This is so painful. I can't stand it, guys! I just can't! *Lord, please give me strength!*

"Melissa, you need to hear the truth, sweetheart", Leigh says, as she fixes three glasses of wine. Cindy must have told her that I love Chardonnay. Chinese food and wine! If this isn't comfort food, I don't know what is.

"The truth about what?"

"I have been talking to a few people about your situation. Like I told you when I first met you, I thought that you and your husband were doing a good job with your children. I didn't like what CCF was doing to you and your family. And Ms. Madeline, honey, that woman is the devil herself!"

"Yeah, tell me about it. Can you believe that she showed up here tonight with Ms. Woods?"

"I am not surprised. She's got it in for you. But I am going to be honest with you. It is very hard to win against CCF. The Judge doesn't care what you say. All they care about is what the child says and what CCF says. They don't care about the facts or anything like that. I heard about your hearing and how that went. I could have told you that they would have taken the kids. It didn't matter what went on in that courtroom. That is just how the system works. You can't beat them. You will have to buckle up and just go through this. They will keep your children as long as the Law allows. Ms. Serchay does not like you. She thinks that you are just another woman who cares more about her husband than her children. And based on stuff that people have been telling her, you have one big ride coming ahead of you."

"So what do you know that I don't know?" I ask, taking bigger sips of my wine.

"I know that you are crazy. You should have made them think that you were done with your husband and move on with your life. When you made that trip to Texas with him, that was what got everyone upset and the balls started rolling from there", she responds.

"But, what is wrong with that? We had a pre-arranged business trip scheduled. It didn't make sense to miss it. We have a great opportunity to get our new business venture off the ground and we were meeting with investors that weekend. What else was I supposed to do?"

"Honey, I know what you are saying, but they don't see it that way. They see it that this is a man who your daughter said touched her inappropriately and you went to Texas with him. Look at it from their perspective", she states.

"I don't care what they think. I don't believe that Kalin did anything wrong to Christy. I just don't believe it!"

"Well, here it is. Ms. Rita started working even before that night to do you in. She has been running her mouth about everything that goes on in this house. She is talking about how she feels that Kalin is a control freak. She says that everything has to be his way or no way. She has told the investigators about yours and his disagreements and how you would always just "back down" from him. She says that he was always making the kids do chores. She told them that he is the one who always disciplines the children. She has a personal vendetta against the two of you, but nobody really knows what it is. Now, that is something that I don't know. I don't know why she hates the two of you so much to destroy you like this. Did you do something to piss her off?" Leigh asks.

"Not that I know of. The only thing that ever happened was when her grandson stayed at our house for a week and ended up getting arrested because he brought drugs into my home. I was pretty upset with her about that. And so was Kalin! But we have recently found out that her grandson was not the problem. That kid went to jail for her! They were her drugs that he was holding. Unbelievable! She and Kalin have disagreed on occasion about the children. I remember one thing that she did that was real lowdown. There was one evening that I went out with a girlfriend to celebrate my birthday and Kalin didn't go with us. It was just me and her. While we were gone, Ms. Rita told my husband that I should be ashamed of myself for going out and she told him how I should be home taking care of my family. But, she turned around and did the same thing when Kalin went out one night."

"Now that is low as hell!" Cindy says, as she sits and listens to our conversation.

"Ain't it?"

"Melissa, this is not the time to lie down and think that they are going to tell the truth about everything. If you ever want to see your children again, you are going to have to fight like hell. Take no prisoners! Trust no one! None of them are there for you. Make no mistake about it. They will say and do anything to win! When are they letting you see the children?" she asks.

"The Judge mentioned that she would review it again at the next Hearing, which is only 2 weeks away."

"Oh, yeah. That is their way of getting in there and brainwashing the children first before you can see them again", she says.

"Wow!" I exclaim. "I will just have to play it the right way. I will end up winning in the end. It may take several weeks or months for this to be over, but I will win", I say, taking another sip of wine.

"Are you already drunk my dear?" Cindy asks.

"No, I am not drunk! I just lost the most important people in my life. I am hurting! I am not going to lie about that. I can't describe this pain that I feel. I just know that I wouldn't wish this on my worst enemy. I just don't want to close my eyes tonight. How can I? I can't go in that room, knowing that ---", I say, as I drop my wine glass on the table.

"Baby, it's alright! Let it all out", says Cindy, as she stands up to get a napkin for me. I am sobbing uncontrollably at this point. I don't know if the wine is causing my emotions to flow or this emotional gathering with these two women who have come here to show me their support has me going. At any rate, I am just not myself right now.

"I'm so sorry guys. I don't mean to ruin our happy gathering, but I am just so hurt right now that my children are gone and the fact that they had to leave in this way. This pain that I feel right now will always be etched in my mind. I won't quit! I won't give up until I end up the victor. I make that promise to myself right now and I know what I am saying. My words may be slurring right now but I know exactly what I am saying. Mark my word!"

"It is okay with us. That is why we are here. But suck it up and go to work! First thing tomorrow, I want you to be all over them about when they will allow you to see your children. They are not going to come to you with that. If you want to see them, you don't stop going after it. Be a pain in their you know what!"

"I got it! I will do just that. I have to meet with Kalin's attorney because he has to start working on his defense."

"Did he get a bond?"

"No, he didn't. He will be in there until the trial happens."

"Are you serious?" Leigh asks.

"Yes, I am serious. I don't know how long it will take, but he will have to be in there until it is over."

"So, how do you feel about all of this?" Leigh asks.

"I don't like to talk about it. I don't want anyone to judge me, so I would much rather not discuss feelings and all of that right now. Right now, I am dealing with the fact that my children are gone and they won't be sleeping in their own beds tonight. My youngest child is five years old and she should be right here with her mother, but instead, I had to peel my daughter away from my waist to go and stay in someone else's house. I want to call there and speak with my children, but how do I know if my niece will let me or if she will turn me in for not following the rules?"

"Well, you really don't know, Melissa, so it is better to just play by the rules and wait until you go back to court to see what the Judge says", Cindy suggests.

"Yeah, you're right. I have to get to work tomorrow, so I better get some sleep."

"Yeah, because you aren't going to let me come in late on tomorrow, are you?" Cindy asks.

"Now you know the answer to that question."

We both laugh.

"Melissa, I am here for you sweetheart. CCF is not going to play fair with you about the children. I am just here to warn you about it. It helps if you already know the games that they will play. And they play a lot of them, trust me", Leigh says.

"Is there anything else I need to know?"

"I will tell you this. Don't trust anybody right now because you never know who may or may not be working for them who will try to use all kinds of information against you", she says.

"Got it!"

"Well, we are going to let you get some rest now. Do you feel better?" Cindy asks.

"I feel so much better because you ladies showed up here tonight. I really appreciate you both for showing your kindness to me. I really needed it tonight, like no other."

Once they leave out that door, my night will not be the same. I really do wish they could stay all night until I pass out on the couch, but they have to get home as well. And how selfish is that of me to want them to spend their entire evening with me!

"Good night, Melissa. I will see you tomorrow", Cindy says as she gives me a tight hug and kiss on the check. "I love you, girl."

"Good night, sweetheart", Leigh says as she makes her way to the front foyer. "And remember, I am here for you. I am definitely going to go through this with you. If you need anything at all, you call me, ok?"

"I will and thanks again ladies."

They make it down the driveway, past my car, and into their cars. Their cars vanish from my cul-de-sac just like my children washed away into the night just earlier. I am now left with only the memory of our conversation. Once they are completely out of sight, I close the door and walk back inside my once again very empty house. Now that I am alone again, I am playing everything over and over in my head.

Dear Lord. I love you Lord. I need you right now. Lord, please watch over my babies tonight. Please wrap your loving arms around them. Please put an angel at each of their beds to keep them safe. Please watch over Christy, Kameron, Darren, Sharell, Amber, and Justice. Be with them on tomorrow as they get up and prepare themselves for school. Thanks you for the food that they will eat and keep them safe when they travel to and from. And Lord, please keep reminding them daily that me and their Dad love them very much. Please, Lord, don't let my kids feel any hurt or pain as a result of this situation. And Lord, please give me strength to make it through this. I know that you won't allow more to come our way than what we can bear. I thank you Lord for that. And God, when we have done all that we can do to stand, please help me to stand still until I hear your voice. In Jesus' name, Amen.

I want total blackness right now, so I turn off all the lights in my bedroom. The television is off and there is not a sound in the room. As dark as it is, I start seeing my husband and children and they are all happy. Kalin has tears in his eyes, though. And so do Justice. I know that my baby needs her mother. Oh how I wish that I were the one who was washing the tears away from her eyes.

The alarm is going off and this starts a new day in my life. This is the day that I start my very own *"good fight of faith".*

CHAPTER 51

"Fifteen Minutes Left"

*T*he alarm is going off, but it is very difficult to make that move to get out of the bed. I keep telling myself that I need to get up and put one foot in front of the other. I know that I have to get to work. I don't want to stay home today because I will be very miserable if I stay in this house all day. *Where's that remote control? I need to watch the news.*

The reporter on the television screen just said something that I just can't believe.

"Local teacher arrested for sleeping with one of her students, local news WKKP, coming up in just 15 minutes", the reporter announces as a middle aged teacher flashes across the screen holding her face in her hands. She appears to be fairly attractive. I know that she has to have somebody in her life. What in the world could she possibly see in a kid that would make her sleep with him?

It is more common to hear about male teachers who sleep with young girls, but how often do we hear about a woman sleeping with young boys? It is bad enough that she got involved with this kid, but she doesn't stop there. She ends up going out of the state with him, which involved his friends in the mix. The funny thing here is that she isn't being arrested. *I wonder if CCF went to that kids' house to speak with his mother. Did she go through half as much as I did? Did they get the mother for failing to protect her child? Probably not!*

While watching the rest of the news, I manage to get some coffee, eat a muffin, and iron my clothes. I just finished applying my makeup, so I might as well get on the road and head for work.

As soon as I make it into the car, my cell phone rings. "Melissa, hey honey; It's JT, how is everything? I haven't talked to you in a couple of days", he states.

"I am doing fine Pops. I am just on my way to work. The kids were removed last night."

"And how did they do?"

"They did fine. They were upset, of course, but we made it just fine."

"Well, that is good to know. I spoke with your hubby last night and he wanted me to call you and let you know that your visit is set up for tonight if you can make it", he states.

"Of course I want to make it. I haven't seen him in over a week and that was when we were at the courthouse. I can't wait to see my baby."

"I knew that you would be. He misses you. That boy is crazy about you. I know my son may say that he wants to see everybody, but the only person he really cares about seeing is his wife. He said that I am scheduled for that time, also, but I want you and him to spend some quality time together. I won't go, just so you all can be alone", he says.

"Are you sure?"

"Yes, I am sure. Just tell him that I love him when you get there", he suggests.

"I sure will and thanks for calling me to let me know."

"You bet!"

"Well, Pops, I am almost at work, so I have to go now."

"Alright then. I will speak with you later on today. When are you meeting with Stuart to start going over Kalin's case?"

"I have to meet with him this afternoon. Why? Do you want to go with me?"

"Yes, I would love to go with you. I will do anything for my son."

"OK, I will pick you up. Be ready around 1:30 or so, ok?"

"OK, see you then."

It seems like an eternity, but I am finally pulling in to the property. Before the day gets started, I can already tell that it may not end up a good one. When I walk into my office, I am shocked at what I see. My eyes must be deceiving me! Waiting for me in my office is Ms. Rita and her daughter!

"Melissa, she insisted that she wait for you in your office. I tried to tell her, but---", Cindy tries to explain, but I have already put up my finger to my mouth signaling for her that no explanation is needed.

"Good morning", I say to Ms. Rita, as I open my office door.

"Hey, Ms. Meme", says Dee. She seems to be so happy to see me. Before I can fully walk into the office, she is already standing in front of me. "Where is Mr. Kalin?" she asks. It doesn't matter where we are, this child is always asking for my husband. She enjoys the times that she spent with him. He always made her feel special.

"He is away right now, but I will tell him that you asked about him." This answer seems to have made her feel better because she finally gives me a hug and rushes back to her seat.

"Well, good morning Ms. Melissa. How are you? You looking good", she says.

"Thank you, Ms. Rita. So, what brings the two of you here today?"

"I just came to see how you were doing and to see if you have received any mail for me", she answers.

"Well, I am doing fine and yes, your mail is at the house. Why didn't you change your address?"

"Honestly, I just don't want to change it", she says so candidly.

"Well, alrighty then", I respond. "I will send it to you. What is your new address?"

"If you don't mind, I would rather you just give it to me", she states.

"Well, like I said, your mail is at my house and I am, obviously, not getting ready to go home and get it for you. So, just let me mail it to you so that you will have it. Is there something wrong with my having your address?" I ask sarcastically.

"Oh no, it is nothing like that sweetie. I will drop by later on in the week to pick it up, so, please just bring it to work with you", she requests.

"I sure will. Are you guys doing okay?"

"Yes ma'am, we are doing just fine. I miss my little children, though", she states. *Did she just mention my children as if she doesn't know that they were recently removed from my home? She knows that all of her meddling is exactly why my children aren't here. I don't want to speak with her at all about my kids.*

"Well, I hate to rush you off, Ms. Rita, but I have a few appointments scheduled for today and I just---"

"Oh it's okay; we are leaving now, but I will see you later on in the week to pick up the mail", she states, as she is getting up from her seat. Her daughter follows behind her but gives me a big hug before she walks out of my office.

I watch them walk past Cindy and out the front door. I know that I have to get my work done so that I can get out of here today because I am scheduled to see Kalin today for a visit and I have an appointment with Stuart to go over the case. I would love to take a detour after visiting Kalin to check on the children but I am trying to go by the rules. I am ordered to have no contact until something has been set up for me by CCF, which I will hear about at the next hearing.

"Cindy, will you come in here, please", I ask over the intercom.

"Sure, I will be right in. I am on a call right now", she answers.

After a few minutes, Cindy makes her way into my office, "Yes ma'am."

"Cindy, I will be working straight through because I have to get out of here a little early today. I have an appointment set for me to meet with Kalin's attorney and then I have an appointment to see Kalin later on this evening.

"Ok, that is great!" she exclaims.

"And I don't want to be disturbed, unless it is the corporate office calling me for something."

"OK, got it! So, what did that lady come here for?"

"She wanted to see if I had some mail for her and when I asked her about giving me the address to forward it to, she didn't want to give it to me. I will bring it in tomorrow and if she comes here when I am not in, the mail will be right here in my top drawer."

"Ok, sounds like a plan. Well go ahead and get back to work."

Because my focus is on my work, I am finally finished with my Budget Proposal and have left it on Cindy's desk for the interoffice mail. This is just the initial draft of it. When the Corporate office gets it, they will, no doubt, make some changes. But, because my property performs so well, I usually get what I ask for during these Budget planning processes. And one thing that I am asking more money for is Payroll! The monthly bonuses are also signed off, as well as my request for Holiday Funds for all of my proposed upcoming festivities.

Mr. Howard, the Owner, just sent me an email. He is coming to Miami in a few weeks and wants to have lunch with me. I love when he and his wife come to town because they take me out to the finest Italian restaurant in Miami and we have a good time. I love working for this couple because they don't have a problem investing in their properties and in their people. They are both very impressed with what I do for the properties during the holiday season. There is no reason to change that just because I am going through hell. The residents deserve a good time and besides, it is what my children would want me to do.

****

I hope that Stuart already has his strategy planned out when I get there because I am most anxious about getting to the Jail to see Kalin and I hope that he is happy with my appearance. I haven't seen him in over 2 weeks already and I am so excited to see him. I wonder if we will get the physical contact visit like we did when he went to jail the last time. I enjoyed that because I got the chance to hold his hands and look into his eyes.

On my way to Stuart's office, I get this sick feeling in my stomach. I am not sure where this feeling is coming from, but I just start praying. My mother always taught me to pray during these kinds of times because I really don't know where the feeling is coming from. I have to hurry up and get over to my father in law's house because he wants to go with me to meet with the attorney.

I make it to JT's house in 15 minutes. He doesn't live that far from my property. When I make it to his front door, I see that the door is slightly open. I don't know if I should go in here or not. What if there is a burglary in process or something? I have been trying to get my father in law out of this neighborhood for years. I told him that he needs to consider moving in with me, but he hasn't answered me yet.

"JT, are you in there?" I say, while peeping around the door. I don't hear anything, not even the dog. I yell out for him again, "JT, where are you?" It sounds like I can hear some muffled sounds coming from the bedroom. I walk toward JT's bedroom and push on the door, but it doesn't move. I push it again and it comes wide open. MY eyes are as big as golf balls when I open the door, to find my father in law in bed, but with a woman. I don't know who yelled louder. I am so shocked! I had no idea that my father in law still had sex. I immediately shut the door and wait for him in the kitchen.

"Melissa, I will be right out", he says, yelling from the bedroom. Moments later, he is standing next to me in the kitchen with a smirk on his face. We don't discuss what just happened. I would rather pretend that I didn't see anything.

After a few more minutes, JT and I head for Stuart's office to discuss Kalin's criminal case. He has done some homework and has a list of witnesses that he will or is thinking about calling to serve as witnesses on Kalin's behalf. I can tell by the types of questions that he is asking, he is not happy with Ms. Rita at all. He is pretty much prepared to destroy her on the stand.

It usually takes 45 minutes or so to get to the Jail. I hope that because this visit is at the end of the day that I don't run into any traffic holdups. I finally make it within 5 miles of the Jail and there is a train. I can't believe it! *Please Lord let this train pass. I hope that this isn't one of those that sit for a while.*

I am finally pulling into the entrance for the Miami County Jail. The parking lot is very full. It looks like this is the time when most people visit. I am not sure what to expect when I get inside. As I am walking to the front entrance, there are other visitors coming out. I assume that these must be the people who were in the slots before the 6pm visit. The visits last for one hour. That is not enough time for me to tell Kalin all that is going on out in the real world.

The line is extremely long. There is a mixture of women who appear to have just gotten off from work, just as I did. This group is also mixed with older men and women, probably here visiting their grandchildren. I can see the stress on everyone's faces, as if there are a hundred other places that they would rather be than right here right now. The lady sitting at the front doesn't look too friendly. She probably hates her job. I probably would hate it too. Are my eyes deceiving me? The lady in the blue suit who is leaving looks like Wendy. This can't be! There must be a mistake. This has to be a woman who resembles Wendy because I am not going to believe that she is coming to see Kalin in Jail. I won't ruin our visit with that discussion, but I will 'table' it for now in my mind.

When I finally make it to the front, it is now my turn to deal with the unfriendly jail attendant.

"Driver's license, please", she demands.

I hand it over to her and she looks at it and compares it to a list that she has. No doubt that she is probably looking over her visitor list to make sure that the name on the license matches the name on the visitor list. I assume that it does because she returns it back to me.

"Do you have keys or cell phones?" she asks.

"Yes, I have keys."

"You must leave the keys here with me and step in the next line to go through the security clearance. Enjoy your visit", she says, without really looking up at me.

I pass through the security clearance and I am one step closer to seeing my husband. I try to look further through the bulletproof windows to see if I can see my husband, but I can't really see anything. The guard walks us to a desk and we hand our driver's license to this attendant as well. She gives me a piece of paper and instructs me to go to the monitor that is marked "16". *Why am I going to a monitor? Where is my husband? I don't see him at all.*

I pull up my desk at the monitor and finally realize that my sweet husband will not be here at all because he is staring at me on a computer screen. *So, I guess there will be no physical contact. So, now this is what visitors have to look forward to when they visit their loved ones. We will talk through a monitor screen. What fun!*

I stare at the monitor and Kalin motions for me to pick up the phone.

"Well, look at the most beautiful woman in Miami", he says, as I pick up the phone.

"Hi honey. How are you? You look great too! Kalin, I love you so much."

Just seeing him makes me cry.

"No tears, no tears, no need. I love you too, Mrs. Thomas and don't you ever forget that for as long as you live. How are the children? Have you heard anything?" he asks.

"No, I haven't. I am waiting for the Hearing to find out when or if the Judge will give me a visit with the children."

"You really do look good, sweetheart", he says, flashing that beautiful smile across the computer screen.

"Thank you, honey. That means so much to hear you say that."

"Bet you can't guess what I wish I were doing?" he asks, with a very sly grin on his face.

"Honey, I am sure that you can't say it. But, I know what you would like to do right now."

"Now, I see who has the dirty mind", he says, laughing at this point.

Our visit continues with more and more talk about the children, until I remember that I have to give him JT's message.

"Oh, your father told me to tell you hello and that he loves you. He told me that you scheduled him for a visit at the same time as my visit but he decided not to come because he said that he knows that you really just want to spend time with me."

"And that would be right", Kalin says, getting closer and closer to the computer screen. I can feel the goose bumps forming on my arms.

"Honey, you always say the nicest and sweetest things."

"But, it is all true. Melissa, my life has not been the same since I met you", he begins to explain.

"Well duh! Look at you now. Because of me and my life, look at where you are now. You wouldn't be here if it were not for me."

"That is nonsense, Mrs. Thomas, and I won't have you speaking that way. This is not your fault. This blame goes to the ruler of darkness that runs this world", he responds.

"Yeah, but he certainly has lots of help getting it done, doesn't he? I can think of one of his ways right off the top of my head - CCF!"

"OK, honey, no more negative talk. Tell me about you. How is my wife *really* doing?" he asks.

"Honestly, I am really struggling honey. I miss you so much. I miss the children. I don't know what I would do if it were not for Cindy. She has been a great friend to me through all of this. She sends a nice hello to you, as well. Guess who showed up at my office today?" I say, changing the subject on purpose.

"Who?"

"Ms. Rita and her daughter! Dee asked about you. You know how much she just loves her Mr. Kalin."

"What did she want?" he asks.

"She just wanted to know if I had her mail. I asked her for her new address, but she refused to give it to me. She said that she will just come back and get it later. I have to admit it, but that was quite weird and suspicious to me."

"Well, you just never know with that woman", he says, in a matter of fact kind of way.

"What is going on with Princess and the whole Middleton thing?" he asks.

"Well, apparently, Mr. Richards heard about what is going on down here and suggested that we get this *"thing"* straightened out first before he submits his recommendation to Foster Care. Apparently, this thing is going to be a lot harder than what we initially thought. Laura didn't do what she should have done to have Princess just automatically come live with us, so the Court is taking jurisdiction of this matter."

"This too shall pass, Mrs. Thomas", he says, with a bright smile.

"Yeah, that is what my girl, Yolanda Adams, says, right?" I say with a half smile on my face. "But how in the world did he find out about what is going on down here?"

"Honey, attorneys have their way of finding things out. Don't think too hard on that", he says. "Princess could not have ended up with a better mother."

"I hope that you are right. So, how are things in here for you? Are they mistreating you?"

"It is jail, sweetheart. There is nothing nice about it. I am holding on. I have my wife and children to think about. I can't give up on life just because of this. I have to admit that it does hurt. It hurts knowing that I am in here because my daughter accused me of something that I know that I did not do. I know that there is some explanation behind this, but I just don't know what it is. All I know is that my daughter must also be hurting", he says, holding down his head.

"So, tell me", I say, forcing him to hold his head up again. "Tell me what it is that you think about mostly", I ask, changing the subject again.

"Do you really want to know the answer to that question?" he asks.

"Yes, I do."

"I think about the day I am set free and how I am going to make love to my wife just like we did the very first time we made love", he answers, with a smile on his face.

"I know."

The words, "FIFTEEN MINUTES LEFT" flash across the screen letting me know that my time is almost up. In fifteen minutes, I will be walking out of this place without my husband only to go home alone without my children as well. I don't really want to go home, but where else can I go? I don't want to go over to Cindy's house because she and her boyfriend are celebrating their anniversary tonight. I can't go to my sister's house because we aren't speaking right now. I can't go over to my niece's house because I will violate the Judge's orders. I don't want to go over to Pops' house because he may have a lady friend there and I certainly do not want to run into the scene I ran into earlier. There is one thing to do and that is to just go home and deal with the loneliness as best I know how.

"Honey, are you okay?" Kalin asks. "You look like you have something on your mind."

"Yes, I am fine. I am just ---", I begin to say before he interrupts me.

"I know, I am going to miss you too, sweetheart. We can do this. Our love has a strong foundation that can withstand anything. We have been through a separation before and we will do it again", he states.

"I know that you are right. I love you, Mr. Thomas", I say, wiping the tears away from my eyes.

"I love you, too, Mrs. Thomas", he says. "Now, you walk out that door knowing that I love you and will think of you tonight."

Our fifteen minutes are up and the visit is over. The monitor automatically takes Kalin off the screen. I am surprised that I made it without crying too much. Walking back to my car suddenly reminds me that I am going home to an empty house to get ready for yet another day.

My court hearing is in a few days and I hope that Stuart is ready for it. He didn't mention it when I was in his office on yesterday. Although we are friends, he is one of the most professional attorneys I have ever met.

I finally make it back home and before going inside, I grab the mail from the mailbox. This must be the letter that Ms. Rita is waiting on to arrive. It is a letter from Social Security Administration, along with a cable bill and a letter from CCF. Right away, I tear open the letter from CCF and it is just a reminder of the court hearing that is to take place in a couple of days. I would; however, love to know why Social Security office is writing Ms. Rita. This is probably why she is so anxious for getting her mail. I would love to know the contents because I have a funny feeling that she is up to something. I just thought about what her sister said the day at the courthouse about her sister and how she wasn't supposed to have her daughter and how it is all about the money. *If the Social Security is so important, why didn't she just change her address?*

The hot bath works wonders! I am finally ready to close my eyes because tomorrow is a new day and I want to be ready for it.

CHAPTER 52

"Move On Counselor!"

*T*he courthouse is packed today. Stuart seems as if something is on his mind. JT decides not to come because he has a situation that just came up at one of his jobsites.

"Stuart, are you okay today?" I finally ask.

"I am fine, Melissa. Just having a little trouble at home", he says.

"What kind of trouble?"

"To be honest with you, I would much rather not talk about it right now. I am on the job and don't want to discuss my personal", he answers.

"Excuse me, Mr. Attorney, but we are friends, remember?"

"Yes, I know that, but we are in a professional environment right now and I need to concentrate on this hearing today", he answers.

"OK, Mr. Attorney, but when this is over, let's do lunch. We are friends and Kalin and I care about you very much. So, are we doing lunch or what?"

"Ok, fine. We will do lunch, but let's go in here and take care of this first", he demands.

In no time, the bailiff is calling all interested parties in the "CCF versus Kalin & Melissa Thomas" case. I didn't notice it until now that we are walking in the door that my niece is actually at the Hearing today. I am curious as to why she is here.

The court bailiff announces the entrance of the Judge. When she sits down, we are all ordered to sit down so that the proceeding can begin.

"Department, are there any new updates?" she asks, looking at their table.

"Yes, Your Honor, there are just a few", he answers, while gathering his notes.

"Proceed, please."

"In the courtroom today is the niece who has taken in the Thomas children and she wants to add a few things", he states.

"Step to the front, ma'am and state your name for the record, please", the Judge orders.

My niece moves to the front and begins to speak. "My name is Nikki Hughes. I just want to say that the children are doing fine. They are safe in my home. The Department helped out with beds and they are all doing fine. They are all enrolled in school and are adjusting very well", she comments.

"Has the Mother been in contact with you to see how the children are doing", asks the attorney for CCF.

"No, she has not called to check on them or anything", she answers.

"So you're telling me that these children have been at your home for 2 weeks and Mrs. Thomas has not showed any interest in their well-being at all?" he says.

"That is correct, sir", she answers.

"Very well, thank you, Ms. Hughes. Mr. Peters, do you have any questions for this witness?"

"Yes, I do", he responds. Stuart directs his questions to Nikki.

"Good morning, Ms. Hughes."

"Good morning", Nikki responds.

"Ms. Hughes, you just mentioned that Mrs. Thomas has not tried to contact the children since they have been with you, right?"

"Yes, I did", she responds, with a slight attitude in her voice.

"Are you aware that the Judge has a no-contact order in this case?"

"No, I am not aware."

"No further questions for this witness", Stuart states, and heads back to his chair.

Mr. Peoples interjects. "Your Honor, it is very clear here that Mrs. Thomas is not interested in the well being of her children. She could have at least called to check on them. They are family and Ms. Hughes has no issues with the mother at least contacting her to see how the children are doing. That is the point that we are trying to make here. But it is very clear, as evidenced by the jail records that she finds the time to visit her husband in jail and quite often, I might add. Three weeks ago was her first visit and she has gone at least 14 times since she began visiting him. This leads the Court to believe that Mrs. Thomas is more concerned about Mr. Thomas than she is for her children", he states.

My mouth is wide open. I can't believe what I am hearing. I didn't call because I was trying to follow the rules. The Judge ordered me to have no contact so that is exactly what I did.

"Your Honor, I object to the assumptions that are being made here about my client", Stuart interjects. "She was not given any authority by this Court to visit these children and my client is simply going by your rules that she is to have no contact with the children."

"Simmer down, Mr. Stuart, I think that Mr. Peoples is just trying to show that the Mother has visited Mr. Thomas but can't find the time to find out what her children are doing. She doesn't have to have contact with the children, but she could have called to at least see how they were doing, that's all. Move on with it, Mr. Peoples? Is there anything else?"

I can't believe that they are discussing me as if I am not in the room. Why isn't anyone interested in what I have to say? How dare they treat me like I don't care about my children? I was thinking the other day to call, but didn't want to disturb anything and break the rules. I can't believe this!

"No, Your Honor, there isn't at this time", he answers.

"Very well. What is the State bringing to the table, if anything, for visitation for the Mother?"

Now, this is why I woke up this morning. I just want to know when I get the opportunity to see my children.

"Based on the mother's schedule, we can set something up for her next Tuesday at 11:00 at the Family Center on Martin Luther King Boulevard", he offers.

"My client will be there at 11 for this appointment. How much time and what will be the frequency of her visits?" Stuart adds.

"This is for an initial visit and we will let her know when the next appointment will be after this visit", Denise says.

"Very well, then. Mrs. Thomas will have her initial visit with all of the children on next Tuesday at 11:00 and will let her know when and how often after that."

"Yes, Your Honor", Mr. Peoples agrees.

"Yes, Your Honor", Stuart follows.

I don't want to look at my niece. I can't believe that she showed up to say this to the Judge. Why in the world would she come in here to try to make me look bad? What is she getting out of this? Is she in cahoots with Ms. Rita or what? Lord, how can my family be so mean and hateful? Do they know how much pain I am in? Do they care?

The hearing is over and I get my first visit with the children. It doesn't matter what any of them think, I am finally going to see my children after 2 very long weeks.

Stuart and I head for the parking garage. He almost forgot that we agreed to lunch but I am not letting him off that easy. He, obviously, needs to talk to someone.

"OK, so you pick where we go to lunch", I demand.

"Oh, Melissa, I really don't want to do this today", he says, trying to get out of it.

"No, Stuart. Stop running. We really need to go somewhere and sit down and talk. I am your friend and I care, so please talk to me. Let's do Chic-Fil-A and it's my treat!"

"Ok, you are not going to give up, are you?"

"And you know that I am not."

Stuart and I cut through traffic to get to the downtown Chic-Fil-A to hopefully beat the crowds. On the way, I gave JT a call just to let him know the outcome of the hearing. He is so excited that I am going to finally see the kids. He wants to see them, but we will have to get him in to visit with them later down the road. Stuart needs my attention now so I quickly hang up the phone with JT.

"Ok, so what is it? What's going on with you? You really do seem preoccupied today. Is Phyllis okay?"

"She is fine", he answers, without looking in my direction. For some reason, the downtown traffic is more interesting to him than what I am saying.

"Come on, Stuart. Don't make be beg. Just tell me what is wrong. I am here for you. You can trust me with whatever it is. You and Phyllis aren't having any problems, are you?"

"It's not her. It is me. Did you know that today is the anniversary of my wife's death? I can't shake the sadness today. I woke up this morning and have been making everyone's life a living hell. It is as if I am angry at everybody because my wife died. She died because of me, Melissa", he explained. By now, Stuart has allowed himself to let go and let his feelings flow. He is sobbing uncontrollably, holding on to the steering wheel tighter and tighter.

"Stuart, please let it go. Let her go, sweetheart. She is gone. Let her rest in peace. What happened that night was an accident. She would not want you to be sitting here blaming yourself for what happened that night."

"Phyllis hasn't done anything wrong. All she ever does is love me and I hurt her this morning. Everything she did or said wasn't right. I even called her by my ex-wife's name. She is so mad at me right now. How do I look her in the eyes and tell her that I still love my wife? How do I tell her that I will always love my wife and that she will never be able to change that?"

"She is not trying to change it, Stuart. She knows that you will always love your ex-wife. She knows that, and what she doesn't know, you have shown her. Don't run off this good woman because of these past hurts and regrets. She loves you and has been there for you. Now, you go home tonight and you need to find a way to make this right with her. She doesn't deserve to be treated like this and you know it. That is a good woman that you have at home. Treat her right, my friend", I continue to say. I can tell that Stuart is listening because he has actually turned his head in my direction and is nodding. The remainder of our ride to Chic-Fil-A is in silence.

By the time, we make it to the restaurant, it is already roaring with the downtown workers. We decide that we won't be able to enjoy our lunch if we stay, so we decide to just get our food "to go". Stuart drops me off at my car and waves goodbye. "Stuart, it's going to be okay, you know that right?"

"Yes, I do, Meme. Thanks so much for the words of encouragement. It means a lot to me."

CHAPTER 53

"How Do You Know Her?"

*T*he day has finally arrived for me to visit with my children and I am not sure why I am so nervous. I haven't spoken to them nor have I seen them since they were removed from the house over 2 weeks ago. I wish that their grandfather, JT, was here with me, but he is not approved to visit with them just yet. I know that Kalin is thinking of us right now and wishing that he could be here too. I believe that the girls really miss him. And more than anything, I truly hope that Christy will show up at the visit. I am feeling so good right now and nothing else in this world matters to me. I am going to be with my children and I am extremely excited about it. It is only for one hour, but that will have to do for now.

My Folgers coffee is brewing, my curlers are getting hot, and my Strawberry Pop Tart is in the toaster oven. Joel Osteen is in the CD player and speaking about how the best is yet to come. This is the time of the day where I make sure to pump my head and heart with more inspiration than I know what to do with. I don't usually like to take phone calls or get on the computer during this part of the day. This time that I spend with God is fuel in my engine. Without it, my mind stops.

Dear God, please be with me as I visit with my children today. Lord, give me the right words to say to them. Give them the right heart to receive it. I pray that Christy shows up today for this visit. I need her to know that I love her no matter what. Please protect the vehicle that they will be in to get to the location of our visitation. Please protect them from any danger. Watch over my car as I travel to the destination. In Jesus' name, Amen.

Traffic is normal and the weather is quite comfortable. I finally make it to the address given to me on Canton Drive on the northeast side of Miami. I am seriously thinking about coming over here again, because I like the shopping centers. There are quite a few twists and turns so I hope that my niece finds it okay. I had to *Map Quest* the directions, but

I found it. I just hope that my niece finds it okay. I am glad that I have a navigational system in the car to help guide me as well.

After what seems like an effortless drive, I have arrived at the Northtown Family Center about 15 minutes early. Unfortunately, I don't see my niece's car yet. I don't know if I should go in or just wait outside. Within 10 minutes of parking, my niece pulls up right beside me. The kids are waving at me as if they are going to wave their hand right out of its socket. I do the same and to my delight, Christy is with them! We all get out of our cars and make it inside.

"Good morning, Mrs. Thomas", says Denise, already waiting inside.

"Good morning."

"Did you have any trouble finding the building?"

"Actually, I didn't have any trouble finding it because I went online and got the directions and I also used the navigational system in my car", I respond.

"Wonderful! Our meeting room is this way." She guides us down the hallway and into our meeting room. Justice can't wait for us to get into the room before she runs up to me and grabs my hand. All of the girls look so pretty in their new outfits that I recently purchased for them.

"Hi Mommy", Justice blurts out.

"Hey, Momma's baby", I say. "You look so pretty."

"You look so pretty, too, Mommy", she responds.

When we make it inside the meeting room, my children, without being told to do so, all make it over to my side of the table. The caseworker begins the meeting with instructions.

"OK, you all have one hour to visit with each other. I am going to step outside. I will be in the room next door making some notes. If you need anything, just step outside and get me", she says, before walking out of the room.

The girls all present their pictures that they had previously drawn for me. Much to my surprise, Christy walks over to my side of the table and gives me a big hug and whispers to me that she loves me. I am expecting to spend time alone with my children, but my niece is still in the room with us. *Was this part of the plan? Do they not trust me with my own children? Why can't we have privacy? I want them to feel at ease to speak with me about how they are feeling. Not only is my niece in the room, but so are her kids. Instead of my children being able to focus on our interactions, they are distracted with their cousins fighting for my attention as well. As unpleasant as this part is, I will have to take what I can get at this point.*

I just remember that I have my digital camera with me. Kalin will certainly appreciate getting these pictures, as well.

"Hey guys, get together for a picture", I say waving the camera in one hand. "Kameron, come on sweetheart, perk up for the picture. What is wrong?"

"Nothing, Ma", he says, sounding so sad. "I just miss you. I like Auntie Nikki and everything, but I miss you too. I don't like everybody asking us so many questions and stuff. I am so tired of it", he whispers, looking around to see if Nikki is listening. Darren goes along with what he was saying as well.

"Yeah, Ma. We didn't do anything to deserve this. I don't care what nobody say, you are the best mother a child can ever have and we miss you so much", he says as he begins to cry.

"Oh, my precious children, you don't have any reason to cry. We will be together again one day. I promise you that I won't stop fighting until we are all together again. Don't cry. Dry your eyes. I need you both to be strong for your sisters. They need you to be strong."

After taking several pictures and hearing all about how things are at their new schools, the meeting is almost up. Christy shares her good news with me about how she is planning to enroll in the Collegiate Academy at her school so that she can earn some college credit during her freshman year. We talk about the upcoming parent meeting regarding the program. I promised Christy that I would be there to support her. To make sure that I don't forget about this meeting, I put in my Daily Planner right away.

My niece stands up, which is an indication to me that our visit is coming to an end. "The kids are all doing well, Melissa. They really miss you. That is all they talk about is their mommy and how much they miss you. You can call to the house whenever you want to speak with them. Sharell cries to sleep almost every night", my niece adds.

"I am sorry to hear that she cries to sleep at night. I turn to Sharell. "Honey, everything is going to be alright. Just say your prayers every night before you go to bed. Mommy prays for you too. With all of that prayer, you are very well protected. So, just close your eyes and go to sleep and we will meet at some point, right there in your dreams." She seems to believe me because she perks up when I finish talking to her. I turn to my niece and respond to her comment.

"Great!" That means a lot to me to know that I can call them regularly. I love my children and I hurt without them", I say, starting to form tears in my eyes.

"I know you do, girl, but they are alright", she says, walking toward the exit.

"OK, guys, it is time for us to say goodbye. I have thoroughly enjoyed this time with you, and –", I am saying before being interrupted by Ms. Woods. She walks into the room with her notepad in her hand. Now, I realize that she was sitting in the next room watching our interactions.

"Come and give me hugs and kisses". The kids run my way with open arms. I don't want to cry right now in front of them. I want to run out of here and scream, but I know that I have to let them see me strong so that they know that it is okay to do the same.

The visit is over and the children are packing into the car and putting on their seatbelts. I watch my niece drive away and then I get into my car and sit for just a moment to take it all in. Before I drive off, I decide to give Attorney Richards a call just to check on Princess' status.

"Hello, Attorney Richards' office, how may I help you?"

"Hello. Is Mr. Richards in?"

"Yes, may I tell him who's calling", she responds.

"It is Melissa Thomas."

"Please hold." She places me on hold and within 30 seconds or so, Mr. Richards picks up the phone.

"Mrs. Thomas, how are you?"

"I am fine. I am just taking one day at a time. I am calling today to check on Princess' status", I explain.

"I am glad that you called. I had called your office and your assistant said that you were at a morning appointment", he begins to say and then I interrupt him.

"Yeah, but I haven't made it back there yet. What is wrong?" I ask, sounding a little anxious.

"Melissa, I hate to tell you this but you are not going to get Princess right now. We received the full report from CCF there in Miami and because of their findings, I can't, rightfully so, recommend her to come with you. Now, being that Laura did leave in her Will for you to have her daughter, you will have to either allow her to stay in Foster Care until your troubles are cleared up or give temporary custody to Brittney Snow, who is somewhat known as next of kin", he continues to say.

"What about Princess' father? Does he have any say-so in this matter?" I ask.

"We have contacted the man who we believe to be Princess' father and he doesn't really have a problem with Princess being with Brittney. But the situation is —", he says before I interrupt him.

"She could have said Brittney, but she didn't. She could have said "Rock", but she didn't. Did it ever dawn on you why she said me in the first place? Think about it. Why would she want me to have her daughter? I live all the way in Miami and she could have chosen Brittney, who is right there, but she didn't. She chose me. She knows that I would be the best mother to her child. Now, if she could see that, why can't you? Why are you so dead set on having Brittney be with this child? Do you know Brittney? What's in this for you?" I ask, sounding upset.

"Melissa, please calm down. You don't have to—", he begins to say.

"I don't have to what? I am so tired of people telling me what to do!! I am so tired of it! I am tired of how unfair everything is sometimes! Fine, do what you have to do and I promise you that you will soon find out why that child needs to be with me. I don't want her to have to stay in Foster care, so what do I have to do to get her out of there?"

"You need to sign off on a temporary guardianship to be granted to Brittney", he answers.

"Send me the paperwork and I will look it over and get it back to you as soon as possible."

"OK, I will have the papers sent to you via FedEx. You will receive them on tomorrow", he says.

"Fine."

"Listen, we can get it all straightened out when you are cleared in this CCF investigation", he says.

"I am sure that we will. Thanks for everything. Goodbye."

"Goodbye".

The phone goes dead. I eventually look up and realize that I am still in the parking lot. I really don't want to move. I should be back at work, but I can't think straight right now. Everything is a blur in my mind. I can't put all of the pieces of this puzzle together just yet, but I am sure that I will find out what is *really* going on. I haven't even figured out how Mr. Richards even found out anything about CCF or that anything was going on here in the first place. I can't think about this right now. I have to figure out how to bring my kids and husband home.

I finally make it back to the office. Cindy informs me that Ms. Rita and her daughter dropped by while I was out. She gave her the mail. According to Cindy, Ms. Rita was very happy with the contents of the mail.

"Ms. Rita is so happy that you left the mail behind for her. She already knew that you weren't going to be here and was worried that maybe you wouldn't have left the mail."

"How did she know that I wasn't going to be here?"

"Not quite sure. Oh, and your friend Leigh called for you. She said to give her a call when you make it in."

"Ok, I am not going to be here too long. I want to go visit my properties that are expecting me today and send in my interoffice paperwork and work on some things at home, if it is okay with you."

"OK with me? You are the boss!" she says, with a deep smile on her face.

"Cindy, I don't know what I would do around here without you. You are not only a great friend, but you are an even better assistant manager. Is there anything that I need to know about?"

"No ma'am, everything is under control. Oh, I almost forgot. The attorney from Alabama called you."

"Yes, I know. I called him and he mentioned that he called here."

"Is everything alright?" Cindy asks.

"It is a long story and I need to focus on some office work right now. It is much better than all the stuff that I am dealing with, so, if you don't mind, I would much rather not talk about any of it. Forget about me! What about your anniversary celebration with your main squeeze?"

"It was fantastic!" she says, holding her hands to her chest. "He and I danced all night on the song that was playing when we met."

"Tell me! What song was that?"

"*Here and Now*" by Luther Vandross. It was so romantic. He walked up to the table where my friends and I were sitting and he came straight to me and asked me if I was with someone and if I wanted to dance. We danced and when our eyes met, I believe I fell in love with him at that moment and believe it or not, I still get goosebumps when I am around him."

"Ah, that is so sweet! You lovebirds! I know what you mean. That is the same way I feel when I am around Kalin. I fall in love with him over and over. Oh no, let me get back to work! If nothing else, I am going to check my emails and get out to my properties. I am going to go home from there. Have a great evening!"

"You too, Melissa."

Driving to the east side of Miami is the area where my favorite properties are. It is so beautiful and I oftentimes stop at one of my favorite parks just to have a "moment". I am not sure how my timing is today, but if there is time for it, I would love to stop and sit by the ocean and just meditate for a moment.

I am finally done with the properties and time has really gotten away from me. The good thing about is that the properties are all in fantastic shape. The curb appeal is on point and the issues that were in question on last week were all resolved. I really do have the best managers in the company. They know how to take care of business. They make my job so easy. I have to get home now, so maybe I will just soak in a hot tub of water with my favorite scent from Victoria's Secret that helps me relax.

The 45 minute drive back home has me starving. I know that I am not going to cook when I get home so I might as well stop in at Crispers to pick up a salad. It is too late to eat from my favorite burger joint. I would only have to pay for it later on. When I walk in Crispers, the ladies in the restaurant are pretty familiar with me being that I am in here picking up my favorite Mediterranean salad at least 4 days out of the week. Eating healthy never tasted so good!

"Well hello Missy", says the clerk, as I approach the counter.

"Well hello Ms. Rachel", I say, sounding happy to see her. I had to look at her name tag because I am not that good at remembering names. I can remember a telephone number from 20 years back, but not a name from 3 or 4 days ago.

"Will you have the usual?"

"Is there anything else? Of course I will!"

I grab my salad and head for home. The house isn't the same to me without my family waiting on me when I get there. Nothing feels the same without my family. I have quite a bit to let sink in from this day. I have to find a way to release it. Now I know what they mean when they say "let go and let God". I truly want to let these hurt feelings and feelings of anger and regret GO and let God replace them with forgiveness and faith.

Dear God, Thank you for this day. Thank you for guiding my steps throughout this day. Lord, I pray that you will allow me to eat this food and have peace in my heart that all things will always work out for good for those who love the Lord and are called according to His purpose. Forgive me where I have fallen short and continue to build me up. Bless this food for my nourishment and bless the hands that prepared it. In Jesus' name, Amen.

I sit down at the dinner table to eat my salad and decide to flip on the television to see what new and interesting things are happening in the news in Miami. *Did I hear what I thought I just heard? I can't be hearing this correctly! I can't believe this!*

The reporter continues to report, "Allegations of sexual abuse continue to rise in Miami. Coach Albert Toler, of Miami Lakes High School, was arrested today for having inappropriate sexual contact with one of the members of his team. The alleged victim's mother found a note in her backpack where she discussed her many sexual encounters with the Coach. The mother took the letter to the local authorities and Coach Toler was arrested from school campus. News reporters went to his home and he declined to speak with our staff. Our reporters spoke with some of the friends of the alleged victim and they all said that the relationship *was* consensual by both the alleged victim and the coach. We caught up with his wife as she was getting into her car today and she declined to speak with our reporters". The television screen shows a very upset woman trying to hide her face from the camera. *She is so beautiful! Why is that not enough for her husband? Why can't he just love her and let that be enough? Why are men always looking for the younger?* The reporter continues, "The alleged victim, who we can't identify, has withdrawn from Miami Lakes High School to avoid scrutiny and further embarrassment. We will keep you updated on this story as it develops", she says.

Right as the reporter is signing off, the phone rings. *Who can this be? I wonder.* On the front of the television screen, it reads *Leigh Bynum*. I wonder if she just saw this report that just aired on the local news.

"Hello."

"Hello, sweetheart. How are you doing?" she asks.

"I am fine. I just got home about 30 minutes ago. I stopped by Crispers and picked up a salad and was just sitting here watching the news. Did you see it?" I ask.

"As a matter of fact, I did see it. Isn't that crazy?"

"Yes, that is pretty wild. I went to that school and I used to work with Coach Toler."

"Well, I have some news for you, honey. I hope I don't upset you with stuff when I call you but I believe that you should always know what is going on with your case because they are *not* going to tell you", she continues.

"What is it now?"

"I found out today from one of my friends at the courthouse that Kalin is now being offered a plea deal, with 15 years. But if he goes to trial and lose, he is looking at life in prison. From what I hear, the State has several witnesses lined up to speak against your husband.

"Oh my God! Are you serious? I don't know what to say!"

My fork slips out of my hand and the food suddenly sours on my stomach.

"I know that it is quite a bit to take in, but your attorney probably knows by now and I am sure that he is speaking with Kalin about his options", she explains. *I don't remember Kalin mentioning anything like this to me. Did Kalin know and just didn't tell me? What are we going to do now? What if he is found guilty of these charges? What if the jury doesn't want to hear anything and has just made a decision without hearing any of the facts? I wonder.*

"Melissa, are you there?"

"I am here, but I am just shocked. How in the world did they come up with a plea for 15 years? Will Kalin take them up on this offer or will he fight it out?" I ask, starting to cry.

"Honey, they can do just about anything they want to do. And I will tell you the truth. CCF is not going to do anything until they have the outcome of Kalin's criminal case. They want to see if he ends up going to prison or not. I can you tell you that if he does, you probably won't have any problems getting your kids back home", she comments.

"I have to go, Leigh, and —", I begin to say before she interrupts.

"Melissa, you shouldn't be alone right now. Why don't you let me come over?" she suggests.

"No, I will be fine. I just really need to go now. I need to spend some time with God right now. I appreciate you for calling me and giving me this information, but I really have to go now", I say, before hanging up the phone. I want to be off the phone and don't give her a chance to say goodbye.

As soon as I put down the receiver, I let out a loud cry and suddenly fall to my knees. I look toward heaven and say, "*God, why? Why, Lord? Why is this happening to my family? I don't know what I have done to make you so angry, but whatever it is, I am sorry! I am sorry, Lord! Please, forgive me! Oh, God, take this pain away! I can't take this anymore! Why have you left me out here? Is this what you saved me for? Oh Lord, you could have let me die when I wanted to die. This is just too much!*

I eventually crawl into my bedroom and end up sitting in the corner of my walk in closet, rocking back and forth and moaning. I can hear the phone ringing in the distance. I know that it is probably just Leigh calling back because of the way that I got off the phone with her. I can't speak to her or anyone else right now.

I have cried so much that my tears feel warm falling down my face. New tears are flowing on top of the dry white lines from where earlier tears have flown. They are dripping off my chin and onto my neck. The only thing I can do right now is pray. I don't have the strength to get up at all. If I could, I would knock a hole in the wall, but that is just more for me to do later. I certainly don't want to talk to my friends. So, I begin to talk to God.

Lord, all I got is you. You are all that I have! There isn't a friend in the world who can take this pain away. The strength that I need to get through this can only come from you. Forgive me Lord for questioning you. Forgive me for doubting you. Lord, you don't make mistakes. I would not be telling the truth if I told you that I understood all of this. The truth is, Lord, is that I don't understand, but I know that I trust you. I know that trouble doesn't last always. Lord, send your comforter. Help me to close my eyes, Lord, and allow me to come into your bosom. In Jesus' name, Amen.

****

The next thing I hear is my alarm going off. I don't remember setting the alarm last night. I wake up and I am still in my closet with my clothes on from yesterday. I have to find a way to get up off this floor, get dressed for work, and start my day all over again. *You can do this, Melissa. You have to do this! You are not going to sit here and whine about your problems. Everybody has problems. You can do this!*

I really need some coffee so that I can go ahead and wake up. In the near distance, my coffee is almost done brewing. My coffeemaker automatically makes coffee for me every morning around 7:30. Before I can make it to the kitchen, I can already smell my Folgers. The commercial is true when it says that it is an eye-opener.

As rough as last night was, I finally make it into the car and head for the office. Doing busy office work is the only thing that takes my mind off my troubles. At some point today, I have to make a connection with Stuart to see if he is aware of the plea deal being offered to Kalin. But for right now, I just want to have pleasant, positive thoughts running through my head. Just like Creflo Dollar would say, what goes through your ears, eventually gets in your heart, and will come out of your mouth, so you have to mindful of what goes in to your ears. I want to make sure that what comes out of my mouth glorifies God because I refuse to let Satan win this battle. I know that the true battle is in my mind. If Satan can get me to believe that there is no hope and that the way it is right now is how it will always be. I have to keep believing that all of this is for a reason.

God knows that I don't know what it is, but I have to trust that it will work out for my good.

It is the beginning of the month and I am sure that I will be more than busy today. There are month end reports to complete for not only my property but for all the properties that I oversee. They have all had a good month, and because of that, my job is so much easier.

"Good morning Jorge", I say, as I drive onto the property. Jorge is my maintenance supervisor and he is making his rounds of the property. They know that I like for the property to always look its best. First impressions are lasting impressions is one thing that I know to be true.

"Good morning boss!" he yells from the golf cart.

I walk into the office and right away, Cindy is bombarding me with so much information that I can hardly grasp it all.

"Melissa, the doctors called about Ms. Rita and - -", she begins before I interrupt her.

"Is she okay?" I ask. Cindy can tell that I am starting to get upset. I ask her again. "Is she okay?"

"She had a stroke and is in the nursing home and she is asking for you", she responds.

"What! She had a stroke? Oh my God! But, why is she asking for me of all people?"

"Apparently, she has been there for a few days and none of her family members or friends has gone to visit her. She feels so alone right now and is extremely depressed and that is why the doctor took it upon himself to call you to see if you would come. *Now this is something? This is the woman who is single handedly trying to destroy me and my family. There is nothing but the love of God that will allow me to visit this woman.*

"And what did you tell them?"

"I told them I was sure that you would be there as soon as you could", Cindy responds.

"And how did you know that?"

"I know just how much you care for others. So, go on and do what you need to do to get there for her. I think you should go now", she suggests.

"I think that you are right. Is there anything else going on that I need to know about?"

"No, I have everything else under control."

Before walking into my office, I decided to just leave out now in order to beat the morning traffic so that I can get back to work. Cindy has already done a Map Quest for me, but I also decide to put the address in my navigational system to help guide me there as well. According to the directions, I am only 42 minutes or so from my destination.

I finally arrive and as I am driving into the facility's parking lot, I can see residents of the facility sitting out in the lawn in wheelchairs, with a resident employee close by watching guard over them. They all seem sad with their heads hung low as if they have already checked out of this world. As I am walking up the sidewalk, I motion for the resident employee to speak with me briefly.

"Good morning sir", I say, as the employee approaches me. "I am looking for the front office."

"Sure, you are heading in the right direction. The front office is straight through the double doors and the first hallway to your right", he responds.

"Thank you so much, Eric", I say, looking at his name tag.

Will she remember me? What condition is she in? I didn't ask Cindy about that. Will she think that I am here to hurt her?

Thoughts race through my mind because I am not quite sure what to expect of this visit. I do as instructed and walk through the double doors and end up at the front office.

"Good morning", I say, as I approach the front desk. "My name is Melissa Thomas and I am here to visit with Rita Gardner. I received a call from a Doctor Patrick Norwood", I begin to explain before being interrupted.

"Yes, he is expecting you", she says, standing to lead me down the hallway. "His office is right this way."

I follow her down the hallway and arrive at his office that clearly reads, "Doctor Norwood", on the door. The receptionist taps on his door and he invites her to come in. As we both walk in the door, he ends his call with the person on the other end of the phone. It sounds like a personal call.

"Doctor Norwood, this is Mrs. Thomas who is here to see Ms. Rita", she says. He motions for me to have a seat. The receptionist leaves the room. I take a seat in his plush leather chair and start looking around and admiring the awards that Dr. Norwood has earned throughout his time as a physician. Like most professionals, he has a picture of his family on his desk. His wife, or so I assume, is beautiful. She has cocoa brown skin and long hair. The little boy in the photo resembles him. Doctor Norwood is very attractive. He has dark hair and emerald green eyes. Because of his striking features, I am curious as to his origin. I am shocked that he is still on his call even though I am in the room with him. His last comment before hanging up his call is, "I have to go because I don't want to get into this with you right now. We will speak later. Goodbye." He now turns his attention to me.

"Thank you for coming so quickly, Mrs. Thomas", he begins to say. "Did your assistant explain why I called?"

"Yes, she did, somewhat. I understand that Rita Gardner had a stroke."

"That is correct. Ms. Rita has named you next of kin and we are to contact you whenever there is an emergency. We always try to reach the immediate family, but for whatever reason, we are never able to reach them."

"I understand that you contacted her other family members and none of them have shown up here, yet, to speak with you."

"That is correct. We have called and left several messages and our calls are unreturned and she is facing a medical emergency and we need to speak with someone about it. When we called your office, your assistant manager informed us that you would be here as soon as you could", he continues.

"I don't really have that much time. Please tell me what is wrong with her. What is going on?"

"Ms. Rita was brought here because she suffered two strokes and she is not doing well. After arriving here in our facility, she started coughing more and more. We thought it was just a cold, but that cold quickly led to pneumonia. Days passed and she became sicker and sicker. We did more tests and the results revealed that that she has AIDS. She has full blown AIDS and we believe that she got it by sharing needles with other substance abusers. She does not have that much time to live", he says. *How am I supposed to feel for this woman who is trying to destroy my family? I can't turn my back on her. She is someone's mother. The love in my heart means that I have to stay and be here for her in the last days that she has here on this earth.*

"What about her daughter? She has a daughter with Down's Syndrome. What will happen to her? Will she be taken in by the family when or if Ms. Rita passes along?"

"I don't have the answers to that. I am assuming that the proper organizations will become involved and find a placement home for her where they will take care of her kind."

"What do you need from me, Doctor?"

"I will start out by telling you what I don't need. Her bill is covered, so we are not looking for any monetary assistance. What I called you here for today is for you to walk with her through this process. She is afraid. She is extremely lonely and sad. She feels as if her entire life was a joke. She feels like everyone deserted her", he explains.

"Ms. Rita has been with my family for many years", I begin to explain. "I am not going to lie to you, Doctor. Ms. Rita broke my heart before she left my home. She has betrayed me and I am still in shock over it. But, I am here because I love her. I love her no matter what she has done or is still doing to me. I love her! And now, she doesn't have that much more time to live. No matter what, I have to be here for you. I will do anything you need for me to do."

"I am so sorry for all that you have gone through with her, but I am so glad that you are now able to put all of that past you to be here for her. There is something else that I think that you need to know", he says.

"What is it?"

"There is a young lady who has been trying to contact her and claims that it is a family emergency, but I am not allowing her to speak with Rita because I am not sure what her urgent matter is. I thought maybe you would be able to shed some light on it for me. If I know a little more about it; perhaps, I can better determine if it is worth allowing her to speak with Rita", he says.

"So, who is the woman that is trying so desperately to contact Ms. Rita?"

"Hold on, I have it written down on a sticky note in my desk", he says, as he opens the desk drawer and pulls out a bright green sticky note. "The name is Brittney Snow from Middleton, AL. She never wants to tell me what it is about but just keeps insisting that there is a family emergency and that she really needs to speak with Rita."

"I know Brittney Snow. She is one of my friends and we grew up together in Alabama, but I am shocked that she knows Rita. She has never met her nor has she spoken to her. Why would she be calling Ms. Rita?"

"If she is your friend, why can't you just contact her to find out?"

"I guess you are right. There must be some misunderstanding, but I will certainly find out."

I am completely puzzled as to why Brittney would be contacting Ms. Rita. How does Brittney know about Ms. Rita? She has never met her. I am still deep in thought and the Doctor comments.

"So, may we contact you whenever we have any issues with Ms. Rita?" he finally asks.

"Yes, you may contact me. I will be here whenever I can visit. Although I have a very hectic schedule, I am more than willing to assist in any way possible for her. Please have my cell phone number as well, 555-325-4545."

"Thank you so much Mrs. Thomas. This is a very kind thing to do. Being faced with any type of sickness is bad, but to have to deal with AIDS is a totally different ballgame. I am glad that you will help out as much as you possibly can. Would you like to see her now?"

"Of course."

"I will need for you to put on a mask and hospital coat before going into the room. I want to warn you that she doesn't quite look the same. She has lost some of her hair and her teeth are practically gone. I was in here awhile ago and she was awake, so let's see", he explains.

"With her stroke, did she completely lose her ability to speak?"

"She only lost it for a little while, but has since regained it. Are you ready?"

"Yes."

As soon as we walk into the room, Ms. Rita opens her eyes and immediately puts out her arms inviting a hug from me. Without hesitating, I walk over to her bed and give her a hug. She starts patting me on the back. She seems to be very excited to see me. I have to admit that I am glad to see her alive. I am glad that she made it through the strokes.

"Hey Ms. Melissa. How you doing baby? I am so glad you done came to see me", she begins to say, before I interrupt her.

"Yeah, but you have to get out of this bed and sit up for me."

She sits up in the bed without much help from me or the nurse assistant. It looks like her hair, what little hair she has left, hasn't been combed in a few weeks. Her feet and hands are so dry.

"So, how are you doing?" I ask, as I sit down in the seat next to her bed, leaving my hand over her hand.

"Ms. Melissa, God is good", she begins to say. "I had two strokes and I am still here!"

"Yes, you are. We always give Him the praise for all He has done and continues to do."

"I feel so much better than I did before. These folks here are taking real good care of me", she says. Right after she makes this comment, she coughs so hard that it hurts my chest to hear it.

"You okay, honey?"

"Yeah, just got a little cold. That's all", she comments. "Ms. Melissa, I would not have blamed you if you had not come to see me."

"Now, why wouldn't I come to see you?"

"I hurt you and I know that you know how I hurt you. It is my fault that your kids left that house! It is my fault that all this mess went on with CCF! I am so sorry for treating you so poorly. You have always been good to me and my child. I need you to forgive me, Ms. Melissa", she says, with tears flowing down her face.

I look into her eyes and jump out of my chair and give her the tightest hug. I don't care that she starts to cough. I don't care how she looks. All I know is that at this moment and time, I am glad that we are connecting like we once did for many years.

"Of course, I forgive you Ms. Rita and I love you so much. We are here for you! You are my family. You were there for me and my children when nobody would have done it. You were there for me when I could pay you and you were there for me when I couldn't pay you. You took care of my family for many years and I will never forget that. Life happens and sometimes, we hurt the people we love. But God is love and in love, we forgive and I forgive you", I say. The tears won't stop falling down my face.

I feel like on this day, a black cloud has moved over and the devil is angry. I feel like a whole lot of pressure is removed.

Ms. Rita and I spend at least an entire hour reminiscing about all of the happy and sad times that we experienced over the years. In the back of my mind, I know that this may be our last time doing it. I know that the next time I see her, she may not remember who I am. But for now, she does and I don't want to lose this moment.

"Where is your lotion?"

"Over here in my drawer", she answers.

"Hand it to me. Your feet are so ashy", I say as we both laugh.

We continue talking while I lotion up her hands and feet. With the hair brush that is still in my purse, I begin to brush her hair and I can tell that she is feeling relaxed. I want to ask her about Brittney, but I don't want to push her away. *Maybe I should wait to ask about Brittney. Have I relaxed her enough to tell me the truth?* "It seems like the people are really nice here", I comment. "Especially Doctor Norwood."

"He sure is, Ms. Melissa. That man sat up with me until I fell asleep one night. He never left my side. I have talked his ear off about you. He has heard so much about you."

"Doctor Patrick asked me a question that I just don't have the answer to and I am hoping that you can help us both with an answer."

"What is it?" she asks.

"Do you have any idea why my friend, Brittney, from Alabama is calling you saying that there is a family emergency? I'll be honest with you. I didn't even know that you knew her."

At first glance, she seems to be very surprised and shocked that this is mentioned. She looks right past me as if she wishes to be anywhere but here right now. There is definitely something here that is bothering Ms. Rita about Brittney calling. She seems to be in mid-thought until I interrupt her. "So, how do you know her?"

"It is a long story and I don't really want to talk about it right now. I don't feel well and really want to get some rest, so if you don't mind, Ms. Melissa, I just want to get some rest", she says, rolling over in the bed.

I realize that I am not going to get anything out of her, at least, not today. I might as well get out of here and get back to work, but it is good to know that I can probably call Brittney now and find out what is going on between her and Rita and perhaps, get some idea, as to what it is that they have in common.

"Ok, dear. I am going to get back to work now. Get some rest and call me if you need anything", I say, as I stand to leave the room. She doesn't bother to turn around to see if I have left the room or not. She faces the wall the entire time of my departure. I walk out of the room and down the hallway. The receptionist turns to wave goodbye to me as I am leaving the facility.

As I am walking to my car, a million thoughts begin to run through my mind. I have so many questions but hardly any answers. *Why is Brittney calling Ms. Rita? What is the emergency? How does Brittney know Ms. Rita? Why won't Ms. Rita tell me how she knows Brittney? What is the big secret? Will I ever know or will Ms. Rita take her secret to her grave?*

On the ride back to the office, my mind is focused on the fact that Stuart is preparing for Kalin's trial and the stress of that trial has me in knots. My husband is facing 7 counts of some type of child felony charges, of which one can send him away for the rest of his life. I don't begin to know how to register this in my mind. For now, I will have to continue to take one day at a time. I am so glad that Stuart and his wife, Phyllis, are finally getting their little situation resolved. He just needs to let go of his dead ex-wife. Cindy and her boyfriend are getting along fine. I am happy that the people close to me are at peace in their lives. I can't help but wonder when I will have my day when my family and me are back together and my husband and I are celebrating our 50th year wedding anniversary. I can hardly wait for the day that all of this is behind us and we can move forward like a normal family should.

I finally make it back to the office and manage to make it past Cindy, who is busy with a resident, and head right for my office. There are a few messages for me. One is from Stuart, and one is marked "URGENT", from Denise with CCF. I need to call Denise first because I am sure that this has something to do with my children.

On the second or third ring, she picks up the phone. "Hello, Woods speaking, how may I help you?" she says on the other end.

"Hello, it is Melissa and I am returning your call."

"I am glad that you called. I called you for a few reasons. There has been an emergency with one of the kids. Before you get upset, it is all under control, but I have to inform you because your children are technically the responsibility of the State and …" she says before I interrupt her.

"What happened to my kids", I ask, starting to get upset.

"Mrs. Thomas, calm down, please", she advises. "It is Sharell. She got into some pills and I guess she thought they were candy and she took quite a few of them. Your niece found her and called the ambulance. She is already home and is resting", she says.

"I need to go see my daughter."

"Just contact your niece and arrange it with her, but your daughter is doing just fine", she says.

"Ok, so you said you called me for a few reasons", I reminded her, sounding a little agitated.

All I really want to do is get off the phone and call my niece to go and see my baby. She needs me right now.

"Your scheduled appointment with the psychiatrist is for Tuesday at 11 a.m. and you are scheduled for a meeting with Nina, a sex therapist, on the following Tuesday at 9:30 a.m. and --", she says, before I interrupt her to get a pen and paper.

"OK, let me go ahead and write this down so that I won't forget it."

"And a family therapist scheduled for the following Tuesday. We set everything apart so that you don't have it all at one time and you are able to have enough time to alert your employer of your upcoming appointments", she continues.

"Can you email me all of this information just to confirm all of these appointments? Why in the world do I have to do all of this?"

"You are being ordered by the Judge to do all of this? If you want your children back, then I suggest you do as ordered by the Judge", she says. "What is your email address?"

Before we hang up, she also mentions that she will soon schedule the Guardian Ad Litem to visit with the children so that she can do her very own evaluation of the children and their placement. As soon as we hang up the phone, I am already calling my niece to see if I can visit my daughter. I call the number several times and still don't get an answer. I am starting to worry, until the phone beeps and it is my niece calling back.

"Hello."

"Melissa, she is fine", she says, before I can ask about Sharell. "She is back in the room playing with the other kids."

"I want to come see her."

"I know that you do, but she is fine. That is really not necessary, but if you want to, you are more than welcome to come see her", she concludes.

"Of course I am coming to see her. I will be right over after work."

My work day is finally completed. The Thanksgiving Can Food Drive is a success! My staff and I decide to deliver the Thanksgiving baskets to the residents as a team. All of us jump on the golf cart and deliver the food to each family, one by one. They are so appreciative of receiving this kind gesture from the Management Staff. I suddenly remember that *my* family won't be with me for the Thanksgiving holidays. Several friends have invited me to their homes, but I have decided to travel to my niece's house to be with my children. I am scheduled for a visit with Kalin on Thanksgiving night. Spending Thanksgiving at the County Jail is not quite what I pictured, but it will have to do for now.

It seems as though I make it to Nikki's house in what seems like 15 minutes or so. Walking in the house with a huge teddy bear in hand makes Sharell's eyes widen. "Mommy! Is that for me?"

"Of course it is and how is the patient?"

"I am fine, Mommy. Mommy, guess what?"

"What?"

"I got a chance to ride in the ambulance. That was kinda fun!"

"I bet it was."

"Where is Christy?"

"She had to stay after school for basketball practice."

"Oh, I see. Give her a big hug and kiss for Mommy when she gets home."

Just as my niece said, Sharell does seem to be fine. But, I am a Mother and nothing was going to keep me from coming here to see it for myself. Now, I can go home and be at peace, seeing that she is just fine.

CHAPTER 54

"And, How is the Main Witness?"

*T*he next morning, I get up and with Thanksgiving only 3 days away, I start feeling a little sad. I walk down the hallway past my kids' bedrooms and start to cry. The emotion of their not being in their rooms begins to overtake me and before I know it, I am sobbing heavily non-stop. I can't believe I am this emotional about it right now. I just remember that I have quite a few appointments coming up so I really need to make sure to get as much done as possible at work.

I start wondering about everything. For the first time in a few days, I start wondering about why Brittney called and was looking for Rita and what was so important that she speak to her? Why wouldn't Ms. Rita tell me what it was all about? What is the big secret? Why do I have to have all of these evaluations and therapy? Do they think that I am an unfit mother or something? What does all of this mean? Why is Christy saying these things about Kalin? Is there something that I missed? Did he put his hands on my daughter and I just didn't notice it? After a few minutes of badgering myself with these thoughts, I decide to check my emails just to make sure that Denise sent me the email confirming all of my upcoming appointments.

There are 264 emails in my "Inbox". After a quick search, I find her email confirming the appointments. I transfer them into my Agenda for work, making sure to have my appointments all in one place. On tomorrow, I will sit in front of a psychiatrist and answer all of their lame questions about my life and why I did this and why I did that. It is all rubbish to me! But, if I want my children home, I will have to play their game.

Cindy is aware of all of my upcoming events and is being very supportive of me during my time that I have to be away from the office. I finally make it to my appointment and I am 20 minutes early. I pick up the Miami Herald and the headliner caught my attention, *"Local coach confesses to*

his relationship with a minor". The article is about Coach Tyler, who I went to school with. He explained about what made him attracted to the minor and why he never ended this forbidden relationship. They met at a pep rally. She flirted with him and he claims he tried to resist her, but she continued to pursue him. He claims that she would wear short skirts to class on purpose just to get his attention. He admitted that he was attracted to her because she made him feel alive and relevant. The affair continued and would still be if she had not told her friends about it.

I can't believe what I just read. I personally know Coach Tyler and he was strictly business back in the day. He wouldn't even talk to a student unless another student or adult was present. I don't know what made him lower his standard and to do this to his wife and children.

As interesting as this story is, I notice that it is already twenty minutes after my scheduled appointment time, so I decide to walk over to the receptionist desk to find out what is going on.

"Yes, Rachel, my appointment is scheduled for 11 and it is already 11:30. Is the doctor in? Is there a problem?"

"What is your name?" she asks.

"Hold on. I see the problem. You are not scheduled for today. You were scheduled for yesterday. You missed your appointment", she says, as she begins to shake her head.

"Missed my appointment! This is the appointment time that I was given. There must be a mistake", I say angrily.

"Ma'am, there is no mistake. See it right here! It says that your appointment was yesterday, which was Monday, at 11 a.m."

I can't believe it! How in the world could I have messed this up? I know that this is the day that Denise gave me to show up for my appointment. I know that I could not have missed the appointment! There is just no way that I could have missed this appointment!

"This is the day that the CCF Caseworker gave me to come here", I say, sounding very frustrated.

"Would you like to go ahead and make another appointment?"

"I guess I will. I don't think that I have a choice."

"Fine. What about next Wednesday? What is better, mornings or afternoons?"

"Morning is better."

"OK, next Wednesday at 11 a.m.", she agrees. She hands me an appointment card and I head for the exit. I can't wait to get to my Agenda book and see what I wrote down for my appointment and then follow up by reviewing the email that I received from Denise.

On my way out of the appointment, my cell phone rings and it is Doctor Norwood.

"Hello."

"Mrs. Thomas, how are you?" he asks.

"I am fine. Is there anything wrong with Ms. Rita? Is she okay?" I ask, almost frantically.

"No, everything is fine. I was just calling you to ask you out for lunch. I have a business meeting on your side of town today and thought we could catch a bite to eat, if you are free, of course."

"Sure, why not? I have had a long morning and would love to get a bite to eat before going back to work. I just need to call the office and let my assistant know where I am in the event someone is looking for me."

"Let's try the new restaurant named "Enchanted" that just opened up over on Firefox Drive, he suggests.

"Sounds fine. I will meet you there around 12:30 or so."

"Great. See ya then!"

I am so shocked that Dr. Norwood has called me for lunch. *Is this a professional lunch date or personal lunch date? I wonder.* He is married and I am too. *My goodness! It's just lunch, Melissa!*

I arrive at the restaurant a few moments early and decide to go inside to the ladies' room to freshen up. I waste no time in letting the waitress know that there is someone else in my party. They, in turn, inform me that my date is *already* sitting at the table.

"Your lunch date is already waiting on you. He is absolutely gorgeous! And his eyes!!! He came in here yesterday to let us know that he would be here today having lunch and wanted to make sure that he got the table that he got. I don't know what is so special about that spot, but he sure did. Girl, work that out!"

I am impressed. Why *would he go through the trouble? How did he know that I would accept his offer?* What confidence!

Since he is not looking, I decide to head to the ladies' room to freshen up. This Florida heat is doing something "bad" to the hair. I walk past the group of waiters and waitresses and head straight for the restroom and freshen up. I finally make it to the table, where Dr. Norwood is patiently waiting.

"You really are a beautiful woman", he says, standing up to greet me.

"Thank you so much. You are not too bad yourself", I respond.

We finally place our orders. It is so hard to make eye contact with Dr. Norwood. He is so attractive. I don't want to look into his eyes because I may see something that I am not equipped to walk away from. Although I am trying to avoid him, I can feel him staring at me. I hope that I don't look up and see him staring at my breast or something. The physical attraction to this man is there! I am sure that anyone who is in his presence would feel the exact same thing. I just have to keep reminding myself that I am a married woman.

"So, how are you, Dr. Norwood?"

"I am fine. Are you wondering why I invited you to lunch?" he asks.

"Well, now that you mention it, the thought did cross my mind", I respond, as we both laugh.

"Honestly, I think that you are a beautiful woman and I like being in the company of a beautiful woman. Is that such a crime? And besides, I was curious about this restaurant and wanted my first time here to be with you", he responds. "And there is another reason as well."

"I am a married woman, Dr. Norwood. And I know you just want to take advantage of me, but I am already taken!" I say jokingly.

"I know that and I respect that. Your husband is a very lucky man and I hope that *he* knows that", he comments.

"To be honest with you Dr. Norwood, I was –", I say, before being interrupted.

"Listen, Dr. Norwood is my father. Please call me Patrick. And do you mind if I call you Melissa?"

"I don't mind at all."

Patrick and I sit in the restaurant for the entire hour of lunch just talking about our dreams, desires, and goals. The more we talk, the more we find out that we have quite a bit in common. We sit down for lunch and one glance at Dr. Norwood and I can see why a woman would fall deeply for him. The safe thing for me is that I am married and so is he.

"Are you enjoying your meal?" he asks.

"It is delicious. Thanks for suggesting that we come here. The service is great. The owner of this restaurant should be proud. They have put it together very nicely."

"You're welcome. It was my pleasure to ask you out to lunch. I am just glad that you said, "yes". Are you wondering about the last reason I asked you out for lunch?"

"It *has* crossed my mind."

"I asked you here because I want to tell you something about your friend", he begins.

"Go on."

"She is dying. She doesn't have much time left and I think that it is time for her to get her affairs in order. I don't know if her family will assist her with that or if you will encourage her to do that, but she is in denial that her situation is as bad as it is. I have tried to explain to her about her condition, but she keeps talking about *God is able* and how she doesn't want to hear anything about dying. I have new information about that other "thing" we were discussing. I found out that the reason the young lady is trying to reach her so desperately has something to do with you.

"With me? What could they be talking about that has *anything* to do with me?

"Of course, I don't know all the facts, but I overheard Ms. Rita discussing an important matter with her on yesterday. I heard something about a child, but nothing more than that. Normally, I would not get involved, but it is important to me that you are safe and protected", he explains.

"I didn't know that you cared so much", I say, with a slight grin on my face.

"Of course, I care. You are a special and I don't like to see good people be mistreated. I watch how you come to visit her and cater to her and that says so many things to me about you. And to be honest with you, I see something wrong with the picture of her involvement with that young lady. I could be wrong, but my gut tells me otherwise. So, I guess that I am warning you to be on the lookout with those two", he advises.

"I appreciate this. I really do. I have no idea what they could be up to that involves me at all. But yes, I will be careful. Thanks for bringing this to my attention", I respond. "And thanks again for lunch. I have thoroughly enjoyed this time with you."

"Then we should do it again, Melissa."

"Are you flirting with me Patrick?"

"I am flirting with you, Melissa. Yes, I am. Is it working?"

"You are just too kind. Are you always this charming?"

"No, just with you. There is something about you that is so intriguing and it makes me want to know more. But, please know that I respect the fact that you are married and --", he responds, before I interrupt him.

"And you are married as well."

"That is another conversation on another day", he responds, looking away.

Patrick and I finish eating lunch and decide that it is time to part our ways. I really do appreciate him for being honest and direct with me, but I really don't have time to think about what Rita and my friend, Brittney, have up their sleeves. He does; however, leave me with some things to think about. I am surprised at how our conversation became so personal. He was flirting with me and for the first time since I have been married to Kalin, I actually wanted him to flirt with me. I feel like I want to see him again, as well. *What is wrong with me?* I need to stay focused because I have an appointment with the psychiatrist soon. All of my other therapies will begin soon and I have to stay focused as to not forget any of them. I am sure that whatever I do is being reported to the Judge. But Patrick is still fine! The thought of him puts a smile on my face.

On my way back to the office, I decide to give Stuart a call to get an update. "Good afternoon Stuart."

"Well, hello Melissa."

"How are things coming with Kalin's trial preparation? Do you need anything from me?"

"No, I don't. And to answer your question, the trial preparations are coming along quite well. I am feeling very confident with everything. We have our witnesses in place and I have submitted the Discovery to the State. I am quite prepared."

"And what about your main witness?"

"He is doing fine. He is ready to face his accusers and he, too, feels very confident with everything. He did; however, mention that the closer it gets to the Trial, he would really like to see you more", he says.

"I don't mind seeing him more, but why did he say that?"

"Come on Melissa. Your husband is facing life in prison for the rest of his natural life if a jury believes your daughter. He wants to have as much time with you as he possibly can. We are dealing with a system that is just simply unfair at times. I can get in that courtroom and can do everything right, but in the end, it is up to the Jury. And if everything doesn't go as planned, he will have at least spent as much time possible with his wife."

"I don't like the way all of that sounds, Stuart." A feeling of sadness has suddenly come over me.

"I understand that but my job is to keep it realistic. Your husband is."

"I guess so, Stuart, I guess so. I have to go now. I was just checking in to see how everything is going."

"Ok, I will talk with you later. Oh, I finally have my psychiatrist appointment rescheduled. Can you believe that woman gave me the wrong appointment date? And then when I showed up, they said that I missed my appointment and that it was the day before. But, I know that I wrote it down correctly?"

"I am sure that you did. That is just another one of their games that they play. Stay in the game, though."

"I appreciate that because I know that I am not crazy."

"Of course, you aren't crazy. They do play silly games sometimes."

"Yeah, but these are real peoples' lives that they are playing with. It is just not right!"

"Just don't miss this second appointment", he orders.

"I won't."

Heading back to the office, I begin to feel a sudden peace come over me. It is almost as if I just found out something good and I am so excited, except that I didn't find out anything. I just feel like everything is okay right now. My spirit is at peace. It is almost as if the rage inside of me is taking a nap or something. *I wonder how Ms. Rita is doing today. Patrick mentioned how she is really dying and she doesn't have much time left. I feel like I need to do something. But, when on earth do I have the time? I am about to start all of these therapy sessions so that I can move on with my life, with my children and then finally bring Princess to live with us in Florida. Should I call Brittney and find out what is going on? Do I really want to know what she is planning? Can my heart take another disappointment? I wonder how the children are doing. Is Kalin eating okay? Is he resting? Are they mistreating him in there?*

So many thoughts are running through my mind. In the end, I know that I have to give all of these *issues* to God. I know that there isn't really anything that I can do but wait on God. I have to trust Him to handle this situation. All I will do is just mess everything up if I start trying to solve it. All I have to do now is just go through the motions and see what happens.

CHAPTER 55

"Nothing Else We Can Do"

*T*oday is my appointment with the psychiatrist. I know that there are no right and wrong answers. I know that whatever happens here will be reported to the Courts to determine my state of mind as it relates to my children. There is; however, something very peculiar about this day. I am really excited about this appointment. I am anxious to get into his office and speak with him so that someone else can see it from my point of view.

Again, I pull into the parking lot and get out of the car. Everything is just as it was a week ago. The construction crew is still working on the building across the street. People are hurrying to and fro. The receptionist is still accommodating and remembers me from last week.

"Good morning again", I say, as I approach the front desk.

"Good morning to you", she responds.

"I am here for my 11:00 appointment with Dr. Rivas", I announce.

"Sign in and wait to be called", she orders. "He should be with you shortly."

I take a seat and pick up the local newspaper and there is picture of my friend, Stevie, on the front cover. It appears as though he is getting more and more movie roles. *LOCAL MODEL TALENT TO BE FEATURED IN THE MOVIE, "THE PUNISHER".* Way to go Steven! It looks like he is really making things happen. I will have to give him a call and congratulate him on his newfound success. The story talks about his family and his experiences thus far. I have to admit that he looks quite dashing in the photo. I get so wrapped up in the story that I realize that it is way past my appointment time. I decide to approach the receptionist to see why we are so past schedule.

"Sweetheart, I haven't been called yet. Is Dr. Rivas running behind time or what?"

"I am not sure. Let me check and see what is going on". I am sure that she can tell that I am just a little agitated. The appointment was for 11 and it is almost 11:30 and nothing!

"Mrs. Thomas, I hope that you don't get too upset", she says.

"Too late. I am getting upset now. "What is it?"

"Dr. Rivas is not at this building today. He is working in the North Miami office", she exclaims.

"Then, why didn't you tell me that when I showed up?"

"I am so sorry. I know that you said that you were here to see him, but it didn't dawn on me at the moment. Please forgive me. This is my mistake. Let me call him and make this right", she exclaims.

"I think that this is the appropriate thing to do. This is my second visit to see this man and both times, there has been an error, which is not my mistake. Please call him and let him know that I will be there because I can't miss this appointment", I say, sounding very upset.

She picks up the phone to dial the North Miami office. I can overhear her explain the purpose of her call to the receptionist who puts her on the phone with the psychiatrist.

"Good morning", she says. "Sir, I am so sorry but one of your appointments is sitting here in this office because I neglected to tell her when I set the appointment last week that you would be in the North Miami office. And then when she came into the office this morning, I still forgot to mention it to her. Can you please see her? She has already taken the time away from work. She can be there in 25 minutes or so. ......okay, doctor? ...Thank you!" she says, before hanging up the phone.

"Everything is fine. He will see you when you make it there. I have already printed out the Map Quest for you. Please drive carefully. Again, I am so sorry", she says apologetically.

"Thank you dear. I know that people make mistakes. Have a great day."

I rush out of the office and head toward the North Miami office. After about 30 minutes or so, I arrive at the location. I will have to break some speed limits to make it here so quickly, but I don't want to give Dr. Rivas an excuse to leave.

The receptionist is pleasant and is expecting me. "I am here to see Dr. Rivas", I begin, before being interrupted.

"Yes, I know. The receptionist from the other office called to let us know to make sure to get you right in when you get here", she mentions.

"The doctor is with another client, but we will get you in as soon as possible. So, have a seat and I will call you up when he is done."

Sitting in the reception area, I can get a good look at the office décor. Everything looks very nice together. I love the brown leather sofas. The paintings on the walls are breathtaking. There are matching accessories all around the office. They really paid attention to detail. The soft music makes the place just that more relaxing. I recognize the song playing over the intercom. It is "Truly" by Lionel Richie. This song takes me way back to sweet high school when I was in love. I wonder how my life would have ended up if I had married Brian. I wonder what he is doing right now. It is so funny because I actually thought that I could not live without him. It is so funny how we say that about every boyfriend that we have. At least back then, I believed that he was my world. I was his cheerleader and he was the captain of the football team. I thought it was the marriage made in heaven!

I am beginning to realize that it has been over an hour and Dr. Rivas is still not done with his appointment. I know that I can't leave. I have to make this appointment happen because when we go back to court, this will, no doubt, be one of the main topics in the courtroom.

"Ma'am, do you have any idea how much longer Dr. Rivas will be?"

"I am not sure. I apologize, but I really thought that he would have completed this appointment by now. Would you like to set something up to come back?" she asks.

She has no idea how upset I am, but I know that I can't show it. I feel as if this was done on purpose just so that I will lose it! I can't lose it!

"No, I will wait because I have already taken the day off to see Dr. Rivas and I am not leaving until I do. Thank you", I say, as I return to my place on the leather sofa.

Fifteen minutes later, a slender young woman comes down the hall with her head down. She walks to the receptionist desk and sets an appointment. They say their goodbyes and the receptionist calls me to the desk.

"Dr. Rivas will see you now", she says. "His office is down the hallway and on your right."

Finally! At last! Ok, Melissa. Get it together. Be yourself! Don't walk in there thinking about how you have gotten the run-around today. Shake that off because it is a trick to get you to lose it. Pull it all back together. Answer the questions asked and call it a day!

I make it to his office and Dr. Rivas looks nothing like I pictured he would.

"Well, hello, Mrs. Thomas. Come in, come in. Thank you for your patience. I know that you have been waiting for quite awhile. Please have a seat."

"I am just glad to be here", I respond.

Dr. Rivas is all about getting to the business at hand. First thing he does is read the history given to him by the Court. He wants to get my feedback on what is written. He also mentions what the Guardian Ad Litem wants to find out from the evaluation. I am very shocked at her assessment of me. She is curious as to why I never showed any emotion in the courtroom. She says that this is of a grave concern because I would show up at court and leave without having cried or anything. She can't understand this because my children were removed and it would have been more typical if I displayed more emotion. He wants to know how I feel about her comments.

The conversation goes quite well with Dr. Rivas. He asks the questions and I answer them. I don't waiver in my responses and I don't change my story at all. My testimony is very consistent with everything I have been saying from the beginning. Right, wrong, or indifferent, I speak what I believe to be my truth.

After an hour or so, our meeting is complete! I am on my way back to work. Having been out of commission for quite a while, I am sure that I have several messages on my phone. I sit in the car, while the A/C is cooling the car off and decide to check my messages. I have a call from Dr. Norwood, Cindy, and last but not least, Brittney! I don't know who to contact first. I pick up the phone to hear the messages. Brittney's message sounds as if she is upset about something. She makes a strong demand that I contact her as soon as I get the message. Dr. Norwood sounds like his message is pretty urgent, so I decide to call Cindy. The phone rings and she answers, "Thank you for calling Lakeview Apartments, this is Cindy speaking, how may I serve you?"

"Cindy, it is me. You called?"

"Yes, I called. I don't know what is going on but Dr. Norwood has been trying to reach you. He said that it is most urgent that you call him as soon as you get in. He really sounds upset, Melissa!" she exclaims.

"Is everything else alright?"

"Yes, everything here is fine. Corporate called a few times looking for you but I told them that you were out on the property doing inspections. There wasn't an emergency or anything. They just wanted to go over budgets with you", she explains.

"Ok, thanks, dear. I am going to take the rest of the day off. I think that I am going to just go by and see Dr. Norwood." *I don't want to contact Brittney right now. I don't know why she is upset and I don't really want to hear about it right now. I don't have time to deal with her drama today.*

There are a million thoughts running through my mind about what I am going to find when I make it to his office. *Is it Rita? Is she getting sicker? Is she finally on her death bed? Is she asking for me or what? How am I going to feel if I am the one who will be with her as she is dying and her daughter isn't there?*

I finally make it to the center and park in the visitors parking space. I rush inside and briefly communicate with the nurse at the front desk. She calls Dr. Norwood and he appears moments later.

"Well, hello Melissa. Don't you look beautiful today? I called you earlier. You didn't have to come all the way out here", he says, leading me to his office.

"I know. I could have called, but I want to see Rita anyway. How is she doing?" *Only if he knew that I wanted an excuse to see him again. I will never admit that, though.*

"Please, step into my office."

"Is she okay?"

"Please sit down, Melissa", he says, leading me to the chair in front of his desk.

"Her condition is getting worse. She is no longer responding to the medications and I want to put her on Morphine drops so that she can be comfortable. She is in so much pain and she is in the last stages of her sickness and I want her last days to be painless. I will need approval of her family and being that none of them will return any of my calls, I have to seek the next of kin, which is, of course, you. I need to know if you will allow me to put her on Morphine to ease the pain."

"So are you saying that there is nothing else you can do for her", I say, with tears in my eyes.

"Yes, that is what I am saying. We have tried everything but the virus has spread to all of her main organs and have pretty much shut them all down. She is at peace and she understands everything. She is ready to go", he says. Dr. Norwood reaches over and takes my hand and looks into my eyes.

"How does she feel about her family not coming by to see her?"

"She is not surprised. She said that you, Kalin, and the kids are all the family that she needs."

"I would like to see her now. Is that okay?"

"Please do so at your pace", he instructs. He leads me down the hallway into the special section marked, "Proceed with extreme caution".

When Patrick and I finally make it into Rita's room she is sitting up in the bed. She doesn't look sick at all. It almost makes one believe that she is not sick at all.

"Well, hello Ms. Melissa. That sure is a pretty dress you have on. I like to see that color on you. It looks real good. You always did look good in green", she says. "Don't she look good, Doctor?"

"She looks very beautiful", he comments, keeping his eyes on Rita, as if he is trying to avoid my eyes.

If I am not mistaken, I believe that the good doctor is flirting with me. I have to admit it, but I like it! Who wouldn't like to have a good looking man such as the Doctor acknowledge your beauty? I am just keeping it real.

"Ok, ladies. I am leaving to go back to my office. And Mrs. Thomas, I'd like to see you before you leave."

"Ok. Sure."

Just as Dr. Norwood has mentioned, it is important that Rita feels comfortable during these last days. So, I want to make sure that she feels loved and cared for. I walk over to her bed and give her a big hug because it is most important to me that she knows that I am not afraid to touch her.

"How is Mr. Kalin?" she asks. I am shocked to hear her mention Kalin's name because she has not mentioned his name since this whole fiasco began.

"He is fine."

"Well, tell him I said hello and I love him. And tell all the children that I love them, too. I know that this is none of my business, but I just want you to keep a good friendship with the Doctor. He really is a nice man, Melissa. He is a very hard working one too. You would think that he would be exhausted by running this place and trying to be there for everyone, but he just opened up a restaurant, too. He has a good staff, so he doesn't go there much."

"Really? What's the name of the restaurant?"

"Oooh Melissa, I don't remember. I think it's called "Enchanted" or something like that? He told me about it one day we were talking. Just continue to be his friend. He is a good guy." *Now it makes sense to me why he was in the restaurant the day before we showed up there together. He owns the place! Impressive! So, he was telling his staff to make sure that we got the table that we ended up with. And that is why he wanted to make sure that I enjoyed the restaurant.*

"I will do just that."

"Ms. Melissa, you know I am dying, right?"

"I don't want to talk about dying. I want to remember the times when we would laugh and would sit up all night watching Lifetime movies. Remember when Kalin would walk down the hallway when he was ready for me to come to bed. We always thought that was so funny!"

"Yes, we did! It wasn't all bad, was it Ms. Melissa?"

"No, it was good. You have always been like family to us, Ms. Rita. You will always be a part of *my* family."

"God wants me to do right by you and I'm going to do that before I leave this world."

Ms. Rita is starting to slur her words. She looks like she is a little tired. Maybe I should let her rest now. The meds are starting to kick in and she is very drowsy. She has closed her eyes and I decide to pray over her.

Dear Father. Thank you for this day. Thank you for life, health, and strength. Lord, I pray a very special blessing over Ms. Rita's life. Lord, I pray that you will take this situation and do what is best for her. Father, she is in a lot of pain and needs the Comforter. Give her peace and comfort. In Jesus' name. Amen.

She is already sleeping so peacefully so I decide to slip out of her room to allow her time to rest. Walking out of her room, a strange feeling overcomes me. It feels like a shadow is following me. It doesn't feel like anything evil at all. It feels like a light spirit that is accompanying me on my way out. I walk down the hall past Dr. Norwood, who looks up from his paperwork and waves for me to come into his office.

"Well, I am on my way out. Rita is tired, so I just slipped out of her room. The morphine should make her feel better now."

"Yes, I am sure it will. Thanks for coming. Although you didn't have to come all the way out here, I am still glad to see you. Do you think that we can see each other again? I mean, other than when you come to the nursing home to see Rita", he asks.

"I don't know about that, Patrick. Maybe one day. You make me a little nervous, you know?"

"Really? Why?"

"It's your eyes. I look into your eyes and I feel things that I should not feel about a married man, especially being that I am a married woman."

"That happens sometimes, but, hey, I respect your decision on that. And by the way, I am no longer married. My divorce was just finalized on yesterday. My ex-wife and I are friends because we still have Evan to think about. We have been going through this divorce for a few months now."

"Oh no! I am so sorry to hear that. Are you okay? Is Evan okay?"

"Yes. Everyone is okay. We have been separated for quite some time now, so it has been over for a couple of years already. We just needed to do it officially. Although I am not looking to be in a relationship, I love special friends and I think of you as a special friend", he explains.

"Really? That's nice. I appreciate it. There are so many things going on right now with me and it's - - -", I begin to say before he completes my sentence.

"Just not the right time! I know. I understand. Well, then, later?"

"Yes, later." Patrick wouldn't believe it if he knew what I was *really* thinking.

"Ok. That is good enough for me", Patrick agrees.

On the way home, I can't help but think that this may just have been my last conversation with Ms. Rita and that the next time I may see her, she will have her eyes closed for good.

CHAPTER 56

"I Can't Do That!"

Because of everything going on around me, I decide against contacting Brittney. Whatever issue she is having needs to be directed towards someone else because I need to focus on getting my children back home with me. I do; however, decide to give Attorney Richards a call regarding Princess. The last time that we talked to each other, he had a concern regarding the removal of my children. He mentioned that he would have to speak with CCF to gain a better understanding of this open case against me and Kalin. When I dial his number, he picks up the phone.

"Attorney Richards?"

"Yes, how may I help you?"

"Hello, Mr. Richards. This is Mrs. Thomas. How are you?"

"I am fine. What is going on in Florida?"

"Oh, nothing really. What is going on with Princess?"

"There will be a hearing on Monday regarding Princess' placement. Because of your open file with CCF, this will be mentioned to the Judge, who will, no doubt, give temporary custody to Brittney. The Judge will not consider you right now because of this open file. She frowns heavily upon this. Like I said, it is temporary custody so that means that once this is all cleared up, she will reconsider placing Princess with you, simply because it was the wish of the deceased mother to have her child with you", he explains.

"I understand. I need to ask you something."

"Sure, go ahead."

"I was informed that Brittney has been calling Florida to speak with Ms. Rita, my former housekeeper. Would you know anything about that?"

There is silence on the phone for a brief moment. Because of his silence, I assume that he does know something. "Are you still there?"

"I won't speak about anything that relates to Ms. Snow. I don't really know anything and I wouldn't discuss it with you even if I did because of my confidentiality agreement to Ms. Snow", he answers.

"So, you do know something?"

"Like I said, I will not get involved."

"I can respect that. If she is up to something, don't you think that I have a right to know?"

"You will have to contact Ms. Snow directly if there is anything that you need or want to know. I won't discuss it with you. She is my client and you will have to respect that professional relationship. Think about it. Would you want me to discuss information about you with someone else? It is my professional courtesy. Is there anything else?"

"No. That should do it. Will you give me a call on tomorrow afternoon just to let me know of the Judge's decision?"

"Of course I will."

I should have known that he would not discuss anything with me regarding Brittney. What I do believe is that his silence leads me to believe that he is; perhaps, aware that Brittney has been calling Florida. I believe that there is definitely some type of link between Ms. Rita and my friend, Brittney. Before it is all over, I will know the truth.

With Kalin's trial coming up, I can't think of anything but his trial. Who will Stuart use as Kalin's witnesses? How will he present Kalin's case? Will he use any scientific evidence? Why hasn't he asked me any questions? Why didn't he use me to prepare for the trial? All of these thoughts are running through my mind. At the same time, I have to keep it all together because I have my first sex therapy class coming up, as well as the Family Therapy session with the girls. How can anyone keep it together with all of this going on? Somehow, I know that I do have to keep it together and stay focused.

Sunday is my regular visit with the children and to surprise them, I have decided to bring their grandfather with me to the visit. They will be surprised. It's the weekend that I have chosen to celebrate their birthday. They are not aware that I will come with cake, and a party. Several of their friends have agreed to come along with me to celebrate with them, which means that I have some shopping to do. JT is excited and asks me to pick him up on Sunday. Kalin's birthday envelope has come in and it includes three birthday cards for Amber, Sharelle, and Justice. He used his artsy skills and has drawn their picture on each one. They will be very happy to receive this mail from their father.

Sunday is almost here and I have finished shopping for the girls' birthday party. Their friends have all received permission from their parents to travel with me to my niece's house. To make sure that everyone is comfortable, I decide to use the company van to transport all of the children and the party supplies. JT is ready to go and we are on our way to visit the girls. My niece is expecting us so when we pull into her driveway, she comes outside to meet us.

"So you came with the company van, huh?" she asks, looking in the van and surprised to see my father in law. "And I see you brought Kalin's father with you?"

"Yeah, I didn't think that it would be a problem. He *is* their grandfather."

One by one, the children peel out of the van just as excited to see the kids as I am. Once they are all settled, we enter into the house. My niece calls for the girls and they rush to the front room, where we are waiting for them and yell, "Surprise!"

"Mommy!" yells Justice and Sharelle at the same time. Amber joins in. The girls all rush to me and plant me with hugs and kisses. Right in the middle of our hugs and kisses, Rachel, Carlos, Victor, and Kimberly, their friends from the neighborhood, walk in right behind me. They are excited and happy to see their friends and immediately start telling their friends how much they miss them. They don't realize that there is one more surprise to go. Moments later, their grandfather walks in. Justice runs and jumps into his arms and gives him the biggest hug ever. The rest of the girls join her. He is so excited that he starts to cry. Watching this happy scene is the best Christmas gift that I can receive. My niece is so inspired by the reunion that she starts to cry as well. The girls have now finally realized that this is their surprise birthday party. We remove the decorations, food, and gifts from the van.

"Well, girls. How's this for a birthday surprise? You couldn't come home for your birthday so we brought your birthday party to you!"

"Mommy, this is perfect. Thank you so much", yells Sharelle.

"Where's Christy?"

"She is gone with her friends", they answer. "And Darren and Kameron are back in the room."

"Well go get them!"

Within a few minutes, my sons come from the back. "Hey Ma!" yells Kameron. He and Darren finally notice that their friends from the neighborhood came along and they get even more excited. "Hey Vic!" yells Darren.

"Hey D and Kam", responds Victor and Carlos.

The table is finally set and we begin to sing "Happy Birthday" to the girls. After two to three hours of eating cake and dancing, it is time for us to head back. JT seems to be happy that he came along. On the way home, the kids talk about how much they missed my kids. My heart is so full right now. I can hardly wait until my next visit with Kalin to tell him about the birthday surprise and how happy they were to receive his handmade birthday cards. They are thrilled at how Kalin is able to draw a picture of them on the card.

The day has been a success. I have dropped everyone off to their destination. I am exhausted! I am going to just drop off the van on tomorrow and pick up my car then. I need a long hot bath, surrounded by my favorite scented candles and a glass of wine. There are a few messages. At first I start to ignore it, but decide that there may be something very important so I push the button and start listening. The first message is from my mother who wants to know how I am doing. The next message is from Denise, the CCF case worker, who is calling to remind me of my appointment with the sex therapist on tomorrow. She is also curious about why my father-in-law made the trip with me today to visit the girls. I can't believe this! Why would my niece call and complain about my father-n-law making the trip? Didn't she see how happy the party made my children? He didn't do anything wrong. How in the world can my niece do this to my kids? I am so upset that I almost miss the next message. It is Ron, the guy I met in Atlanta who wants to write my story. He is calling me because he is in Miami and wants to have lunch with me on tomorrow to discuss further what we discussed in Atlanta. I think that this is the best time to speak with him. These people took my children away from me for no reason. I have never mistreated my children. They have told numerous untruths to the Judge and everyone tells me that "I just can't win against the State of Florida. As a matter of fact, even some of the most professional people I know have told me to just do as CCF says and before long, my children will be home. But what does that do for me? Why would I admit that I am a bad parent when I know that I am not? Am I supposed to just quit and give up because CCF says that I should? I am starting to think that it is not such a bad idea to let people know that they don't have to just sit back and allow this system to continue taking their children away, forcing us into all of these programs just to get our children back when they know that their decisions are simply personal and have nothing to do with the children.

I am going to call him first thing tomorrow morning to meet him for lunch. I hope that this deal works out for the best. Now, I know that I have to get my bath. Before I know it, I have already soaked in the bathtub for at least an hour. The quietness in my home causes me to relax and forces me to think about how to approach a book deal and what it is that I want to accomplish by allowing someone into my personal life to reach an audience with a message. My truths will have to be exposed. What will Kalin think about all of this? Will my children understand? These thoughts are too much to think about at one time. Before I know it, I am falling asleep in my bath. My mind starts to drift back to the day that I met Kalin and how much in love we were back then. We were both young and really loved each other. When we got married, we couldn't keep our hands off each other. We did everything together. Although there have been bumps and bruises along the way, we always managed to mend it together with our love and faith. What will happen to him? His life is on the line. Our future is on the line. Stuart has done a great job on Kalin's case so far but in the end, it is up to the Jury. They are the ones who will decide his fate. I heard it straight from Stuart. If Kalin is found guilty of one of the counts leveled against him, he will go to prison for life. What if that happens? What will happen to our relationship? Will he expect me to stay married to him? Will I stay married to him? Will our love survive a prison life sentence? These thoughts are starting to make me cry because I have to remain positive for Kalin. If I am hurting this way, just imagine what he must be feeling at night. I am here taking a bubble bath, but he is suffering in jail, sleeping on stained sheets, and wearing stained shorts, and having to take a shower while everyone in his pod is watching. To everyone's surprise, he still finds a way to say that he trusts God with this situation. Kalin shares the Word of God with the men he comes in contact with in Jail who don't know God.

It seems like I just got home, but the alarm clock is going off and I do not have the strength to get up to turn it off. My coffee is starting to brew. That will certainly get me out of bed and on my way with a new day.

CHAPTER 57

"Ordered To Attend"

My appointment with Fran, the sex therapist, is first thing this morning and I can't say that I am looking forward to this meeting. I have said it before and I will say it again and that is I will do whatever I have to do to bring my children home and if I have to glide through, yet another hoop, I will do just that. My personal days haven't been used so I might as well use it for the purpose of meeting with Ron about the potential book deal.

It's been a long time since I have gone to the Market Cafe to get a muffin. They make the best blueberry muffins I have ever tasted. Because I have a few minutes to spare, this is the best time to find my favorite booth, drink my coffee, and eat my muffin. It also gives me an opportunity to read the paper before getting my day started. What do you know! Who is in the spotlight today? It's CCF! The headline reads, *"LOCAL CCF WORKER ACCUSED OF FALSIFYING REPORTS AND NOW ONE CHILD IS DEAD".* I can't believe this! My heart goes out to the parents of this child. This 6 year old child, Camille Stanton, was removed from her family because she was disciplined by her stepfather. When the mother was charged with neglect and the stepfather charged with child abuse, the State's CCF Department intervened and removed Camille from her mother's home and placed her in foster care. What appeared to be a loving foster care home turned out to be a disaster! The State's worker was supposed to visit the child in foster care every other week and was turning in her reports that she was doing so. Unfortunately, that worker was not able to make her rounds one week because she was assigned to another case. The new State worker discovered that Camille was no longer at the residence. Upon speaking with the foster parents, the new State worker was informed that the child had, in fact, been missing for a few weeks, of which was during the time that the previous worker's reports says that she was visited. Because of these false reports, not only is the foster mother potentially facing charges, but the 24 year old CCF worker is definitely facing some serious charges.

It is time for me to be on my way so that I don't miss my appointment. I think that it is a great idea for Ron to see just what issues there really are in the System so I decide to take the article with me. Maybe this will help him see why telling my story may save a child's life. When I call him up, he is thrilled! My appointment is only 35 minutes away and I make it there in 25 minutes. Walking up to the office, I start thinking about how my life has taken this turn. How did I end up here? Why did I end up here? I didn't do anything sexually inappropriate to my children, nor have I ever allowed anyone to do anything sexually inappropriate to my children, but for some reason, the State feels that I will benefit from this class. I finally make it inside. The office feels damp and almost abandoned inside. There are other women waiting in this small waiting area. The room is filled with a very diverse group of women. No one is making eye contact with one another. I am assuming that we are all here because we have been court ordered to be here. The instructor walks in. She introduces herself to the group as Fran Griffith.

"Good morning everyone. My name is Fran Griffith and I will be the instructor for this class that each of you have been ordered by the Court to attend. Our sessions will begin every Wednesday at 5:00 pm. This is the only session that we will have during the morning hours. I appreciate all of you for coming and for being on time. Please follow me into our classroom. Please take a seat wherever you are comfortable and let's get started."

Everyone finds a seat and quietly looks around at the person sitting next to them. The classroom is small and our seats are like cafeteria chairs. The chairs are grouped into a semi-circle. Fran begins the class.

"Each of you is here because the Court feels as though you require some training on sex offenders. You will learn about their behaviors so that you will be equipped better to protect your children. *Did she say what I just thought she said? Sexual offenders and protecting your children? Now I see it. The State put me here because they believe that Kalin was sexually inappropriate with Christy and this is to make sure that I understand how to protect my children in the future. This is so uncomfortable and I can feel my attitude is starting to change. What am I going to do about it anyway? I have to be here so I might as well get used to the idea of completing this class and moving on.* "Feel free to raise your hands if you have any questions. One of the requirements is that each of you participates in the class. So, with all that said, let's get started. I want each of you to introduce yourself to the class and tell why you are here."

One by one, each lady stands up and introduces herself. I am not a lone ranger because each of the women in this class has had their children removed from them. Some of them have not lived with their children for several months already. There is one woman in the class who claims that her caseworker won't return her children until she gets an apartment big enough. She doesn't have any extra income to afford it. She doesn't get any child support from their father, but is still required to do as instructed by the State. *There has to be something I can do to help this young woman. I will need to speak with her after the class to get more information from her. I know that I can get her into one of my properties that ares designed for families with low income.*

It's my turn! "My name is Melissa Thomas and I am here because, just like all of you, I was ordered by the Court to attend this class. Although I do not believe there is anything appropriate that happened in my household, I look forward to learning about the behaviors of a sexual offender so that my children will always be protected."

Fran jumps in. "Welcome to the class, Mrs. Thomas. I know that it is hard to believe, but you are here in this class because there was some type of evidence that made the Courts believe that your husband is guilty of inappropriate sexual activity. This is not the court and we are not going to try the case, but hopefully you will learn how to protect your children in the future." *I am so moved by these words that she just said to me. I don't know whether to be angry or what. She, too, believes that I truly need to be here. But, to be honest, most of the women here don't believe that they should be here.*

She begins the class with the common examples of how predators win over their prey. She speaks about the preferential treatment that these victims receive. The class is very informational, but I just don't believe the class is for me. I want to complete this course as quickly as possible to put me one step closer to bringing my children home with me.

I have officially survived the first class. The instructor announces that part of the rules of being in the class is that we aren't allowed to communicate with each other outside the class. She explains that our comments to one another are limited to the classroom only. *Well, there goes my idea of wanting to help the young lady find housing. I will just have to figure it out another way.* The class is dismissed and everyone heads to their vehicles to leave the facility. The young lady who spoke about needing a bigger apartment just sat down at the bus stop. I believe it is easier to speak with her away from the class, so I walk by her and give her my card and wrote, "Give me a call, 786-555-4548, to help with apartment". It does my heart good to help other people when they have a need. My mother always taught me to *give* when you hurt instead of *hate* when you hurt. The expression on her face is one of extreme gratitude. I finally drive off in excitement that I am finally going to meet with Ron about the potential book deal.

I am at Panera Bread and have already forgotten how upset I am about the comments made by the Sex Therapist. I am just very excited that I may have a book deal. Interruption is usually inevitable because right in the middle of our conversation, my phone rings and it is Stuart.

"Excuse me Ron, but I have to take this call", I say, getting up and walking away from the table.

"Hello Stuart, Melissa speaking."

"Hey there, how are you?"

"I am okay. Is everything okay?"

"I just called to tell you that we finally have a trial date. It will begin on April 24th. On the first day is when the jury will be picked and the trial will begin immediately afterwards", he explains.

"And how is my husband with this news?"

"He is excited to finally get through this, once and for all. He said that he is ready to come home to his wife and children and get his life back together."

"Yes, me too. So, do you have a list of witnesses yet?"

"Yes. My list is very short. It consists of only you and Kalin", he answers.

"Just me and Kalin. Nobody else?"

"No. I don't think it is necessary. It doesn't get any better than having the mother of the alleged victim", he says.

"I would love to go into details with you, but I am right in the middle of a meeting and I excused myself to take this call."

"Ok, that is all that I wanted. Have you heard anything else about the open case in Alabama?"

"The Judge has ruled that Princess will temporarily live with Brittney. Attorney Richards had already prepared me for it. He said that the Judge on the case will not consider granting anything to me as long as this case is still open in Florida. And CCF is not going to allow my children back home until this criminal case is decided."

"That is true. CCF is hoping that he goes away to prison and it will make their job so much easier."

"I know. But anyway, I have to go. I will call you later."

"Ok."

By the time I make it back to the table, Ron is also on his cell phone. He puts up a finger to let me know that he will be done in a minute. After a few minutes, he wraps up his phone call and looks at me and says, "Now, where were we?"

"Let's talk about the writing of this book. Why do you want your story told? Why do you think it is necessary? Is your main reason for wanting to write this book for money?"

"I want this story told because people don't realize how the System is *really* designed to work against you. They say that they are for families, but they don't do anything to build the family, but work like hell to tear it down. Writing this book is not just about the money, but is moreso about the message. When I go to Court, the Judge doesn't want to hear what I have to say. She is only interested in what the men and women who represent Florida have to say. She doesn't care whether they are telling her the truth or not. Regardless to what they believe, I matter! My children matter! They have no right to tear families apart the way that they have. They are in the media more and more for their very own careless behaviors. Because of their inconsistencies, children are dying. It is insane and there needs to be some attention brought to this matter. The entire time I am explaining myself, Ron is nodding his head in agreement.

"Mrs. Thomas, it was wonderful meeting with you today. I feel as though I have a better understanding of why this book is important to you. I think that this is a very sensitive and private matter for your family and if you are willing to share it with the world, as far as I am concerned, that makes it even more amazing. I would be honored to write this book for you", he says.

This feels so good! It has been a long time since I have felt victorious with anything. Being successful with this makes all the waiting and all the crying worth the while. I will finally be able to be heard. People will see what I went through with my children and how we survived it and know that they can make it too. Just like the song that we used to sing back at Beulah Baptist, *"If I can help somebody as I go along, then my living shall not be in vain…"*

Dear Lord, Thank you for, yet, another day. Thank you for all the good that happens and help me to deal with all the bad that creeps our way. Lord, help me to forgive those who despitefully abuse me. Help me to continue to show love to those who find joy in my sorrows. Forgive them, Lord, for they know not what they do. And when it is all said and done, I will continue to give you the praise, honor, and the glory. In Jesus' name. Amen.

CHAPTER 58

"Letter For You"

M ost of my sex therapy appointments have passed. The family counseling sessions are going quite well. My schedule continues to be stretched because I am desperately trying to maintain all of the court requirements as well as my day to day job. I am not able to see Kalin as much and he is usually disappointed when I finally do show up to see him. Although I understand why he is upset when I don't show up, I am also very disappointed that he isn't a little happy when I do make it to a visit. During the visit, he just pouts about why I didn't show up, as opposed to just enjoying his time with me. It is so frustrating because at some of our visits, the computer monitors aren't working properly so we spend the hour long visit writing notes to one another instead of speaking. If I were a gambling person, I would say that they were doing it on purpose.

With the criminal trial coming up soon, I am really starting to get nervous. I can only imagine what Kalin is feeling. I can only imagine what Christy is feeling about all of this. I don't want either of my children to go through the agony of sitting in the courtroom and being questioned. I really don't want them to see their father this way either. I need to call Denise and speak with her about this. As I begin to dial her number, a call is coming in and it is Patrick. I wonder why Dr. Norwood is calling. I wonder if there is yet, another, form that I need to fill out for Rita. I will just have to call him back when I get off the phone.

"Hello", she says.

"Hello, Denise. This is Melissa Thomas and I am calling because I really need to speak with you about my children and the possibility of them being in the courtroom."

"What is it?" she asks.

"I don't want my children involved in this. It has nothing to do with them. Christy is the only one who needs to be involved."

"Mrs. Thomas. Your daughter was molested by your husband and if there is anything that went on that the other children knows about, then, it is only fair that the Judge hears that also", she says without hesitation.

"How can you say this when nothing has been proven? There is not one shred of evidence to suggest any wrongdoing. How can you say this?"

"Based on your daughter and the babysitter, it did and I don't really care what you say because our protection is for the child", she says.

"The babysitter?" I ask, sounding surprised. "What do you mean the babysitter?"

"That is correct! The babysitter corroborated your daughter's story. Your other children are being interviewed by mental health professionals to see if we can get a better understanding of the dynamics of the home", she explains.

"Did you get my permission from me for my children to speak with a mental health professional? Might I remind you that I have not lost any of my parental rights? I am still their mother!"

"We don't need your permission and that is why we went to the Judge to get permission and it was granted. They are meeting with Medstaff Mental this afternoon at the foster home. These reports will be handed over to the Judge and discussed at the next hearing. The Judge is interested to see what the other children in the home have to say about everything", she responds.

"I really wish that I had known because I could have made arrangements to be there with my children."

"No one is allowed to be in on the meeting with the children when the therapist is speaking with them. They don't want the children to be influenced in any kind of way", she explains.

"That is crazy. They are my children! I have the right to be with my children when they are being questioned. Like I say, I have not lost my rights as a parent. How is it that you all can do anything that you want?"

"Is there anything else, Mrs. Thomas? You are more than welcome to see the reports when they are completed. We have to do a thorough investigation before the children will be allowed to come home with you", she goes on to say.

"Since I have you on the phone, I might as well go ahead and speak with you about this. I am almost done with my sex therapy classes as well as the family sessions. After these are completed, I will have completed everything asked of me. At that time, will my children be allowed to finally come home?"

"Mrs. Thomas, there are other factors involved besides you completing these classes and –", she says before being interrupted.

"Like what Ms. Woods? What else do I have to do to prove that I will do whatever it takes for my children?"

"Are you going to divorce your husband?" she asks, without hesitation. There is silence on the phone. I don't know if she is asking me this because I am beginning to make her upset or if she really means this.

"What does that have to do with anything?"

"We don't want him in the home with these children. We feel as if the home is an unsafe environment if he is there. There is a lengthy history of abuse in the home and once we know the outcome of his criminal case, we are more apt to make a decision about their placement", she explains.

"I don't believe this. So you are saying that I need to choose between my husband and my children?" She doesn't answer my question. There is, again, silence on the phone. "Is this what you are saying? Are you telling me that as long as I am married to Kalin, there is no chance in hell of my getting my children returned to me?" I ask, with an angry tone in my voice.

"I am telling you that we are not going to return your children to you until we feel as though the environment is a safe one", she answers.

"So what if he is found not guilty of the charges?"

"We will figure that out if and /or when it happens", she answers. "The children are doing just fine in their placement and we don't see any need to rush them home to live with you. I met with them on yesterday and they seem to be adjusting quite well to their foster home", she adds.

"How do you know that? How do you know how happy they are in their placement? I get a totally different picture from my children when I am around. They are constantly telling me that they feel bad when they hear family members talk about their father. Justice told me that when she says her prayers at night and decides to mention her father in her prayer, she is told to shut up and go to sleep. What kind of environment is that for a child to have to adjust to? And what about the fact that I decide to take their grandfather over for a visit and instead of it being embraced, he is told that not only can he not visit them anymore, but he has to go through a fingerprint background check. And get this. When he goes to get the background check, he is told that he doesn't really need it, but he still has to set something up through CCF if he wants to visit them. You have no idea what my children are being subjected to! How dare you sit there and act like you even care about my children! I will find out when the reports are completed and will request to have my very own copy."

"That is fine", she responds.

"And when I have completed what is required of me, based on the written case plan, I will want a meeting to discuss having my children returned to me", I comment. She does not respond to what I just said. I don't know what is going on in her mind. It seems to me that they are going to drag their feet until there is a resolution on the criminal charges pending against Kalin.

"Good day, Ms. Thomas", she says, ending our call. *I don't why it is that every time I get on the phone with CCF, I let them get to me. I already know that this is what they are trying to do anyway. I just have to take Leigh's advice and do what they are asking of me and then come out fighting. That is exactly what I intend to do.*

With all of this going on, I almost forgot that Patrick called. I wonder what he wants. Maybe he wants to take me out for a real dinner this time. I dial his number with all kinds of thoughts running through my mind as to what it can possibly be that he wants. In no time, he answers the phone. I just realize that he called me from his cell phone.

"Hello, Mrs. Thomas", he says, obviously recognizing my number.

"Hello, Mr. Norwood. How are you?"

"Patrick, please? With all that we have been through, I think we should at least be on a first name basis", he says.

"I forgot. Please forgive me. Ok, how are you doing Patrick?"

"I am fine, but I have some sad news for you", he says.

"What is it now?"

"It's Rita. She is gone, Melissa. She passed away early this morning. I had to call her immediate family members before I could speak with anyone else. They finally contacted me after a few hours. I spoke with her sister and they agreed to come to the office to pick up her things", he begins. "Are you okay, Melissa?"

"I am shocked, I guess. I am saddened to hear of this news. She is like family to us. I knew that this day was coming, but now that it is here, I am just sad. I will be just fine."

"Don't cry. She is finally at peace. She is no longer in pain. But if you will allow me, I will tell you that the happiest I have seen her was when you were coming to visit her. She would be so happy after you would leave. I heard all the stories about your children and how she has been with Amy and Justice since they were babies. There is something that she wants me to give you and she gave me specific instructions to give it to you after she has passed. She did not reveal the contents of the letter. She did mention that this letter will finally give you the peace that you have been looking for and that she took it away from you and in her death, she is glad to be able to give it back to you. I have the letter here for you whenever you are ready to get it", he explains.

"A letter? Do you know what the letter says?"

"No. I don't know what it says. Would you like to pick it up tonight?"

"Oh no! I am actually on my way to an afternoon appointment, but I will call you and let you know when I am ready to get the letter. Do you have any idea how her daughter is?"

"I don't think that her daughter really understands what is going on. When they came to the office this morning to get Rita's things, her daughter was asking for her mother", Dr. Norwood responds.

"I will have to go over there and explain it to her. I have a way of getting her to understand. Thank you so much, Patrick, for everything that you have done for Ms. Rita. I really appreciate how comfortable you made it for her in her last days."

"Are you going to be okay? Do you need a friend right now?" he asks.

"In more ways than one, but I will have to pass on it. I have quite a few things to do right now, but I appreciate the offer."

"That is an open offer, you understand?"

"Yes I do. Thanks."

After hanging up the phone with Patrick, I try hard to recollect my thoughts. I don't know what to feel right now as I am truly saddened for her daughter because I just don't know how she will survive without her mother. I need to reach out to her family and offer my support to them. Instead of just calling, the next best thing is to show up with some chicken and sodas. And besides, Maryland Chicken is on the way to Rita's apartment, so I will stop there for the food. I am sure that by now, many of the family members and friends have gathered at Ms. Rita's apartment. When I pull into the community, there is a strange feeling that overcomes me. *What if they don't want me there? What has she told them about me? How will they feel or what will they say when they see me?* I can't turn around now! I just pulled into the parking lot. There are some people standing outside, but I don't recognize any of them. "Is Ms. Rita's family inside", I ask the two young men sitting on the porch.

"Yeah, they are all inside", he answers.

After the first knock, the first person who runs to the door is Ms. Rita's daughter, Dee. She recognizes me right away. "Hey Ms. Melissa, how you?" she asks.

"I am fine, sweetheart. How are you? It is so good to see you again."

"Ms. 'Lissa', Momma gone with Jesus now. She gone! She happy too! She told me she'll be happy when she flies away", she says.

"Is that right? Well she is with Jesus now and she *is* so happy! She is not hurting anymore. She will never be sad again. She is much better off than being here and hurting", I tell her. She seems to understand what I am saying to her. I can tell that she is enjoying having all of her family together.

The rest of the family joins in by saying "hello".

"I have chicken for you all. I thought that you would enjoy not having to cook today. Send one of the kids to my car. I have a case of sodas in the back seat."

"Nu-nu, ya'll go out to Ms. Melissa's car and look in the back seat and get them sodas and bring them in the house", one of the ladies yell. I don't recognize anyone here right now. I am looking around to see if I see her sister. She is nowhere in sight.

"I just wanted to stop by and offer my support to all of you. I will miss Ms. Rita, too. She will always be a part of my family, and you too, Dee."

"I don't know why. She was nasty as hell to yo family. That woman ain't mean you no good!" one of the ladies proclaim. "She was nasty as hell. That's why didn't nobody go see her when she was in that nursing home. Hell, you the only one who cared."

"Well, that is alright. I just wanted to stop by with the chicken. I am going to go now because I really have to get back to work. If you need anything, please call me. Here is my number". I hand my card to the lady sitting at the table who yelled to the children outside. Dee tears away from her cousins to give me a bear hug as I am leaving. I really want to continue to be in her life because I know that she still needs me.

I leave the apartment feeling very sad, but at peace too. I don't know if her testimony would have helped or hurt in Kalin's trial. I am curious to know what is in the letter that she left behind for me and why it is that she only wanted Patrick to give it to me after she was gone. I have a visit scheduled with Kalin tonight and I will give him the news when I see him. When I call JT to give him the sad news, he is already aware of her passing. The word of her death spreads quickly throughout the community.

Even if Ms. Rita did what she did to me, I am still concerned for her well-being so I decide to contact the funeral home to make sure that her burial is squared away, only to find out that it isn't. When I finally get in touch with Ms. Roberts, who is the family's representative, she informs me that the family is short $2,500.00. Without any hesitation, I agree to pay this balance, but ask that my identity remain confidential. She assures me that she will keep it confidential and will contact the family and let them know that the financial obligation is fulfilled.

Dear God. Thank you for your many blessings that are meant to be shared with others. I thank you for my quarterly bonus that I am able to give back to help out this family. Please, Lord, receive it as seed. In Jesus' name. Amen.

My phone is ringing and it's Brittney! I wonder why she is calling me. This time, I decide to answer the phone.

"Hello."

"Hello Meme. What's going on? I haven't talked to you in a while. Is everything okay?" she asks, sounding sincere.

"Everything is fine. One of my closest friends just passed away and I am a little saddened by it."

"Really, who?" she asks.

"Remember the lady who watched my children for me all those years? Yeah, she passed away this morning. I just left her apartment where all of her family is gathered and dropped off some chicken and sodas for them."

"That is so sad. I am sorry to hear of it. Was she sick or something?"

"Yes, she was sick. She had been in the nursing home for a couple of months. She was very sick, but at least she is no longer in pain. Besides, she was ready to go. She had made peace with everyone and got everything off her chest that she needed to."

"Well, that's good! The reason I called is because Princess often asks about her Auntie Meme all the time. She loves the gifts that you send to her. When we were playing at the park today, she mentioned that she wanted to come to Florida to visit. I told her that I would have to give you a call to see if that is okay with you", she says.

"Of course, I would love to see her. She is welcomed here anytime. I can get some tickets to Universal Studios and Disney. We can make a weekend of it in Orlando. I think that she will get a big kick out of it."

"Too bad that your kids won't be there", she adds.

"Yeah, but I can take her over to visit with them."

I can't believe that Brittney is sitting here on the phone speaking with me as if she doesn't have a clue who Ms. Rita is when she knows all along that she has been communicating with her, or at least been trying to communicate with her. I am very curious as to what her conversations with Ms. Rita were about that involved me. Maybe Ms. Rita addresses it in her letter that she left behind for me.

Now that Brittney has called me, I am even more anxious to get the letter that Patrick is holding onto from Rita.

"That will be fun! I can't wait to see your kids. I bet they are so big now", Brittney mentions.

"Yes, they have grown. And will you be bringing your kids on the trip as well?"

"If it is okay with you", she responds.

"Of course, it is okay with me. We will have one big family reunion. I am really looking forward to it."

"So, about your friend? Did you get a chance to visit with Rita while she was in the nursing home?"

"Did I say that she was in a nursing home?" I ask "B". She has gotten extremely quiet for a second.

"B, are you there? How do you know that she was in a nursing home?"

"I thought you said that once before", she responds, hesitantly.

"Nah, I don't think that I did, but yes, I visited her there quite often. Her doctor became very concerned about her because she was starting to get calls that were beginning to upset her."

"Really? Did he ever say anything to you about it?"

"No, he just spoke with me about her health. You know how it is - that confidentiality thing. At any rate, just let me know exactly what weekend you want to travel to Florida and I can make sure that the weekend is planned. We will have a good time. Let me go, dear. I have to make a few calls."

"Alright sweetie. I will talk to you later. Goodbye!"

"Goodbye!"

CHAPTER 59

"Is He Flirting With You?"

*M*y visit with Kalin is a little more relaxed tonight. He is saddened by the news of Ms. Rita but he is looking forward to the trial so that our family can finally move forward to begin the healing process. He is very confident that the truth will be revealed. He does not speak with me much about the strategy that he and Stuart have. He just tells me that they have gone over every possibility that the State can present.

"Ms. Williams, you look beautiful tonight. Do you have any idea how much I love you and have missed you? I wake up thinking about you. I go to sleep thinking about you. I am so in love with you. I can't wait to get out of here to take you in my arms and make love to you", he says.

"I know what you mean. I love you too, Mr. Thomas. I miss you terribly. It is so difficult to wake up each morning and look on your side of the bed and see that you are not there. But what makes it easier to deal with is the fact that I am extremely busy with the family therapy, sex therapy, visits to the children, and my demanding job."

"Is that right?"

"Yes, that's right. I forgot to tell you. Rita's doctor, Patrick, called me to inform me that she left behind a letter for me and asked him to only give it to me after she is gone."

"Patrick, huh? So, how is it that you are on first name basis with the doctor?"

"Please don't make a fuss out of that. It is nothing. Because of Rita's illness, you have to know that I have spoken to him quite a few times. So, he felt comfortable telling me to call him Patrick. Please don't make a fuss about that. Back to the issue at hand. He is holding onto a letter that Ms. Rita has left behind for me that he claims that she wants me to have that will set me free once and for all. What do you think about this? Do you think that there may be information in this letter than can help in the upcoming trial?"

"I don't like the fact that he wants you to call him Patrick. Has he flirted with you?"

"Kalin! Will you please move past this? I didn't come here to fight with you. Our time is limited, so please don't do this! I am trying to get our lives back on track and you are sitting here acting like a school boy. So, are you going to answer my question?"

"OK. I just get like this because I love you so much. I know what he is trying to do and ---", he says before I interrupt him.

"You are the man I love! You are my husband and my best friend in the world. When I lay my head on my pillow at night, it is you that I think about. You are the one who my body aches for. Do you get that? Do you think you can handle that, Kalin?"

"I'm sorry, Mrs. Thomas! I am just losing it, I guess", he responds.

"And besides, he is not interested in relationships. He is recently divorced."

"And how the hell do you know so much about his personal life? You are supposed to be there for Rita and here you are having conversations with this man about something personal."

"Ok. Just like you, right? So you want to go there? We can go there! Let me say this. I need to say this right now. See, I know how you feel because these are the exact same feelings that I have had over the years about Wendy. This is a woman that you slept with and when you needed somewhere to go, you ended up at her house. And then to make matters worse, she felt comfortable enough to call my house at 9:30 at night and tell you God knows what and you went running! You tell me that you are going to Home Depot, but the tracking device to the car says otherwise!" *Kalin has struck a nerve with me this time. I know that this is not the time nor the place to discuss this. I need to change the subject. And I need to do it quickly because the look on his face says that he is ready for one hell of a fight!* "Kalin, let's talk about something else. This is not the time for this. I don't want to talk about anything right now, but us!"

"Wow! It sounds like you really needed to get something off your chest. But you know what, Melissa. Fine! Go get the letter from Patrick", he says sarcastically. "If you think it will help, get the letter. But, personally, I don't think it is that important! Stuart and I have all that we need", he answers. *I know that Kalin is only saying this because he doesn't want me to see Patrick. That is his issue with this letter. I know one thing. I certainly can't deny the fact that I miss being held by a man and have him look into my eyes and tell me that he loves me. I miss a man's touch. And the truth of the matter is this. The chemistry between the two of us is unbelievable and we both sense it. But I am married and the dangerous part is that he isn't married.*

"So, moving on to something else. How are you holding up in here? Is anyone mistreating you?"

"No. Everything is fine. I ran into one of my students in here from when I was teaching. That was an awkward moment", he admits.

"I bet it was. What is Stuart's strategy for trial?"

"Now, sweetheart. You know that I am not going to discuss that on this phone. Call Stuart and speak with him about it."

"How are the children?" he asks.

"They are doing just fine. They are all scheduled to meet with a mental health expert and get this, I didn't know about it because they went to the Judge to get permission as opposed to calling me and getting my permission."

"I am not surprised by anything that they do. I am not worried about that because there is nothing going on and there is nothing for them to find out other than the fact that the children were not harmed in any way whatsoever", he responds.

"That is true. I am going to get a copy of the final report upon completion", I say in a matter of fact kind of way.

"Well good. Honey, do me a favor."

"What?"

"Stand up so that I can look at you."

I waste no time in giving my husband what he wants. He hasn't seen me in a little while and it is important for him to know that I still adore him, respect him, and want only him. He knows that it is possible for me to desire other men because he has been in jail for 3 years awaiting this trial, but I don't want him to think that there is anyone else out here for me.

"You look fabulous! And thanks for wearing a skirt. I wish I could put my hands up that skirt right now", he says jokingly.

"I bet you do! You are so crazy, Kalin."

"About you!"

Our visit is coming to an end and the clock on the monitor reads that we have less than one minute for the visit to be over. Kalin puts a pouty look on his face letting me know that he is sad that I will leave soon.

"I love you Mr. Kalin Thomas. I can hardly wait to have you in my arms again. Hang in there and we will be together soon. I just know it!"

"Goodnight, Melissa."

"Ok, sweetheart. The next time you visit with the children, please give them all a hug and kiss from their father."

"I certainly will!"

This very awkward visit is over and I head for the parking lot. The attendant returns my cell phone to me and I notice that I have a few messages. I missed calls from Rock, Brittney, Patrick, and a call from an unknown "private" number. Rock simply called to check on his son. Patrick said to give him a call, and Brittney wants to let me know when she and the kids have decided to travel to Florida.

I am so tired. I just want to go home and take a warm bath, listen to my oldies station and soak for at least an hour. I don't feel like talking to anyone else today. It has been a very long day, with Ms. Rita passing away, CCF getting on my nerves more and more, and Patrick tempting me with his good looks and charm. I know that I definitely need to go home now. Before I am out of the parking lot, my phone is ringing and it is Patrick calling again. I wonder why he didn't wait for me to return his call. This must be an important matter. But what could be so important now? Rita has already passed! I decide to answer, but thinking in the back of my mind that perhaps, I probably should ignore the call and continue home.

"Hello".

"Hello Melissa. It's Patrick. How are you doing?"

"I am fine. I am just leaving an early evening appointment. *Now why didn't I tell him that I am leaving the jail from visiting with my husband? What on earth made me say what I said?*"

"So you are on your way home, huh?"

"Yes. I am extremely tired. It has been a long day and I just want to get in a nice hot bath and relax."

"Yeah, I can understand that. I was just making sure that you were okay. I called earlier and now I see why you didn't answer. I hope that you have a good night. Enjoy your bath."

"I will. Thank you. So, are you on your way home or what?"

"I just finished a meeting with my board of directors and was calling to see if you wanted to share a cup of coffee or something at Starbucks. I am actually on your side of town. But I do understand if you are busy. I can bring the letter with me if you would like."

"Do you have the letter with you?"

"Yes. I thought that you might agree to meet with me, so I brought the letter to keep you from having to travel all the way out to my office to pick it up."

"Sure. I guess it's not that big of a hassle. I mean, this *is* on my way home. I should be there in about 15 minutes or so."

"Great. It's a date!" he exclaims.

"I will see you when I get there."

"Drive carefully", Patrick says.

"Ok." *What am I doing? This man is too much of a temptation for me. I feel as though this meeting is more than what he is saying. This would not be this difficult if he were not so charming. The man knows all the right things to say. Don't get it twisted, Melissa! You are in love with your husband. He is in jail right now. Don't do anything to hurt him. You have to resist this temptation. I need to call Lena! She will know just what to say to keep me on track.*

Within 20 minutes, I am pulling into the parking lot at Starbucks. I have located Patrick's black Mercedes in the parking lot. After finding a park, I freshen up my makeup and go inside. He is already seated at the table. I rush past him to order my latte and he waves me over to the table. He has already ordered it for me.

"So you made it?"

"Yes. I am here. So, you must have been close by. How long have *you* been here?"

"I was here only five minutes before you", he answers, looking me up and down.

"And how did you know to order me a latte?"

"Your friend, Cindy, mentioned it the day I called you at your office. She said that she was headed out to pick up a latte for you and I just remembered that I asked her what kind. So, I already knew what you liked. Sorry for being so attentive."

"No. It's fine. Thanks!" I say, with a huge grin on my face.

"Melissa, I don't mean to be disrespectful, but you *are* a beautiful woman, and very intriguing, I might add. Your husband is a very lucky man to have you and I hope that he knows that", he comments.

"Thank you, Patrick. But, the truth is that I feel that I am the lucky one."

"Is that right?"

"Yes. What did it for you and your ex-wife? What caused your marriage to fail?"

"She cheated on me with one of my colleagues. I guess I saw it coming. She dated him in college before she and I met. We were all friends, though. When I went away on a missionary trip to Africa and was gone for a year, I returned to find out that she had fallen in love with him. I wish them the best. Don't get me wrong. I will find a way to move on with my life. I refuse to let this get me down. I have my Nursing Center and our children and nothing else matters right now", he says.

"You are holding up pretty well. I would be devastated if that happened to me and Kalin. I love him so much. I can't imagine being with another man. We have been through so much together. I have to admit that there are times when I will meet someone who I am completely attracted to, but I know that he is off limits to me. I know that I can't cross that line, no matter how much I may want to", I respond.

"You mean like now?" he boldly asks.

Patrick's comment causes me to choke. Patrick leans over to pat me on the back because the coffee went down the wrong pipe. When he leans over, I get a sniff of his cologne. He smells so good!

"What do you mean?"

"Come on Melissa. You and I both know what is going on here. Believe me when I say that the attraction is mutual, but I respect the fact that you are married. I love being in your space and I know that if you were not married, you are certainly the type of woman that I would want to share my life with. Because we are both adults, it is not abnormal for us to have this attraction to each other. I understand why you won't cross that line and I respect it. Different time, different place, who knows?"

"I don't know what to say, Patrick."

"You don't have to say anything, sweetie. Your silence says it all. Enjoy your latte. Before I forget, I have the letter here", he says, as he hands me the sealed envelope that reads, "For Ms. Melissa", on the outside.

I don't know if I want to read it now or wait until I get home. I guess Patrick can tell that I am hesitating a little.

"Go ahead and read it now. I want to be here for you if there is something that is just too hard for you. Please, let me be here for you", he pleads.

I open the letter and begin to read.

Dear Ms. Melissa,
If you are reading this letter, I have already passed this life. I want to first of all say, thank you for everything. Thanks

to both you and Mr. Kalin for allowing me to be a part of your family for all of these years. You were there for me when my very own family turned its back on me. You brought me and my daughter into your home and I am most grateful for that. The truth of the matter is that you are a very special woman and more than that, I now know that you are a woman of God. In my time of being in this facility and having my talks with God, He made me see who you really are and He told me that I have to make it right with you before I leave this world. I may have made your life hell while I was on earth but I have to give you the peace you need in my death.

Ms. Melissa, I hurt you badly. I can't take back what I did to you and your family. I allowed greed to take over and it caused you and your family so much pain. The funny thing is that no matter what I did to you, you still showed love to me and my daughter.

Mr. Kalin is fighting for his life and it is my fault. Here is the truth and I pray that you find it in your heart to forgive me. I made up this lie to get Kalin arrested so that he would be out of the way and so would you. Moving the two of you out of the way was what had to happen to make my destruction plan go through. Do keep in mind that I had help to do this. Your family was more than willing to help because they hate Mr. Kalin. CCF was even more willing to participate because they hate him too. The trial that is going on right now for Mr. Kalin will end when this letter is presented to the court. Mr. Kalin did not do anything to Christy and this is what happened.

Christy and I were talking one day and she was upset about the fact that you and Kalin told her that she couldn't go to a dance at her school. It just went from there. During that conversation, she mentioned that Mr. Kalin assisted her with a tampon when neither of us were home. She tried to tell me that nothing bad happened with that but me and your family turned it all around to make it bad. We started adding stuff to it just to get CCF involved and forced Christy to go along with it. CCF already had it in for Kalin because they have been trying to get him for years, so they saw this as a great opportunity to see him off to prison. They made everything fit just perfectly to keep the case open. You have raised a good child because Christy never wanted to go along with this, but she listened to me. The real culprits were me, your sister Diana, and your friend Brittney. Everybody had a benefit in bringing this hurt and shame to you.

Your sister did it because she just hates Kalin and always did and she felt like this was the way to get him once and for all. For me, I was working with Brittney to hurt you because with you out of the way looking like an unfit mother, she would get full custody of Princess and inherit all of the money that her mother left behind for her. She promised me some expensive gifts for helping her to ruin you. The lawyer in Alabama helped her do this. She has a big secret on him about some video that she made years ago that could ruin his career. He told her all about Laura's Will and the financials associated with it and that is how she knows all about what the woman left behind for her daughter. The last time we talked, she said that she is going to come to Florida and put the final nail in the coffin. Even I don't know what that means, so please don't let her come here to your home. She hates you. She said that when you all were growing up, yall were the best of friends but that you were always more popular and she has always resented you for it.

So, there you have it. Show this letter to the court. I was behind this accusation. I love you and Mr. Kalin. You two are the best parents that a child could ever have. You took care of me all these years and have never asked me for anything. This one is on me. I am gone and I am not there to make this right. I hope that you can find it in your heart to forgive me. You have had to go through a lot behind this accusation and I sat there and watched you for three years crying, going to court, fighting with all you have for your kids and I respect you, Ms. Melissa. I love you and I pray that you will find it in your heart to forgive me. And to the courts...Please end this nightmare for this family. This was all my fault.

Love Always,
Rita

By the time I am done reading the letter, my tears are unstoppable. I truly believe that God spoke to her on my behalf. He worked it out! Oh

God! Thank you Jesus! Patrick stands me up and leads me outside. With all of the crying, we are getting quite a bit of attention from the other people in the restaurant.

"Melissa, come on sweetheart. Let's walk outside", he says, leading me to his car.

He takes my face in his hands and wipes away my tears.

"You just don't know what I have been through over the last few years because of a false accusation. In this woman's death, she made it right. I am so shocked right now, Patrick. Oh God! Oh God, thank you! Thank you Jesus! You are awesome! I am so caught up on this moment that I lift my hands to heaven because I exalt Jesus. I know that there is no way this could be happening right now if it were not for God's goodness. I am overjoyed!

"I don't know what is in that letter, but I am so glad to see you so happy. I am happy for you, Melissa and - - -", he says, before I lean over to give him a kiss on the lips. The kiss lasts for what seems like 10 minutes. I am obviously caught up in this moment. He has an old school CD playing with Al Green in the background and the moment just seems right. I know that it has to end here, but I needed to know what it would feel like to press my lips against his lips. The truth is that I have wanted to do that since the day I met him. I know that I have crossed a line that I should not have crossed.

"I am sorry, Patrick. I should not have done that. I was way –", I say, before he pulls my face to his and returns more kisses on my lips. We kiss for even longer. We are sitting in the parking lot of Starbucks, sitting in his Mercedes, with Al Green's old school CD playing in the background and sharing these tiny bits of forbidden passion together.

When we finally come up for air, he looks me in the eyes and says how he has wanted to do that since the day we met.

"Patrick, you know that our night has to end here. I am so tempted to make love to you right now, but I can't. I love my husband and he needs me now more than ever. So, I will say goodnight."

"I understand, Melissa. Goodnight. Let me walk you to your car", he offers.

"No. That is fine. I will say goodnight right here because if you walk me to my car, I may not be able to resist you. I will say this. You are an amazing kisser", I say, as I open the door to his car to leave.

"You are, too, baby."

I walk away and head for my car. This special moment with Patrick is just that. It is special and sweet, but I know that it can never happen again. I believe that this was just something that we both needed. He is missing his wife and I am certainly missing my husband. I will always remember him, though, for giving me what I needed at the right time. I have the letter that will bring my family home and he delivered it to me. I don't think I will ever forget him.

I am too excited to sleep now. I immediately give Stuart a call. It is late so I don't expect him to answer, so I leave a message for him. I am finally home and coming home on this night is different than any other night. I have a letter than will set my husband free and bring my children home. God did it. It has been three years of crying, praying, and patiently waiting for an answer, but God worked it out.

I am so happy that I put in a Yolanda Adams CD. The words that she says so eloquently in her song, "I'm Gonna Be Ready", are on high volume -*"I was free to do what I wanted to, lost everything but I still had you . . "You showed me your grace and now my life's renewed and I thank you. so I will tell anyone who will listen, I'll testify about how good you were to me when so called friends passed me by...the fact that you would show somebody so broke down so much mercy...sight beyond what I see, you know what's best for me, prepare my mind, prepare my heart for whatever comes...strength to pass any test...* THANK YOU JESUS!

I prepare my bath and soak for at least an hour. Tomorrow is the beginning of the end. Now, I know what Joel Osteen means when he says that the latter will be better!

CHAPTER 60

"Cindy, Don't Go There!"

I wake up today feeling like everything is going to be alright. I am now reminded of the song by Florida Mass Choir when they sing that 'the sufferings of this present time are not worthy to be compared to the glory that we shall receive'. I am ready for the glory! I am opening up my heart to receive from God. I thank you Lord for having a spirit of forgiveness because it is through your love that all blessings flow.

The phone rings and it is Stuart. "Stuart, are you sitting down?"

"Why, what now?" he asks.

"Stuart, I have a letter in my hand that was delivered to me last night by Ms. Rita's doctor. She wrote a letter to me on her death bed breaking down how she was directly involved with this false accusation leveled against Kalin. She mentions all of the people involved with bringing this shame to my family, including CCF. I want the prosecuting attorney to get this and drop the charges against my family. God has told me that it is time for them to all come home. It is over, Stuart! It is over! I don't want Kalin to know about this letter until it is read in court", I explain.

"Are you serious?!!!"

"Yes, I am. She even had the letter notarized so that it gives more credibility. There is also a video that her doctor delivered to the Courthouse already. She said that she needed her life to count for something good and if she was able to help the one family who cared for her and her daughter, she would do whatever it took to give us our freedom from a system that plagued us for many years.

"Well, I need that letter right away. I don't want anything to happen to it! This is great news Melissa. I am so happy for you all. You really deserve it! "

"Thank you so much Stuart. Thank you!"

I decide to give my niece a call to see if I can come see my children for a special visit tonight even though it is not my usual visitation day. She agrees. I need to call Cindy and give her the news. I am so excited that this nightmare is finally coming to an end. Just as usual, Cindy is busy running the office. I walk past her and go to my office to check my messages.

"Good morning Melissa", she says, looking up briefly from her paperwork.

"Good morning, Cynthia."

"Cynthia? What has you so happy this morning?"

"When you are done, please come into my office. I have great news!"

"Ok."

Before I can put all of my things down, Cindy is already walking into my office. "What happened?"

"Please sit down to hear this. The sad news is that Ms. Rita passed away yesterday, but what she left behind will finally bring my family together. She wrote a letter and gave it to Dr. Norwood and told him to give it to me when she passes away. Well, he did. He gave it to me last night. She confessed in the letter that she was behind this big lie to try to destroy me and Kalin and she used my friend, Brittney, my sister Diana, and CCF to help her do it. They all went along with it because they wanted Kalin's final destruction to come to him. And get this! My friend's secret agenda is that she wanted to make me look like an unfit parent so that the courts in Alabama would not give me custody of Princess. She doesn't really care about the child but her mother left her everything and Laura had a lot. She told me all about it in the letter. I am getting ready to take it to Stuart, but Dr. Norwood told me last night that the video is already in the hands of the State Attorney. She did a notarized letter, and a video to make sure that the documents are authentic. Can you believe this?"

Cindy is speechless. She is sitting with her mouth hanging open.

"I know, right? This is just God! I am so excited and very appreciative of Dr. Norwood.

"Well, you might as well know this. He called here this morning and he just wanted me to tell you that last night was special and he said that you would know what that means", she says, with a skeptical look on her face.

"No, no, no, don't go there. What we shared was special but not sexual. We had a very special kiss and that was it! I am a married woman and I haven't forgotten that. I am not going to lie about it. He is any woman's temptation and if I were not married, I would love to see what could happen between us. But I am married and nothing more can happen with Patrick other than the sweet moment that we shared on last evening. So, there! That was it! So what do you think?"

"Melissa, I think that you are human! What you felt with him last night was a normal reaction for a woman who has not been intimate for 3 years. It has been a long time coming. It is about time!"

"That's not what I am talking about, crazy girl. I am talking about the letter written by Ms. Rita. What do you think about that?"

"Oh! Of course! That is wonderful, sweetheart. It is about time! I am so happy for you. I really am. So now what?"

"We wait! I told Stuart that Kalin is not to find out about this until the trial. I just don't want to get his hopes all up and everything."

"True! True! That makes sense. I am sorry to hear about Ms. Rita. How is her family doing?"

"They are doing just fine. How is everything here at the office? I am sorry that I have not been here, but when all of this is over, you won't be able to get rid of me."

"I know! That is what I am afraid of."

"Ha ha. Too funny!"

"Any messages or anything before I get my day started?"

"No, but your friend Brittney has called here a couple of times. She said something about getting the address to come here to Florida. She said that she had spoken with you about it. I would not tell her anything, of course. So, she may be calling back."

"And I hope that I am here when she calls, so I can let her know that the game is over!"

My work day is totally different for me today. I feel like God has opened up Heaven and let the light shine through. I am at so much peace that it feels like the warmth from Heaven is around my neck. I feel like the angels are sitting on my shoulders and have taken the hurt away. I feel like, perhaps, Ms. Rita is right here with me. I am so excited that I feel like I want to just run and scream through the streets of Miami and tell everyone how good God is. I need to call Ron to see where we are with the book deal and tell him of the potentially dynamic ending to the story.

The criminal trial is only 2 days away and so is the Children's Status Request Hearing. I am so glad that I have finally finished all of my family therapy sessions, as well as the Sex therapy sessions. The Judge will have to return my children to me now, especially with Ms. Rita's signed confession letter. It is safe and sound in Stuart's hands now.

CHAPTER 61

"Dear Ms. Melissa"

Stuart meets me in the downstairs lobby of the courthouse on Tuesday, April 24th. We have been waiting on this day for quite some time. We take each other's hands and begin to pray.

Dear God. Father of our Lord and Savior Jesus Christ. Lord, this journey, no matter how hard it became, I always knew that you had it. Father, we ask you to show up today and show out! Lord, I want you to know that no matter what happens in either one of these courtrooms, I walk away from this place today still trusting you. You are the author and finisher of our faith. I know that I never would have made it right here at this moment without you. You wiped away the tears when people talked about me, when people doubted me, but you gave me forgiveness in my heart and I thank you for it. You watched over my children. You protected my husband and I give you all the praise and honor and glory for it. Go ahead of us today Lord. Put the right words in Stuart's mouth. Give him wisdom, Lord. And when it is all said and done, we will be very careful to give you the praise. In Jesus' name. Amen.

"Let's do this, Mrs. Thomas", says Stuart, as he grabs tightly to my hands. I look to heaven and give God a wink. We are on the elevator on our way to the fourth floor. It feels differently today and I know that it is because God is out front. We get off the elevator and not much has changed since the last time I was here. There are still tons of people sitting and waiting to be called. When you show up with a private attorney, you are the first to be called. We wait for only 15 minutes and Stuart and I are escorted to the back where the courtrooms are. Within 30 minutes, he and I are sitting in courtroom 4D being sworn in and attesting that the statements that we are about to make are true to the best of our knowledge.

"Ms. Woods, please address the court with what this hearing is about today", the Judge requests.

"Your Honor, in light of the fact that Mr. Thomas has a criminal trial being held today, we would really like to see the outcome of that trial before we make any recommendations to the court on behalf of the Williams/Thomas children", the caseworker states.

"Can you at least give me an update of the requirements placed upon Mrs. Thomas by this Court?"

"Sure, Your Honor. Mrs. Thomas completed the family therapy sessions successfully. Her therapist said that she did not miss any appointments and was very cooperative with the suggestions given to her to bring more cohesiveness to her family. She sent in her letter as a follow-up to her recommendation for Mrs. Thomas. We will present this as Exhibit A."

"Does she feel that Mrs. Thomas is in any way a threat to her children?" the Judge asks.

"No, Your Honor. She does not", she answers.

"What else was required of Mrs. Thomas?"

"She was required to attend an 8 week program for sex therapy awareness."

"And did she complete that?"

"Yes, she did, Your Honor. She gave the recommendation that Mrs. Thomas is loving and caring towards her children, but does feel that she is in denial regarding the charges leveled against her husband. She went on to say that Mrs. Thomas is certainly "straddle the fence" and will probably never admit that her husband did these things that her daughter claims were done to her."

"Is that true, Mrs. Thomas?" the Judge asks.

"Your Honor, I do not believe that my husband was ever inappropriate with my daughter. I have been very consistent with that from the very beginning. I believe deep down in my heart that he would never do anything to hurt, not only my children, but any child."

The courtroom becomes very quiet. All eyes are on me. I can feel their eyes piercing through me, but for some reason, I don't feel ashamed or hurt anymore.

"With all due respect, Mrs. Thomas is not on trial here, your Honor. She has a right to believe what she believes. She has successfully completed the requirements of the court and I feel that it is now in the best interest of the children that they be returned to their mother", he goes on to say.

"Mr. Peters, the State has requested of the Court to await the outcome of Mr. Thomas' criminal hearing before they make their recommendation to the Court. What do you think of this request?"

"Your Honor. I guess there is no better time than the present to present a notarized letter that my office received that was written by the former housekeeper before she passed away. This letter is being presented as my Exhibit A."

"Ms. Woods, are you aware of this letter that Mr. Peters' office received?"

"No. This is our first time seeing this", she answers.

"Please hand it over to Ms. Woods so that they can take a moment to review the letter. I would like to take a look at the letter as well."

Stuart hands the letter to the Judge. The courtroom is quiet for a moment. You can tell when CCF got to the part about them because they become very agitated and try with all of their might to discredit the letter.

"How do we know that she wasn't pushed into signing this letter? Where did it come from? How did the Doctor get the letter?"

"Your Honor. This letter was handed over to my client by Dr. Patrick Norwood, Ms. Rita's physician who cared for her before she passed. There is also a videotape that clearly states her position on this matter if anyone is interested in viewing it", he adds.

"I have already read the letter and I have witnessed the video. In light of this new evidence, the State requests that the Wiliams/Thomas children be removed from the foster home and returned to their mother, effective immediately", she announces.

Did I just hear what I thought I heard? Did the State just ask the Judge to return my children home to me? OOhhh Glory to God!

"Mrs. Thomas, your children are coming home. After 3 years, I certainly think that it is time for you to reunite with your children. You have done everything asked of you by this Court; therefore, you are free to pick up your children whenever you want to. And Ms. Woods, you need to contact the foster mother and inform her of the ruling of this Court so that the children are ready to leave when Mrs. Thomas arrives", she orders.

"Is there anything else from either of you?"

"No, Your Honor", Stuart says.

"No, Your Honor. The State is happy to oblige", she says.

Stuart and I get up and walk towards the door to leave the courtroom and my legs are shaking. I am so happy! Thank you Jesus! Once we are out of the courtroom, I give Stuart a very tight brotherly hug.

"Thank you Stuart. God did it! God did it!"

"Now, let's go get your husband!"

As we are walking towards the elevator, the CCF caseworker approaches us and extends her hand as a peace offering.

"Congratulations Mrs. Thomas. We have seen many mothers come through these doors, but never have we seen a mother fight so hard for her children the way that you have. And it is very clear that there is nothing left to fight here. You need to know that we never meant any harm, but it is always our position to "protect the children". I personally wish you the best of luck with your family", she continues.

"Thank you. I appreciate what you are saying. Thank you so much!" I say, with tears freely flowing down my face. "I am not sad. I am just so happy right now to see that God is true to His Word. You have no idea what my life has been like without my children. They are my life, but I am not angry. What I have been through over the last three years has made me a much stronger woman. You know what they say, 'what doesn't kill you just makes you stronger'. I made it through this simply because of my faith in God. I never would have made it, without Him."

She gives me a nod and walks away into the crowd of people heading for the elevator.

Stuart turns to me and we decide to take the stairs. We have at least 2 hours before the criminal trial takes place. Kalin's family will be here today for the Trial and none of them know about the letter. Kalin is going to be shocked when he realizes that I have known this for 2 days and didn't tell him about it. To pass time away, we go to the Courthouse Cafeteria. But now that I am here, I can't eat. I am simply not in the mood to eat. The only thing I want to do is walk into that courtroom and bring my husband out of there. It is time for him to come home to me and his children. This Hearing today is in God's hands. We showed up together for a Criminal trial, but with the evidence that is being presented, the Judge can decide to accept it and throw out these charges. This will be over and everyone goes home. If the Judge doesn't accept this new evidence and feel that it's not authentic, the Trial will begin today as planned.

I just received a text message from Kalin's family. They are in the courthouse and want to know exactly where I am. I send a text back to them that I am in the cafeteria on the 2nd floor. They text back for me to sit tight because they are on their way to meet me in the cafeteria. Kalin has no idea that his mother is coming here today. He is aware that his sisters and brothers are coming, but his Mother decided to come at the last minute.

"Hello Mom. I am so glad that you all made it safely. We just finished in Family Court and your grandchildren are coming home! God did His thing in that courtroom this morning. Now, we just have to get Kalin home. Excuse my manners. Stuart, this is Valerie, Ken's mother, his sisters, Cheryl and Angela, his father JT, which you already know, and his twin brother Kenneth. They came all the way from Alabama to be here for Kalin."

"It is nice to meet all of you", Stuart says.

We sit and chat for at least an hour and decide it is best to go ahead and head for the courtroom. Hopefully, Kalin has already made it inside and we will get to see him. I am sure that it will make him so proud to see his family represented in the courtroom.

Outside the courtroom, Christy and my niece are sitting on one of the benches for the witnesses. My daughter doesn't care that I am surrounded by everyone, because she still comes up to me and gives me a hug and tells me that she loves me. I know that Kalin's family may not understand this, but she is still my daughter and I will never refuse her my love. Spectators begin to fill the courtroom. We walk inside and the very first person in the courtroom that I connect with is my husband of 13 years. He spots me right away, but what brings tears to his eyes is when he recognizes that his mother is standing right next to me. He starts crying. I notice that the bailiff bends down and says something to him.

Now that the Judge has entered the courtroom, everyone stands to show respect.

"Please be seated", instructs the Judge. "Good morning everyone. Considering the fact that new evidence has been presented, we will review this evidence and if it is accepted into evidence, it will weigh heavily on whether there will be a trial or not. Therefore, we will have to postpone the selection of the Jury, which is what we would have been doing first thing. Apparently, the Defense has presented into evidence a letter that was written by the late Rita Gardner, a State Witness, along with a videotape to accompany the letter. We will read that letter in the courtroom as well as view the videotape. Any objections?"

"No, Your Honor", says Shatner, the State Prosecutor.

Kalin turns his total attention to me. He can see that I am in tears. He looks puzzled. I mouth the words, "I love you" to Kalin, as he stares at me. His family is looking at me in total disbelief. Nobody had any idea about this new evidence.

"Melissa, did you know about this?" Angela whispers into my ear.

"Yes. I knew about this. I just didn't want anyone else to know about it until court. God is merciful. Don't ever forget it."

The court reporter picks up the letter and begins to read.

"Dear Ms. Melissa,

If you are reading this letter, I have already passed this life. I want to first of all say, thank you for everything. Thanks to both you and Mr. Kalin for allowing me to be a part of your family for all of these years. You were there for me when my very own family turned its back on me. You brought me and my daughter into your home and I am most grateful for that. The truth of the matter is that you are a very special woman and more than that, I now know that you are a woman of God. In my time of being in this facility and having my talks with God, He made me see who you really are and He told me that I have to make it right with you before I leave this world. I may have made your life hell while I was on earth but I have to give you the peace you need in my death . . ."

Love Always, Rita.

By the time the court reporter is finished reading the letter, the entire courtoom is in tears. The Judge clears his throat and reminds the audience to have order. Kalin's eyes are locked on mine. He is in shock!

"And now for the viewing of the video", the Judge announces.

The video begins. Once I bend down to get tissue out of my purse, I am now in shock because I can't believe what I am hearing. *Is that Patrick that I hear and see in the video?* It *is* Patrick! He is the person interviewing Ms. Rita! He knew all along! He knew exactly what the letter was about. Why didn't he tell me that he interviewed Ms. Rita? He kept that from me, but why? He was part of this entire process!

Patrick asks Ms. Rita, "Why is it that you feel that is necessary to make this video for the Court?"

"I wrote a letter and even though I got it notarized, I still want to make sure that everyone knows that what I said in the letter comes from me", she answers.

"What is it that you want the Court to know?" he asks her.

"I want the Court to know that I am responsible for Mr. Kalin sitting in jail. I made up the whole thing. I got people to lie and say that they saw things that never really happened. I brainwashed Christy to say what she said because I convinced her that it would get Mr. Kalin out of the house. She was mad at him anyway, so it was easy. Ms. Melissa's sister went along with it because she never really liked him either. She said that after her sister married Kalin, she has never been the same with the family. We all got together and contacted CCF and gave them our made up story. They never asked any questions or required any evidence. They even helped us make sure that everything fit together and was consistent. They presented a case to the Judge that was bound to get the children removed and Mr. Kalin in jail. They added things to the story and we just went along with it. CCF never meant for the children to be removed as long as they were, but Ms. Melissa didn't do quite like we thought she would have. She fought very hard for her children and that was not supposed to happen. We were trying to do any and everything possible to break her, but she kept fighting. The plan was for Melissa to lose her children permanently, Kalin go to Prison for the rest of his life, and all of this would have prevented Melissa from gaining custody of her friend's daughter in Alabama. There is quite a bit of money connected to the child in Alabama and the money will go to the person who is, of course, raising the child. The child's mother wanted Melissa. But Melissa's friend, Brittney Snow, wanted Ms. Melissa to look like an unfit mother so that she would not receive full custody. Brittney knew every detail of what was going on here because of me. As I was feeding the information to her, she was informing the Attorney in Alabama. He would have done anything for Brittney because she had some very damaging evidence against the attorney. She promised me some of the money when she finally got full custody of the child. The reason her attorney was so willing to help her is because she was blackmailing him about this sex video that they made. Brittney was all about money and she didn't care who it hurt to get it", she explains.

"So, are you saying that you never witnessed any inappropriate behavior between Mr. Thomas and Christy?"

"That is correct, sir."

"And what about the other children?" he asks.

"Nothing! Ever! Mr. Kalin was great with all of the children", she answers.

"But Christy was the one saying these things to the Judge and to CCF. Why did she do that?"

"She trusted me. She would have done anything that I said to do. She didn't want to do it, because she didn't want to hurt her mother, but I convinced her to do it anyway", she answers. "What made it so easy for us is because even though Christy was inconsistent in her statements with the Judge and with the police, the Judge always agreed with the State."

"Is there anything else that you would like to say to the Court?"

"Ms. Melissa is a great mother and Mr. Kalin is a great father. They didn't do anything to their children. If there is ever a woman who is close to God, it's Ms. Melissa. She is a great mother. She is the type of woman that I would want to raise my daughter if I needed her to do so. Give these people back their life. I took it away from them and I was wrong for doing that because I have seen them go through so much as a result of my selfishness. They deserve to finally live in peace. Give them back their children and let this man go home to his wife and kids. Sending this man to prison would be the biggest mistake you could ever make."

"And why did you come out with this information now?"

"Because I am dying and I am the only one who is willing to share the information and if I didn't tell the truth, this family would have been destroyed for nothing", she says, starting to cry. "This woman has been nothing but nice to me. When I found out that I was dying, my real family didn't care whether I lived or died, but Ms. Melissa was right here visiting me and sending money to my daughter. She thought she was being anonymous about it, but I have friends everywhere and I found out that she was sending money to my daughter. A woman who can be in so much pain herself and still find it in her heart to give deserves to have the peace of God return to her life and that is why I had to make this video and write this letter. I needed to at least let my life count for something."

"Bailiff, please stop the video. Let's take a short break."

The entire courtroom is in tears as everyone walks out into the hallway. Kalin is so overtaken with the news that he has to leave the courtroom to refresh himself. Kalin's family is also in tears. They are speechless.

"Melissa, we had no idea that all of this was going on here. This woman lied! She did this on purpose! It is a good thing that she is dead because I would be right there in that nursing home whooping her ass!" exclaims Cheryl, Kalin's sister.

Patrick exits the courtroom and makes eye contact with me. I want to run up to him and thank him for what he has done, but I don't want Kalin's family to notice that there is a connection between me and Patrick. *Did I just say connection between me and Patrick? Was that kiss an innocent as I want to believe it was?* I know that he is off limits to me. I know that we had an intimate moment, but that is all that can or will ever happen between us. He knows that I am obligated to be with my husband's family and understands that we can't talk right now; however, I will just politely thank him.

"Excuse me, sir. Thank you for what you did in there. I had no idea that you were part of the video. You knew all along, didn't you?"

"Yes, I did. I did my homework and I knew that you were getting the short end of the stick. I started digging around after the young lady continued to call the Center for Rita. And when I approached Rita about it, she confessed to me. During our many conversations together, I convinced her to do the right thing by you and the rest is history!" he answers.

"I just want to thank you for what you have done here. My family thanks you!"

"It was nothing. You would have done it for me, right?" he asks.

DEJAVU! That is the same thing that I said to my sister when I called CCF and lied that I was watching her children. It is funny how things come around full circle. The bailiff has just come out to inform us that court is back in session and to return to the courtroom.

"Ladies and gentleman of the courtroom, I need to bring the author of this video up to ask some questions as to determine the credibility of this video presented in the courtroom. Please have the Doctor come in, please", the Judge instructs the Bailiff.

The room is quiet as Patrick makes his way to the witness stand.

"Sir, please state your name for the Court", the Judge says.

"Patrick John Norwood."

"And please state how you came to know Rita Gardner."

"She was my patient at Norwood Nursing Facility."

"Please give the facts surrounding the making of this video."

"Mrs. Thomas was the only visitor who would come to see Ms. Rita. After every visit, I began to notice how happy she was, and for awhile, her health was progressing. It just seemed as though her health was stronger as long as Mrs. Thomas was visiting her. But then, I began to notice a sudden decline in her health when the young lady, Brittney, would call her. She would become very upset after those phone calls. Against my wishes, she had started refusing to take her medications. It was almost as if she wanted to die. She would cry and become sad. I became very concerned and decided to exercise my authority as her doctor and listened in on one of her phone calls with Brittney. This is when I learned that there was some type of connection to Mrs. Thomas and her family. I learned that there was a conspiracy against this woman and I knew that I had to do something."

"And, why, if you don't mind my asking, did this concern you?" asks the Judge.

"Mrs. Thomas is a good woman and I just didn't feel that she deserved to have any wrongdoing placed upon her and I wanted to do whatever I could to eliminate any harm to come to her", he answers. As Patrick is making this comment, he turns his attention towards me. I hope that Kalin nor his family notice the connection between me and Patrick.

"And did you, at that time, approach Ms. Rita?" the Judge asks.

"Yes. I approached her and demanded to know the truth. She confessed to me about her part in the plot to destroy this family."

"And that is when you decided to make the video?"

"That is correct, Your Honor."

"OK, Mr. Norwood. You may step down now."

"We have seen the video and have read the letter from Rita Gardner, the deceased witness who has recently presented evidence in the case against Kalin Thomas. I would like for both attorneys to make some closing arguments regarding what we have witnessed here today and I will deliberate and make a decision as to whether this evidence will be submitted. Mr. Shatner, you are up first."

"Judge, this trial comes at a time after so many events have taken place. Three years ago, Mr. Kalin was arrested for what was believed to be true events that took place, not just collaborated by a few witness but several, of which one included the victim, Christy Williams. According to her testimony, her stepfather, on more than one occasion, touched her inappropriately. Her story was corroborated by this same lady, who lived in the same household for years, but in the end, submitted a video to the Court to retract her statements. Who do we believe? A child who lived in the Thomas household for many years, who was so brave to testify in Children's Court with all of the details of the inappropriate sexual activity, as well as a child who saw more than her share of abuse by that man over there, Kalin Thomas, … or do we believe a video tape of a ghost? You decide!

Once the prosecuting attorney finishes his closing arguments, there is a silence that overcomes the courtroom. Kalin looks flatlined. He shows no emotion after this final remark by Mr. Shatner. Stuart now approaches the center of the courtroom to deliver *his* final comments to the Judge.

"Judge, we have all heard the comments made by the Prosecuting Attorney. After we have listened to the reading of the letter, and have witnessed the video that Rita Gardner, before her death, presented to the Court, I honestly believe that you are all smart enough to see that she was not forced into this, no one promised her anything, nor did she gain anything out of this, except that the family who loved her unconditionally will finally be at peace. As Mr. Shatner so eloquently states, "that man over there". Let me tell you about "that man over there". Mr. Thomas and his wife, Melissa, took me into their home when I was a crack head with no reason to live. They believed in me and allowed me to live in their home to get sober. They fed me. They made sure that I was well taken care of when I lived with them. And not only that, but they took on the expenses of having me be in a rehabilitation center to get my life on track. When I lived with them, they were nothing but loving towards their children. I am asking that each of you will dig deep into your hearts, review the letter and the video and see that this woman is finally doing for the Thomases what they have been doing for many all along the way. Thank you."

There are some cheers from the audience, but the Judge quickly dismisses it.

"Order in the courtroom! Order in the courtroom!" he says, as he bangs down his gavel.

"I am now calling a recess so that I can deliberate over the information presented to the Court." The Judge stands and leaves the courtroom.

Dear God, It has come down to this moment. You and I have been going through this for 3 years. I have cried, and you have wiped away every single tear. I have worried and you have always delivered an answer. I need you today, Lord. I need to have peace in my heart, no matter what happens in this courtroom today. Lord, please be with this Judge as he deliberates over this evidence. Help him to see what needs to be seen. Watch over Kalin. Give him strength to deal with whatever happens. These and other blessings I ask in Jesus' name, Amen.

Everyone stands and leaves the courtroom. Kalin makes eye contact with me and our eyes say that we can't wait to hold each other again. I want my husband to feel my warm body against his. It has been three years since we were intimate. Until this kiss with Patrick, I have not thought of being with another man.

Outside the courtroom, I become quiet and withdrawn from everyone. I don't walk to talk to anyone. All I want to do is run out of here and get my children and then go by the Jail and pick up my husband. I want this over. It has been a long time coming. The nerve of Brittney to do what she did! Every dog has its day is what I have always heard. I can't think of her right now. The Judge in Alabama will get the video, along with the letter and before we know it, Princess will be here in Miami, with the rest of her family.

"Melissa, are you okay?" asks Kalin's mother.

"Yes, Mom. I am doing as well as can be expected."

"You did a good job honey. We don't blame you for any of this. And that man who got Rita to tell the truth, well, that was the best thing that could have happened", she says.

"Yes, I know. I had no idea that he was working on that at all. He never said anything. I would go see her in the nursing home and he never told me that he was working on this."

"It just goes to show that God brings people into our lives for certain reasons. We have to just leave things in His hands and He will work it out for us. It is almost as if God sent this man to be your angel, right? That sure is what it seems like."

"Since I have been in this world, God has done nothing but look out for me, no matter how many times I messed up", I say, with tears in my eyes. "And now I need Him more than I ever have. I need him to free my husband so that we can pick up our family and move on with our lives."

"I know, baby."

I look down at my fish sandwich and I can't eat it! I am getting sick to my stomach. I decide that I don't want to eat and would much rather wait outside the courtroom. This is very hard because the waiting is killing me. I try to read my magazines to pass time away. The words are running together. I call Cynthia to try to talk to her, but I am not really talking but just listening to her talk. I pick up the phone and to my surprise, there is a "New Text Message". I hit the button to view it and the message is from "Patrick". It reads,

"I love you and that is why I did what I did. I knew that she was up to no good from the moment she came to my nursing home and after I met you, I knew then that I was put into your life to protect you. I hope that the verdict is in your favor and that you will go on and live your life in happiness.
Love, Patrick".

I look up to see if he is anywhere around but I don't see him. He must have left the courthouse. I wonder if I will ever see him again. I want to tell him that I love him, too, but I can't. That will definitely cross the line. I finally reply to his text, *"Thank you, Patrick, for everything!"*

After 2 ½ hours, the bailiff walks out into the hallway and announces that the Judge has reached a verdict. I can't move!

"Melissa, come on, honey. It is time to go inside", whispers JT. "Are you okay? This is it! It will be over soon and we will all know."

I build the strength and I follow JT inside. The Judge is already speaking. "I have reviewed the video again, along with the letter submitted to the Court, and I would like to personally say to Mr. Thomas how sorry I am that he has sat in Jail for 3 years for something that he did not do. I can't give you back those three years that you have missed from being with your wife and children. On behalf of the State of Florida, I am truly sorry", he states.

This is the moment where everything flashes before me. I can still see my children being torn away from our home. I see Kalin being taken away in handcuffs, an act that causes him to lose his job and discredits his name by many who respected him. I can see the tears that I have shed going back and forth to court for the children and for Kalin. I can still see the friends who walked out on me because I chose to stand by Kalin. I can see it all. I am without emotion, now that the Judge is about to render his verdict. Although I can clearly see the movements of those around me, it feels like I am looking down at myself.

The Judge continues. "It is my decision that Mr. Thomas be released from custody, immediately. All charges are being dropped!

Kalin is crying out of control at this point. They are removing the handcuffs and shackles. He is headed towards me. I move everyone out of my way to get to my husband. It seems as though he is running in slow motion. We are finally embracing each other after 3 years.

"Honey, I love you. I love you so much, baby", he says as he is kissing my face.

"I love you too, Kalin. I have missed you so much and can't wait to get you home."

Kalin's family surrounds him and gives him hugs and kisses for what seems like 20 minutes.

"Order in the courtroom! Order in the courtroom!" the Judge shouts.

The courtroom quiets down.

Me, Kalin, his mother and father, sisters and brothers, exit the courtroom for one final time.

"I am hungry!" Kalin exclaims.

"I bet you are. Where would like to eat?"

"Let's go to the Longhorn Steakhouse. I want a fat juicy steak!" he shouts.

After 3 long and painful years, my family is together again. We walk into our home as one big happy family. Everything feel s right! Christy is the first one that Kalin hugs. He makes sure that she knows that he loves her.

The words of Yolanda Adams seem more real now than they have ever been. "The battle is not yours, it belongs to the Lord."

EPILOGUE

Five Years Later.

"Mr. Peters, you may now offer to the Court your Final Statements."

"Five years ago, Kalin Thomas was charged with 7 counts of sexual crimes, punishable by 30 years to life in prison. He did not have to go to trial because Rita Gardner, who before she passed, sent in a letter, as well as a video to the Court, outlining how she was part of the conspiracy to destroy Mr. Thomas and his family with her lies. In her confession that was accepted by the Court, she mentioned that part of that conspiracy was shared with CCF, Florida's organization that is supposed to work with families to keep them together. They maliciously attacked this family with lies presented to the Court, kept their children in foster care for almost 3 years, and left this family to deal with the hurt and pain all on their own. Upon the return of the children, the damage was already done. They had to get extensive family therapy and to make matters worse, they were left with a financial obligation to the State for child support to repay over $10,000 for the time the children were in foster care. This family was wronged! They deserve to live out the rest of their life with no further interferences from the State of Florida's Department of CCF. This family deserves to have their name renewed. And what better way to do that than with a settlement that will prove, once and for all, that the State made a tremendous mistake in the way it mis-handled the Thomas family. I think that today is the day that we will send a message to the state of Florida that it needs to pay close attention to the facts before they decide to remove children from their families. It is time to send a message to individuals who decide to take the law into their own hands and decide what is best for another person. No more! No more! Go back in the Jury Room and bring back a "guilty" verdict proving that the State of Florida should have to pay for the 3 years that it took from this family. No family should ever again have to deal with this. Thank you."

Stuart delivers an award winning Final Argument. The audience applauds.

"Order in the court! Order in the court!" the Judge announces.

The State responds with how they do not feel that they are responsible. They bring up every case that CCF has brought against the Thomas family. They talk about how they had every reason to have removed the children based on what they were told. They mention they didn't feel obligated to investigate to see if it was true. They believed that to be the criminal court's course of action and not theirs.

The case is now handed over to the Jury. It is their decision as to whether the Jury believes that the State of Florida could have handled this situation differently.

All of the children are present for this hearing. We have quite a few supporters in the audience. When Amy was sentenced to Fed Time, she took advantage of the opportunity and earned a Law Degree and being that she has it, she is afforded the opportunity to sit on the team of lawyers fighting this case, right alongside Stuart and the team of lawyers that he put together. I am so proud of her because she just recently accepted her proposal to work for Johnny Cochran.

Christy recently graduated from the University of Southern California, with an Engineering degree and just accepted a job with the largest engineering firm in Atlanta. She came home just for this hearing.

Darren's big game is this weekend. He is playing in the Super Bowl as a member of the Philadelphia Eagles football team. The game is being held right here in Miami. Several family members have come home for Darren's first Super Bowl appearance. All of those days of playing football with the neighborhood kids finally paid off for him. Kameron is hanging out in Philadelphia with Darren and is working with a top fashion designer. Sharell, Amber, Justice, and Princess are all still home with me and Kalin. Sharell is now in her teenager phase and it looks like we have Christy all over again! Princess is turning out to be quite a ballerina. The older she gets, the more she resembles Laura. She has a giant sized portrait of her mother in her bedroom and every year, we travel to Middleton to commemorate her mother's death. Amber is now in the Collegiate Academy, with Justice building a name for herself at the Miami Performing School of Arts as an actress.

Several hours later, the Jury is re-entering the courtroom.

"Mr. Foreman, I understand that you have reached a verdict?"

"Yes, we have."

"I want to remind all of the spectators that there are to be no outbursts after the reading of this verdict. Will both sides please stand?" he instructs.

I don't know what I feel at this moment. I always knew that I felt like the State of Florida should pay for all the hurt that was caused to us, but this is the final moment. Everything that we have gone through as a family boils down to this final moment. Whatever happens, I am very proud of Stuart. Look at him. He is a man who was once on crack and now he is standing in this very courtroom standing toe to toe in a lawsuit against the state of Florida. He is excited to have such a big case. He knows that after this win, he will be able to open up his own firm and perhaps, give Johnny Cochran a run for his money. And who knows, maybe Amy will leave Johnny and follow Stuart.

"In the case #2007-CFS3587441, Kalin A. Thomas versus the State of Florida, we find that the State of Florida is guilty of malicious intent to cause harm to Mr. Thomas. As a result of this guilty verdict, we find that Mr. Thomas should be awarded punitive damages of $3 million", he says, before being interrupted by the Judge.

"Order in the court! Order in the court!"

Did I just hear $3 million dollars? Oh God, did I just hear $3 million dollars?

Tears begin to flow down my face uncontrollably. I finally lose it! I can no longer hide what has been in my heart for these last 8 years. Each of my children rushes up to me and kiss me. Christy walks up to Kalin and gives him a big hug and says, "Congratulations, daddy!" This is the moment I have dreamt of for so many years and it is finally here! Seeing her grow into a beautiful young woman throughout this entire process and making her very own mark in this world is all I ever wanted.

"Honey, we did it! We did it! All the crying, all the waiting, all the stress, all the late nights of sitting in that jail without seeing my wife and children - it is all worth it right now! The sufferings of this present time are not worthy to be compared to the glory that we shall receive! In Jesus name!"

Kalin raises his arms to heaven and gives God praise right there. I am crying. Stuart is crying. Amy is crying. The people who know us best are crying with us. Cynthia knows more than anyone what this whole ordeal did to me. She never gave up on me. She never stopped believing in me. I am glad that she took the time off to be here, but she is family to me. She is my sister and my dearest friend.

"Melissa, it is over, sweetheart! It is finally over! We talked about this day and look at you. Cry, baby! Get it all out! It is over!" Everyone is congratulating us, when all of a sudden, my cell phone vibrates. The phone reads, "New Text Message". Before clicking on "View", I get this feeling in my stomach that this is Patrick. Even though we have had no communication over the last 5 years, I feel that he is with me. *Snap out of it, Melissa! He is not here. This is probably from someone else.* As curious as I am about who this text message is from, I don't want to alarm Kalin, especially if this is Patrick.

Kalin is distracted with talking with Stuart and I decide to click on "View" to see who it is that is sending me a text message.

"Melissa, I love you. For me, the kiss was not innocent. From the moment I first laid eyes upon you, I have wanted nothing more than to kiss you. I have tried to forget about you. But I can't. And now, I want you. I don't want to live without you. And if you give me this opportunity to love you, you will grow to love me, too. Congratulations on your win!
Love, Patrick."

I can't believe this! He must be here! How will he know the verdict if he is not in the courtroom? I look around to see if I can find him, but I don't see him anywhere. I can't believe this!

"Melissa, are you okay?" Kalin asks. He can tell that something is wrong. "Did you get a call?"

"Everything is fine."

What an awkward position right now. I am here with my husband celebrating our victory, and mind you, a victory that everyone said would never happen because, according to them, nobody can win against the State. My three older children are doing well in their careers and the four left at home are doing well and are all college bound. My son is playing in the Super Bowl this weekend. Everything is going just great in my life. After all these years, I finally think about Wendy, who was also in the courtroom today, without her husband. *Was she here for Kalin? Are they seeing each other?* I can't forget about what Kayla said to me before she died. It seems like, perhaps, Kalin has some type of connection with Wendy. *Why else would she be here?* To think about it, she never really says anything to me. My thoughts are a little confusing to me right now. I know that it is because of the text from Patrick. As happy and excited as I am about this win, I have to admit that I am glad that Patrick is here. I miss him and I, too, can't stop thinking about that night we kissed.

After all of the celebrating, we finally leave the courtroom. I look to Heaven and say, "It is finished. Thank you Jesus."

Once we make it through the courtroom doors, I look up and right into Patrick's beautiful eyes that have always made me weak. He is standing there and crying, with his cell phone in his hand. Kalin sees this connection and looks at me and I look back at him. We both look at Patrick.

Patrick looks into my eyes and senses my confusion. Neither of us can say a word. I think I fell in love with him. I didn't mean for it to happen. Because he is the gentleman that he is, he says, "Chao for now!" He winks at me and walks away.....

Book Club Reading Guide

1. Although Melissa had troubling experiences in high school, do you think that this may have impacted her life as an adult? If so, how and why?
2. How did you feel about Melissa's decision to attempt an abortion, not once, but twice?
3. What did you feel about her encounters with the angels? Do you believe that these were real life encounters or just a figment of her imagination?
4. How do you feel about Mark's arrangement with Melissa while is wife was dying? Do you think it was okay being that his wife agreed to it? What if he had decided to leave his wife for Melissa during that time?
5. What was your first impression of Kalin? Did you believe that he had good intentions for Melissa and her children? Was he just looking for something stable or was he really looking for love?
6. How do you feel about Kalin disciplining Melissa's children? How did you feel when he disciplined Sharelle and CCF had to come to their home?
7. What did you think when the children were being removed by CCF? Was Melissa right for disciplining Darren for stealing money out of the woman's purse?
8. Should Melissa have gone to Kalin's ex-wife's funeral service?
9. Would you have stayed with Kalin after an accusation like Christy's?
10. What did you think of Rita, the babysitter? Should Melissa have fired her? If so, when and why?
11. Cindy was not only Melissa's employee, but a very good friend. Do you have any friends like Cindy who sticks closer than a sister? If so, praise her! Do you have any friends like Brittney? How do you handle people like her?
12. When Melissa's children were being removed the second time, how did you feel? Did you want to cry and scream right along with her? Can

you relate to this at all or do you know of someone who has had their children removed?

13. Should Melissa have gone to visit Rita at the nursing home? Would you have shown this type of compassion for her?

14. What did you think of Patrick? Was his friendship with Melissa appropriate? Was he simply being a friend or do you think he had other ideas about Melissa?

15. What did you think about Wendy? How would you have felt if she had called your husband late at night and he left home to tend to her needs?

16. What do you think Melissa felt when she learned that Kalin went to Wendy's house instead of Home Depot like he said? Would you have confronted him about it?

17. Were you expecting that Patrick was responsible for the videotaping of Rita's confession? Should Melissa have been more grateful towards him? Would she have been wrong if she had given in and slept with him?

18. What about Melissa and Patrick's first kiss? Should Melissa feel bad about it? Should she continue to explore her feelings for Patrick?

19. When Melissa didn't tell Kalin what was really going on with Patrick, was she wrong for this even though she knew that he suspected something?

20. Were you expecting that after 5 years, Patrick would still be interested in Melissa? Where would you like to see their relationship end?

Printed in the United States
By Bookmasters